Architecture 1980

ARCHITECTURE 1980

The Presence of the Past

Venice Biennale

RIZZOLI
NEW YORK

We express our thanks to all the people who gave
their contribution to the realization of the exhibition,
and in particular:
for authorizing the use of the Corderia in the
Arsenale, thanks to:
Francesco Reviglio, Minister of Finance
Lelio Lagorio, Minister of Defence
Attilio Ruffini, Former Minister of Defence
Calogero Pumilia, Assistant Secretary of the
Ministry of the Treasury
Ferruccio Benucci, Captain and Commander of the
Italian Navy in Venice
Egisto Grassi, Colonel and Member of the Naval
Engineers in Ancona
Vito Tarantini, Colonel and Member of the Naval
Engineering Division in Venice
Giuseppe Pallone, Venice's Inland Revenue Officer
Giuliano Zanovelli, Engineer of the Technical
Revenue Office of Venice Town Council;
for allowing the Corderia's restoration, thanks to:
Mario Rigo, Mayor of Venice
Giovanni Pellicani, Vice-Mayor of Venice
Renato Nardi, Municipal Councillor for Public
Works in Venice
Renato Padoan, Professor and Member of the
Sovrintendenza to Venice's Environmental and
Architectural Properties
Francesco Prosperetti, Architect and Member of
the Sovrintendenza to Venice's Environmental and
Architectural Properties;
for allowing the construction of the "Strada
Novissima," thanks to:
Pasquale Lancia, Lawyer and Chief Executive of
the "Ente Gestione per il Cinema"
Pietro Ponti, Engineer and Chief Executive of
Cinecittà S.p.A.;
for the cooperation in putting up Ignazio Gardella's
exhibition special thanks is given to the Centre for
Studies at the Archives of Communication in
Parma, headed by Professor Arturo Carlo Quintavalle.

Translations Thomas Becker, Maria Camilla Bianchini,
Nicholas Herdon, Armando Pajalich, Giannina Perrucchini,
Margit Preuss Cacciapaglia, Ellen Shapiro.

Design Diego Birelli
Editor Gabriella Borsano
Publishing Director Carlo Pirovano
Technical co-ordination Carlo Mion
Collaborators Rita D'Alessio, Gail Swerling

Original edition published in Italy by
Electa Editrice via Goldoni 1, Milan
under the imprint
©1980 - Edizioni «La Biennale di Venezia» Venice
Published in the United States of America in 1980 by
Rizzoli International Publications, Inc.
712 Fifth Avenue, New York, N.Y. 10019
LC: 80-51736
ISBN: 0-8478-0356-2

ARCHITECTURE 1980
The Presence of the Past
Venice Biennale

Chairman
Giuseppe Galasso

Board of Directors
Matteo Ajassa
Fernando Bandini
Maurizio Calvesi
Giovanni Cesari
Piero Craveri
Wladimiro Dorigo
Augusto Premoli
Massimo Rendina
Amerigo Restucci
Mario Rigo, *Vice-Chairman*
Carlo Ripa di Meana
Giuseppe Rossini
Luigi Ruggiu
Ettore Scola
Vittorio Spinazzola
Ernesto Talentino
Roberto Tonini
Maurizio Trevisan

Board of Inspectors
Filippo Alfano D'Andrea, *Chairman*
Luigi Saporito
Vincenzo Fralleone
Antonio Foscari

General Secretary
Sisto Dalla Palma

Director of the Architectural Section
Paolo Portoghesi

Architectural Section
Eugenia Fiorin
Paolo Cimarosti

Advisory Commission for the Architectural Section
Costantino Dardi
Rosario Giuffré
Udo Kultermann
Giuseppe Mazzariol
Robert Stern

The exhibition has been edited by the Director of the Architectural Section together with the Advisory Commission and Charles Jencks, Christian Norberg-Schulz, Vincent Scully

The exhibition has been organized by the Director of the Architectural Section together with Francesco Cellini, Claudio D'Amato, Antonio De Bonis and Paolo Farina

Preparatory Researches have been developed by Francesco Cellini and Claudio D'Amato together with Paolo Farina

The relationships with the participants of the exhibition from Germany and the United States have been dealt with by Emilio Battisti, Alessandra Latour and Burkhard Grashorn

The catalogue has been edited by Francesco Cellini, Claudio D'Amato, Antonio De Bonis and Paolo Farina

Ignazio Gardella's one-man show has been set up by Paolo Farina

Philip Johnson's one-man show has been designed by Massimo Vignelli

Mario Ridolfi's one-man show has been set up by Francesco Cellini and Claudio D'Amato

The exhibition on the Corderia in the Arsenale has been set up by Manlio Brusatin

The general layout and the supervision of the exhibition has been realized by Francesco Cellini and Claudio D'Amato

Staging
The "Strada Novissima" has been constructed by Cinecittà S.p.A. It has been staged by the following firms: Bastianon, Boem, Elenia Elettricità, Favero, Vettore, Giacomelli, MP Foto, Colorificio Giorgione

The Corderia's restoration has been supervised by Claudio Rebeschini

Other collaborators
Wladimiro Dorigo, *Curator of the Historical Archive of Contemporary Arts*
Luigi Scarpa, *Director of the Section for General and Institutional Activities*

General and Institutional Activities
Marina Borghi, Giorgio Boscolo, Vincenzina Brugnolo, Roberto Chia, Paolo Cimarosti, Osvaldo De Nunzio, Adriano Donaggio, Eugenia Fiorin, Giuseppe Foti, Luigina Franco, Maria Cristina Lion, Carla Mariotto, Donato Mendolia, Rita Musacco, Giulio Passoni, Anna Maria Porazzini, Antonia Possamai, Roberto Rosolen, Fiorella Tagliapietra, Marina Tesser, Antonio Turin, Dario Ventimiglia, Gianfranco Venturini, Wanda Zanirato, Alfredo Zanolla, Silvano Zaranto, Alessandro Zen

Historical Archive of Contemporary Arts
Angelo Bacci, Giuseppe Barban, Gioachino Bonardo, Erminia Bressan, Gabriella Cecchini, Roberto Conte, Espedito D'Agostini, Aldo De Martin, Daniela Ducceschi, Enrico Fanti, Sonia Finzi, Marie George Gervasoni, Antonio Ginetto, Paola Gonzo, Giovanni Maccarrone, Sergio Pozzati, Giuseppe Simeoni, Chiara Simonato, Loris Talpo, Pierluigi Varisco, Giancarlo Zamattio, Giorgio Zucchiatti.

Administration
Aldo Beltrame, Anna Claut, Luigi Lion, Gabriella Marchesin, Giuseppina Maugeri, Lucio Ramelli, Gualtiero Seggi, Daniela Venturini, Giorgio Vergombello, Antonio Zanchet, Leandro Zennaro

The Biennale's decision to set up, alongside the other activities, a sector dedicated specifically and autonomously to Architecture, was the result of an experience and a necessity. The experience showed that including Architecture among the other Visual Arts created considerable problems of balance and involvement in the set themes.

In such a context, tradition rather tended to undervalue the facts of architecture and put them on a lower level. All the same, and this is a paradox perhaps worth more than a fleeting mention, in the most recent Biennales it was more the other artists or operators in the field of the arts who complained of encroachment by the architects, something that even seemed sanctioned in the tasks which the architects, obviously, were allotted — staging shows and exhibitions.

Living together had, in other words, become difficult: not, certainly, because of mere incompatibility of a corporate or — even less — a personal nature. It was necessary to take note of a technical, expressive and functional specificness which, no matter how ancient it was (and seeing as how it was at the origin, it was ancient), had qualified Architecture in an ever more complex fashion compared with the Fine Arts: they had been joined to it by ancient aesthetic and rhetorical tradition. While the work of art was progressively being transformed into an event, gradually but on a very large scale losing its features as a manufactured article (sculpture, painting, etc.), the architectural product, energetically removed from all monumentalist concepts, appeared ever more to be part of a much more complex subject which on the one hand flowed into the whole, vast subject formed by town planning, land management, "landscape architecture" and so on, while on the other hand it ran into the problems of "material culture," the social and individual use of time and resources, etc. All this was naturally felt well beyond the Biennale, and much more prematurely. All the same, the Biennale became aware of this along with another particularly important element concerning the nature and installation of the cultural events. Here, too, the element of paradox was not missing. The old method of putting the Visual Arts on show, with exhibitions, reviews, or whatever other names were dreamt up, collapsed and entered a deep and as yet unsolved crisis (not easy for the Biennale to solve, nor for anyone else). Meanwhile, the exhibitory methods of Architecture, no matter how much they have been or will be revised, demonstrated a remarkable sensitivity for new articulation and constant vitality, which was another reason for the uneasy alliance between Architecture and... the rest.

It is precisely with an exhibition that Architecture is today inaugurating its activity as an autonomous sector within the Biennale, just like Cinema in far-off 1932 and then Theatre and Music, all branching out from the Arts. By coincidence this beginning has taken place in the year of the celebrations of Palladio, which can be highly symbolical in every way (from permanence to extreme diversification) for architectural tradition. The Biennale's conscious choice, following a suggestion by Paolo Portoghesi, the sector's Director, has in its turn dedicated the theme of the exhibition to the so-called Post-Modern Movement, or rather, to one of the main and most significant expressions of contemporary art.

At the same time a determined and marked remembrance of Ernesto Basile takes us back to considering the aspects and problems of Italian regional history as well as contemporary architecture, going beyond the Post-Modern and even the Modern Movement. It should virtually only be seen as a spatial and chronological matching, but it also seeks to serve as an opportunity for further analysis, as does the whole event, gathering connections, substance, directions in the whole vast reality — which is expressive and artistic, but more than ever social and anthropologically cultural, too — which the experience of work in architecture gives proof of today.

As it offers these themes in its first architectural exhibition the Biennale is aware of the critical risk it is exposed to. It is aware of the complexity of the material offered, which can lead to reflection over and above specific analysis related to the proposed theme. The Biennale can only submit to the widest and frankest debate possible on the achievement and presentation of these themes, as with whatever may lead to reflection on contemporary culture and on our age: it can only repeat, as it does, the assertion that it harbours no established or normative ambition. The Biennale only wants to offer tools for work, opportunities for thought and movements of more intense aesthetic and social life.

Giuseppe Galasso

The End of Prohibitionism
Paolo Portoghesi

The architecture section of the Venice Biennale, after its debut with the theater section in the exhibition dedicated to "Venice and scenic space," has its first autonomous initiative at the beginning of the penultimate decade: the First International Exhibition of Architecture. Every two years, the same kind of exhibition will be held in conjunction with the principal manifestations of the Visual Arts section. In this way, tribute will be paid to the continuity of a public institution of historic dimensions, and its original periodicity will be maintained, even if the programs of this section are not exhausted in this first engagement. Rather, they provide for permanent laboratories and for a series of manifestations that strengthen the link between the institution, the city, and its territory, and confirm the function of the Biennale as a center for the elaboration and promotion of architectural debate and research.

Rather than attempt a systematic, neutral review of architectural "quality" wherever it can be found in the complex phenomenology of present architecture in the world — a notarial task requiring measuring instruments discredited by the crisis of the discipline — we preferred to choose a theme, and hence a "movement." With this last work, we do not intend an organized tendency endowed with an orthodoxy of its own, but rather a grasped phenomenon coming into being, to be listened to and understood, more than to force and direct, where problems, discomforts, and even the discoveries and desires of a certain time are explained; "our time," with regard to which — as Benjamin wrote about his own experiences — it is important, without deluding oneself, "to state one's opinion without reservations." With the title of the exhibition "The Presence of the Past," we hope to take hold of a phenomenon which has its symptoms in the fifties, in the courageous turn of direction in the researches of the masters of modern architecture, but has carried on, with a slow and arduous rhythm, transformed only in the past few years into a radical and definitive effort. This phenomenon is the direct comparison, with no defences or inhibitions, with architecture as one of man's permanent institutions, and therefore with the history of architecture as a unitary system where the experiences of the relationship between man and earth, the operative and cognitive conquests of a defined sector of human work converge.

The ideology of modern architecture thought it had rid itself of this whole of languages and language, human institutions and conventions with a stroke of the eraser, proclaiming its obsolescence in the new times. But it had actually continued to live in the memory of man, renewing itself constantly since it was fed by the "presence of the past," by messages that continue to originate from that set of tangible things called historical heritage as a whole, and from a new viewpoint produced by the contents of the "human condition."

The return of architecture to the womb of history and its recycling in new syntactic contexts of the traditional forms is one of the symptoms that has produced a profound "difference" in a series of works and projects in the past few years understood by some critics in the ambiguous but efficacious category of Post-Modern.

The word modern, originally designating continual change, has undergone a process of sclerosis in identifying itself with a style, contaminated by the stasis of an unproductive situation.

Paradoxically, it has become the symbol of an abstract power to be fought and overturned.

In choosing a title different from Post-Modern, this exhibition proposes a clarification. In fact, in choosing a sphere both vaster and at the same time more restricted within a great area of phenomena still only temporarily classified, it intends to point to the changes of the specific disciplining of linguistic exigencies rather than to the psychological attitude with which the forms, whatever they are, are used. A "Post-Modern condition" exists, created by the rapid structural change of our civilization. It is easy to foresee that other, more precise and appropriate philosophical diagnoses will be added to the first ones.

This new condition can be explained in architecture in two ways, one totally ideological, concentrating on what has changed inside us, and therefore on the inevitably different way we perform the same acts we performed before. The architect lives this presence observing himself, describing himself, noting that the collapse of illusions modifies his sense of work, gives new meanings to the old operations of the avant-garde, creates around these operations a halo of silence or a magic play of mirrors which satisfies both the desire for play and the need for tragedy.

The other way is that of looking beyond oneself and observing that architects are not the only "priests" who change the reality of architecture, but everyone else, and it is not only they who work in this sector of human endeavor, but it is also they who suffer, use, and consume it. It is enough to accept this principle to realize that the axe invented by historians to divide ancient from modern architecture never existed in the minds of the users of architecture, but only in the minds and intentions of the "employees." Recognizing the "Post-Modern condition" in this second way, through architecture and not through ideology, means both denying any definitive break in the concreteness of architectural institutions and recovering that character-rightly emphasized by Robert Venturi — of "expert in conventions" through which it is possible to "communicate" not verbal messages, but architectural thoughts, there by socializing intellectual work without outdated populist aspirations.

The choices made and the inclusions and exclusions in the group of architects invited begin from this basic hypothesis which privileges transformations of language and the abandonment of Modernist orthodoxy, and singles out in the "relationship with history" the central knot which permits the establishment of the boundaries of a movement and the perception of a "before" and an "after" regarding something precise that happened in architecture.

This does not mean that the choice of the architects invited to participate corresponds rigorously to a homogeneous design.

The advisory committee of the section, comprised of Nino Dardi, Rosario Giuffré, Giuseppe Mazzariol, Udo Kultermann and Robert Stern, decided to involve critics like Vincent Scully, Christian Norberg-Schulz, Charles Jencks and Kenneth Frampton in the organization of the exhibition, in order to guarantee a range of different and at times diverging interpretations of the theme proposed by the director of the section. These can be compared to one another in the preparatory debate, and clearly communicated to the visitors to the "Presence of the Past" through special shows they see for the first time.

Kenneth Frampton's progressive detachment and eventual withdrawal of his participation in the choices for the exhibition (due among other things to his proposal to include Rem Koolhaas in the twenty planners of the "Strada Novissima") indicates how the resulting picture, even in its plurality, is not so neutral that it does not produce disagreements and incompatibility. Originally perplexed by the excessive openness ("I see this Biennale as a pluralist-cum Post-Modernist manifestation; I am not at all sure that I subscribe to this position, and I think I will have to keep my distance from it"), Frampton then cultivated a clearer refusal of the comprehensive viewpoint of the exhibition, and even decided to exclude his prepared text from the catalogue. ("The critical position it adopts is so extremely opposed to all that could be summed up under the category Post-Modernist, that I realized it would be absurd for me to advance the essay in this context.")

This exhibition really attempts to cast doubt on the first aggregations made in function of a category like Post-Modern, all the more useful the more it extends beyond the boundaries of architecture, trying to form a relationship with what is happening in converging directions in the most diverse disciplines, and has made the magic work ricochet from philosophy magazines to literary, economic, and political magazines, in so far as it is possible to reconstruct history.

Getting rid of a category because of its ambiguity, or because "others" whose company we don't want have taken shelter under it (and perhaps they try to elbow out those preceding them) is understandable. But it doesn't help us to understand or clarify such a complex and hardly controllable reality. The reign of architectural magazines and their power groups has in the past few years become a sounding board for a strongly guided radical turning point.

But by now, the undulatory motion is too strong to be brought back to order and canalized into preconstituted designs. For years we have opted for a "criticism of listening" whose objective is change, and not the forecast or the illusory planning of some consultory "final solution," and less than ever the sterile game of verifying the correspondence between what happens and the great central schemes of philosophy and history. In the sphere of a strategy of listening, the exhibition on "the presence of the past" will help as many people as possible to a better understanding of the fact that several important things have changed even in architecture and that the "subjects" of architecture are not only the architects. It will serve — and in this the direct interlocutor is Italian culture — to announce the end of that "prohibitionism" which for years has repressed the instinct to use everyone who agrees to communicate with us as materials for the present, without preconceived discrimination, to involve memory and imagination with the maximum effectiveness, the projection into the future and the desire for the environmental quality of citizens.

In Italy today, official criticism, with its judicial methods, is still ready to catch a glimpse of the dangers of involution, infantile regression, the return to the academy, wherever research leads to the recognition of the fundamental role of memory in the process of the communication of architecture. The prefix "neo" applicable to any "style," ancient or modern, has served to brand with infamy and to break off at birth all attempts at opposition to the conformism of a culture that oscillates, like a mad pendulum, between arbitrary invention and the passive acceptance of technological mythologies. The priests of the Modern Movement continue to recite their litanies on the basis of untenable identifications between classicism and authoritarian regimes, between eclecticism and creative sterility, as if thirty years of research hadn't definitively rid the historian's desk of the opposing pairs of concepts dear to old high-school teachers and of the mechanical connections between political contents and artistic forms.

Even so, the barrier of prejudices circulating with such patient continuity is no longer effective. The young no longer believe in the totems or taboos of this withered religion. By now, the excommunications and invectives, the slanderous tricks of judicial criticism remind us of the police tricks of the prohibitionists. They bring to mind the famous Izzy Einstein Chew who, disguised as a longshoreman, arrested an Italian who had carefully hidden tiny bottles of liquor in his cash register; or, another time, entering the Half Past Nine Club in New York playing the part of a rich poultry merchant, found a large quantity of illegal beverages in a huge stuffed bear. By now, there are so many stuffed bears around that the work of critic-policemen is difficult, and prohibition seems over forever. As we predicted, its end has carried with it many intoxications and exaggerations, but also a certain type of enthusiasm that will perhaps make us remember these years (and the Venice exhibition) as full of vital ferment where irony and nostalgia, disenchantment and "sympathy for things" are mixed. In a certain sense, these are the years of "refound time," to use a Proustian image.

The negation of the past, or rather the rigid morphological separation between present and past desired by the Modern Movement was a typical defense mechanism, to use the Freudian term for negation. "The cathartic illusion — wrote Marcello Pignatelli — of freeing ourselves from all dross and obstacles, of cutting the knots of conditioning and guilt, of waking up different tomorrow, destroying yesterday's house full of unbearable memories, really means projecting the internal conflict onto a magical act, in the impossibility of elaborating on it."

The re-proposed "presence of the past" is neither simply ironic, nor, least of all, purely unnecessary and consumerist. It contains a lot of truth because it realizes its impotence in elaborating a real psychological conflict. The possibility of confronting and resolving the problem of replanning the city depends on overcoming this conflict. This is seen in the unresolved contradiction between historic centers and periphery, berween the space of meaning and quality (that of the ancient city) and the space of quantity and the absence of meaning (that of the periphery). Closed in the ghetto of the ancient city, memory has become inoperative, a factor of separation and privilege. Circulating once again in the present city beyond the fences erected to defend its alleged purity, memory can help us leave our impotence behind, and exchange the magical act that once deluded us into exorcizing the past and building a new world without roots, for the lucid and rational act of the reappropriation of the forbidden fruit.

We can already predict the reactions to the exhibition. There will be an attempt to proclaim the consumption of the Post-Modern Category, or an attempt to classify the recycling of historical forms as reproductions of the Surrealist avant-garde, or the Beaux Arts method. And there will certainly be someone who, making a connection between what is going on with the symptoms of the fifties, from New Sensualism to Decorativism, to neo-Liberty, will predict the marginality of an elitist movement seemingly unable to upset the consolidated establishment of official architecture indentured to the International Style. As always, whoever is forced "out of bounds" in his field of research by something he had not foreseen, tries for a "removal" as a last defense, and expects his revenge from time and from the mistakes of others. But the objective of the exhibition is so ephemeral and untriumphal that these objections or prophecies only confirm its timeliness.

If this is an elite phenomenon, then why not verify its capacities for enlargement, involvement, contagion? If its mythologies are far from the real problems of the growth and reorganization of the territory, then why not verify it by observing, studying, trying to understand if instead it contains indirect indications for the solution of these problems? If everything we can observe in this exhibition were simply the cyclical reflowering of a nostalgia that has already demonstrated its ephemeral character many times, then why not realize with our own eyes if the diagnosis is correct, if those emergency elements are really missing that allow us to consider this culture of the image, this approach to the past, by now qualitatively incomparable to the symptoms and anticipations advanced?

The strategy of listening, the critical willingness to attentively consider the results of any new regrouping of works, even the least approved and authorized, eliminates even the fears and accusations regarding inclusions and exclusions. The choice was made collectively and is therefore inevitably compromising. It has the merit, though, of being a dialogical choice, and so has the advantage of bringing together things born in different climates and sensibilities. It also helps let us see intellectual work as a symptom of a common lymph circulating not only in the ordered network of canals that our minds can imagine, but also in the labyrinthine circulatory system of the ideas of a new human condition, experienced before it is interpreted and made conscious.

Other objections will be raised concerning the forced coexistence of at least three tendencies with different declared programs. I allude to European neo-rationalism, whose ramified structure descends from the teaching of Rossi and from what is called "la tendenza," to the semiological poetics of the first "five," to urban classicism flowing into the anti-industrial resistence which constitutes a partial branching out within the tendency, to the radical eclecticism theorized by Charles Jencks. The opinions of the other directors of the exhibition concerning these classificatory hypotheses are revealed in their writings and in their direct participation in the exhibition. We assume full responsibility for temporarily setting aside the categories mentioned, since we feel it more opportune to consider discriminating not intentions and theories, but architectural facts, morphological choices: that is, the way of thinking with architecture and not about architecture. The consequence is certainly the heterogeneity of the contents and principles underlying the forms. But it was much more important for us to propose the demythologization of a method that, putting forms and ideologies together and considering the indissolubly tied, ended up in a ridiculous court of history, condemning structures, methods, and collective patrimonies, comparable to those conquests of science whose only fault is having been adopted by people with not very recommendable police records. It seems strange, but in a world which has become more tolerant and comprehensive about deviance, and where no one would dream of disdaining Caravaggio's work because the artist was violent, or the work of Michelangelo for his particular inclinations, symmetry is still branded and considered synonymous with homosexuality, and classicism as something irremediably contaminated by the use made of it by certain political regimes.

The declarations of poetics in this catalogue are an extraordinary illustration of the variability of intentions that can inspire intellectual work. And, given the singular adherence to the proposed theme of the exhibition, these declarations also illustrate the different attitudes towards the past marking the personalities and groups identifiable on the basis of geographic and cultural areas. We are really interested in declaring the richness of the motivations and thoughts that animate a great common effort: that of linking old and new, of contaminating memory and the present, of gradually focusing a set of contrasting methods, a patrimony of experiences which, summed up and compared, already make possible the identification of a long road of collective research. This writer holds it opportune to set aside the sectarian attitude which would lead to setting the protagonists of the front singled out by the exhibition against one another. The reopening of boundaries that delimited the language of uncontaminated geometry and separated it from the forest of symbols and connections of historic memory has at times been interpreted, in theoretical propositions, as the reopening of a one-way street towards other firm certainties, towards an orthodoxy of an opposite, but no less risky, sign. A new classicism as a moment of the "eternal return," or an architecture of illuministic reason as little adapt to present reality as the dogmas of the functionalist statute and the myths of technology. No less illusory is the romantic return to the healthy virtues of the pioneers in a world which the energy crisis ought to make move backwards.

The past whose presence we claim is not a golden age to be recuperated. It is not Greece as the "childhood of the world" which Marx talked about, ascertaining the universality, duration, and exemplariness of certain aspects of European tradition. The past with its "presence" that can today contribute to making us children of our time is the past of the world. In our field, it is the whole system of architecture with its finite but inexhaustible sum of experiences connected or connectable by a society which has refused a monocentric culture, a main tradition with no competition.

Nineteenth-century eclecticism had already recognized this curvilinear horizon that makes us embrace a visual field of 360° and denies us the privilege of a fixed orientation with respect to which everything is measured. But the eclecticism of that time, like old imperialism, proceeded from a sort of natural history of civilization, from a systematic cataloguing of closed repertoires or from their naïve mixture directed towards the realization of characteristic beauty or towards assigning styles a value of illusionistic contents in the great history of urban typologies.

The relationship with the history of architecture which the "post-modern" condition makes possible doesn't need the eclectic method anymore, because it can count on a form of "disenchantment," on a much greater psychological detachment. The civilization of the quantified image, the civilization of sacred images that knows the barbarities of the new imperialism and its progressive shattering can use the past without being more involved in illusory revivals or in naïve philological operations. History is the "material" of logical and constructive operations whose only purpose is that of joining the real and the imaginary through communication mechanisms whose effectiveness can be verified; it is material utilizable for the socialization of aesthetic experience, since it presents sign systems of great conventional value which make it possible to think and make others think through architecture.

In this sense, architecture can once again be returned to the places and regions of the earth without a return to a racial or religious metaphysic. It can be the means of removal of the old Eurocentric system based on the myth of classicism. It can also be the recognition of the relative and partial validity of all conventional systems

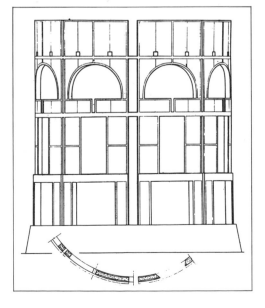

1. Ernesto Basile, detail of the Basile cottage in Palermo, 1904.
2. Roberto Gabetti and Aimaro Isola, Villa in Pino Torinese, 1968.
3. Louis I. Kahn, drawing for the Salk Laboratories, San Diego (Cal.), 1964.

provided that one accepts belonging to a polycentric network of experiences, all deserving to be heard.

Entering post-industrial society, knowledge changes its statute.

The process of "getting informed" which characterized the past few decades symbolizes a new Copernican revolution whose constructive and destructive consequences we are only beginning to understand. The intense and continuous circulation of images and data, the possibility of more and more easily approaching complete statistical knowledge, the resorting to probablistic methods which in successive attempts simulate once quite long processes of comparison and elaboration.

The acceleration of many processes and the miniaturization of instruments, the use of models and analytic programs have accelerated the crisis of the great systems centered in the field of epistemology. And it is easy to predict that the same thing will happen in a short time for the methodological patrimony of the human sciences and specific operative techniques.

"It can be suggested – wrote Lyotard – that the problems of internal communication that the scientific community meets in its work, to take apart and put back together its languages, are comparable in nature to those of social collectivity when, deprived of the culture of "récits", it must test communication with itself and interrogate itself about the legitimacy of decisions made in its name.

The collapse of the great summarizing discourses that propose unitary interpretations and programmatic prophecies, and the incredibility towards them that qualifies the post-modern position according to Lyotard makes the strategy of listening obligatory, and the intellectuals can regain a specific role in the self-interrogation of real society as regards its desires and objectives.

The architects' interest in history and in the recycling of forms and traditional compositional systems should also be seen in relation to this self-interrogation, to this census of still valid or confirmable conventions, to the restitution of the role of subject to the community of its users, after the long parenthesis of the claim of this role only by the "technicians of form," made legitimate by the theory of the Modern Movement.

Mass culture produces a continuous wave of information and images that reproduce originals, but that also tend to substitute and underrate them, rather than create scared auras around them. Seeing a purely negative phenomenon in this underrating and quantification of access means simply continuing to use an aristocratic viewpoint and not knowing how to grasp the liberating result and the egalitarian charge of this profanation of the myth. Together with the inhibitions imposed by prohibitionism, the devotional attitude towards history hidden behind the negation of its real value also collapses. Like the Renaissance, with the reawakening of critical conscience and the birth of philology, it has marked the true definitive separation from the ancient world (to which, paradoxically, it wanted to link up again); thus, the end of prohibition and the recycling of traditional forms

marks the definitive separation in architecture from the near past, from the inextricable mixture of Illuminism and Romanticism making up the modern tradition.

A decisive step ahead is thus made towards the laicization of the discipline.

It is not the task of this introduction to effect the historic reconstruction of the "movement" which the exhibition attempts to outline with the force of its images, or to establish the role of the protagonists and the quality of their contributions. In organizing the exhibition, we preferred not the place of the critic or historian, but of the architect who "puts into action" his discipline, builds a platform to speak first of all with his language. Elsewhere, we tried not to make history but to systematically display some aspects of the movement (cfr. P. Portoghesi, *Dopo l'architettura moderna*, Bari, 1980); we would especially like to clarify the objectives and the method that inspired the exhibition of 76 architects – is a section of "tributes" ideally placed first, comprised of Philip Johnson, Ignazio Gardella, and Mario Ridolfi. The organizers intended to complete this section with a show of Carlo Scarpa's drawings, but a hurried and reductive effort was discouraged for reasons of organization, and also because a large retrospective of Scarpa's work will be held in 1982. The choice of Johnson, Gardella, and Scarpa is the recognition of their importance in the creative reintegration of historical heredity and repudiation of the binding orthodoxy of the International Style. In Johnson, we wanted to especially remember his lucid work of testimony that, after interpreting the concrete result of the Modern Movement in a well-defined practice, was the first at the beginning of the sixties to declare with no regrets the sterilization and death of a by now immobilized movement. The proximity of the exhibition dedicated to Ernesto Basile completes the section of the tributes with a reminder of the importance that the revaluation and study of Art Nouveau had in the cultural formation of many architects of the last generation included in the central exhibition. The initial intention to put on other exhibitions dedicated to Joseph Hoffmann and Bruno Taut next to the Basile show but later postponed because of organizational difficulties, would have clarified how it is possible to identity a vein of self-criticism of fundamental importance within the modern tradition, and very similar to the present revisionist orientation. Even the first project for the central exhibition included names which are missing from the final cast, cancelled after ample discussion by the consulting committee, whose results were rigorously respected by the director (but not by the directive council, which voted by a majority for the inclusion of two other names in the list of the twenty architects of the facades of the "Strada Novissima").

I feel it my duty to mention that in the initial proposal, the following were included in the twenty names selected for the street project: Roberto Gabetti and Aimaro d'Isola, Ricardo Porro, Hassan Fathy, and in that of the exhibitors, Piero De Rossi, Uberto Siola, Nicola Pagliara.

The idea of the "Strada Novissima," with its twenty facades, answers the intention immediately im-

mersed in the preparatory discussions, of insisting on the possibility of its realization, and of involving the architects invited to the show in a concrete operation offering the public the chance for direct tactile and spatial contact with architecture. At first, we thought of suggesting one or two themes related to the Venetian territory. Among the hypotheses was that of redesigning the steamboat landings.

The hypothesis of the street was born in December in Berlin, in the climate of the Christmas festivities, during a seminar organized by Paul Kleihues in which Carlo Aymonino and Aldo Rossi participated. After a dutiful tribute to Schinkel, and near the Alexander Platz, between the echo of the late Behrens and the outlines of the Stalin-Allee, we discovered a marvellous enclosed amusement park with a small piazza surrounded by small stands that imitated facades of houses in temporary materials, the ground floor in true scale and the others in a scale of 1:2: a paradoxical answer to one of the needs of the city, a need for closed and inviting space at the center of one of the cross-roads of modern architecture.

The desire to build a "space of the imaginary" in the center of the exhibition has its immediate result in the image of that temporary architecture made for play, animated by the crowd and where, as on a stage, there was always an inside and an outside, a part for the employees and another for everyone else. The fair seemed to be a simple eloquent metaphor for the relationship between architect and client, mediated by the group of facades that are also faces, the sign of an identity transferred to an object. In this way, the idea came up for the street inside La Corderia of the Arsenal, a gallery of architectural self-portraits made for play, for rediscovering the very serious game of architecture, a game on which even the quality of our life depends somewhat.

It is not by chance that the "Strada Novissima" was realized by the Organization for the Administration of Cinema in the laboratories of Cinecittà. Since its birth, cinema has been the factory of the imaginary, and for many generations it was the only possible access to an aspect of life exorcized from the other sectors of human life. The street is built in temporary materials using refined artisan techniques that the world of cinema has miraculously saved. But what was seen unanimously as an element of weakness can today be seen instead as an element of interest and strength. As a temporary and transportable piece, a machine in the ancient sense, the "Strada Novissima" links up again with the tradition of temporary urban furnishings that gave the city a different face, with its seasons and recurrent or exceptional events. The making private of urban space, the abolition of the street and the piazza as places established for meetings and exchanges has pushed aside the temporary urban space, reducing it for the most part to the fanciful illuminations of patronal feasts. In a city reinterpreted in function of the new collective needs, the temporary space can reacquire its importance and become an instrument for the socialization of urban space and the continual creative reinterpretation of its appearance. The experience of the Venetian

Carnival in 1979 administered by the Theater section of the Biennale directed by Maurizio Scaparro, is one demonstration of this potential for rediscovery, interpreted also by the great sign of the Theater of the World. Of all Italian cities, Venice is perhaps the one with the richest and most significant tradition of temporary space, seen in the floating machines and in the structures that can be reassembled in the fair of the "SENSA" and which can be considered prefigurations of our street.

The result of planning provocation lies completely along the lines of irony and autobiography, but has a strong communicative impact: it is a happily scandalous result that promises to stir up discussions and arguments, and to involve visitors not in a useless and anachronistic agreement, but in a critical adhesion, in a reawakening of a conscious question of the imaginary as an antidote to urban sterility. Naturally, the exhibition has not produced and does not propose models. It does not intend to resolve "the problem of housing," but to propose through graphic evidence the "problem of the city," to affirm the principle that the problem of housing can be resolved only through the confrontation of the problems concerning the quality of the urban environment and its symbolic recodification. Architecture in action was the "Theater of the World" that Aldo Rossi designed, forcing the impossible scenery of the San Marco basin to reopen a dialogue, interrupted for centuries, in a new way. Architecture in action is the "Strada Novissima" that reaffirms the centrality of the theme of the street as an instrument for the reintegration of the urban organism. Architecture in action is also the choice of the Arsenal, the splendid space of La Corderia that seems to contain Piranesian space "in nuce." Realizing the First International Exhibition of Architecture in the Arsenal, and symbolically projecting a piece of the city onto it, the Biennale intends to be a Trojan horse in a desirable restitution to Venice of one of its most vital organs.

The military authorities and the Revenue Office have demonstrated far-sightedness and sensibility for the public interest, conceding such a prestigious space for an exhibition. And the city of Venice, allowing for an initial restoration, has crowned this gesture of solidarity towards this new-born sector of the Biennale, making its immediate use possible. Now, the future of the Arsenal acquires a new value and concreteness. Its future destination could open up the narrow spaces of a city that can grow only within itself, and on the other hand, cannot be happy with surviving only for others.

This great structure of Venice, which has always been a prohibited space and an unadmired wonder, finally opens its doors to the public.

We would like the birth of the architecture section of the Biennale to be identified with this symbolic act.

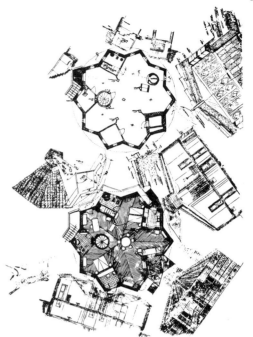

4. Ricardo Porro, school of dancing in Avana, 1962-1963.

5. Ignazio Gardella, housing complex in Punta Ala (Grosseto), 1961 (together with Alberto Mazzoni).

6. Mario Ridolfi, preparatory drawings for Lina House in Marmore (Terni), 1966.

7. The interior space in the Corderia at the Arsenale (June 1980).

14

How things got to be the way they are now
Vincent Scully

1. Pan Am Building from Park Avenue, New York.
2. Oak Street Connector in New Haven (Conn.).
3. Louis I. Kahn, Trenton Bath House, Trenton (N.J.), 1955.

The events of the past fifteen years have been truly amazing. An entire way of thinking about architecture has been called into question and, in many instances, has already been almost entirely replaced by other sets of ideas in the minds of the young. I refer in general to what Europeans have normally called the Modern Movement but specifically to that aspect of it which has in America usually been described as the International Style. That style was rigorously exclusive and puristically hermetic and, it must be admitted, rather paranoiac in its conceptual stance. Its urbanism was therefore destructive of the traditional city, while its individual buildings were normally hostile to those which preceded them and with which in consequence they got along very badly. In Europe those catastrophic results were rationalized as a necessary clearing away of old styles of life, and the levelling process which ensued was patiently suffered as an inevitable step toward the creation of a new, socialist society. The old architecture was seen as the embodiment of upper class attitudes, the new, however as yet partial and faulty, as the first signs of a new proletarian language of form. Those hopes, or illusions, have by now been sadly deceived. Modern architecture has accommodated itself most comfortably to the objectives and methods of the capitalist entrepreneur, the ruthless *developpeur* at his worst.

It has enabled him to build sloppily, nastily, and without love for anyone or anything, neither for those who use his constructions nor for the materials out of which they are made. Applied urbanistically in somewhat more idealistic, governmental terms, the principles of modern urbanism have produced ever more thorough-going horrors. One notes the nightmare of Créteil.

In America, the Modern Movement was seen in more purely formalistic rather than in sociological or even in methodological terms. This was at least a more realistic view, since intentions and methods in architecture must be judged by the environments they produce — by, that is, their forms. It is true that some European pedagogues in America, especially Gropius, confused the shape of the problem by in fact separating form and method: the latter functionally and structurally deterministic, the former neo-De Stijl. Because of this, and because few social hopes ever really rode on the International Style in American thinking, it came as little surprise that Modern Architecture was soon perceived to be serving Mammon more successfully than it did Marx, and that Gropius himself was able to produce one of the most urbanistically destructive of all corporate skyscrapers, the Pan American building. This, like a typical Bauhaus design object, and over the objections of Emory Roth, the hardnosed collaborating architect, was placed on a cross axis to the existing tower of the Grand Central Office Building and so destroyed the shape and the sweep of Park Avenue forever. It is a sign of the developing power of cities to protect themselves and of the growing determination of their citizens to fight for their existence that New York was later able, through legal means, to prevent the destruction of the rest of Grand Central Station by Gropius'

disciple, Marcel Breuer. Since that time, the preservation, conservation, and rehabilitation of old buildings and of old neighborhoods as a whole has become the major hallmark of advanced urbanistic thinking in America. Only the remaining bureaucrats of the Redevelopment Agencies, who obdurately continue to wear headlights for brains, are still trying to rip cities apart for those ravishing high speed connectors which Le Corbusier and Giedion hailed. They are still doing enormous damage, but their days are numbered for many deep reasons, ranging from ethics to energy, which can best be discussed later. Too late, however, for millions of America's poor, who were dispossessed of their neighborhoods under Redevelopment's Middle-Class Socialism of the nineteen-sixties, whereby a coalition of suburbanites with Center City merchants and bankers tore the fabric of our towns apart for the benefit of the automobile and its shopping center trade. How like the Ville Radieuse the result came to look: cars rushing through the empty space, large corporate structures standing in vast areas of parking. And why not? Le Corbusier's vision had finally come to pass, since the poor, as he had demanded long ago, had at last been banished from the town.

The same thing happened in the new Corbusian city of Brasilia. It is no wonder that young European architects like the Kriers, with those awful examples before their eyes, have turned back to traditional European urbanism, as in Leon Krier's project for La Villette, where solid blocks of housing and traditionally scaled streets — from which, however, the automobile has largely been banished — reassert traditional, pre-Modern Movement values once more. One can only applaud the intentions of such architects no less than the stern beauty of their forms. It is true, perhaps, that the polemic they now support was proposed in America fifteen years or more ago, when the ravages of Redevelopment first became apparent there. Plenty of American writing in this vein exists from that period, some of it published in *Zodiac* and other European publications. It is sometimes forgotten, too, that the suburb and the strip are fundamental urbanistic realities in America, entities of their own which need not destroy Center City, and they are not likely to change except under the pressure of energy shortages whose effects may conceivably lead, however, toward more decentralization rather than less if the problem of transportation can be solved. Hence American architects have had to deal realistically with America's existing urbanistic patterns, and in the past fifteen years, largely through the example of Robert Venturi, they have increasingly learned how to do so and how to create a reasonable and humane architecture out of the process. That is why architects like Robert Stern can propose "Subway Suburbs" rather than new Karl Marx Houses for the devastated centers of our towns. The symbol of freedom and achievement in America is still the single-family house, and the fact that the Nazis, for example, consciously made use both of that program and of vernacular forms in order to disperse the solidarity of the working class should not blind Europeans to the different set of

conditions obtaining in the United States. There the population does not like to think of itself as working class, but leaving that perhaps regrettable turn of mind aside for a moment, it does not want to inhabit large project blocks either and has none of the sense of unity, pride, and defiance in their Gemeinde Bauten that the working people of Social Democratic Vienna so heroically showed and so splendidly embodied in their buildings.

The Viennese workers were living as they wanted to live; that is exactly what American workers need to do, and what they want, rightly or wrongly — and his sorry performance as a social engineer during the International Style period indicates that it is not for the architect to say — is a house. Moreover, it is not easy to grasp, unless one has seen it, how devastated urban America has become, what vast empty areas, as in the South Bronx, are now available on existing rapid mass transit lines for building up in quite moderate density as single family homes with the symbolic values which those who will inhabit them want to have.

Here we touch on one of the terrible facts of the present moment, especially in the United States. It is the agony of the black population, now legislated into civil equality but crushingly disadvantaged, under-employed, badly educated, isolated in fearsome ghettoes, and rapidly coming to the conclusion that they have nothing whatever to hope for from society. Their desperation and the terror of their anger haunt urban America in ways few Europeans have had occasion to experience. Only a massive program of jobs, housing, and education at the national level has the slightest hope of saving them (which means, of course, everyone else as well), and such a program is highly unlikely in the state of public opinion and government policy. Priorities lie with non-productive military spending, and this, coupled with the rising price of oil, is creating a runaway inflation which is rapidly destroying the middle class and may well end by bringing the whole economic structure down. Somehow, though, there is still work for architects to do — more than there was a few years ago, and the rising prices are still finding customers to pay them. Yet, under these threatening circumstances, it is no wonder that "The Presence of the Past" as it is now functioning in American architecture, has to do largely with a reassessment of traditional, vernacular values by architects and critics alike. There is a strong feeling, comparable to that which produced the first Shingle Style in the eighteen-seventies and eighties, that America has forgotten some of its most important virtues and that they need to be revived once more. Among these is a resistance to consumerism, a belief that we once got along well with a lot less and would be better off to do so again. Related to that point of view, now as in the eighteen-seventies, has come a new interest in the forms of vernacular architecture, especially those deriving from the American tradition of domestic building in wood. The most striking fact to be observed in architecture throughout the country is precisely this reappearance of vernacular and traditional forms, from the Shingle Style of Venturi, Moore, and Stern (though they all do other things

as well) to the hallucinatory combinations of styles practised by T. Gordon Smith and the academically "correct" if rather Lutyens-like classicism of Allan Greenberg. It is clear that a liberation has occurred in the United States which is, simply in terms of conceptual freedom, far beyond anything which has happened in Europe during the past fifteen years. That liberation began to take shape through the work and teaching of a man whose reputation throughout the world has now attained mythic proportions. I refer of course to Louis I. Kahn. It is especially striking that the influence of Kahn has been one thing in America and another in Europe. The facts are apparent: Kahn broke up the International Style as a set of forms. He brought mass and weight back to architecture, not in terms of late Corbusian sculptural gymnastics but in directly structural terms. As he developed, Kahn began to take the process of building itself apart and to reconstitute it in beautifully clear, lucid, rationalized ways, in terms of structure and function alike. In the Yale Art Gallery of 1951-53 he stated his intention, even if the results were as yet not wholly clear. At Trenton in 1955 he penetrated back to the ultimate questions: geometry and material, ideal and real, man in the center and the first archetypal environmental shapes of square and circle taking position around him. By 1960, at the University of Pennsylvania, the function has reshaped the building as a set of towers — a wholly non-International Style form. The structure articulates the mass into a totally integrated body, the product of a system — or so it appears — rather than of a whim. A tragic solemnity results. Yet the functional analysis is highly arbitrary. It doesn't really work too well: the work spaces are small, the services complicated and there is no sun protection. But Kahn goes on. At Rochester he reshapes the wall in terms of environmental layering, reconstitutes the space and massing in terms of his newly conceived theory of Form and Design.

Through this he reconciles the idealist neo-Platonic abstraction of the International Style with a realistic concern for material reality and functional particularity. Ideal Form is in the mind: it is subjected to pressure from the specific demands of the program and so deforms itself to a certain extent. If it is pushed too far to retain its integrity as a shape, a new Form is sought. An equilibrium is found, for Kahn always a geometric one. The principles of the Beaux-Arts in which Kahn had been trained at the University of Pennsylvania in the 1920's now reassert themselves. Space is analyzed according to function but is systematized according to the demands of the structural fabric. An eloquent dialogue is set up between frame and screen. The method is very close to that of the neo-Greek of Labrouste at the Bibliotheque Ste. Genevieve of 1843-50, since brilliantly studied by Neil Levine. (Arthur Drexler's enormously influential exhibition of Beaux-Arts drawings at the Museum of Modern Art in 1975 derived in large part from these developments.) By the early sixties Kahn's reassessment of the past had given him a new grasp on what he wanted to do, and the mature masterpieces appeared: Bryn Mawr, Salk, Fort Worth, the Mellon

Center — the latter his last building and the most strictly neo-Greek of all. In it the pervasive presence and influence of Mies van der Rohe's work in America is recalled.

If we see Mies' American buildings for what they were, a union in the schematic terms of the Modern Movement of the neo-Greek and classicizing traditions which had both had a place within the old Beaux Arts academic system — and which were indeed of its Real and Ideal sides — we can perhaps understand how the pre-conditions for Kahn's further breakthrough, back to traditional mass and body, existed in the United States more than they did in Europe. Still, Kahn's work, like Mies', remained abstract and schematic in detail. He too rigorously avoided eclectic quotations or, in other than structural terms, decoration of any kind. If he goes back to Rome, as he does from 1950 onward, under the influence of Frank E. Brown and others, the results are structural and geometric. He develops Roman brickwork and reverses the Roman relieving-arch and lintel technique to produce his Brick Order for India and Bangladesh. With all this his buildings there become more and more abstract. Their scale is universal, hard to particularize. Though developed out of considerations of function (primarily the reception of light) and structure, they seem to escape such rational identifications and to move out into some timeless, motionless landscape of dream. This is clearly what Kahn wanted. So he ignored Roman decoration and Roman semiotics alike, avoiding the gesture of the building as symbolic embodiment or urban sign.

His buildings must be still, wholly silent, essential, immanent, not compromised by action. This quality in Kahn's work was to exert the strongest influence in Europe, perhaps in part because it was easier to idealize Kahn at that distance, or, perhaps, more basically, because of the deeply seated European tradition of Ideal, Neo-Platonic design. In America, among Kahn's most important students, colleagues and followers, the effect was different. Kahn's new forms became suggestions for active gestures. A good example is his famous project for Roman "ruins wrapped around buildings" as sun protectors for the Salk Community Center. They are pure façades but are organized in an ideal, abstract, timeless context. Venturi takes them, as in his Guild House of 1960, and turns them into the American false front to set the scale of Main Street and to gesture toward it as a sign. "Main Street is almost all right," Venturi was to say, so turning right around the International Style's destructive contempt for the urban vernacular. To enhance the point of his decisive gesture Venturi calls the abstract metal sculpture which crowns his façade a television aerial (which it is not), so endowing it with sign values at once realistic, popular, and ironic. Kahn reacted bitterly to that realism and attacked it in public. His design remained Ideal, and abstract, and was thus still linked in part to International Style puristic objectives. Venturi's moves to the real and the associational and thus brings back the third component of 19th-century Beaux-Arts style: the associational and symbolic one.

4. Louis I. Kahn, Richard Medical Laboratories, University of Pennsylvania (Penn.), 1960.
5. Henry Labrouste, S.te Geneviève's Library, Paris (France), 1843-1850.
6. Louis I. Kahn, Yale Center for British Art, New Haven (Conn.), 1970-1978.
7. Louis I. Kahn, Dacca (Bangladesh), 1966: detail.

Labrouste's Bibliotheque Ste. Genevieve, for example, was not only functional and structural but also consciously descriptive and symbolic, invoking with its spare but dense decoration the heroic and civilized graces of the past and inscribing the names of the writers of its books upon its screening walls.

It was precisely in this turn toward symbol that Venturi's work exerted its greatest impact. It was the essential component needed to bring architecture wholly to life once more, because human beings live by symbols, and when those are touched the core of the human adjustment to life is affected. So Venturi's epoch-making *Complexity and Contradiction in Architecture*, of 1966, which dealt largely with our physical responses to architectural form, was joined by his *Learning From Las Vegas*, of 1972 (written with Denise Scott-Brown and Steve Izenour), which dealt largely with symbolism in associational terms. In his enthusiasm for this renewed dimension, Venturi may sometimes have tended to separate the physical and associational effects of form more than they in reality can or should be (they are both learned responses, largely culturally coded, and they both cannot help but convey and embody meaning — so that ignoring the empathetically physical, for example, can reduce the semiotics of architecture to an overly restrictive linguistic mode), but his ability to derive architectural expression from the popular culture was the final break with the International Style's snobbery of form. So his work picked up the vernacular, whether of New York apartment houses at Brighton Beach (such a magnificent adjustment to the site and so terrifying to some of its jurors) or of the signs of the strip in the leap and shout of his Fire Station No. 4 for Columbus, Indiana. Starting back exactly where Frank Lloyd Wright had begun in 1889, with the archetypal frontal gable, he revived the Shingle Style tradition and produced new examples of a living vernacular in his Trubek and Wislocki houses on Nantucket. As the old symbols come alive the attitude toward creation changes. Where, for example, is the architect as romantically conceived if a true vernacular holds sway? In a healthier position, one might answer, but the bulk of the architectural profession, trained to believe that it was not only the guardian of esoteric experience but also reinvented the wheel in every design, at first did not think so. Hence the rage which Venturi's work aroused among professionals was unequalled for knee-jerk violence since that which had been directed against Le Corbusier almost two generations before. And, despite the 180° difference in objectives and forms, the reason was the same: the nerve had been touched. One could not help but realize that the rules of the game had changed. Architecture was wholly real and dangerous once more. Out of this revitalization has grown the lively dialogue which now exists among architects in the United States. They, of all artists and critics (with of course some spectacularly sullen exceptions), are now the most liberated and therefore have the most to say, the liveliest ideas, and the greatest capacity to sustain argument and disagreement with wit and good humor, avoiding the paranoid reactions of the International Style period. That old way had indeed come to be a shouting of slogans, precisely because it had unrealistically sought to exlude vast and natural areas of artistic experience, especially those related to associational values. The new way is, as Charles Moore pointed out, an inclusive one. It is interested in everything. Anything may be of value and may suggest new and better things. Those European architects and critics who are most wedded to ideological considerations have tended to become irritated at this American attitude.

It is my belief that they should not be. Concern for truth wherever it may lead, for reality however upsetting, for experience and knowledge however counter to preconceptual patterns, cannot help but lead toward a better grasp of the substractural facts of things and thus toward a better architecture no less than a juster society and a more rational world. They surely cannot help, in any event, but set the stage for a more varied, resonant, and effective architecture, and it seems to me that this present exhibition in Venice offers enormous promise for that. It is not the decayed detritus of a betrayed Modern Movement, as some would probably like to see it, but the yeasty material, just beginning to rise, of the more humanly complex architecture which could, under proper economic and political conditions, help shape a better human future. Perhaps many other important architects should have been included in it, but were excluded because their work did not seem especially relevant to the chosen theme. One thinks in Europe of any number of people from Böhm to Lasdun, in America of Roche Dinkeloo, Richard Meier, Eisenman, and many others. Among them the absence of Jaquelin Robertson is especially regrettable not only because of Robertson's special link with Southern traditions but also because his Seltzer house of almost a decade ago was one of the first and best examples of the new movement toward traditionally based forms.

With that qualification, the present selection is enormously rich and various and, it seems to me, shows a greater concordance of objectives and methods between Europeans and Americans than might at first sight be apparent. If, for example, Neo-Rationalism may seem Idealist in method, and the Americans we have so far mentioned Realist, that distinction can break down when we consider the relation of both sides to the central issue, which has to be the urban structure and its architectural vernacular.

Here, as we have noted, the Kriers, Culot, and others have rejected Le Corbusier's cataclysmic automobile urbanism out of respect for traditional and vernacular values. This parallels Venturi's revival of Main Street. Archetypal differences remain: the European tradition of the solid city, the American passion for the open road.

Hence plaza vs. strip. Which is more realistic than the other depends purely on the cultural context. Ethical differences between them might be a matter of dispute. But both are in revolt from the International Style. Or take vernacular forms. Ungers' eloquent studies of typologies, followed by those of

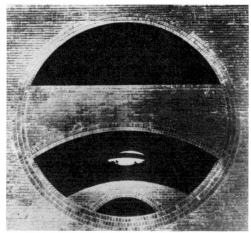

Kleihues and others, are concerned with contextual urbanistic relationships in traditional situations rather than with puristic style. This parallels the new American interest in preservation and contextual design.

Similar principles now seem to guide Stirling's recent work, strengthened and solidified by its close contact with Neo-Rationalism and with contextual urbanistic requirements such as those which helped shape his great entries in the various German museum competitions. It is regrettable that his magnificent entry for Cologne, the most spectacular of all those urban settings, did not receive the prize. Rossi most of all, the very heart of the Neo-Rationalist movement, seems to owe much of his poetic power to his ability to tap, with De Chirico, the hauntingly evocative tradition of Italian historical and vernacular architecture. True enough, there is a tragic dimension to his work which is most rare in America. Le Corbusier's late buildings embodied a rather muscular heroic activism at once French and Hellenic, but Rossi's buildings and projects have in them a special Italian sweetness and sorrow. They are drenched in time and memory, in the deprivations no less than the splendors of the centuries and, half in love with death, in the somber recollection of Fascism's perversion of the Italian dream. At last, artfully seeming to cast the flatulent subtleties of "design" aside, Rossi penetrates to the simplest of archetypal and vernacular shapes, as if discovering them for the first time like a child. Out of this comes the little theater for the Biennale, as pure as a child's castle floating on the lagoon. Inside, the tubular structure creaks and deforms according to the swelling of the waters, moving counter to the movement of the wooden shell that encloses it.

At the same time, it may be surpising to note that Rossi's gables, his square windows with crossed mullions, and his general adaptation of "dumb" vernacular forms, can all be matched in Venturi's work, as in the Trubek House, and the two find a common ancestor in some of Wright's early buildings, such as the house of Spring Green for his aunts, of 1887. Again, Neo-Rationalism and Venturi connect, and indeed they both look quite solid, conservative, and sternly neo-classical in comparison with a good deal else that is going on at the moment, from the Gaudi-like choreographies of Bofill and Portoghesi in Europe to the whole extraordinary scramble of activity in the United States. Here the career of Charles Moore is instructive. Moore is surely, with Venturi, the major architect of the new liberation. His early espousal of Shingle Style influence and his exploitation of the system of formal deformation first described by Kahn has clarified itself over the years into a kind of design that is increasingly receptive to the special needs of particular situations. In pursuit of that particularity Moore has on the one hand moved toward the vernacular forms of the area in which he is working while on the other he has developed a lively method of client participation, most significantly that of the citizens who will be affected by urban planning projects. Moore has used television to make such contacts with the public and, armed by

the extraordinary quickness of his intellect and of his capacity to perceive relationships, will design and re-design the area under consideration before their delighted eyes and according to their every suggestion. His Piazza d'Italia in New Orleans should be seen in this light as an urban fantasy, a community stage set, one of the most recent spin-offs of that influence of Hadrian's Villa at Tivoli which was so curiously important in America for a while during the nineteen-fifties. With quick-change urbanism of this kind, involving free play with forms of every conceivable cultural coding, Moore has succeeded in turning architecture into a kind of happening. This may well be the most intelligent and appropriate of his many contributions to the contemporary scene. It makes architecture at once immediately responsive — not to say responsible — to public taste and de-mythologizes it to the point where it can readily be seen as the construction of the entire environment and so directly susceptible to change according to social requirements and symbolic needs. Venturi and Scott-Brown have also been aproaching urbanistic question in similar ways, working directly with the inhabitants of disadvantaged neighborhoods to help explore methods through which more directly symbolic forms can be achieved. Hence Moore's play has a serious social and economic base. Sterns's Subway Suburb project, referred to earlier, should be seen in much the same light. The vernacular layout and houses that Stern proposes are right in that line of thinking and are symptomatic of the general development of his design. This is significant beyond itself because of the fundamental shift it demonstrates away from an early desire to be inventive at all costs toward the present natural preference for vernacular propriety and traditional order. Stern has played, along with Jencks, a considerable role in the formulation of the Post-Modern theoretical position, and such is mirrored in his work. He now seeks not the abstract originality of the Modern Movement but the cultural code (should we once again say "style") which is involved in each design instance. Stated in older architectural terms, he is now openly eclectic and looks for those precedents, types, and directly traditional forms which seem appropriate to the program and situation at hand. Much of his work is straight Shingle Style down to the original details, and it should be contrasted with his earlier New Shingle Style work where he derived general suggestions from the older buildings and then at once abstracted and distorted them. He has always had a gift for adaptation, as his truly grand and tragically baffled project for Welfare Island showed, but he is now seeking to adapt directly from tradition rather than, as he did in that instance, from the work of Venturi, who was his original and essential master in theory and design.

Frank Gehry's work seems much more modern in the way the Post-Modernists use the term, but it shares the happy-go-lucky character that they tend to applaud. It is indeed a collision between modern architecture and the omnipresent Stick-Style, Shingle-Style, Shack-Style traditions of the West Coast. It seems to celebrate the structurally complex conjunction of all the many virtues that have

kept the level of domestic architecture in California so high and interesting now for more than a hundred years. Thought it actually resembles less the lively vernacular of the region than Moore's brilliant essays do, it still seems to symbolize the rebelliously *ad hoc* state of mind which has sustained that vernacular throughout the years. It is crankily anti-elitist, so recalling aberrant proletarian philosophers of the region such as Hofer. In that context the outrageously eclectic combinations of T. Gordon Smith seem almost a mainstream effort, hardly strange at all. Smith's classical orders begin to resemble those of Maybeck in their Baroque-Primitive power while his interweaving of styles, though usually more purposely staccato than those of the past, can still seem obdurately Californian. But Smith stands alone in America, I think, in the haunting aura with which he can endow his images. The same is true of his baroque planning, which delights such generous Romanists and students of the Baroque as Norberg-Schulz. For an American critic of my age it recalls the clandestine essays in the reverse curve that used to be made thirty years ago, suggested by the intersecting cuvilinear patterns of Hadrian's Villa or by their European Baroque successors. But, characteristically for this generation, though with an idiosyncratic command of their rhythms which is apparently all his own, T. Gordon Smith dares to bring them forward and to sustain them as serious architectural proposals.

His parody of classical forms suggests those initiated by Venturi in some highly influential colored drawings of a few years ago, and like those they seem to make the antique and Renaissance traditions intellectually accessible to us through their irony. Such parody is rigorously condemned by Greenberg. He wants to have his classic tradition straight — even though, of course, the scale of his forms is strongly influenced by his pioneering studies of Edwin Lutyens, who was clearly, at his best, a distinguished parodist himself. It now seems true that Lutyen's greatest work, such as his memorial to the dead of the Somme at Thiegual, achieves a tragic grandeur beyond that attained by any other architects of the twentieth century, including Le Corbusier and Frank Lloyd Wright. But it is his inspired wit and freedom with Renaissance details which account for much of his enormous vogue today. He is the semi-divinity of the Post-Modernists, a role which he himself would in all likelihood have found appropriately ridiculous. But Greenberg sees nothing strange in a direct, non-parodied revival of the classical tradition. He points out that architects continued to practise it right through much of the Modern Movement. In this his stand parallels that of a fairly coherent group of young English architects (among a few of whom, it is true, a repellently reactionary stance, smelling of the whip and irrelevant to the issue, may unfortunately be sometimes distinguished), but Greenberg is now in the process of completing a commission, a new Brant House, in which the viability of his method will be tested at full scale as he adapts the client's chosen model, Mount Vernon, to a contemporary situation. This is as far from the Modern Movement as anyone can get and

as directly involved with bringing the past unashamedly into the present. One awaits the controversy which will erupt when the house is completed. It should be an interesting one, involving as it must do the assumption of some basic attitude toward non-ironic historicism.

All this is very far from the suave games played with past and present by Tigermann in Chicago, which have driven the dominant Miesians of the region into the usual paroxysms. But the most challenging and problematical of the younger middle-aged talents right now seems to me to be that of Michael Graves. Here it is clearly a garden tradition which is parodied, a tradition of rustication and mouldering ruins at once melancholy and picturesque. The feeling is of eighteenth-century Romantic-Classicism, so that Graves' design accompanies (and perhaps reflects) the dominant concerns of some of the most interesting critics of the present time, such as Frampton and Rykwert, who have taught at Princeton with Graves. But Graves has his own special poetry, as well as remarkable pictorial gifts. It is in fact a painter's freedom with which he endows his architecture, embellishing its surface with boldly conceived decoration on an outrageous scale, employing forms unthinkable in contemporary architecture a few years ago, and involving types of associations which were once even more wholly suspect. His massive two-dimensionality (if one may be allowed that conjunction) is also involved in the renewed interest in architecture as sign, and this connects Graves' work to that of Venturi. It should indeed be pointed out that such "rusticated" design was revived precisely when Venturi tacked the curved one-by-one to the façade of his mother's house and began thereby to evoke signs and associations related to experiences of the classical past. The enormously scaled details of the temple and palace façades for Venturi's little minimal house project to which I referred earlier, also play a part in this sequence. In Graves' work the rustication takes on new richness, freedom, and plastic power. The great keystones drop; the colors turn autumnal, deep and earthy. The cavern returns in memories of Serlio's horrendous doorways, and as the shapes recombine the mass as a whole begins to develop contour rather than merely silhouette. The whole begins to respond. The pencil excavates the paper, digging out grottoes, pushing back the forest (usually mythical, but the gardener's instinct is sound) which surrounds the dwelling, setting up responses of plan to elevation that are beginning to make an intrinsic organism out of the natural and the man-made components of the design. Much yet remains purely pictorial: how long would the tacked-on rustication survive in the rain? And that graphic dominance, in which Graves is clearly one of the leaders, now shapes a considerable amount of contemporary work. As in the later eighteenth century, a large percentage of the projects shown by younger architects are fundamentally fantastic in character. They are eye-stopping precisely because they are conceived of as drawings, and these are now regarded as works of art themselves and are sold as such. Graves is thought to support his office in this way. The in-

fluence of the neo-Rationalists from Rossi to the Kriers has reinforced that direction; it perhaps even initiated it. Rossi's incomparably evocative cityscapes and awesome projects, Leon Krier's highly articulated, primitively powerful buildings as little cities, have set a standard of graphic imagination and power hard for the young to resist, even when the forms involved have little to do with the particular programs they are working on. It is the pull of the visual, which all artists must feel.

But it is even more the tug of the archetypal, the recognition — among the compromises and complexities of modern life — of primitive simplicities, landscapes, and sculptural beings. It is a fascinating development, and in many ways, as we have noted, it parallels that of the eighteenth century, especially of the period just before the revolutions occurred but when their future scenes and processes were already being imaged in artists' prophetic eyes.

Yet, lest the present graphic renaissance be viewed too freely in terms of imminent social catastrophe, mention should be made of the extraordinary architectural accomplishment of Rem Koolhaas, who, with his OMA group, has brought the skyscrapers of New York to life. Something more than ten years ago skyscrapers had begun to rehabilitate their reputation, which had always been high among the public but low among modern critics obsessed with the Ville Radieuse and Chicago. Now the work of Koolhaas and his group has turned them into persons. They come crowding before our eyes as loved and benevolent beings, each more charming than the next, all of them now seen by us as consummate achievements of human art. Koolhaas has not only humanized them but has also made them accessible once more as models, not only for his own glowing projects but also for skyscraper building in general. It is safe to say that if skyscrapers continue to be built, the Art Deco sweethearts of New York, the Chrysler Building and the Empire State, the RCA Building and all of Rockefeller Center, will suggest forms even stronger than Johnson's AT & T project to challenge Citicorp's graph paper and suburban shopping mall. It is a splendid example of how a portion of the recent past which was lost can be brought back into contention and of how everyday living and simple joy in the environment can be immeasurably enriched thereby.

It is salutary, though, that another, more rigorously pragmatic set of suggestions for architectural form now exists as a counterweight to the graphic, the romantic, and the linguistic-symbolic tendencies.

I refer here to those proposed by the challenge of the energy shortage, which may yet entirely reshape the way of life of the urban world. In America those young architects (and they are by and large all young) who concern themselves with energy problems tend to be a totally different group from that which now practices the most avant-garde pictorial and linguistic design in New York, Princeton and New Haven.

They tend to be young people who graduated from architecture schools during the revolutionary years of the late sixties and early seventies and who

wished to explore vernacular building and, often, more agrarian ways of life. David Sellers was one of the first of those architects and indeed, going to Vermont after graduating from Yale in 1965, he was well before his time. He tried then to redesign architecture from the ground up but came into his own as the problem began to shape itself around the house as a recycling eco-system and a creator rather than simply a consumer of energy. Now groups of younger designers such as those who form the Total Environmental Action office in Harrisville, New Hampshire, have carried the movement along what seems to be its logical path: toward a simple vernacular architecture which is deformed and reconstituted according to the requirements of new passive and active energy systems. It is remarkable how close the vernacular itself everywhere is already adapted to some requirements, which are fundamentally those of living with nature where possible, against it (as with insulation) only where absolutely necessary. This attitude is apparently counter to the needs of big business, at least as it probably incorrectly understands its own problems. Solar energy, for example, has so far received very little intelligent assistance from government. The latter reflects the objectives of the large corporations which it serves and therefore prefers energy sources which take enormous sums of money to harness and which can be sold at a profit. Hence it puts its money on nuclear power, and, where forced into the solar field, tends to favor fantastic schemes like those for space stations reflecting the sun's heat down to the earth and distributing it, for a price, through one of the well-known brand names. But the very essence of the harnessing of solar energy lies in its applicability to small individual units, the installation of such passive and simple systems costing nothing to run (though as yet something substantially additional to construct).

Such systems can supply more than two-thirds of the energy requirements, for example, of any house anywhere in the United States right now: bringing sun into the house where it can heat some substance (water, tile, whatever) which can store such heat and then give it off inside the volume of the building during the hours of darkness when the external skin of the house can, conversely, be closed against its loss.

Thus the building begins to breathe in and out; it opens and closes.

Its forms evolve according to the suggestions of that process and are thereby linked to their vernacular forebears with their central fireplaces, taut skins, and operable shutters. The fact that small buildings can so far be most efficiently developed for solar energy is itself suggestive of future urbanistic patterns as a whole. The decentralization that Wright so consistently demanded is now suggested, but here the question of transportation comes to the fore. How can the automobile either become energy efficient or be replaced by various types of mass transit? The latter will probably take place sooner of later in any event. The result need not be catastrophic. Such systems can be infinitely more flexible in terms of scattered living than the automobile lobbies would like us to believe. It was once possible, for example, to travel all over the state of Connecticut, U.S.A., by trolley cars.

Their abandoned roadbeds can still be seen deep in the woods of far-off rural areas. The system apparently reached almost everywhere. It could do so again.

The challenge is there. The crisis in energy is one of the realities which must shape the environment of the future if it is to function at all. Architects, no doubt, will prefer the more spectacular and concentrated urban forms which an architecture attuned to energy problems will surely make it possible to design some day: vast shining collectors for metropolitan groupings, windmills massed along the ridges, whirling in the updraft, a whole science-fiction landscape out of Archigram, delightful to imagine. Some of this architectural dream, a tenacious one over the past hundred years, may indeed come about, but it is more likely that the reality will be gentler, smaller in scale, humbler, and more like the way things used to be before consumerism shaped the world. In the United States especially it might well play a part in reviving that spare, thrifty, threadbare way of life that was once the American's pride. The steps that architects are now taking to renew contact with tradition and with the vernacular may therefore be the first acts in a long process, one which will eventually involve political and social reformation as well.

Towards an authentic architecture
Christian Norberg-Schulz

One cannot become an architect today without having gome through the needle eye of modern art.
S. Giedion

The demand for meaning

The many tendencies and currents which make up "post-modern" architecture have one thing in common: the demand for *meaning*.

During the last decades our environment has not only been subject to pollution and urban sprawl, but also to a loss of those qualities which allow for man's sense of belonging and participation. As a result many feel that their life is "meaningless," and has become "alienated."

The term "meaning" evidently implies something that cannot be quantified. Man does not identify with quantities, but with values which go beyond mere utility. As an *art*, architecture has always been concerned with such qualities. Today, however, the artistic dimension of architecture seems to have been mostly forgotten. Environmental monotony is one aspect of this situation; our places become ever more alike, and lose what in the past was known as thier *genius loci*. On the other hand we also experience many surroundings as chaotic, and are unable to develop any satisfactory environmental "images." Monotony and chaos are apparently contradictory phenomena, but at a closer scrutiny reveal themselves as interrelated aspects of a more general crisis, which may be called the "loss of place." This loss is generally interpreted as the manifestation of the "failure" of modern architecture. As a consequence, Post-Modernism demands a "meaningful" environment, and rejects the functionalist belief that architecture may be reduced to a translation of practical, social and economical conditions into form.[1]

Among the many attempts at coming to grips with this problem, two are particularly symptomatic: the pluralistic "complexity" of Robert Venturi and the rationalistic "typology" of Aldo Rossi. Both architects have acted as catalysts to the professional milieu during the last 10-15 years, not only because of their controversial works, but through written statements which explain and support their respective approaches. Venturi takes a reaction against monotony as his point of departure, and advocates a complex architecture which expresses the "richness and ambiguity of modern experience."[2] Rossi rather protests against liberal diversity, and wants a return to simple, typical forms which may be understood by everybody.[3]
Thus the two architects propose diametrically opposed solutions to the same problem. A comparison may therefore offer a useful clue to a better understanding of the present demand for meaning. In the introduction to Venturi's early book *Complexity and Contradiction in Architecture*, Vincent Scully points out that Venturi "opens our eyes to the nature of things as they are in the United States, and out of our common, confused, mass-produced fabric he makes a solid architecture; he makes an art."[4] In other words, Venturi takes the given everyday life as his point of departure, rather than an ideal image of a "better world." Thus he likes "ele-

ments which are hybrid rather than "pure," compromising rather than "clean," distorted rather than "straightforward," ambiguous rather than "articulated"...;[5] in general he prefers "both-and" to "either-or," and advocates the "difficult unity of inclusion rather than the easy unity of exclusion."[6] In his book Venturi illustrates this approach with analyses of buildings from the past and the present. The analyses serve to explain general principles of architectural composition, such as "accomodation," "adaptation" and "inflection;" all of which substantiate his interest in "the circumstantial contradictions of a complex reality." In general Venturi wants a "subtle compromise between order and circumstance, outside and inside, and private and public functions," and says: "Designing from the outside in as well as the inside out creates necessary tension, which helps make architecture. Architecture occurs at the meeting of interior and exterior forces of use and space. The wall becomes an architectural event."[7] It is certainly a great merit of Venturi's to have reminded us of the importance of the wall, as where architecture "takes place." Thus he has opened up for a more concrete understanding of architectural form. Of particular importance to Venturi is the use of "conventional elements," such as quotations from past architecture. Thus he says: "Familiar things seen in an unfamiliar context become perceptually new as well as old."[8] By introducing conventional elements, Venturi initiated what has been called "Radical Eclecticism."[9] The term implies that meaning mainly has to do with "memories." As far as we can see, Venturi refers to two kinds of meanings: the spatial ones which stem from the interaction of "interior and exterior forces," and the "iconographic" ones, which are determined by memories. As he neither explains the nature of the forces nor the memories, however, his theoretical basis remains somewhat vague.

More recently Venturi has arrived at the definition of architecture as "shelter with decoration on it."[10] The shelter (spatially simple or complex) accomodates the functions, whereas the applied decoration expresses a meaning. An iconography which relates to present-day life is more important than spatial relationships, he maintains, and hence "it is when you see the buildings as symbols in space, not forms in space, that the landscape takes on quality and meaning." Venturi also points out that a shelter with decoration on it may be built by means of modern technology, whereby the structural system becomes "a grid for decoration."
The works of Venturi illustrate his approach.[11] Thus the plans are characterized by subtle interactions of spaces as well as varied inside-outside relationships, at the same time as complex functional demands are accomodated. The façades often combine a striking image-quality with details which suggest a wide range of contents. In general we may characterize his architecture as "pluralistic." It is not based on ideal forms, but expresses the individual situation.

In his early book *The Architecture of the City*, Aldo Rossi explains his approach to architecture, discussing its "philosophical" basis as well as its prac-

3. Between sky and earth: Khartoum.
4. Between sky and earth: Denmark.
5. The architectural thing: Subiaco.
6. The architectural thing: Bieda.

"autonomy" evidently consists in the ars combinatoria just mentioned, but its relationship to human life is not explained. What is most disturbing in Rossi's book is in fact the total absence of man. [18] The Platonic origin of Rossi's theory is obvious; what he is looking for is a timeless essence, which determines the meaning of individual phenomena. He adopts this approach from the theorists of the French Enlightenment, from which he also learns the method of decomposition into pieces and the classification of such. Hence it is justified to characterize his approach as "rationalistic." [19]

The ideas of Venturi and Rossi represent interesting attempts at facing the demand for meaning in architecture. Whereas Venturi tries to uncover the contents which are implicit in any given life situation, Rossi looks for "eternal truth." Venturi is "vital" and concrete, and makes direct use of past experience. Rossi is "rational" and abstract, and acts in an ideal world where experience does not count. Venturi "accomodates" interior and exterior forces by making the parts of the building interdependent, while Rossi adds independent "pieces" together.

Our comparison shows that each of them may be characterized as one-sided, an as such they may even be "dangerous." "Complexity and contradiction" easily degenerates into a new kind of superficial play with forms, and typology tends towards sterile schematism. Thus we may end up with chaos and monotony again, and must conclude that Post-Modernism has failed too.

A more complete understanding of the dimension of meaning is evidently needed, also to be able to evaluate the contributions of Venturi and Rossi. As the present situation is related to the supposed "failure" of modern architecture, such an understanding has to take an analysis of the ends and means of Modernism as its point of departure.

The two faces of modern architecture

The criticism of modern architecture is usually focused on the concept of *functionalism*. "Modern architecture" and "functionalism" are taken as synonyms, and as a consequence it is asserted that the modern movement above all was interested in utility and efficiency. Some critics even maintain that it became a servant to "the ruling power of capitalism" and that it "sacrificed architecture." [20] What, then, did the term "functionalism" imply? The word was certainly not used exactly the same way by everybody, and the concept of "functional" has been given a more or less comprehensive interpretation, sometimes denoting physical and practical functions only, sometimes including psychological and cultural factors as well. [21] The most important point, however, is not the definition of "function" as such, but its relation to architectural form. Thus the slogan "form follows function" is usually presented as the creed of functionalism, with the implication that forms may be deduced logically from *quantifiable* needs and resources. Design thus becomes to "fit" a form to a collection of "data." [22] Evidently such an approach does not take any "complexities" and "contradictions" into consideration, and if we assert that meaning con-

tical implementation. [12] The title already offers a clue to his intentions. By taking the *city* as his point of departure, his urban Italian background comes forth, as well as his understanding of the "collective nature of architecture." [13] In spite of his Marxist outlook, however, he does not define the city in economical and social terms. Rather he stresses that we have to deal with an *architectural* fact which has "permanence" and "meaning," and which comprises "monuments" which serve as environmental foci and generate urban form. Thus he regards the city as a "work of art" which has to be analyzed and defined.

The analysis is carried out through a process of "decomposition," whereby the totality is split into "urban facts" (primarily buildings) which consist of "pieces" (*pezzi*), such as cylinder-columns, pillars, wall slabs, triangular and semicircular pediments, girder-bridges, open galleries and porticoes, windows (usually square with cross-shaped mullions), flat and conical roofs, as well as hemisperical domes. [14] The "decomposition" is done in a theoretical rather than a concrete way. In contrast to Venturi, Rossi hardly offers any analysis of examples, but arrives at his elements by "reason" alone. Thus the elements are reduced to the simplest possible "typical" form. A building comes into being through an *addition* of such "pieces," a process which in the works of Rossi appears as absolutely pure; in fact he shuns all kinds of "inflections," interpenetrations and joints, and places the elements next to each other without letting them interact in any way. Not to disturb the ideal nature of the composition, he also avoids decoration and hardly gives emphasis to material texture. The result is an architecture of utmost simplicity, based on typical elements which through different combinations constitute superior types. The works which are thus created may appear as kinds of *archetypal image*, which are supposed to represent the "essence" of architecture. In fact Rossi says: "The type is the very idea of architecture, that is, what is closer to its essence." [15] Quoting Quatremère de Quincey he stresses that the type does not represent a concrete "model" to be imitated, but a general idea which is common to many works. [16]

The concept of typology represents an important contribution to the recovery of meaning in architecture. Thus it reminds us of the fact that the architecture of the past in general was based on the variation of types. As far as we can see, however, Rossi and his followers do not develop the idea in a satisfactory way. The origin of the types is not explained, and their meaning therefore remains vague. Although the word *locus* appears frequently in Rossi's book, he does not investigate the structure and character of places. Therefore he cannot approach the problem of adapting a type to local circumstances. The types are instead used as fixed "models" (in spite of the warning of Quatremère) which participate in a mechanistic *ars combinatoria*.

In general Rossi defines architecture as an "autonomous" discipline, although he also says that it is an "integral part of man." [17] The

sists in *qualitative* relations between phenomena, functionalism may indeed be responsible for the present "loss of place." Or perhaps the real reason is a more general attitude to life which stands behind functionalism. For the hope that architecture may be rationalized does not come from nowhere. In general it is a consequence of the belief in logic and scientific method which has ruled our approach to reality since the Enlightenment. During the last two centuries analysis and "planning" have in fact come to dominate all human enterprises. What is thereby lost is the concrete everyday world, and with it the sense of existential meaning. Already Max Weber realized that rationalism implies *disenchantment*.

It is not correct, however, to put a sign of equation between "functionalism" and "modern architecture." In the writings of the pioneers of the modern movement the word "functionalism" does not appear, and when the need for a rational or scientific approach is asserted, it is generally added that it only represents one of the faces of modern architecture. In 1935 Gropius wrote: "...rationalization, which many people imagine to be the New Architecture's cardinal principle, is really only its purifying agent... the other, the aesthetic satisfaction of the human soul is just as important as the material." [23] Even Mies van der Rohe said: "Architecture depends on facts, but its real field of activity is in the realm of significance." [24] It was mainly the Marxist Hannes Meyer who wanted to reduce architecture to its "measurable" aspects: "Everything in the world is a product of the formula *function times economy*. All art is composition and therefore unfunctional. All life is function and therefore unartistic." [25] We may conclude that functionalism was only one of the aspects of modern architecture, and possibly not the most important. What, then, was its other face? Gropius and Mies tell us that the real aim had to do with "aesthetic satisfaction" and "significance." In other words, the modern movement was primarily of *artistic* nature. Its spokesman, S. Giedion, maintained that modern man, in spite of his power of scientific thought, has lost a true relationship to the world in which he lives. The estrangement first became manifest as an art and architecture based on "devaluated symbols." The "ruling taste" of the nineteenth century borrowed the forms of the historical styles to give the "self-made man" of industrial society a "humanistic alibi." [26] Man thereby became a split personality. He adopted the aims and methods of the Enlightenment in his thought, but his feelings did not get a new basis through a corresponding assimilation of meanings. As a consequence his self-expression became a superficial play with motifs, which Henri van de Velde characterized as a *mensogne des formes*.

The Modern Movement started as a protest against this "devaluation." Over and over again Giedion emphasized that its aim was to conquer the "split of thought and feeling," and to restore man as a *whole* personality. And he added: "It would however be a fundamental mistake to believe that socio-political change would itself cause today's maladjusted man, the product of century-long rupture of think-

7. The architectural thing: Chia.

8. Settlement: Monteriggioni.

9. Urban characters: Procida.

10. Urban characters: Amsterdam.

11. The wall: Vitorchiano.

12. The roof: Florence.

ing and feeling, to disappear." [27] What man needed as a help was rather a new "honest" and meaningful art and architecture. Thus it was the task of modern architecture to "give expression to the emotional content of the period."

The problem was interpreted in concrete terms, and first of all as a need for a "new dwelling." At the Exposition Internationale des Arts Décoratifs in Paris in 1925, Le Corbusier did not demonstrate the "spirit" of the new age by means of a didactic exhibition or a monumental symbol, but with a standard dwelling for the common man, which he called *Pavillon de l'esprit nouveau*. Evidently the "new spirit" he had in mind was directly related to the human and social problems of the time. It may seem surprising or even incomprehensible to our politicized period that the Modern Movement approached such problems in artistic terms. The Movement simply recognized that it is an illusion to believe that real improvements may be obtained through rationalistic planning. Improvements have to grow out of life itself, that is, from a deepened sense of being in the world. Therefore the Modern Movement also rejected the abstract education offered at the *academies*, and instead gave emphasis to "visual training" and "learning by doing." The preliminary course at the Bauhaus in fact aimed at the development of "observation, emotion and fantasy," [28] and when the work was continued in Chicago by Moholy-Nagy, the motto chosen was "design for life." In general we may say that the Modern Movement wanted to develop man's *imagination*. "Contemporary architecture had to take the hard way. As with painting and sculpture, it had to begin anew. It had to reconquer the most primitive things, as if nothing had ever been done before." [29] It is in this sense we must understand Mies van der Rohe's dictum: "Less is more," and we may also be reminded of Brancusi who said: "Simplicity is not an end in art, but one arrives at simplicity in spite of oneself, in approaching the real sense of things." In the new dwelling this kind of simplicity was concretized.

The aims of the movement were not restricted however to the dwelling. Giedion defined the second stage of the development of modern architecture as the "humanization of urban life," and the third as the manifestation of a "new monumentality," that is, the creation of buildings which symbolize man's social, ceremonial and community life. [30] In 1954 he added the "new regionalism" as a fourth point, and stated that the architect before he makes any plans has to study the way of life of the *place*. [31] Today the urban milieu, the symbolic or expressive form, and the local character have become major issues, but hardly anybody remembers that they were already part of the aims of the Modern Movement. Together the four stages constitute what Giedion called "the new tradition," that is, a development which makes the "hidden synthesis" of our period manifest. [32] It may be added that Giedion also was one of the first to demand the preservation of our historical *milieu*. After the war he fought against the demolition of old houses in his home-town Zürich, and we may also recall that his book *Space, Time and Architecture*

starts with a discussion of those historical phenomena he considered "constituent facts" to the development of modern architecture.

Over and over again the pioneers of the Modern Movement state that the means to heal the split between thought and feeling was a "new conception of space." [33] It may seem superfluous to mention again this well-known fact, but unfortunately the new space conception tends to get lost in the present confusion. Evidently its purpose was to make manifest the image of an open and dynamic world, as well as a new ideal of human freedom. In general, the "open plan" should "make room" for modern life, including its complexities and contradictions, which means something quite different from the general openness favoured by the vulgarizers of modern architecture. But the open plan only satisfies one aspect of the new conception of space. Any plan needs concrete embodiment, and, accordingly, Mies van der Rohe developed the concept of "clear construction," saying: "The structure is the backbone of the whole and makes the free plan possible. Without that backbone the plan would not be free, but chaotic and therefore constipated." [34] Clear construction implies that a building knows "what it wants to be," to use Louis Kahn's words. The vulgarizers, however, made clear construction degenerate into modular schematism. Together, open plan and clear construction satisfy the demand for a new conception of space.

We understand that the Modern Movement from the very beginning was concerned with the problem of meaning. When Giedion used the word "feeling," he evidently had in mind an authentic relationship with a meaningful environment. The "cult of the minimum" characteristic of much modern work thus expressed the wish for a return to something genuine. At the same time the modern movement accepted science and technology as necessary and useful aids. As a "purifying agent," rational analysis should give the new environment an objective basis. The pioneers however realized that thought alone would produce a meaningless world. Thought has to be inspired, and true inspiration can only come from life itself. Therefore the Modern Movement defined its aims in concrete, environmental terms.

The present criticism of modern architecture, however, proves that its results were less convincing than the aims and means. Although the Modern Movement certainly did not "sacrifice" architecture, the loss of place is a fact. Except for the works of particularly talented protagonists, the results are mostly characterized by monotony or by a new kind of play with devaluated (modern) motifs. Our discussion of the two faces of modern architecture makes it easy to understand what has happened. Environmental monotony, thus, stems from a one sided dominance of the "functional" approach, whereas visual chaos is due to a superficial understanding of the artistic side. In other words, the loss of place has come about because the Modern Movement did not succeed in healing the split between thought and feeling.

Our discussion moreover shows that the ap-

proaches of Venturi and Rossi are also rooted in the split. Venturi thus cultivates the artistic side, and aims at the expression of contents which cannot be rationalized. In general he renews the original aim of the Modern Movement, and hence finds a place within the "new tradition." His conception of the "decorated shed," however, may be understood as a resigned acceptance of the split; the shed being a functional-technical frame to which meanings are "superficially" added. [35] Rossi, instead, does not belong to the new tradition. His idealized architecture does not have any artistic dimension, but represents an extreme intepretation of the rationalistic approach. Evidently the aim is to proceed beyond the circumstantial logic of functionalism, and to establish an absolute basis. To do this, however, Rossi has to leave out our everyday world, and accordingly his works become the manifestation of a total alienation from life. [36]

Today the split of thought and feeling seems stronger than ever before. Various "design methodologies" have brought the functional approach to its culmination, and "architectural semiology" has reduced the dimension of meaning to a mere question of habit and taste. Whereas the design methodologies do not have to be considered in this context, semiology needs some comment.

In contrast to the approaches mentioned above, architectural semiology did not grow out of architectural practise. Rather it has been developed as a method of analysis and criticism, that is, of interpretation. [37]

As such, however, it may become important to practical work, and its influence is in fact already considerable, in particular with regard to the demand for meaning. Basically the semiologists consider meaning an aspect of communication, and hence a *linguistic* problem. Architecture "speaks," and uses "signs" which may be compared with the words and phrases of spoken language. One of the foremost advocates of architectural semiology, Charles Jencks, explains the approach thus: "People invariably see one building in terms of another, or in terms of a similar object; in short as a metaphor." [38] In other words, the meaning of a building consists in its "looking like" something else. This is considered to hold true for a building as a whole, or for parts of it. Jencks thus refers to buildings which look like "a marble doughnut," "stacked television sets" or "a big black piano," and a dome which looks like an "onion." The building or the part accordingly acts as a sign or "signifier" which is related to a "signified," and the "language of architecture" is a system of such signs. Language primarily develops through choice and habit, and may therefore be understood as a "code" which represents a particular "taste culture." [39] Evidently this implies a general relativization of meanings, although some semiologists do not exclude the existence of "archetypal" signs.

In our opinion semiology reduces the problem of meaning to one of its more superficial aspects. If the meaning of a thing (building) consists in its relationship to other things, this relationship evidently comprises much more than similar "looks." A jug is related to water and wine, but it does not look like a fluid! And still we are able to grasp its "meaning." Hence we do *not* primarily see one thing in terms of another, or as a metaphor. This is well known by philosophers concerned with the problem of meaning and interpretation. Thus Gaston Bachelard says: "A metaphor should be no more than an accident of expression, and it is dangerous to make a thought of it. A metaphor is a false image.[40] The remark of Bachelard suggests that semiology may not be sufficient to explain language, in particular poetical language, and also implies that the arts may not be considered "languages" at all.

In general it is doubtful whether much is gained by basing architectural interpretation on a method borrowed from another field. We may also add that semiology is not really concerned with *meaning*, but only discusses certain mechanisms of communication. As a typical product of the split of thought and feeling it reduces the dimension of meaning to one of its instrumental aspects.

The Modern Movement wanted to make architecture part of our everyday life-world, and thus to help man to gain a new existential foothold.

It failed, however, because it did not understand the structures of that world. Rather than developing a unified approach to reality, it continued to separate "art" and "science." Thus its philosophical basis remained vague, and the quality of its products depended entirely on the talent of the individual architect. We do not solve the problem, however, by accepting the split of thought and feeling as an irreversible fact, thus betraying the original aims of the movement. The new tradition is basically sound, but it needs a better foundation to become fertile. This foundation can only be based on a deeper understanding of that everyday life-world of which man and architecture form part.

Meaning in Architecture
When we use the term "life-world," we have in mind the everyday world of natural and man-made things, and of human action and interaction.[41] To describe the structure of this world, a new kind of approach is needed. Scientific concepts cannot be used, because science as a matter of principle abstracts from given reality to arrive at generalizations and "natural laws." Our aim is rather to reveal more clearly the nature of what is immediately given, and therefore our descriptions have to be concrete rather than abstract. The discipline which makes this possible, is known as *phenomenology*. "To the things themselves," was chosen as the battle-cry of early phenomenology, and the aim was to grasp the "thingness of things."[42] So far, however, phenomenology has been mostly concerned with problems of ontology and psychology, without giving much attention to the "environment" as such.[43] What we need is an "environmental phenomenology," that is a study of the "spatial" aspects of the life-world.[44]

The common expression to "take place," may serve as a point of departure for our discussion. When something happens, we say that it "takes place." This saying implies that "place" forms an

intrinsic part of the life-world. Thus we do not have "life" on the one hand and "place" on the other, but have to do with an integrated totality. In common usage the word "place" denotes a kind of "concrete" space, which is different from isotropic mathematical space, and has defined properties. The word is also used to name natural as well as man-made localities. In general we may say that *the subject-matter of environmental phenomenology is the nature and structure of place*, in relation to "life."

The concrete, non-Euclidean spatiality of the life-world is revealed by our everyday language. Thus we say that a thing, such as a building, is *on* the ground, *among* the trees, *next to* the hill, *under* the sky, and, more generally, *in* the landscape. The spatial relations in question in general refer to qualitative differences, such as the difference between "up" and "down." We could also grasp the same relations by saying that the thing *stands*, *rises* and *extends*. In both cases we indicate how the thing "is" in the world.

The spatial relations have to be unified in more comprehensive concepts. In our context it is useful to introduce "earth" and "sky" as general terms.[45] Life necessarily occurs "on the earth and under the sky," and is related to the general and local properties of the two realms.

In general the earth extends towards the horizon, or it rises towards the sky. Locally it comprises rocks, vegetation and water in different combinations. The sky is less tangible, but nevertheless has properties such as colour, "height" and quality of light. Together earth and sky constitute a "landscape," which is the basic form of concrete space.[46] Evidently landscapes are structured and comprise places of different kinds, such as valleys, bays, promontories, hilltops, groves and glades.

All places are defined by "things" which have particular properties. We have already suggested that the properties of things primarily consist in their being between earth and sky in a certain way. They "are in the world," and the relationships implied constitute their identity. We could also say that they "have a world," intending that the world of a thing consists in its relationship to other things. Rather than understanding the thing as an "imperfect" reflection of an archetype in the Platonic sense, we thus define it as a concentration or "gathering" of a world. "Gathering" is in fact the original meaning of the word "thing."[47] *The world which a thing gathers is its meaning*, and the meaning of a place is determined (*be-dingt*) by the things which constitute its "boundaries." Meaning is hence an intrinsic property of the world.

When we say that life "takes place," we imply that man may be considered a thing among other things, and that the spatiality of his being in the world is related to the spatiality of concrete space. The term "take place" thus implies places or "centres" from which paths extend horizontally into the environment, defining man's concrete world of action.

Life, however, does not only occur on earth but also under the sky, and thus implies the qualitatively different direction of the vertical.

13. Frank Lloyd Wright: Johnson Wax, Racine.
14. Le Corbusier: Ronchamp.

The simplest model of man's "existential space" is therefore a horizontal plane pierced by a vertical axis. [48]

As "existence," man is evidently something more than a thing among things. He is also in the world as "mood," "understanding" and "discourse," and as "being-with" others. [49] The life-world cannot be understood without taking these structures into consideration, because man is related to its other "elements" through these structures. The term "mood" here denotes the immediate state-of-mind which is the primordial relation between man and his environment, "understanding" comprises cognition as well as other practical and intellectual faculties, "discourse" denotes the revealing and communication of meaning, whereas "being-with" refers to the structures of social intercourse and association. It has to be emphasized that all the terms name basic structures of a life-world where man forms part, rather than aspects of "human nature." Thus the split between subject and object is abolished, and a comprehensive environmental phenomenology becomes possible.

The existential structures also have spatial implications. "Mood" implies that man *identifies* with a given environmental character, "understanding" that he *orientates* in space, "discourse" means that he *expresses* the spatiality of the situation, and "being-with" that he *shares* this spatiality with others. We could also say that he identifies with the things that constitute the environment by grasping their meaning, and that he orientates to their spatial relations by standing "under" or among them. "Mood" and "understanding" are interdependent aspects of man's being in the world, and indicate the basic unity of thought and feeling.

In our context, "discourse" is of particular interest. As part of human "discourse," *works of architecture reveal a spatiality of the life-world*. This "revelation" has two aspects. Firstly, any taking place presupposes that a space is available for the occurrence. The German word *einräumen*, which means "provide room for" or "admit," names this aspect well. [50] Originally *einräumen* meant to cut a glade in the forest, but it could also mean the building of an enclosure. In both cases the space provided is delimited by a boundary which determines its character or meaning. The second aspect therefore refers to the making of the boundary. As a composition of concrete "things" the boundary *embodies* the character relevant to the occurrence. Together provision of space and embodiment of character constitute a place.

Places are part of different life-situations. Evidently the more important are forms of togetherness. Following Louis Kahn, we shall call these forms "human institutions." As "home," "school," "shop," "church," "piazza" or "street," the place becomes the house of an institution.

Any institution demands a particular spatiality. A relevant character is especially important, as it embodies the "mood" which belongs to the institution in question. The spatiality of an institution, however, also relates to the spatiality of the locality where the institution is implanted. A man-made place is therefore to be understood as an institution which

has been adapted to a concrete locality "on earth under the sky." It may be inferred that places possess a structure which is both general and circumstantial.

Architecture is the making of places. It provides space and embodies characters. The places created are the houses of human institutions. Thus they form part of a *typology*. A type represents in other words the spatiality of a basic life-situation. As such the type is an abstraction, but in the single work it is "concretized" as a particular room or building. The city is a system of such concretizations, or, in Kahn's words, the place of "assembled institutions". The description of the structure of a place, typical or particular, has to be done in terms of spatial order and embodied character, that is in terms of "topology" and "morphology." It has to be emphasized that these aspects are interdependent and cannot be separated, except for analytic purposes. [51]

Topology is concerned with spatial order and comprises the problem of providing room for institutions. In the single work, it means a particular "spatial organization." By leaving out the built character, topology is concerned with the more abstract aspects of the structure of place. It does not, however, treat space in mathematical terms, but investigates the properties and possibilities of "lived" or "concrete" space. The point of departure is the model of existential space, that is, the motions of "centre" and "path." Definitions of spatial elements and interrelations are worked out, as well as the analysis of comprehensive types of such. As examples of topological types we may mention the non-geometrical groupings of farms and villages (cluster, row, enclosure), the axial symmetry of Roman lay-outs, the radiating patterns of Baroque plans, and the "open," fluid space of modern architecture. Of particular importance in topological description is the distinction between "outside" and "inside." In general, topology is founded on the spatiality of "understanding," which we have called "orientation." Psychological orientation implies an "environmental image," which makes spatial understanding possible. [52] Topology uses Gestalt principles and geometry as tools of description.

Morphology is concerned with the "how" of architectural form, and in the single work is concretized as "formal articulation." A spatial organization may be embodied in infinitely many ways, and accordingly the character changes. In general, the character of an architectural form is determined by how it "is" between earth and sky. The word "form" here denotes the well-known "elements" of a building: floor, wall and roof (ceiling). Together they make up what we have called the spatial *boundaries*. [53] Morphology is hence concerned with the articulation of the boundaries, as a means of defining an environmental character. Morphology asks the question: *How do buildings stand, rise, extend, open and close*? The word "stand" denotes the relationship to the earth, "rise" the relationship to the sky, "extend" the relationship to the horizon, and "open" and "close" the relationship between outside and inside. Standing is embodied through the treatment of the base and the wall. A massive

15. Louis I. Kahn: First Unitarian Church, Rochester.
16-17. Paolo Portoghesi: Baldi House, Rome.
18. Paolo Portoghesi: Papanice House, Rome.
19. Pietila: Dipoli.
20. MLTW: Johnson House.

and perhaps concave base ties the building to the ground, whereas emphasis on the vertical direction tends to make it "free." Vertical, rising lines and forms (such as a serrate silhouette) express an active relationship with the sky and a wish for receiving light. Verticalism and religious aspiration have in fact always gone together. The outside-inside relationship is first of all expressed by the treatment of the openings in the wall. In the wall, thus, earth and sky meet, and the spatial meanings of a life-world are embodied in this meeting.

Traditionally façades show a tripartite division: a ground floor or basement which is related to the earth, a top floor or attic which is related to the sky (also as "gable"), and between them a main floor (*piano nobile*) which represents the human domain proper. It is interesting to notice that the basement is mostly suppressed in churches, whereas the top floor may be reduced to a subordinate attic in classical palaces. Thus the two institutions are expressed by the articulation of the wall. Moreover we may point out that there exists a certain number of basic relationships between base and cornice, which are again related to types of site topography. But a building is not between earth and sky only in terms of horizontal rhythms and vertical tensions. "Earth" and "sky" also imply concrete properties such as material texture and colour. Morphology therefore understands embodiment as *built structure*. Through building, a character gets real presence. To the Greeks the word *techne*, technique, in fact meant to make something appear as what it is, a notion which is renewed in Kahn's concept of "inspired technology."[54] In general, morphology is founded on the spatiality of "mood," which psychologically implies an identification with the environment. Formal articulation is therefore a basic property of the life-world.

Together typology, topology and morphology make up "the language of architecture." The scope of the language of architecture is in general to translate the spatiality of the life-world into built form. This translation happens through a process of *gathering*. As a thing, a building "gathers world." We understand that what is gathered is earth and sky, as well as man in his relation to things and in his "being-with" others. We may also say that what is gathered is an *inhabited landscape*. The gathering is done by means of "visualization," "complementation" and "symbolization." *Visualization* means that the spatiality (order and character) of the environment is emphasized or explained by the work of architecture. *Complementation* means that the building adds something which is "lacking" in the environment, as when an "artificial oasis" is made in the desert. *Symbolization*, finally, serves to move an "understood world" from one location to another. From time immemorial man discovered basic structures of the life-world in particular places, which were thus considered "holy." By means of the language of architecture he could transfer his understanding to man-made centres, which thereby became gathering foci of civilization. Symbolization does not mean, however, that the architectural form is a "sign" in the semiological sense. As a "thing" it *is* in the world in a certain way, and thus becomes

an *imago mundi*.[55]

The use of conventional elements or quotations from the past, evidently belongs to symbolization. A quotation reminds of a gathering of world that is already done, and implies that man makes use of previous experiences.

Thus we recognize that certain gatherings, be they spatial organizations or articulate forms, remain valid through history. The quotation is hence employed to integrate the work in a general or local context. To do this, however, it has to *belong* to the new building, which means that the quotation has to relate to the way the new work is between earth and sky. If the quotation is arbitrarily "applied," it remains anachronistic. When the quotation visualizes or complements the new gathering it becomes meaningful, and shows us that to be in the world is always a situation which is new *and* old.[56]

The structure of a place, that is, the "dimension" where life "takes place," is the *genius loci*. According to ancient Roman belief every being has its genius, its guardian spirit. This spirit gives life to people and places, accompanies them from birth to death, and determines their character. The *genius* thus corresponds to what a thing *is*. We do not, however, understand the *genius* as an "essence" in the Platonic sense, but define it in terms of the world it gathers. Thus we have freed the concept of place from the extremes of idealism and relativism, and made it part of living reality.

It is a necessity for man to come to terms with the *genius* of the locality where his life takes place. We have to be "friends" with the environment to gain an existential foothold. The inhabitants of the desert have to be friends with the infinitely extended sand and the burning sun, whereas those of the nordic forest have to love fog, snow and cold winds. Such a "friendship" implies that the environment is experienced as *meaningful*. A correspondence between outer and inner world is thus established, which means that man's psyche is founded on understanding as a standing under, among, meaningful things. When things are thus "understood," they come close, the world becomes a world and man finds its identity.

Environmental friendship implies a respect for the place. We have to "listen" to the place, and try to understand its *genius*.[57] Only in this way we may give it a new (and old) interpretation and contribute to its self-realization. The "creative adaptation" implied ought to become the basis of architectural practise, as it was in the past.[58] An analytic, scientific understanding does not suffice to this end, nor does a semiological interpretation of architectural form. A new phenomenological approach is needed, which understands things in terms of what they gather. To respect the *genius loci* does not mean to *"freeze"* the place and negate history. On the contrary it means that life at any time is *rooted*, and that history becomes something more than a series of accidents.

To be friends with a place means to *care* for the place. To care implies to "take care," which in our context has been understood as "creative adaptation." An authentic architecture is an architecture

of care. An architecture of care, however, is necessarily an architecture of *participation*. As togetherness is a basic existential structure, a place is always something we share with others. "Participation" means to "take part," that is, to share a common value. Place is such a value of communal sharing, and an architecture of participation can only be defined in terms of place. The place is in fact used to define one's identity, as when we say: "I am a Roman", or, "I am a New Yorker." To be on earth under the sky means to be located, and human identity goes together with the identity of place. To have a place in common means to possess a common (but not identical) identity, that is, to belong to a fellowship. The places we share are of different sizes, and form a hierarchy of "enviromental levels." "Landscape," "settlement," "urban space," "building" and "interior" are the words commonly used to name these levels. [59]
When man belongs to a place we say that he *dwells*. Firstly this means that he understands the place, and secondly that he is able to "concretize" his understanding in works of architecture.
An authentic architecture is an architecture which helps man into dwelling. Man dwells when he builds. As a thing, the building brings the inhabited landscape close to man, so that he may experience his existence as meaningful. "Meaning in architecture" is therefore not a problem of communication. Meaning in architecture is accomplished when the work of architecture reveals the spatiality of the life-world. This revelation depends on how a work of architecture is in the world, that is, how it stands, rises, extends, opens and closes, in a concrete sense of space and embodiment. When a work of architecture reveals the spatiality of the life-world, it becomes a work of *art*.

Towards an authentic architecture

As "design for life," modern architecture wanted to offer an answer to the demand for meaning. When it failed, it was because it did not develop an adequate understanding of the life-world, and rather relapsed into quantification and formalism. In the works of some protagonists, however, a new authentic architecture has been realized. Not to lose the "new tradition" out of sight, it is important to recall the most important contributions.
When Frank Lloyd Wright wanted to explain his approach to architecture, he said: "I was born an American child of the ground and of space." [60] In this phrase, a complete life-world is implied. The open natural space of the great American plains is there, as well as the "frontier" as a dimension of human conquest. But the need to settle and get rooted is also included. Accordingly Wright "destroyed the box" and transformed the house into a juxtaposition of vertical and horizontal planes, which serve both to guide the spatial extension and to mediate between earth and sky. And he introduced the vertical chimney-stack at the centre to make the house stand and rise while it extends. This centre also serves as a meaningful core to the open plan. Thus Wright wrote: "It comforted me to see the fire burning deep in the solid masonry of the house itself." [61] We could also say that the jux-taposed planes visualize open space, whereas the chimney-stack complements this openness by offering a point of identification.
Wright's approach to the world evidently did not consist in the observation and analysis of European rationalism, but rather in a direct experience of "meanings," or in Wright's own words, in "a hunger for reality." And he knew how to translate this experience into built form. Wright was not alone, however, in this authentic approach to architecture. Mackintosh, Gaudi, Saarinen the elder, Horta, Guimard, Olbrich and Behrens also knew how to gather and translate an understood life-world. [62] All of them were concerned with the contents of a new epoch, but as they were locally rooted, they arrived at different interpretations. At the outset of the modern movement we thus encounter works which offer a promise of a new unity of thought and feeling, and may hail the birth of a genuine *art nouveau*.
During the second stage of the development, that is, between the two wars, the new architecture however underwent a transformation: it became "international." Rather than taking the immediate situation as a point of departure, attention was now concentrated on the definition of a new, generally valid, language of architecture. [63] The "five points" of Le Corbusier are representative of this search. His *pilotis* and *fenêtre en longeur* embody a new kind of standing and rising, and a new openness. The *pilotis* preserve the continuity of the earth at the same time as they define the building as spatial organization.
The traditional enclosed ground floor is thus transformed into an "open place" where a general order becomes visible. The *fenêtre en longeur* articulates this order without contradicting the general openness. In his buildings, Le Corbusier developed the articulation into a rich and complex interplay of forms, with the purpose of "moving the sensitive heart." His famous dictum from *Vers une Architecture* expresses this aim: "My house is practical. I thank you as I might thank Railway engineers, or the Telephone service. You have not touched my heart. But suppose that walls rise towards heaven in such a way that I am moved. I perceive your intentions. Your mood has been gentle, brutal, charming or noble. The stones you have erected tell me so... This is architecture."
We understand that it would be wrong to reject the works of the "international" phase of the modern development because it did not give due attention to local conditions and traditions. Architecture is circumstantial *and* general, and works of architecture may have great value, even if circumstances are excluded. The strength of the early works of Le Corbusier, Gropius and Mies van der Rohe in fact consists in such an "exclusion."
It was not the intention, however, that architecture should go on being exclusively general. Gropius always rejected the notion of an "international style," and Le Corbusier in his later works demonstrated a growing interest in local and circumstantial factors. The creation of true places evidently presupposes that buildings are "rooted," in the sense that the general is adapted to the situa-tion.
The need for a synthesis of the general and the local was felt already in the thirties. The great protagonist in this third phase of the modern development was Alvar Aalto. Coming from a country with a strong local character, Aalto from the very outset aimed at creating a regional modern architecture. To fulfill this aim, he transformed the general openness of modern space into complex organisms, which open and close while they extend, just like the continuous patterns of the Finnish forests and lakes. And he visualized the standing and rising of the local rocks and trees in the built form. Thus Giedion said: "Finland is with Aalto wherever he goes. It provides him with that inner source of energy which always flows through his work. It is as Spain is to Picasso or Ireland to James Joyce." [64]
In the works of the "third generation" of modern architects, the creation of authentic places has been continued. A regionally valid modern architecture is today found in many countries, from the "Finnish" works of Pietilä, to the "British" buildings of Stirling, the "Dutch" lay-outs of van Eyck, the "German" projects of Ungers, the "Catalan" inventions of Bofill, and the "American" houses of MLTW. Three architects deserve special mention in this context: Robert Venturi, Paolo Portoghesi and Jørn Utzon. We do not have to repeat what has already been said on Venturi's use of "conventional elements" and recognition of the wall as where architecture "takes place," but should just add that his ideas have opened up for a more subtle interpretation of the new spatiality.
Portoghesi has also taken interest in the articulation of the facade as an embodiment of being between earth and sky. Thus he has used curved tufa walls to combine basic traits of the Roman tradition with modern openness, and has decorated similar walls with coloured vertical stripes to express how the building rises up from the ground to receive the light of the sky. The most important contribution of Portoghesi, however, is his notion of space as a "system of places," an idea which he has developed theoretically in terms of interacting spatial "fields," and realized in several interesting buildings. [65]
Jørn Utzon has also been deeply concerned with spatial problems.
His juxtaposition of solid platforms and hovering roofs reveas a true understanding of what it means to be between earth and sky. [66] This juxtaposition constitutes a general theme in Utzon's works, a theme which is however varied according to the local situation. The idea represents something more than a metaphor of rocks and clouds. Its true importance resides in its bringing back to life the basic "dimensions" of architecture. In his platforms, Utzon makes the earth become alive again. The abstract quality of the floor in early functionalist architecture here gives way to a concrete *ground* which offers man a sense of security and possibilities of movement. Moreover he gives back to the roof its space-creating role. Whereas early Modernism mostly reduced the roof to an abstract horizontal plane, Utzon's roofs are a manifestation

of man's being *under the sky*. In his projects Utzon has used these general concepts to create true places which recover the figural quality of a "thing" in relation to an understood landscape.

Whereas the architects mentioned have contributed significantly to the development of a new formal language, Louis Kahn approached the demand for an authentic architecture in a more complete, philosophical way. Although he presented his ideas in aphoristic form, they constitute a coherent "theory." [67] Thus he tackled the problems of provision of room and embodiment of character in terms of the spatiality of human institutions, saying: "If you create the realm of spaces you make the institution alive." His famous question: "What does the building want to be?," concentrates his integral approach in a simple formula.

In his buildings and projects Kahn shows that his approach leads to rich and varied spatial and formal solutions. Thus he proves that a meaningful, authentic architecture does not consist in a combination of codified "signs" or "archetypal elements," but in the revelation of the spatiality of the life-world. This revelation implies that the works are new as well as old. "I am trying to find new expressions of old institutions," Kahn said. In general Kahn develops the notions of "open space" and "clear construction," and thus belongs to the "new tradition."

Modern architecture is alive. Its basic aim has always been to heal the split between thought and feeling, which implies the creation of places which allow for human orientation. The architects who have contributed to fulfilling this aim, have abolished the abstract "planning" of radical functionalism to base their work on environmental understanding and care. Thus they have satisfied the demand for meaning.

Modern architecture is alive. Its basic aim has always been to heal the split of thought and feeling, which implies the creation of places which allow for human orientation and identification. Today we are able to distinguish between the true contributions to this end and the abstract, "functional" planning which is responsible for the destruction of our environment. We also understand that rationalism and materialism are forms of human alienation, and that an authentic architecture rather presupposes a return "to the things themselves," that is, a poetic approach to reality. This approach has always been at the root of modern architecture, and today it again comes forth. [68] In the works of architects such as Robert Stern, Stanley Tigermann, Michael Graves and Ricardo Bofill, architecture is recovered as a circumstantial embodiment of a general language. Although they protest against degenerate Modernism, these architects belong to the new tradition, and their artistic creations satisfy the demand for meaning.

1. A "radical functionalism" was proposed by C. Alexander in *Notes on the Synthesis of Form*, Cambridge, Mass. 1964.
2. R. Venturi: *Complexity and Contradiction in Architecture*, New York 1967.
3. A. Rossi: *L'architettura della città*, Padua 1966.
4. Venturi: op. cit. p. 15.
5. Venturi: op. cit. p. 22.
6. Venturi: op. cit. p. 23.
7. Venturi: op. cit. p. 88.
8. Venturi: op. cit. p. 50.
9. C. Jencks: *The Language of Post-Modern Architecture*, 2nd ed. London 1978. pp. 131ff.
10. R. Venturi: "Une définition de l'architecture comme abri décoré," *L'architecture d'aujourd'hui* 178.
11. Venturi: *Complexity...* cit.
12. Rossi: op. cit. passim.
13. Rossi: op. cit. p. 11.
14. Rossi's own presentation of his method remains vague. For a good introduction see: E. Bonfanti: "Elementi e costruzione," *Controspazio* 10, 1970.
15. Rossi: op. cit. p. 33.
16. Rossi: op. cit. p. 31.
17. Rossi: op. cit. p. 13.
18. It has often been observed that the buildings of Rossi hardly allow for human life to "take place."
19. In general see *Architecture rationelle*, Bruxelles, 1978.
20. A. Lorenzer in H. Berndt, A. Lorenzer, K. Horn: *Architecktur als Ideologie*, Frankfurt am Main 1968.
21. C. Norberg-Schulz: *Intentions in Architecture*, London 1964.
22. C. Alexander: op. cit.
23. W. Gropius: *The New Architecture and the Bauhaus*, London, 1935, p. 19.
24. Mies van der Rohe: "On Technology," *L'architecture d'aujourd'hui* 79.
25. H. Meyer: "Bauen," *Bauhaus* Vol. 2, nr. 4.
26. S. Giedion: "Napoleon and the Devaluation of Symbols." *Architectural Review* 11, 1947.
27. S. Giedion: *Space, Time and Architecture*, 5th ed. Harvard 1967, p. 879.
28. L. Moholy-Nagy: *The New Vision*, New York 1947.
29. S. Giedion: *Architecture, you and me*, Harvard 1958. p. 29.
30. Giedion: op. cit. p. 27.
31. Giedion: op. cit. pp. 138ff.
32. S. Giedion: *Constancy, Change and Architecture*, Harvard 1961.
33. Gropius: op. cit. p. 20.
34. C. Norberg-Schulz: "Rencontre avec Mies van der Rohe," *L'architecture d'aujourd'hui* 79.
35. The Early Christian basilica is something more than a "decorated shed."
36. Rossi shares: the negation of life "as it is" with totalitarian ideologies such as Fascism, a fact which undoubtedly counts for general similarities of architectural expression.
37. See C. Jencks, G. Baird (eds.): *Meaning in Architecture*, London 1969. Also G. Broadbet, R. Bunt, C. Jencks: *Signs, Symbols and Architecture*, New York 1980.
38. Jencks: *The Language...* cit. p. 40.
39. Jencks: op. cit. p. 42.
40. G. Bachelard: *The Poetics of Space*. Boston 1964. p. 77.
41. The term *Lebenswelt* was introduced by E. Husserl in *Die Krisis der europäischen Wissenschaften* (1936).
42. M. Heidegger: *Sein und Zeit* (1927), Introduction II, 7.
43. Valuable hints are however given in Bachelard: op. cit. and in O.F. Bollnow: *Mensch und Raum*, Stuttgart 1963.
44. C. Norberg-Schulz: *Genius Loci*, Milan 1979.
45. M. Heidegger: "Bauen Wohnen Denken," *Vorträge und Aufsätze*, Pfullingen 1954.
46. Norberg-Schulz: op. cit.
47. M. Heidegger: "Das Ding", *Vorträge und Aufsätze*, Pfullingen 1954.
48. C. Norberg-Schulz: *Existence, Space and Architecture*, London 1971, p. 21.
49. Heidegger: *Sein und Zeit*, cit.
50. Heiddegger: *Die Kunst und der Raum*, St. Gallen 1969.
51. C. Norberg-Schulz: *Louis I. Kahn, Idea ed immagine*, Rome 1980.
52. We use the word "image" in the sense of Kevin Lynch.
53. "A boundary is not that at which something stops but, as the Greeks recognized, the boundary is that from which something begins its *presencing*." Heidegger: "Bauen Wohnen Denken," cit.
54. Norberg-Schulz: *Louis I. Kahn*, cit.
55. M. Heidegger: *Hebel der Hausfreund*, Pfullingen 1957.
56. Norberg-Schulz: Genius Loci, in particular the chapter on Rome.
57. P. Portoghesi: *Le inibizioni dell'architettura moderna*, Bari 1974.
58. C. Norberg-Schulz: "Bauen als Problem des Ortes," *Anpassendes Bauen*, Munich 1978.
59. We cannot here discuss how the interior concentrates and "explains" the "exterior" world. See C. Norberg-Schulz: *Pieter de Bruyne and the Meaning of Furniture*, Ghent 1980.
60. F. L. Wright: *The Natural House*, New York 1954. Also: C. Norberg-Schulz: "La casa e il movimento moderno," *Lotus* 9.
61. Wright: op. cit. p. 37.
62. C. Norberg-Schulz: *Casa Behrens*, Rome 1980.
63. In general see Giedion: *Space, Time and Architecture*, cit.
64. Giedion: op. cit. p. 620.
65. C. Norberg-Schulz: *On the Search for Lost Architecture*, Rome 1975.
66. J. Utzon: "Platforms and Plateaus," *Zodiac* 10.
67. Norberg-Schulz: *Louis I. Kahn*, cit.
68. A stimulating introduction to the current tendencies is given in C. Jencks: The Language of Post-Modern Architecture, London 1978.

Towards radical eclecticism
Charles Jencks

Architects today are looking for an eclecticism which goes beyond the easy shuffling of styles that characterized building in the 19th century. They are approaching a style I would call Radical Eclecticism, one that seeks to enhance a pluralist society in all its richness and diversity and one that looks for a deeper justification for its use of various languages of architecture that existed in the past. In the nineteenth century there were many attacks on the facile mixing of styles, attacks on a weak aestheticism and permissive jumbling of this and that (just as in the fifties and sixties of this century there were attacks on a frivolous historicism). Eclecticism when so opportunistic was called "indifferentism," its botched hybrids were called "mongrel" architecture or, even worse, "macaronic." Positively it was seen as the Queen Anne Revival ("a Gothic game played with Neo-Classical counters" as Goodhardt-Rendel put it) and later the Yachting Style, Youth Style, Liberty Style, Art Nouveau and Free Style. Between opportunism and freedom, shallowness and creativity, this eclecticism swung, never reaching a firm philosophical basis and teachable body of theory. This Radical Eclecticism aspires to do, to put the illicit practice into the academy where it can be taught and talked about with conviction – at the moment a hope for the future. Here I will develop three of the fundamental arguments for Radical Eclecticism – its basis in the context of the building, the character of the functions and the taste-culture of the users – and show its fortunes in America and Europe, how it varies in quality and depth. To bring out the fundamental split in attributes towards the past, I will contrast Late-Modern with Post-Modern architecture.

Late and Post Modernism in America
Late-Modern architecture is an exaggeration of a previously existing language of architecture, whereas Post-Modernism is the combination of this language with others (vernacular, historical or commercial) and is thus "doubly-coded." Quite obviously Late-Modern architects have reacted against the failures of Modern architecture just as much as other groups. Where Modern architects produced the "dumb box," the blank parallelopiped of glass and steel, they have produced the sensuous, shaped box, a slick-tech skyscraper of mirror-plate which is humorous rather than dull. Or they have resorted to articulating the surface to give visual delight, extreme articulation, which makes them once again, Late rather than High Modernists.

The most convincing of these Late-Modernists, as well as one of the first, was Louis Kahn who, in the late fifties, started designing buildings around exaggerated joints and technical elements such as the extract ventilators. Where Modern architecture was brittle and flat, his buildings were heavy and powerful; they embodied the sculptural weight of the Classical tradition, its *gravitas*. Louis Kahn also looked to traditional architecture for cues – to San Gimignano, Mycenae and Rome – but he kept this historical reminiscence very much in the background as a Modernist would. Thus one of his last buildings, the Kimball Art Museum in Fort Worth, Texas, has its Roman barrel-vaults and Beaux-Arts symmetry, but these references are completely absorbed within the primitive forms, the black surfaces, the reinforced concrete and primary forms. This is not real eclecticism or Post-Modernism, it is the clever and implicit use of history which Mies and Le Corbusier would have allowed themselves. And the results are as entirely convincing as the work of these Modernists; that is as long as one looks clearly at the spiritual expression of building and doesn't ask embarrassing questions such as – "Where is the entrance? How does the building relate to Fort Worth, the Texan culture and the variety of art displayed within?" Such issues of content were not addressed by Kahn any more than they are by Modernists and Late-Modernists. The content of their architecture is the structure, space and pure form and it is these values which they hope to substitute for the missing ones. When these values are successfully realised we overlook the obvious faults; convincing architecture makes hypocrites of us all, makes us "suspend our disbelief" and balance aesthetic gains against symbolic shortcomings.

Late-Modernism is dependent on such trade-offs for its appreciation. Obviously weighted with the problems of Modernism – the overscaled commissions of Late-Capitalism, the £ 50 million quick-built monolith, the symbolic poverty, the malapropism – it mitigates these problems with an aesthetic sweetner, and anaesthetic some would say. Most clearly this produces the main styles of Late-Modernism: besides the slick-tech facade, there is the extreme articulation of surfaces, the expression of every joint, every different function, every different constructional element. The work of Gerhard Kallmann, a follower of Kahn, and the work of José Lluis Sert, a follower of Le Corbusier, shows how dynamic and fractured such articulation can be. For the "dumb box" of Modernism it substitutes the voluble talking-machine which may tell us more than we want to know: where every room is, where heat circulates and people flow. In Late-Modernism the content often is movement itself: you are always going somewhere, to paraphrase Gertrude Stein, but never getting anywhere. In addition the hallmarks of this style are a treatment of structure as ornament and overall form as sculptural mass.

Whereas Hitchcock and Johnson defined the International Style as an emphasis on volume rather than mass, the structure and skin rather than the heavy masonry wall, we now have once again an emphasis on constructional weight. Pre-eminently it is massive sculpture in reinforced concrete. The work of I.M. Pei, overvalued often as Amercia's best architecture, characterizes this style of Late-Modernism. Its major competition is the much more light-weight but deeper work of the New York Five, the revival of Le Corbusier's early period as complicated sculptural form. John Hejduk, Richard Meier and Peter Eisenman take this early Modernism to an extreme as they elaborate axes of rotation and other formal devices such as frontal layering.

Finally and most obviously there is the style I have mentioned above, the supersensual slick-tech style of skyscrapers and other fragmented megabuildings. It is appropriate that this form of Late-Modernism has flourished mostly in one centre of Late-Capitalism, Texas, as well as Japan, and produced two of its masterpieces (if we once again avoid embarrassing questions). Philip Johnson's twin towers in Houston, the Pennzoil skywedges, are obvious distortions and exaggerations of Modern skyscrapers: two triangular, minimalist black wedges are placed ten feet apart on edge. The tension created between these two sharp angles is electric, to use a metaphor prompted by these nodes of mechanical power. From one angle the diagonal chamfers of the roofs line up to produce a "double-whole," one building out of two, an interpretation which is supported by the left-over triangle of space between the towers (that forms the suggestion of a whole void). More precisely, the space enclosed on two sides is itself a mirror image of the two wedges. Add to these visual illusions the reflective glass and the optical buzz created by the space-frame and one has an aesthetic vertigo that is opposite to the stability of Miesian skyscrapers. Where they were harmonious, Johnson's are dissonant, where they repeated a visual element to create order, Johnson multiplies the repetition to create optical vibrations, a shimmering surface and space. Still the Pennzoil is a simple building (or two) like Modernist ones, but it is a "complex simplicity" responding to the boring box as Post-Modernists did with another kind of complexity.

Complex simplicity, the visual paradox or oxymoron of Late-Modernism can also be seen in the Hyatt Hotel in Dallas designed in silver reflective glass by Welton Becket Associates. Conceptually it is a simple slab block, but one broken into seven fragments which stagger up and down in profile and turn to the side in plan. This, "the largest glass sculpture in the World," a necessity for Texas, is still a simple building. It's constructed from the exaggerated repetition of a single element – the suare mirrorplate block. Its atrium plan, its bedrooms and corridors are all very familiar, and simple elements are borrowed from other Late-Modern hotels, those of John Portman. It is only in the fracture and juxtaposition, the shimmer and dazzle, that one finds a vanishing complexity, and one imagines that the historical overtones, the Art Deco echelons, and the anthropomorphism, the animal image, are unintended.

Post-Modernists, by contrast, intend their metaphorical imagery and in the most effective cases tie it to purely architectural meanings. Thus Caesar Pelli and Stanley Tigermann mix body imagery with constructional expression. The former's "Blue Whale" is also an "architectural moulding," the latter's "Daisy House" is both "male and female," and these metaphors are mixed with crisply detailed window elements which call attention to themselves as windows. Since I have written on the importance of this mixed and suggested metaphor elsewhere, I might just point out one aspect of the anthropomorphism, usually referred to as empathetic. The argument of Post-Modernists, which is widely shared now, is that we project bodily states into architectural form, finding a correspondence between our own structure and that of a building, its facade and our face, its columns and our torso or legs, its decoration and our own (eyebrows, lips and hair to name three ornamental elements). The empathetic projection may be childish or naive as it often is with the popular American bungalow where these features are exaggerated; or it may be complicated and subliminal as it is in much classical architecture and the work of Michael Graves. In either case it is a quite natural response, one suppressed by the Modernists (except for Le Corbusier and occasionally Aalto) and one emphasized by the Post-Modernists. The latter focus on it for the quite obvious reason that it is so universal. Since we are so apt to see ourselves in architecture, this projection can be one element in humanizing abstract form. It is perhaps the most powerful means of gaining the inhabitant's confidence, or engaging the passerby. An immediate rapport is felt between the inanimate building and our body. Classical architecture recognized this in its exaggeration of columns and mouldings, in its profusion of caryatids and sculptural figures, while Post-Modernists are investing their own buildings with an equal variety of body images.

Many of them are raw and too obvious, denying the truth of this empathetic response that it is most effective when felt and not explicitly seen. But a case can also be made for literal body images, the face house, and so forth. If discreetly used in parts of a building they can cue the inhabitant to the implicit metaphors: the way the "body of the house," the plan, might have its own life, the way views are "framed," the way entrances welcome and "enclose." Effective body imagery is thus a subtle blending of implicit and explicit metaphor.

Several American architects are exploring this anthropomorphism while keeping a residual commitment to Modern architecture. Their work can be seen as transitional, as one-half Post-Modern, to split an already split hair. Michael Graves designs esoteric and complicated buildings which have a breadth of architectural reference perhaps best perceived by the architectural historian, although all of his work has some witty and obvious reference. Frank Gehry, with his *ad hoc* industrial aesthetic, wraps corrugated aluminium boxes around traditional buildings producing a complex and humorous set of juxtapositions. Eugene Kupper, another West-Coast architect, also creates spaces full of ambiguity and surprise. An extensive analysis of any of their recent buildings would show the characteristic Post-Modern space: fragmented, rich with symbols, ambiguous, layered with cut-out screens and ordered for an experience of continuous surprise much like an English landscape garden. These aspects should be contrasted with the "universal space" of Mies and Modernism, but they can only be alluded to in this brief analysis. An important point, which is raised by so much eclectic work today concerns the question of pastiche and it is to this I would like to turn in show-

ing the work of the Post-Modernists. Pastiche has two popular meanings, both of which are rather pejorative: it means a work of art which is a medley of various sources, and a work which recalls the style or subject matter of a well-known author. In short either a hodge-podge or a cliché, or more likely both together, a mish-mash of stereotypes. Involved in these judgements, however, is the truism that one man's pastiche is another man's creative interpretation of tradition: e.g. Mozart's re-use of comic opera. For Post-Modernists then, involved with tradition, the distinction between good and bad pastiche is crucial: let us use the positive word re-invention when it is successful. How do we judge this?

Philip Johnson, who spoke in London, 1979, about his "twelve twists" on tradition, is an opportune case for treatment. His Dallas Chapel in the form of a spiral ziggurat, one of his twelve thefts from the past, borrows quite directly from the ninth-century minaret at Samarra. It recalls this building explicitly along with the Tower of Babel and a host of other well-known spirals. In fact it recalls other buildings more than it calls out for attention in its own right. Partly this is due to the flat surface and blank detailing, the reduction of the building to an archetype and diagram. The minimal inventiveness — one enters through the lowest wing of the form, and stained glass spirals, predictably, up to the centre point — is not enough to recharge these shapes with new meaning. They remain past references and very incongruous in Dallas at that. To generalize, a pastiche fails when it recalls a previous building more than it convinces one that its present re-use of form is inventive and suitable. Johnson's more controversial AT & T building is also more convincing. Here he has borrowed from Brunelleschi, Ledoux and the skyscraper architect Raymond Hood — the references are obvious and freely admitted. But they have more relevance in this New York context than the previous ones do in Dallas because they relate to the workings of a skyscraper (with its customary tripartite division) and the New York tradition of these buildings. The AT & T caps the sky with a temple form as skyscrapers did in New York for fifty years, from 1880-1930. Its bottom piers, multiplied beyond the necessity of structural support, create a sheltered space at street level. This semi-public place may become, with its arcade in the rear, a new form of transitional urban space, half open and protected. It is hard to judge before completion, but at least it looks in model form like an inventive variation on the atrium and arcade of Portman's work. The side elevation and the gilded statue within are another matter. Here we have a banal revivalism. The statue located on an axis, where the altar would be in Brunelleschi's chapel, is a pastiche, the "Winged Goddess of AT & T" as it were.

This is the kind of devaluation of symbols which Siegfried Giedion attacked and which the Modern Movement was invented in order to stop.

Robert Venturi, among the Post-Modernists, has been most articulate in his re-use of symbols and the problems this creates. Much of his work plays with pastiche, but in a more knowing way than

Johnson. He is careful to use a traditional motif, a cliché, so that it both communicates conventionally and differently. This has an obvious advantage over Modernism, which eschewed conventional symbolism, and Straight Revivalism, which fell into a stereotype, both of which failed to communicate effectively with the user of buildings for exactly opposite reasons. Venturi has steered a middle course, not always successfully, between these extremes of non-communication.

In his house for his mother (another one of these Post-Modern commissions) he has used applied ornament and traditional house forms in a symbolic way. For instance the exterior shows a Palladian symmetry and various other signs of homestead: the pitched roof, the off-centre chimney and gable. With these essential stereotypes of the house he has produced unstereotypical variation. Some windows are exaggerated in size, e, the top floor lunette, to increase the scale. An exterior dado, or string-course, bisects windows also to increase the size of the small building and make it more formal. Further decoration is applied to signify the public entrance, or front door, but it consists of a "false arch," a broken slat of wood which also has a signifying function: to indicate further distortions in conventional usage. One enters not straight ahead under the arch, but at right angles to it. The shifted axis, signalled by a curve to one side, has since become a conventional device for Post-Modernists.

Two followers of Venturi, Robert Stern and Thomas Gordon Smith (an architect still in his twenties) have developed the same complicated spatial motifs, use of historical styles and applied ornament.

Stern uses decorative mouldings in a Venturian way to bisect the windows, increase the scale and symbolise important areas such as the front door. He adds to these functions an older one, the role of ornament to symbolise well-being, to "hide a fault in construction," to take the eyes off an otherwise cheap and ugly facade. The question of ugliness, previously raised in the 19th century as a sometimes positive contribution, has once again been formulated by Venturi and Stern. Their buildings are often calculatedly awkward. This can result from an attempt at "inclusivism" trying to include and show as much different content as possible, the contradictions of functional requirements, even the different tastes of the users; in short ugliness may be a by-product of a straightforward approach to a pluralistic society. Or, more questionably, it may be a simple reaction against the too-facile beauty of Modernism, the policy to which they contrast on their own the "exclusivism" of Mies. There is a reactive tinge within some Post-Modernism which makes it more complicated and awkward than it has to be, even according to Venturi's doctrine of "inclusivism and the difficult whole." Against this trend the quite powerful work of Thomas Gordon Smith is refreshing. Using very strong colours, part of the San Francisco tradition, and an eclectic mix of fragments — Michelangelo, Dientzenhofer, Baroque, Modern, Vernacular — he manages to incorporate this diversity with elegance and strength.

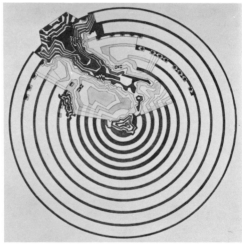

We see in these Post-Modernists an implicit trend towards incorporating more and more style from the past. In the early sixties this eclecticism was hesitant and embarrassed, the first tentative steps into a previously prohibited area. Today the re-use of historical motifs is frank and confident, we have achieved a more easy-going relation to our traditions and the stage is being set for eclecticism itself. The question is no longer whether to use any and all styles, but how to use them with conviction and this must depend in part on a philosophy. As mentioned at the onset, there are three clear justifications for choosing a style, or mixing them as the case may be: the context of the building, the character of the functions and the taste-culture of the users. We can see these three aspects in Charles Moore's half-completed Piazza d'Italia, New Orleans, an example of Radical Eclecticism worth analysing in depth.

As the aerial view of the urban context reveals, this piazza is set in a mixed area of New Orleans. To one side is a Modern skyscraper, the black and white graphics of which have been taken up as a motif to generate a graduating circle of rings. This circular form, at once a Modern "bull's-eye" and Baroque urban form (*Place des Victoires*, Paris), permeates out into three streets giving a cue to the passer-by that something unusual occurs behind the existing buildings. This setting up of an expectation, and the use of veiling devices that at once proclaim and hide — the archway, the pergola — dramatise the approach. We are pulled towards the centre of the bull's-eye and expect to find there a symmetrical, circular culmination. What actually occurs both satisfies and contradicts this supposition. There are indeed a centre and circular forms, but instead of them confirming a Baroque centrality, they set up certain new expectancies. The circles are partial discs, screens of columns that spin asymmetrically on the diagonal of movement towards a new culmination point, the tallest form, an archway, in fact a Modern *Serliana*. This diagonal is reinforced by the cascade of broken forms, — the boot of Italy — which focuses on the highest plateau, the Italian Alps. Thus we have a clear organisation of form and content. As Italy rises towards the Northern Alps, so too do the Five Orders of *Italian* columns, and they culminate in a new, Sixth Order, which enframes the future restaurant. This invention for a German Restaurant (they will hang sausages in the windows) Moore calls the Deli Order. Neon necklaces around the neck of these columns further indicate that this is the twentieth century, and the fact that commercial "bad taste" is a vart of it. Moore is quite committed to architectural whimsy and building-puns (he calls watering metopes "wetopes") and it is a credit to his teamwork that these calculated lapses in judgement don't get the upper hand. They are part of a rich mix of meanings rather in the way similar elements are absorbed into Shakespearean drama. A point worth stressing is that the plurality of meanings in this scheme could not have been invented by one designer. Moore has teamed up with two local architects from the firm of Perez and Associates and these designers supplied much of the peculiar cultural knowledge. They were the ones to stress the importance of the annual St. Joseph's festival — the pretext for the fountain and piazza. Once a year the Italian community comes to the fore to celebrate its presence and they do so by selling Italian specialites and local concoctions (muffalattas, salami, cheese, etc.) on the day of their patron saint. Since the ostensible reason for the piazza was to give identity to the Italian Community in a city where other ethnic groups dominate (the French, the Spanish, the blacks and Anglos), there was an opportunity for historicist rhetoric. There was important social content ready to be symbolised if the designer knew what to symbolise and had the rhetorical skill to carry it through. (We should note in passing that Late-Modernists end up signifying "technique, construction, movement," because they have no great interest in social content).

What was the content in this case? "Italianness" clearly, as symbolised by the echoes of the Trevi fountain, the Five rather than Three Orders, the strong earth colouring, the Latin inscription ("This fountain was given by the citizens of New Orleans as a gift to all the people") and above all the plan of Italy, (with the Adriatic and Tyrrhenian seas and rivers represented by moving water). Since the community is made up mostly of Sicilians this island occupies the centre of the bull's-eye and becomes also another focal point — set against "the Swiss Alps" and "the German Restaurant." It also rises in black and white granite and slate and turns into a speaker's rostrum from which the mayor can address an audience on St. Joseph's day. This peculiar conceit, like the idea of setting up an area for selling food (the Italian community use wagons on tracks for this) is the kind of detailed social content that emerges only after patient enquiry into a local culture. These particular functions give the rhetorical forms a credibility they would otherwise lack. Indeed some Modern architects have perceived this work as pure pastiche, partly, I think, because they haven't visited the piazza and seen the rationale for each form. These rationales exist, once again, on many levels.

To return to the urban context we can see how the piazza, void, not only provides a contrast to the rehabilitated fabric, solid, but becomes another New Orleans centre in contrast to the 18th-century French square a mile to the east. Basically we have a mixed urban type here: a more or less solid *poché* of infill space, warehouses and offices which is carved out by the disc-screens and, to one side, by a pie-segment of brick and granite. A sliver of this pie is framed by a pergola-temple of concrete columns and open pipe-work, which is skewed in plan to conform to the pie-shape. The proportions and details of this "temple" are at once ancient and modern, classically scaled and more slender than the marble prototypes. This, the major gateway, carries the name Piazza d'Italia in a straightforward way. It is balanced asymmetrically by the twenty-two storey tower to one side and a "campanile" on the corner, to the other. Thus again there is a pleasant mixture of old and new meanings, symmetrical Baroque and asymmetrical Modern, enclosed and open, low and high. This is a plural architecture that tries to include everything.

For historians there are references to the Marine Theatre of Hadrian and the triumphal gateways of Schinkel; for the Sicilians there are references to archetypal piazzas and fountains; for the Modernists there is an acknowledgement of skyscrapers and the use of current technologies (the neon and concrete); for the lover of pure architectural form there are cutaway imposts finished in speckled marble and a most sensuous use of polished stainless steel. Column capitals glisten with this material as water shoots out of the acanthus leaves; or the stern, squat Tuscan columns are cut from this material, leaving razor-sharp, "paramilitary" images, the silhouettes of Greek helmets.[1] The overall impression finally is a sensuous and rhetorical one every bit as mixed and rich as the Trevi fountain, another example of architecture, sculpture, writing, fountain, landscape and urban form. If the background to the Piazza is finished, its rhetoric will find the intended contrast.

We see, to conclude, that the Piazza is a successful example of Radical Eclecticism; it fits into and extends the urban context, it characterizes the various functions, symbolic and practical, with various styles, and it takes its cues for content and form from the local taste-culture, the Italian community. Moreover it provides this community with a centre, a location, a "heart" to reiterate the Post-Modern catchword. On the questions of pastiche when borrowing from the bank of previous architecture, especially in a time of inflation, one has to repay the loan with interest; that is reinvent previous meanings while *also* using them conventionally. Otherwise the forms are devalued. Finally, and on a predictive note, it foreshadows an architecture like the Baroque, when different arts were combined together to produce a rhetorical whole. Clearly the success of this rhetoric depends on an area outside of architecture: the belief in a social or metaphysical content. Otherwise the energy necessary to bring the arts together will not be expended and the images will lack conviction — be in fact *pasticcio*.

Late and Post Modernism in Europe

The explosion in the architectural culture of America has its counterpart in Europe although, as one would expect, the metaphor of cultural explosion, a sudden burst of creative energy, has to be modified to suit the prevailing conditions — mental and economic. Europe also has had its chain reaction but this has resulted in, not the buildings of America and Japan, but a megaton of writings: books, articles, manifestoes and exhibitions — instead of architecture.

The written work, the drawn project, have intentionally or not, dominated over the constructed artefact. These writings are largely concerned with the city: *L'Architettura della Città* (Aldo Rossi), *Delirious New York* (Rem Koolhaas), *Collage City* (Colin Rowe) — or with rediscovering a European tradition, *Architettura razionale* (Rossi again), *Rational Architecture* (Leon Krier), *La Tendenza* (French, Italian and Swiss magazines), or with both

together, thus giving the eclecticism a more contextual basis than it has in America.

While completed buildings remain few and somewhat unconvincing, we should not underestimate the effect of architectural publication. Vitruvius, Alberti, Serlio, Viollet-le-Duc, all marginal builders, need only be recalled to illustrate the truth that present writing creates architecture just as much as current building practice. And it is my contention that we are living through a renaissance of architectural *thinking*, a rebirth in theory that awaits expectantly, and longingly, for a corresponding rebirth in practice. It is a *re-naissance* not of classical antiquity, but of architectural history in its variety; not of one tradition, but many heterogeneous ones, displaced from their previous contexts. Paradoxically the content of this architecture, the problem for an agnostic age, is the repository of architectural form. We fill up the empty centre of the city, the place previously occupied by the church and palace, with the recapitulation of many cultures — that is the museum, "the museum city," or its political equivalent, the democratic forum and public realm, where a plurality of cultures contend. These are the new icons of architecture, part fantasy and part very real institutions: the city as a collection of artistic fragments and contentious subcultures.

In sketching out this "renaissance of the Renaissance" and other traditions, I will once again show the gradual development from Late to Post-Modern architecture, from the first, tentative modifications of Modernism to its more radical transformation. The first steps took place in Italy and Germany with the extreme and even terrifying projects of Aldo Rossi, Mathias Ungers and a group called Superstudio. On the one hand, and in a very Modernist way, they revived the primitive Rationalism of Abbé Laugier, the notion that architecture could and must be reduced to certain fundamentals. Hence their constant invocation of Laugier's Primitive Hut and its lesson that architecture lies in the column, the colonnade and the triangular truss, that is structural universals and necessities. Of course these universals were invoked by Le Corbusier and the Modernists, along with their attendant qualities of simplicity and nobility. These combined virtues, always present in Laugier's engraving, were presumed to exist in the simple constructions of the Noble Savage, that bare-foot architect who supposedly kept as close to the "needs" of the people as to the "rawness" of nature. That no bare-foot architect can exist in an industrial society does not make him any the less attractive as a fiction, and it is as a fiction that his presence looms large in the work of the present Rationalists. Aldo Rossi calls forth his virtues in large, anonymous housing schemes that repeat the simple structural support more than is structurally necessary. Leon Krier actually promotes a building industry which has returned to rustic huts and a craftsmanship that celebrates knotted logs, a kind of log-cabinism built on the scale of the Crystal Palace. The contradictions are disarming and, taken at face value, absurd. Krier, a Marxist, supports the classical revivalism of Quinlan Terry, the architect of Palla-

dian Country Houses. Or Aldo Rossi and the Italian members of Superstudio, also Marxists, support the Fascist architecture of the thirties, including the work of Stalin. We shall see many such incongruous contradictions in this Rationalism and although much can be said against them, I shall concentrate on the positive anomalies to which they give rebirth.[2]

Aldo Rossi was instrumental in turning architects' attention back to city morphology and the way the city and its monuments form a collective memory. Street, arcade, piazza, monument — these traditional elements reappeared in his work along with "the constant elements of architecture: the column, the architrave, the wall, the roof," that is Laugier's elements. Their reappearance was transformed by the new technologies — basically white planar reinforced concrete — and Rossi's particular, indeed peculiar, fascination with Lombardy farmhouses, barns and anonymous structures.

So, although memory of the traditional city was invoked, it was subtly displaced towards a primitive Modernism. Rossi's Gallaratese neighbourhood is a case in point. For him it recalls Italian arcades and the traditional street, whereas for the working class community it may recall mass housing and the Fascist stripped classicism of the thirties. Rossi's misapprehension of popular codes of architecture mark him as Late-Modernist, whereas his theory of city memory has contributed to the Post-Modern notion of the contextual city. All of his buildings approach the condition of the grave and the monument; his most influential scheme, the Modena cemetery, 1971, was in fact both a giant mausoleum and urban landmark. Laid out as a series of primary elements organized on a grid, adopting an axial approach which focused on "the house of the dead" and a stark cone-shaped funnel, it gave an ultimate image to death. Black shadows replaced windows, a striking image of the burnt-out ruin: empty piazzas with long shadows evoked the silent urban spaces and metaphysical loneliness of De Chirico paintings. The finality of these images might be appropriate to death, although one could argue that even in a cemetery life and variety should be celebrated. In any case all Rossi's building seems like an illustration of Adolf Loos' statement that architecture resides in the monument and grave, and they depend for their power on the striking incongruity of evoking images of death for life.

Since Modernism was ostensibly anti-monumental in the twenties, the work of Rossi and his followers has sought to rectify this failing by turning modernist housing schemes into monuments. Giorgio Grassi and others have designed housing blocks as long arcaded streetscapes. Again the ornament, such as it is, consists in the play of solid and void, white pier and black shadow, and the looming emptiness of De Chirico is recalled. Their scheme, for student housing, 1976, is reduced to Rationalist fundamentals: street, arcade, balcony and window. If one compares it to Weinbrenner's streetscape for Karlsruhe, 1808, the obvious prototype, then its relative austerity becomes more pronounced. Where Weinbrenner allowed himself minimal orna-

4. Charles Moore, Piazza d'Italia, New Orleans (Lou.).
5. Robert A.M. Stern, Lang House.
6. Ricardo Bofill, Le Lac, 1977: final project.

ment, a cornice, podium, dentil frieze and string-course, Grassi has allowed himself nothing except balconies and mullions. This makes his architecture, like Rossi's, reminiscent of the prison and death camp, unintended meanings which he might deny. It also resembles, again, Fascist architecture equally abhorrent to the authors on a political level. The argument in favour of this architectural language, apart from its powerful imagery, rests on the idea that these forms can be resemanticized with new usage.

That prisons, concentration camps and Fascists made use of stripped Neo-Classical forms does not contaminate their meaning forever; in fact the Rationalist programme is to resemanticize these "universal" forms by tying them to new socialist housing schemes, and new functional *types* of the city. Leon Krier, in his book *Rational Architecture* 1978, illustrates these schemes with a dogmatic pronouncement, emphasized in capital letters, on how the language of types is supposed to work.

The street and the square represent the only and necessary model for the reconstruction of a Public Realm. In this context, we also stress the necessary dialectical relationship of Building Typology and Morphology of Urban Space and inside that dialectic, the Correct Relationship of Monuments (public buildings) and the More Anonymous Urban Fabric (buildings for private use).[3]

So street and square along with primary building forms and a chosen urban morphology are meant to re-establish urban identity. The ideas are exemplary although they hardly go far enough (since the form remains abstract, not cultural or local). And since many people continue to perceive the work of the Rationalists as Fascist, because of its style, one would have thought minor modifications in the language, such as ornament, might have been introduced to change the message. Yet the Rationalists, unlike the American and Japanese designers, have been loath to take this next step. Although they will revive many classical antecedents — Palladio, Ledoux, Schinkel are the favoured three — they will not yet revive their system of ornament because they regard it as kitsch, or as contrary to constructional reality. One presumes this contradiction will not last and that in the next few years the Rationalists will accept their whole patrimony, not just the fundamentalist part.

By 1975 the Rationalist movement had spread across Europe and there were major centres in Berlin, Paris, Milan, Venice, Rome, Brussels and Barcelona, centres which kept in touch with each other through publications, lectures and exhibits. One exhibition in Barcelona was called, I believe, "21 followers of Aldo Rossi," while Leon Krier and his students who redesigned the morphology of this city, were given a major showing in 1978. Local Barcelona architects, in any case, had been practising by name a form of rational architecture since the late fifties and this work culminated in the Surrationalism of Bofill's extraordinary schemes. Giant housing blocks, called Xanadu or Walden 7 were lifted out of a city context and stuck like a Surrealist *objet trouvé* in a stark, rocky landscape. The simplicity, and organisational logic were both rational, while the image and scale were surreal: hence my term surrational for this compound of reason and madness. Indeed the strength of much Rationalist work depends precisely on this mixture, and the semantic contradictions mentioned above are just one more powerful instance ot it. The most convincing examples of surrationalism, besides Bofill's architecture, are the projects of OMA, the Office for Metropolitan Architecture. For instance Elia Zenghelis' Hotel Sphinx, 1975, mixes several urban types with the barely visible image of an animal, perhaps a sphinx. The legs are escalators, the tails are twin towers, the head that "turns and stares" at important civic events is a health club, the whole animal is a "luxury hotel designed as a model for mass housing." This might be any one of the thirty Hyatt Hotels springing up across America except it is considerably more colourful and witty. In its mixture of real urban functions and existing urban fantasies it summarizes the tendencies towards surrationalism both on the commercial and artistic planes. Like other anthropomorphic buildings it animates potentially overpowering large-scale form.

Rem Koolhaas, perhaps the ultimate surrationalist with his book and designs on *Delirious New York*, shows the poetry behind the mixture of logic and commercial dreams. His rational fantasies consist in taking artificiality and urban congestion to an extreme; continuing thereby the tradition of the Rockefeller Center and the Waldorf Astoria Hotel.

There is a side to European urbanism which is not surrational; the same designers have their practical side which treats city problems in a very realistic way, as a problem in morphology. During the early sixties many architects started looking at Hadrian's Villa and its complex plan for its morphological implication. What they found of interest was the mixture of geometric form and accident, formal set-piece and informality, axial planning and the picturesque, foreground and background, monument and infill — in short the set of dualities which later were to be summarized and turned into a theory of *Collage City* and a book of that name by Colin Rowe. The idea of collage city was dualism itself, an incorporation of opposite qualities which modern city planning in its utopian, or totalistic phase, had denied. Thus there was a place for utopian or "ideal" urban form, in fragments, set within a background of private buildings, or urban *poché*. Besides Hadrian's Villa, the Nolli plan of Rome, 1748, was a model of such urban morphology. As Rowe pointed out the collage technique had the further advantage of "permitting us the enjoyment of utopian poetics without our being obliged to suffer the embarrassment of utopian politics." That is it could incorporate vest-pocket utopias — Swiss canton, New England village, Dome of the Rock, Place Vendome, Campidoglio, the set-pieces of totalistic ideologies without having to put up with their inherent totalitarianism.[4] The resultant morphology could best be represented in figure-ground city maps which showed, like Nolli's plan, a relation of private to public which was roughly four to one. Modern planning, on the other hand, set monuments in a park, or more likely, in a parking

lot, so that the fabric was destroyed and the set-piece had nothing with which to contrast.

Oswald Mathias Ungers, James Stirling and then the Krier brothers took up these morphological ideas and applied them to existing cities, especially the parts that had been destroyed by Modern planning. In addition to their characteristic figure / ground drawings and rich collage of primary, "utopian" shapes, there was a recurring leitmotif which almost became the trademark of the Rationalists; this was, most basically, the circle set against the square.

This primary opposition, adopted from the Mandala as much as Hadrianic architecture, was used to carve out a positive urban void from a conceptually solid block of urban tissue — foreground curve against background square. One finds the opposition in Ungers' Student Hostel Competition of 1963, in Stirling and Kriers' Derby Civic Centre of 1970, in Charles Moore's Piazza d'Italia of 1975 and many of the recent Stirling schemes for German cities. The circular form often takes the function of a pedestrian route under a glass-covered arcade, or rather a curved *galleria*. This revival of the nineteenth-century arcade in a new form is itself a devastating critique of recent development which has seen the destruction of so many of these pleasant urban places. The curved *galleria* has a potential in providing a strong sense of place. It encloses or envelopes, womb-like, a piazza to one side, the favoured *res publica* of the Rationalists, while on its inside it provides a certain degree of expectation to a walk through the city. The eye and mind are continually pulled around the corner. The centre of the circle, or more often semi-circle, is felt as the "heart" of the city, again a favourite theme of Post-Modernists. But it is the opposition circle to square, feminine to masculine, which gives communicational weight to this pattern and a universality it would otherwise lack.

The Krier brothers have revived, or "recuperated" as they say in Europe, almost all such urban forms thrown out by the Modern Movement. Robert Krier has made countless morphological studies of existing historic cities to show the importance of crescents, arcades, streets and squares and it is these "universals" he not surprisingly uses to stitch together disrupted fabric. In a series of before and after drawings, like those of Humphrey Repton, he shows what particular advantage can be had by reinventing and then adding the old elements to a destroyed "centre," such as that of Stuttgart. Other Rationalists fill up the empty spaces in the modern cities of Oscar Niemeyer and Le Corbusier, doubling the density, increasing the "culture of congestion," as Rem Koolhaas has termed it.

Leon Krier, in an extraordinary outburst of city drawing reminiscent of Le Corbusier's unsolicited plans, has provided urban icons which are meant to stimulate political action. He has drawn seductive aerial views of London, Echternach, Rome, Bremen, Barcelona and Luxembourg which concerned citizens are meant to use against those who would continue modern, comprehensive redevelopment. Aerial views, like 18th-century tourist maps, become critical tools, *aide-memoires*,

icons, and finally "counter-schemes" to stop that insidious marriage between speculators and Modernists. No urban authority has yet intervened to commission a Krier mend and modify job, just as no authority commissioned Le Corbusier for forty years, but his influence has nonetheless been effective and, like that of ARAU, a Brussels group, enough to deflect some of the more destructive plans.

His most poetic intervention in terms of imagery is his modification of the 1748 Nolli plan of Rome, an intervention supported by the mayor Carlo Argan in an exhibition "Roma Interrotta," 1978, an exhibition of twelve architects' proposals for the city. Krier has, Laugier-like, reinvented the primitive hut of columns and triangular roof trusses, but this time each column is the size of an eight-storey tower and the pyramidal roof encloses an awesome public realm — a cross between a train-shed and an open-air market. The drawings when seen collaged into the Roman perspectives of Piranesi actually stand up to these grand and disturbing images. The buildings have the breadth of scale and the heavy gestural quality typical of the Roman tradition. They consist of three basic types: the square, semi-circular and triangular shed inserted respectively into the "centre" of Rome, the end of Piazza Navona and the open end of St. Peter's, a triangular wedge thrusting towards the church (actually a rather "Modern" completion when compared with those offered since 1660). The triangular shed, like the others, is a new social centre meant to revive and support a local form of civic organization, the *rione*, an alternative to the centralized bureaucracy, church and *municipio*. It would have restaurants, clubs, rooms for games and large top floor studios for artists. These craftsmen of the new grass-roots democracy would "work on the adornment of their *rione*. Their creative work will naturally spread (in final stages of elaboration) into the square, and for short periods these spaces will be filled with some vast fresco or sculpture before they are taken to their location."[5]

Here we have then a typical "vest-pocket utopia" a form of syndicalism and local organization being collaged into the existing fabric, both formally and politically. The idea, as Krier makes clear, is to revive the *res publica* and create new civic institutions which can support it, ones on a par with the 17th-century churches of Rome, which would be, ironically, converted back into Thermae. If this social idealism is both realistic, "embarrassing" (as Rowe would term it) and unrealized, the Rationalists have nevertheless built small, imperfect versions of their white, utopian dreams. Georgia Benamo and Christian de Portzamparc have completed a small urban scheme on the edge of Paris, the Rue des Hautes-Formes, 1975-9. This inevitably seeks to create "the street, the square, the urban place" with that density or congestion beloved by the Rationalists. Tower and slab blocks of Modernism are combined and given a Post-Modern formal treatment of cut-out screens à la Moore, false hanging arches to signify entry à la Venturi, and a variety of window treatments à la mode. The last is further justified to keep a thousand windows from

Progetto per il Cimitero di Modena 2/30   A. Rossi 73

watching you, the many eyes of the scheme from seeming oppressively large and homogeneous (three types of window are used behind a screen wall). If there are Rationalist doubts about this scheme they concern the leaky space, the small size of the piazza and *res publica*, and the rather neutralized relation of solid to void, urban *poché* to monument (the scheme lacks monuments). Still we have here an idea and summary of Rationalism in its Late-Modern phase just as it's coming to grips with the problems of communication, of signification based on traditional and local codes.

The next stage of European urbanism overlaps temporally with the previous one, but is more explicit in its attempt to deal with local understanding or the way architecture is a language that must be decoded, however imperfectly, by those who use it. In short these are the Post-Modern architects, or else the same Rationalists we've looked at in their new-found interest in architectural communication. Again the ideas of Colin Rowe are relevant, for their dualism contains the binary logic which is essential to all communications systems. Urban form is significant partly because it consists in a series of contiguous opposites, an obvious truth which perhaps only needs statement at a time when the environment has become too homogeneous.

During the last few years many architects and theorists have attacked excessive homogeneity with countervailing strategies which they have termed variously townscape philosophy, adhocism, bricolage, collision city, and the new empiricism. These philosophies are counter to both Modernism and Rationalism because of their exaggerated emphasis on geometric order and repetition. By contrast the new consciousness favours the Picturesque and inevitably makes use of ideas from this tradition amongst which are, notably, variety, surprise and contrast. If there is an addition to this triad it concerns the notion of the "interest group," or the idea that any city contains many sub-cultures which have opposed interests. The urbanist's role is to design fragments of the city which reflect the culture and ideals of these groups while contrasting them with other orders — pragmatic or architectural. Perhaps this strategy was only articulated by Advocacy planners and a few politically inclined architects, but it was implicitly shared by many designers who favoured participation and consultation in design.

The architectural results were especially hybrid. In Amsterdam, Zwolle and other Dutch cities, interest groups formed with architects to produce a hybrid Modern/Traditional urban infill, the tall thin brick houses of the traditional city with several modifications. These included flat-top gables (Modernist signs), large bay windows, internal courtyards, double-height spaces and garden extensions; otherwise the morphology was the traditional urban pattern of street and square, and the language deferred to the local vernacular. At its most tepid this tendency became the Neo-Vernacular, that mix of regional style and modern amenity which was unassertive and accomodating in the extreme. More aggressively it became the adhocism of Ralph Erskine and Lucien Kroll, a dramatic juxtaposition of styles and ideologies more pluralistic in its variety. The buildings of these two architects and their extended design teams were created in continual consultation with the ultimate inhabitants. More purely architectural in intention, but still locally based, were the urban schemes of James Stirling, Jeremy Dixon and a Viennese group known as Missing Link (they seek to become a link with the past of their city). Stirling proposed an *ad hoc* attachment to an open space in Berlin which had been partly created by modern planners and the aerial bombardment of a huge parking garage. Onto this desolate structure Stirling attached a thin city fabric of shops and urban tissue. He took the scale and picturesque variety of the remaining Berlin houses and manipulated the form so that it underwent a musical development, a type of sonata-allegro organization. Reading from left to right down the street and around the corner, one could see an analogous pattern of "introduction, exposition, development, recapitulation and coda."[6] Bay windows, doorways and roof exits became the musical themes which were transformed in each section. Because Stirling is more committed to architecture than the other designers playing on a local vernacular his schemes are more highly ordered and syncopated than the others.

There is one London version of this urban architecture which is finished, the infill housing of Jeremy Dixon in the Notting Hill Gate area. Like the Neo-Vernacular Dutch examples this is a traditional brick type, even having a Dutch gable and crowstep articulation. Like the nineteenth-century Queen Anne Revival, the English style is allowed to be eclectically foreign while it is still British. Other historicist quotes include Art Deco ziggurats and Rationalist grids, but it is the local contextualism which is most relevant. Accepting the street lines and the traditional layout (except for unfortunate diagonals in plan), accepting the bay windows of the adjoining houses and their emphasis on stairway, door and front stoop, the scheme manages to be both acceptably familiar and inventive. The inhabitants can recognize their traditional language and requirements; the stereotypes are used in a relatively straightforward way, as stock as the London brick. But then, on further inspection and in an esoteric code there are meanings more directly accessible to the architect, or the inhabitant who cares to search for them: the physiognomic visage, the stare of the "face" now divided between two houses; the repetition of the aedicule, "the little house," that image of domesticity which goes back to the Greeks and which has signified homestead ever since; the stained glass and colour syncopations in blues and greens which give interest and identify a house; the aedicular entrance gates which hide garbage cans. The scheme is modest and one shouldn't make immodest claims for it, but it does illustrate the level that Post-Modern urbanism had reached by the middle seventies.

There are two other schemes which also show this degree of knowing eclecticism: Hans Hollein's Travel Bureau in Vienna, completed in 1978, and James Stirling's Stuttgart Museum, under construction.

Hollein has characteristically preserved the urban fabric and subtly collaged signs of the new function into the old framework. Polished bronze gleams out of the grey neutral grid of the street block. On the inside the various tourist fantasies, and stereotypes, become an excuse for an eclecticism I would once again term Radical because of its semantic appropriateness: ruined columns impaled by chrome shafts signify travel in Greece and Italy; desert travel is communicated by bronze versions of the palm columns at Brighton; India by a bronze solartopee, theatre tickets by a stage curtain and, ironically, the place where one pays for all of this, the cashier's desk, is signified by the outlines of a Rolls Royce radiator grill. All of this is sheltered under a light-filled coffered vault reminiscent of the home-town Post Office, the magnificent "Modern" space Otto Wagner built in 1906. Thus local reference is set against foreign, modern images against stereotype and existing urban fabric against infill. Because of the precision craftmanship the clichés are not kitsch; or rather, the elements of pastiche, which are used to communicate directly to a mass-culture, are lifted above their station.

James Stirling's museum in Stuttgart is, like his other German projects, an essay in urban contextualism. It picks up formal cues from the surrounding context, in this case the height and grain of adjacent buildings and the basic axial relationship to the main street. From this entrance axis it layers a sequence of space frontally and at right angles to movement; as in a Rationalist building the grid is felt conceptually throughout although one is forced to move around it in circles and diagonals. Thus a basic dualism is set up between rectilinear and rotational elements. One moves under an entrance arch, a primitive hut, a Shinkelesque gateway, but then to left or right off axis. The U-shaped, symmetrical gallery is in front, but one has to approach it diagonally up a ramp; the circular, open-air sculpture court can be reached on the axis, but one moves through it on a perimetrical, semicircular ramp. This connects up finally with a walkway into the more domestic urban fabric. In this circuitous way the public is brought informally right into the heart of the museum.

It is an unusual heart, at once familiar like a circular Neo-Classical Museum, and strange, as a dome without a top. Basically the language is Schinkelesque and as eclectic as was this architect, although it is a subdued eclecticism. Barely recognisable Romanesque arches open onto the sculpture court, while slightly Egyptian cornices edge the painting galleries. The references signify "museum," "art," in the stereotypical way that Hollein's generalized images referred to foreign travel. And of course the overall reference to Schinkel's Neo-Classicism, a German sign of "culture," is also justifiable. In a sense this plurality of styles with this function creates a miniature of the "museum city" itself.

The handling of this language is at once dramatic and easy-going. The public is brought into the building informally, as mentioned, and then given a straightforward chronological journey through the history of art with no discontinuities — just as there is a continuous flow between new and old buildings, those he has designed and those he has attached to. The exceptions to this ordinariness (and we would have preferred adding ornament to this list) are the ramps, curves, views across layered space and the paradox of the "domeless dome," the inside-out space, the room towards which one moves to find oneself outside, cut-off from urban noise and in touch with sculpture or the sky. The ideas behind this, the Mandala, "the dome of heaven — the sky," the "heart of the city" and the circular *res publica* are, as we've seen, the key ideas of many Post-Modernists. They are as much ideas of content as purely architectural ideas, and in this sense seek to raise, if not answer, a fundamental question of our time: "what is architecture to be about?"

This is the question facing architects in a consumer society. The basic problems are social, political and metaphysical, not formal and technical. Our society is quite adept at reaching formal and technical standards of excellence, at least in Japan and America, but it has not brought forth either very exciting building tasks or metaphysical mandates. Hence the Surrationalist fantasies, trying to fill a vacuum; hence the syndacalist utopias or modest attempts at participation; hence the great American attempt at revivalism and significant cultural form. All these Post-Modern tendencies are trying to give birth to a new architecture before consumer society has given it a mandate; it is the sound, as the saying goes, of one hand clapping. It may be, however, the only sound a consumer society is willing to allow, immersed as it is in the joys of private life. This culture is essentially passive, waiting for the directions from its self-appointed elites. What messages it receives today are extraordinary in their plurality and breadth. To discriminate among these messages, as well as send them, has also fallen to an elite, that is the "communications industry." So we are at a most curious juncture in history that isn't in fact a turning point at all. Rather we are in for "more of the same," much more, in fact a recapitulation of all historical architecture including that of the recent past. We are, as you will guess, in a Radically Eclectic age, an age that makes the 1870's with its relative paucity of fifteen styles look like an integrated culture. We have more styles and ideologies than they did then and they probably mean less; have less conviction and semantic meaning. Gothic-Revival is now a-religious and doesn't carry Pugin's moralistic fervour; Stirling at one time had Gothic arcades for his Stuttgart Museum before they were changed into Romanesque. In our *Musée imaginaire*, in our museum city that has recapitulated world history, styles have lost their overall meaning and become instead genres — classifiers of mood and theme. This is a major point of Radical Eclecticism; it substitutes a time-bound semiotic view of architectural form for the monolithic view of the past, the Modern and Neo-Gothic views. Its approach to style and meaning is relativistic, related to the context of the culture being designed for, and this entails changing those styles and meanings perhaps after they have swung too far one way, or, by contrast, need support and confirmation. The two ideas behind

this are plenitude and pluralism, the idea that, given the choice, people would rather have a variety of experiences and that, as history proceeds, a plenitude of values, a richness, is created on which it is possible to draw. These architectural loans must, to repeat a point, be repaid with interest, that is reinvention. In short the content of our building is not the Space Age or the Energy Problem, not the Machine Age or High Technology, but the variety of cultural experience, the plurality of psychic, social and metaphysical states possible to people. For the museum we have the museum city, for a single meaning of history we have all of history, for a single political view we have the *res publica* and for architecture we hope to have an Eclecticism that is radical.

This paper is adapted from two of the three Bossom Lectures given at the Royal Society of Arts, London, May - June 1979.

1. Several of these meanings were pointed out to me by Charles Moore in a discussion, March 1979; others can be found in Martin Filler's excellent article on the Piazza in *Progressive Architecture*, Nov. 1978, pp. 81-7.
2. Elsewhere I have criticized the coercive and reductive aspects of these architects; see "The Irrational Rationalists — The Rats Since 1960" in *The Rationalists*, ed. Dennis Sharp, The Architectural Press, London, 1978, and *Late-Modern Architecture*, Academy Editions London, and Rizzoli, New York, 1980.
3. *Rational Architecture* The Reconstruction of the European City, Brussels, 1978, p. 58. Texts by Robert L. Deleroy, Anthony Vidler and Leon Krier.
4. Colin Rowe and Fred Koetner. *Collage City*, Cambridge, Mass., 1978, p. 149.
5. See "Roma Interrotta," *Architectural Design*, Vol. 49, Nos. 3-4, 1979, p. 163.
6. Unpublished essay by A.B.K. Quan, "The Five Projects in Germany by James Stirling," Architectural Association, April 1979.

The "Strada Novissima"

The central fact of the First International Exhibition of Architecture is formed by the "Strada Novissima," a real street built with temporary materials inside the Rope Factories of the Arsenale, which have been made accessible to the public for the first time.

The aim was to enable the visitors to verify directly "the return to the street" as a formative element of the city and one of the fundamental aims of Post-Modern research.

The Commission of the Architecture Sector of the Venice Biennale, with the support of the Critics' Committee, has entrusted the planning of the "Strada Novissima" to 20 architects from all over the world. Each one of them has been asked to design a "Facade" expressing his own particular sense of form, with special reference to the theme of the "Presence of the Past," that is, the role that has now returned to take on the reflection on history as an active basis for planning.

The order of facades on the "Strada Novissima" runs as follows:

left

Dardi, Graves, Gehry, Ungers, Venturi, Krier, Kleihues, Hollein, Portzamparc, Greenberg;

right

Koolhaas, Bofill, Moore, Stern, Purini, Tigermann, Grau, Smith, Isozaki.

Behind the facade is a one-man exhibition of the designing architect.

The facade relating to the entry area, which has no exhibition space, has been designed by Paolo Portoghesi, Francesco Cellini and Claudio D'Amato.

The entrance portal was designed by Aldo Rossi.

There follow the building regulations and the graphic documentation sent to the designing architects, and the individual projects sent back.

1. The Theme

The street can be thought of as a sequence of houses; each house can be:

a. the architect's dwelling, with the place where he works, or a personal museum, or a space for the exhibition and "sale" of his own ideas;

b. simply a "dwelling," a place for everyday and private life;

c. a façade (maybe only partial) of a building destined for meetings (for work or study), gatherings, entertainment.

2. Size and distribution of the space available

— The "street" is 70 metres long;

— It lies in the central nave of the rope factories;

— It will be defined by a sequence of 20 façades, 10 on each side (see table 1);

— The street is 4.50 m wide: this section is limited by the cross interaxis of the columns measuring 7.00 m (see table 2);

— The height of the façade along the street can vary from a minimum of 7.20 m to a maximum of 9.50 m. It is limited by the floor and by the lower plane of the truss (the beam) see table 2;

— For the building of his façade each architect can use the distance between two columns in the longitudinal sense, which is 7 metres long and a maximum of 1.60 m wide (see tables 3 and 4).

3. Architectural characteristics required

— The façade will be in full-scale;

— Each architect is free to indicate the number of storeys which cannot however be more than three (according to the maximum height allowed);

— There must be an entrance to the back (and the entrance must be at level 0.00 from the floor)

N.B.: through the façade the audience has access to the "one-man" exhibition

— The columns of the central nave cannot be part of the façade (they stay "covered")

— The composition is entirely free; as an example, if several storeys are planned, the ground floor could be a "porch," it could have a "plinth," and so on; the first floor could have windows of different sizes and shapes; the second floor (the one between the gallery and the beam of the trusses) must necessarily have at least one opening in order to give the possibility of seeing through it onto the street. However, this opening can be situated at a uniform height, or it can be at a variable height or it may be mixtilinear.

4. Budget and building techniques

The cost of each façade should be about 3.500.000 liras ($4.000). Building techniques may be of every sort, but they must be easy to carry out. In order to keep within the budget, we advise the use of low-cost and easily accessible materials (first of all wood, such as pine or ply-wood, etc.; cloth; metal, etc.)

— Colour can be used.

— The façades will be fixed to the columns and the gallery.

— The back of the façades must have only absolutely necessary finishings.

1-4. Technical drawings showing the "building regulation" for the design of the façades of the "Strada Novissima" in the Corderia at the Arsenale.

5. The interior space in the Corderia from the gallery above.

6. Georgia Benamo, Christian De Portzamparc.

7. Ricardo Bofill/Taller de Arquitectura.

8. Costantino Dardi.

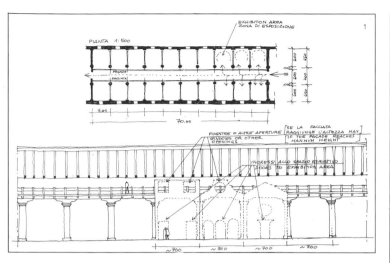

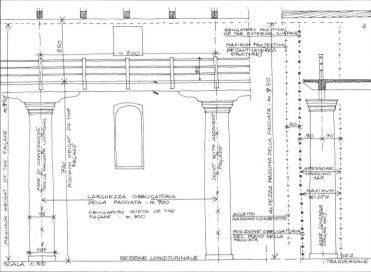

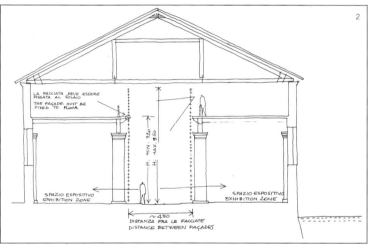

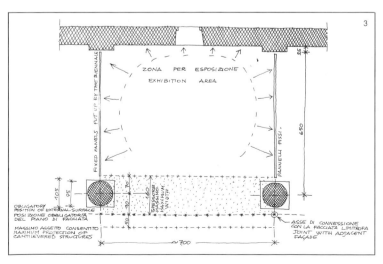

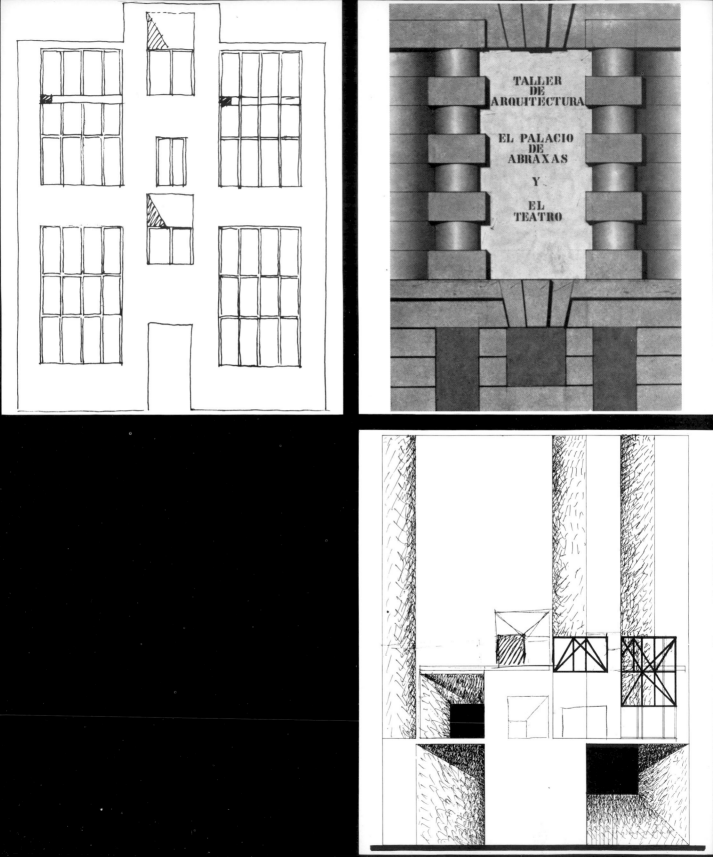

TALLER
DE
ARQUITECTURA

EL PALACIO
DE
ABRAXAS

Y

EL
TEATRO

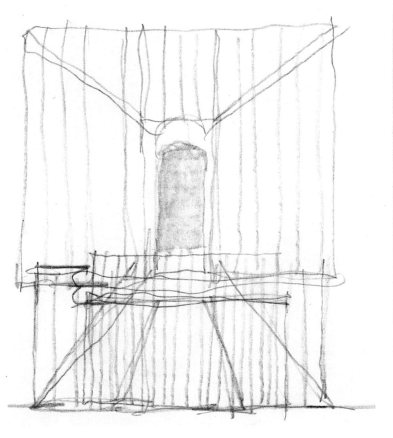

9. Frank O. Gehry.   10. Studio G.R.A.U.

Venice Biennale · 1980

11. Michael Graves.   12. Allan Greenberg.

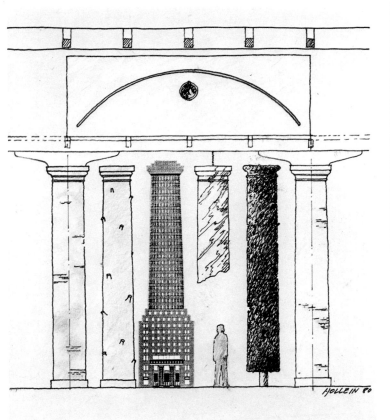

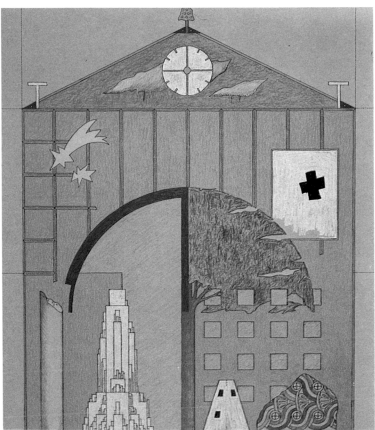

13. Hans Hollein.　　　　14. Joseph Paul Kleihues.

15. Rem Koolhaas/OMA.   16. Léon Krier.

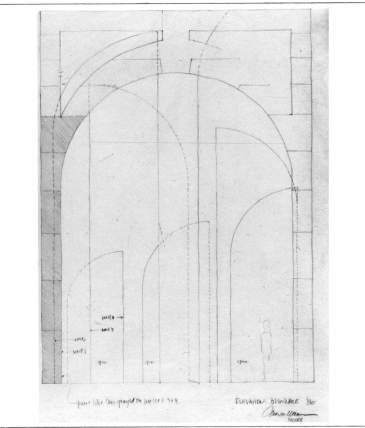

17. Arata Isozaki.

18. Charles Moore.

20. Massimo Scolari.

19. Franco Purini, Laura Thermes.   21. Thomas Gordon Smith.

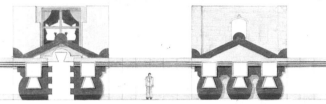

22. Robert A. M. Stern.   23. Stanley Tigerman.

47

24. Oswald Mathias Ungers.   25. Robert Venturi, John Rauch, Denise Scott-Brown.

Homage to Gardella, Johnson, Ridolfi

The fascination of the present
Paolo Farina

"Seen from close-by, our history is uncertain and intricate, like a marsh that has only been half reclaimed," wrote Musil.

This statement has considerable importance, for it warns us that we base our judgement on what barely emerges or is on ground that has already been drained, and it makes us suspicious of labels and syntheses that are too brief and hasty. Modern architecture has still not been rescued from the unacceptable mortgage that has kept too many of its interpreters and leading characters locked up in cages that are more or less gilded, put there beforehand to balance the accounts. Ever since the sixties Ignazio Gardella has been put in one of these cages — the one for the "prudent," which is certainly gilded — confirming the caution with which many critics assessed a production that put the accounts into no little disorder.

A caution which, having become open reserve, has liquidated the positive worries and the interests with as many facets as "scandals" that have matured in the post-war period; it is branded en masse and without appeal as "poetry of ambiguousness," "intimism," "a flirt with history," a movement of "petty Prousts," "new sensualism," or more openly as nothing less than a "retreat from the Modern Movement," "a return to Giovannini" under the guise of an artful continuity of the crisis-stricken appeals inherited from the thirties. In fact the "betrayal" could not be proved, unless at the cost of sacrificing reality. Gardella asserted that "The very diversity of architecture and the impossibility of reducing it to a stencil is one of the proofs of its validity and of its navigating in the same waters in which all the most lively architects can be found, ignoring the fact of their physiological age." One of the most frequent accusations made against Gardella was that he looked back the past "too much." The fact is that he has repeatedly declared to look at it with interest "not so much as the past but as the present." The announcement, which could have a prophetical flavour, in the context of the Venetian exhibition, is clearly verifiable in all his work and is the symptom of a coherence that should not be seen as an arid cliché, but as a deeply rooted vocation. The impossibility of analyzing a clear evolutionary process in Gardella's work, the absence of unexpected loves and trumpeted second thoughts (it has been said that "he has never been an abstractionist"), indicates continuity of a method that does not seek results, rather approaches problems. The family tradition — an uninterrupted series of architects starting with the Ignazio Gardella who, with Carlo Barabino, was one of the protagonists of Genoa's solemn, Neoclassical appearance —, the extremely precocious drawing habit ("Ever since I was eight," Gardella, who was born in 1905, tells us "my grandfather made me copy the plates from treatises in pencil and then colour them with watercolours"), the familiar and genially understanding relationship with two extremely rich and complex urban civilizations like Genoa and Venice (the former matured through family tradition, the latter through "inhibition"), are only a few of the stages in a relationship with history that has developed without resorting to the solutions of continuity. The past is indispensable to Gardella because only through it can communication be established. The big-hearted effort towards an Esperanto, a new and universal language, failed because by questioning the traditional city ("Nous tuerons la rue...") he showed himself to be unprepared and inadequate to measure up to urban contexts over a long period; they can be compared to a house where we tend to attribute a special value to the objects that have always been there. The link with the context, the juxtaposition of old and new and the way they react have always been Gardella's most intentional and explicit interests. By following a procedure that is objective and arbitrary, analytical and concise, and always very selective (he has never believed, for example, in the myths of spontaneous architecture), Gardella tends to gather in a place's culture and the visual habits of its users, then, instead of placing his trust in a positivist principle of derivation, he guarantees himself a wide margin for development that does not deductively eschew any direction. The result is the "direct grasp" of the environment that Argan noticed in his house in Venice, a lesson that others only saw as a betrayal or as an example whose "imitation was severely forbidden." Gardella approaches data from the context and elements of the language synchronically and vertically, rather than by studyng the context systematically. Because of this, next to the fascinating limit of not having any utopian or prophetic outbursts, his works have more of the past and the fascination of the present, a present that perhaps is contradictory but is always rich and emotional, and never decimated. Gardella wrote that "There is always the risk of slowly losing the balancing contact with life and in the end not responding to society's wants, not only as regards use but also, and equally fundamentally for every civilization, as regards emotion." Rather than admit this, the majority of critics has preferred to admit the quality of Gardella's work while denying its up-to-dateness, thus neatly cutting his field up.

Gardella's taste for juxtaposition, counterpoint and underlining are some of the most interesting techniques in his language. The figure, the adjective, the well-calibrated drawing of a detail or a decoration are sometimes concentrated and defined, or else he plays around with them on different levels from their background, so that they lend themselves alternately to close observation and to distant viewing, to attentiveness or to distraction — they are all the heritage of architecture and of the city precious perceptive truths.

In the theatre of Busto Arsizio, Gardella cuts out some figures from the nineteenth-century decoration on the ceiling and sows them again like fantastic fragments over the new, pale pink background; the slender cast-iron columns, preserved and painted green with white capitals stand out from the white gallery. What was the usual practice in those years — the "convenient cleaning-up," the brutal superimposition of the "rational arrangement" as a tranquillizing remedy — had been questioned. Ever since his first works, for Gardella history neither represents a heritage to be exploited, according to the procedure typical of the most old-fashioned restoration which approaches it with sham "neutrality," nor is it a theatre for exhibiting novelties, gestures; rather it is an extremely sensitive instrument that makes what is new react through a diligent process of analysis, calibration and underlining, making it speak.

Here we should recognize that Gardella is not insensitive to the attraction of the most cultured and aristocratic restoration — like what D'Andrade does — and, at the same time, to the taste of Metaphysical painting with its silent objets trouvés immersed in light or marked by clear chiaroscuro. This art of making things speak, things that belong to a History that is not necessarily always spelt with a capital H, but is also everyday — what we would now call événementielle — achieves great intensity in a work from the immediate post-war period: the Queen Isabella Baths at Lacco Ameno on the island of Ischia. Here the "figure," the fragment, formed by the old whitewashed nineteenth-century columns, stands right out from the "background," represented by the rosy façade of the new building. The relationship between the two planes is quite, perhaps involuntarily, similar to the one established in Milan over the centuries between the columns of S. Lorenzo and the compact screening building that separated them from the close-by Basilica. Accumulation, superimposition and stratification are equally important elements of the project for Gardella. In many ways the Parco delle Mura in Genoa offers us a similar attitude, in the dialectical relationship between the wings represented by the irregular walls with their many-coloured bands (slate and stone from Finale), and the Neoclassical wash-house of Barabino, found in a warehouse where it had been relegated by building speculation, and put together again piece by piece. All this is a clear indication of the deep seduction and influence that the classical language of architecture exercised on Gardella, with its syntax and its rules, but also with the limitless degrees of freedom that it allows inside rigorous criticism, hard discipline and creative sensitivity. From the Baths at Ischia to the Mura Park we can transparently distinguish the desire, which is only unconfessed to a certain extent, not to give up complexity and contradictions, or even the right to confirm not only the validity, but also the novelty and originality of a disciplinary heritage, a knowledge that was being lost and a period that was extremely rich. Faced with the dilapidation and drying up of modern architecture, Gardella vindicates the role of a history that cannot be summed up in a few stereotypes and, at the same time, a "tradition of the new" that cannot be reduced to a handful of unvarying elements. From this his whole production is marked by a series of interests, themes that are now decisively favoured or are referred to en passant. A provisional and largely incomplete list could be drawn up: the use of the cornice (as a frequent comment on the openings), the outline, the moulding, the pilaster strip, which not only are valued for what they are but also for the chiaroscuro they create, and which are considered a heritage of tradition in the same way as other lexical and typological elements; the cornice

1. Building project designed for the thesis, 1927.
2. Transformation of the theater in Busto Arsizio (Varese), 1934: the interior space with nineteenth century "fragments."

3. Anti-tuberculous clinic, Alessandria, 1937: elevation with the brick wall.
4. Competition for a tower in the plaza of Milan's cathedral, 1934: model.

5. Addition to the Senator Borletti's house, Milan, 1935: view of the "addition" showing the walls covered with Ticino's pebbles.
6. House for a viticulturist, Castana (Alessandria), 1947.

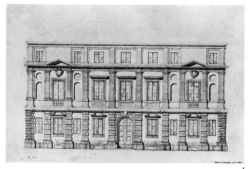

1

2

3

4

5

6

as an adjective, sometimes given its rhythm by dentils, and others joined to the wall with the emphasis of a shell, as in the "square" at Arenzano; the gradation, stratification and hierarchy of full and empty spaces (there is no avoiding the subtle analogy between the Agriculture Building at the Fair of Milan and the Ducal Palace in Venice, while Argan has already noticed the rising effect in his house on the Zattere in Venice that should be linked to the tradition of High Gothic and its most severe revivals); the treatment of the edge, be it furrowed by chiaroscuro or lightened and almost pierced by windows that open spaces in the pagination of the façade; some concave-convex solutions, as in the church at Gela, which reinterpretes eastern Sicily's Baroque tradition; the compression and expansion of space and volume sometimes obtained with slight inflexions (the house at Alessandria for the employees of the Borsalino company) and sometimes with close intervals (the Olivetti hall at Düsseldorf), or more solemn and "gigantic" ones (the church of S. Enrico, near Milan, probably not oblivious to the Lombard seventeenth century and, in particular, to Ricchino); the use of the modulus ("the charming Muse of architecture or, if badly interpreted, the enchantress Circe, who can turn the architect's language into a grunt" was how Gardella once defined it); but also, and more often, several moduli at the same time; the experiments on the stereometric block, truly a constant theme in Genoan tradition, as has been synthetically recorded by famous perspective views of the Strada Nova. His research into the window, extremely rich and refined, has made Gardella one of the precursors of the renewed interest which this "episode" has aroused in these last years: Gardella's window links up again consciously with the tradition of stressed verticalism that belongs to Lombard tradition; sometimes it is Venetian, but above all it is Genoan, and it also finds confirmation in some experiences belonging to the less-acclaimed "tradition of the new, as in some of Siren's Finnish buildings that breathe the same dry, Neoclassical air as does the Tognella house in the Park of Milan. Sometimes his complex research into the order and arrangement of the windows interprets the rhythms of courtly tradition, and on other occasions lesser tradition, putting his faith in what Portoghesi has called "dishevelment," that is, challenging the vertical alignment, as in his Venetian house; one of constant themes in Gardella's work is his trust in the capacity the form has of communication: Gardella believes it tautological to put form and content together, for form is only one of the contents that comes into play with all its autonomy, sometimes as part of the crowd, and others as the leading actor.

This leads to a research that sweeps from the most elementary forms (like the square, with all its possibilities of being rotated with respect to an alignment, which has always fascinated him on all scales, from the little windows at the base of the Venetian house to the Theatre of Vicenza and the Alfa Romeo offices), to the most complex ones (the elliptical staircase in the Grassi Collection in Milan), right up to his exotic repertoire. His use of colour is

9-12. Cicogna House in the Zattere, Venice, 1957-1958: model of the first version; elevation facing the Giudecca's channel; view from the Fondamenta in the Zattere; detail of the balcony at the top floor.

13-14. Low-income district INA/Case, Cesate (Milan), 1954; the church (1958) and one of the residential buildings.

9

10

11

12

15-17. Hotel, restaurant and swimming-pool in Punta S. Martino, Arenzano (Genoa), 1956: views from outside (together with M. Zanuso).

18. Building with housing and stores around a "plaza," Arenzano (Genoa), 1957; view of the courtyards.

19. Arrangement of the Raccolta Grassi inside the Royal Villa in Via Palestro, Milan, 1958: elliptic staircase.

20. Building for the Olivetti's canteen, Ivrea (Turin), 1955-1958, interior paths.

21. Church in Gela (Agrigento), 1960: sketch for the entrance hall.

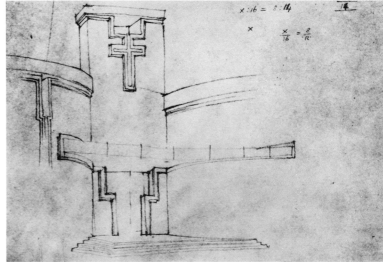

fundamental in commenting on and evoking an atmosphere; most of it ties in with Genoan tradition, which uses it impartially even to the extent of substituting architectural decoration in its most plastic effects. Gardella opposes the diaphanous, blinding white surfaces of the Rationalists with a measured, yet decided motion for colour: yellow at Casale soft blue on the façades of the Dispensary at Alessandria, the "impasti" of the plaster now with punded earthenware (in the Venetian house and the "square" at Arenzano), now with Finale stone, and the recurrent Ligurian pink, which are the backgrounds of window and door frames that are almost always white and shutters that are dark green; the burnt brown of the clinker in the "full" volumes, certain chromatic underscorings of architecture (the green majolicas on the base of the baths at Ischia, the intradoses of the layers in the pavilions and on the roof-terraces at Arenzano, which are vividly painted); stone, too, is used for its tonal properties, for the contrasts and detachment it may give against the plastered background: Vicenza stone for the balconies and cornices of the Venetian house, slate that is often matched with stone from Finale or white marble, as in the high base to the Olivetti canteen at Ivrea; round, white pebbles from the Ticino that cover the walls of the extension to the Borletti house, which add an unheard-of surface vibration to the tonal effect. The choice of material with which Gardella made the most impact, however, was probably a refusal. One cannot in fact help but notice the programmatic, almost total, absence of one of the most widespread materials in the language of modern architecture – concrete –, which is loved by so many Masters who, especially ever since the postwar period, have used it to offer Rationalism once more in more aggressive and material clothing when compared to that of the smooth, plastered surfaces. The absence of reinforced concrete in Gardella's vocabulary confirms another disconcerting statement, the fall of another of the Modern Movement's taboos: the structure never has a conclusive meaning for Gardella and not only must it not be exhibited, but it is not even indispensable to "declare it," as an architect would say; structural "sincerity" loses its untouchable function as architecture's "form." This is why the arcades of the porticoes at Arenzano, which are set on visible cement dadoes protruding from the pilasters, are above all a highly refined syntactical solution. This universe of technology, materials and details is the surest indication of the more radically rationalizing hypotheses of the Modern Movement, which can be seen as instruments in the hands of the economic forces for cutting all the bridges with the past irretrievably, first on a structural and then on a superstructural level. By basing himself on the precious help of a vast and well-tested technical repertoire, a constant relationship with the building world, vindicating things that are well-made and designed to last, and aware of the reality of production whose task it is in different times and different contexts to give body to the project, Gardella can only be suspicious of the ideology of the machine for living in, the pre-fabricated house that resem-

bles "so many Meccano sets." Once again the presence of the past plays the double role of barrier and opening. If a synthesis of Gardella's attitude to history had to be made, one could in fact say that he has always known how to relinquish the "wise diet" that conformism has prescribed every so often, without ever losing the necessary tension. He has always known how to oppose the renuncia-

tion and sense of guilt of those afraid to be accused of escapism with the defence of the song and poetry that belong to all the most vital periods of history, when, as Gardella himself wrote "it could be said, with a thought of Pascal's of striking freshness, that there was 'un rapport parfait entre une chanson et une maison'."

24-26. Building for the Alfa Romeo's technical offices, Arese (Milan), 1968: sketches for the site plan; partial view of the elevation.

27. Project for the new theater in Vicenza, 1970: plan.

28. Settlement of the Parco delle Mura, 1977-1978: general elevation.

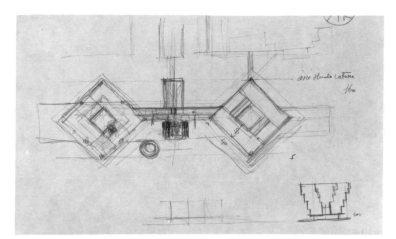

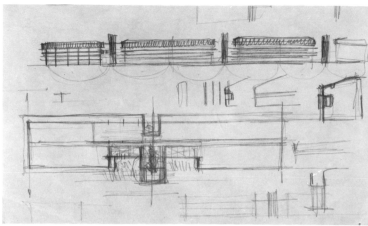

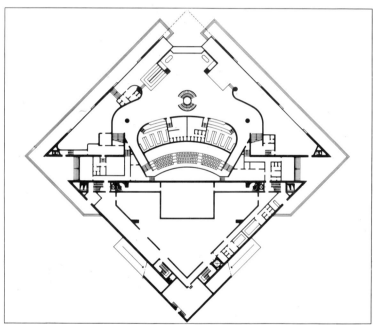

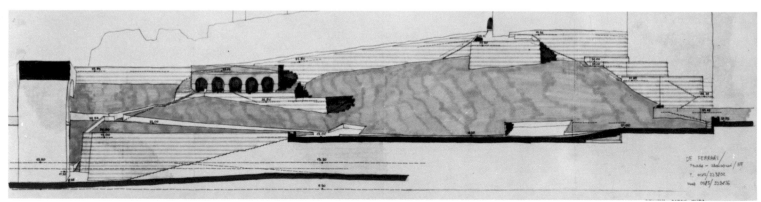

Philip Johnson: images
Emilio Battisti

In January 1979 *Time*, the American magazine which is most read internationally, dedicated its front cover to Philip Cortelyou Johnson.

In the past, excluding Buckminster Fuller, who cannot exactly be considered an architect, only Frank Lloyd Wright had received the same privilege. In the image on the cover mentioned Philip Johnson appears in a rigid position, almost at attention, taken slightly from below so as to emphasize the prominence of his figure; on his left arm is propped the model of the facade of his latest building — the skyscraper headquarters of AT&T — which is at present under construction in New York.

I am no iconologist but this image gave me more elements for valuation and information than did the ten pages in the same magazine dedicated to the new tendencies in American architecture, and I would even say more than what was offered me by the official public relations office in the books dedicated to his works, his writings and in the catalogues to his exhibitions.

We are a long way away from the portraits adopted by *Time* covers where every famous personality is shown in the foreground, without a real context for reference. In this case, for those who know how to read, there is a context, and it is the inside of the Seagram Building, where Johnson has his studio; he built it together with Mies van der Rohe over twenty years ago and it represents one of the greatest universally recognized masterpieces of architecture in the field of skyscrapers and the highest expression and application of the poetry and rational purism of one of the masters of architecture and of the Modern Movement.

From this pulpit Johnson, at the age of 73, dominates an inevitably cowed audience with his lean figure, staring through his severe, black-rimmed glasses at each potential interlocutor and displaying the silvery model balanced on his left arm as if it were the tablets of the law. He throws out a message that was formulated twenty years ago as a theoretical proposition and is now a precise, imperious commandment that almost seems to paraphrase the introduction to the ten commandments: "You cannot not know History." This image, the latest I have seen, is the last of a long process of carefully rationed and planned appearances by the man in the cultural and formal scenario defined by his architecture. This autographical relationship with his own work does not have the judicial and abstract dimension of author's rights, but is related to behaviour involving existential participation, as though the author were assimilated inseparably inside his own masterpiece. There is no doubt that Johnson is the architect who has portayed himself most decisively as an anthropological modulus for the architecture that he himself has designed.

His eruption into the open on the *Time* cover is the final effect of a long transmigration, from private space inside his architecture to the public arena of the general social and cultural space. His architecture — carried out by himself for himself — is the receptacle for his image, the scenario for sociocultural conduct that Johnson plans with the same precision and essentiality as his works.

Johnson makes his first appearance in his first complete critical biography which documents his work up to the beginning of the sixties. In a presentation of the Glass House due to Arnold Newman, called "transparencies and reflections of the glass wall" in a faded scenario with the outlines of trees and architectural elements, which are silhouetted on levels placed at a varying depth, is the clear outline of a man sitting engrossed in reading who dominates this illusory picture made solely of reflections by his presence, the only active and concrete form.

By way of a subtle metaphor this image tells us about the choice which is the basis of his cultural commitment, one that was born out by himself in 1960 when he declared himself to be "first of all a historian and only an architect by coincidence."

Thus we can recognise the cultural meaning of the architect's work: an intellectual who acts by way of his own tools in the world of ideas, knowledge and art, rather than a craftsman whose job it is to transform material and social reality.

It is my belief that this figure of the intellectual and critical architect represents the historical defeat of the cultural and professional model defined by the Modern Movement and has now become a marked characteristic of second-generation architects.

It is no longer possible to express the activism of the masters or promote and carry on their project which asserts the political and social role of architecture, but it is necessary to get through a crisis which even has a subjective and existential dimension. By abandoning worldly ideals like the hypothesis of using architecture to transform the world it will at least be possible to save and revalue aspects of its superstructure, the cultural and artistic values that are at the heart of the subject. This first image, where the figure of Johnson expresses a subdued yet positive and reflective presence in the multiple mirrors of the glass house, is followed by an appearance that is clearly silhouetted yet mirrored, melancholy and reflective, tragically trapped inside the glass box, forced there by the purist idelogy that characterizes it, which does not allow errors, trespassing, exceptions or simple poetic licence.

"A glass box can belong to our time, but it has no history" is the quote that bears witness to the whole drama of being condemned to live in the immanence of the present. Nevertheless this cannot be forced on the intellectual critic, the historian that he recognizes himself to be before anything else.

I believe there is an obvious analogy between the disquieting cultural complexity of this character and the kind of intellectual, critical architect personified by Ernesto Nathan Rogers in those very same years: he too is an active architect as well as a subtle theorist, a polemicist and a proposer of the concept of "continuity" that managed in such a dialectical manner to mediate between the desire not to destroy the heritage of ideas worked out by the Modern Movement and the vital need to re-establish an active relationship with the historical tradition. It is my opinion that the controversy aroused over Johnson's cultural responsibilities with regards to his presumed "betrayal" of the

International Style and of the purist poetry of Mies van der Rohe can be considered a pretext and without foundation, as were the accusations made against Rogers and the so-called "Neoliberty" tendency of having caused "the Italian withdrawal from modern architecture."

Instead we can now admit that both of them, in their respective contexts, took on the responsibility and the task of explaining the processes of mutation that were coming about in the architects' concrete work, contributing to the historical evolution of the discipline. The last image of the series taken by Arnold Newman at New Canaan finally shows us Johnson in person; he is no longer presented in a reflected fashion, but is portrayed behind a partially open door. Behind him shining brightness traces a ray of light on the floor, almost as though it were a demarcation line. It appears that the image of this photograph represents the moment of a fundamental choice: the exit from the closed yet sure and luminous world of architectural ideas and the entrance into the real world where things are in areas of light and shade and there is contamination.

In this image he seems to be still balancing between the two realities, keeping himself in position so as not to lose sight of the discipline's context, while he explores and scrutinizes the outside world. The choice is difficult but necessary; his face betrays neither enthusiasm nor excitement, but quiet, thoughtful concentration. His hand keeps the door open: if it were the case, it could be closed again.

After a process of meditation and torment lasting five years, Philip Johnson came out of his "glass box" and questioned the ordered picture of his discipline, overthrowing the system of conventional references as practised in planning.

The apologue of the "Seven crutches of modern architecture" made to the students of Harvard in 1954 was without a doubt more of a risky political manoeuvre than a clear theoretical proposal, through which he freed himself from his spiritual fathers, who as such could "be hated," whose work had by then become "tradition" and had fallen behind those who worked as architects, who were faced by a field of action that was completely clear of methodological obstacles, theoretical limitations or formal references. In this sense, the only crutch that Johnson seems to have saved at the end of his apologue, history, seems more than anything else to be a weapon with which he demolishes the rigid disciplinary frame of the Modern Movement in the name of the very masters who set it up and imposed it.

This consideration regarding the political character of the position Johnson assumed effectively involves more than its specific content.

From that moment on he planned his own cultural behaviour: architecture as well became an element of this labour of planning his social personality.

Once the historical references began fading away and history had been, so to speak, put into movement again, it was no longer a problem of following in the wake traced by recognized tradition: if anything it was to put himself resolutely at the head

JANUARY 8, 1979
$1.25
TIME
IRAN
Violence and Chaos
U.S. Architects
Doing Their Own Thing
US INFO AGENCY
830 3RD AV
BLK 45

of the historical process, no longer accepting to perform a socially recognized historical role, but emerging instead at the level of a historic personage with a particular, pre-eminent character.

So architecture began to become a vehicle that could be used in a very unprejudiced way to plan and promote his own image. In the photograph Saul Leiter took more than a decade later to accompany the presentation of the new pavilion attached to the Glass House at New Canaan, the illusion of proportions that results, which could have been totally to the detriment of the architectural scale, turns out instead to the entire advantage of Johnson's stature.

He towers over a background that is an architectural capriccio, whose function seems to be merely what is represented in this photograph, and the expression on Johnson's face looks like satisfaction at the sense of wonder that he causes; the shrewd and amused expression of a man who is certain of the success of the instruments he uses and who is positioned wisely in his space for his own personal ends; the photograph also reveals his narcissistic attitude, reflected in water surrounded by columns and well aware of not running the risk of Narcissus' mythical destiny.

It is evident that an essential component of Johnson's personality is indeed represented by his narcissism, whose dimensions are self-contemplative and knowingly exhibitionist: any person worthy of this designation must of necessity express this.

Philip Cortelyou Johnson is now one of the architects who is able to express real power in the cultural and professional environment of architecture and the other arts.

His qualification as "guest of honour" at this international exhibition of Architecture organized by the Biennale of Venice, unlike the analogous recognition awarded to other Senior Architects like Gardella and Ridolfi, which corresponds to the final seal to a career, rather confirms his acme and the moment of his greatest success. He is definitely recognized to be the leader of the "American team" of Post-Modern architects which, in virtue of this fact, appears extremely compact despite the presence in its ranks of extremely varied and contradictory design philosophies and architectural products, ranging from the technical reductionism and pessimism of the Californian Frank Gehry to the self-satisfied and aggressive decorativism of the New Yorker, Robert Stern, to the sophisticated and ironic historicism of the Bostonian Michael Graves, not to mention the variety of positions in existence among the minor presences.

With his authority and prestige Philip Johnson holds up the huge umbrella under which these positions cohabit and this fact shows us how powerful he really is: nowadays he is undoubtedly the architect who internationally is endowed with most power, and there is no other architect who, outside the narrow professional confines, exercises such an incisive influence on a cultural level and particularly in the world of architectural culture.

I have tried to approach the character by examining his public image and have also sought to identify

6. Model of "Transco II" in Houston (Tex.).
7. Philip Johnson, Roofless Church, New Armony (Ind.), 1961.
8. Pavillion for the house in New Canaan (Conn.).

whatever existential elements appear.

The meaning of the work of Johnson the architect cannot be understood without knowing his character and the public figure of great social prominence that it embodies. While most architects, even the famous ones, are exclusively known for their works, Johnson is an architect whose image as a real person can be associated with his works by even the non-specialized public.

In constructing this synthesis he has not only resorted to the "crutch of history," which he declares not to disdain, but also to the "crutch of power," which he has used in a well-disguised and sophisticated way, no longer as an architectural historian but as a "historic man."

I believe that Johnson has demonstrated in an extremely cultured and historically meaningful way that architecture and power are terms that can still be united.

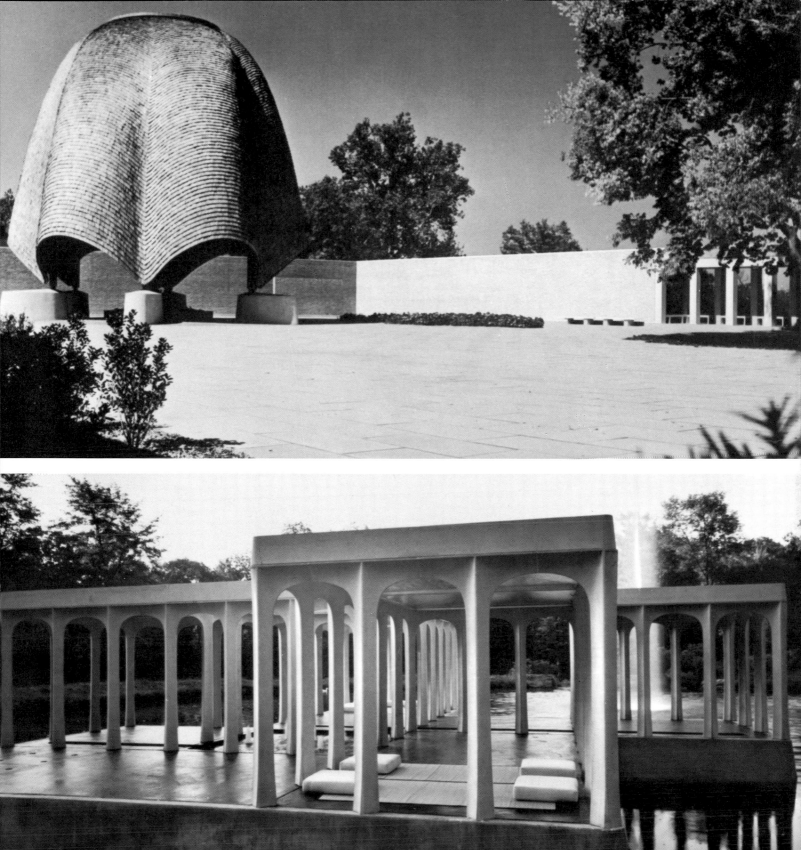

10. Preparatory drawing for the Philip Johnson's House in Big Sur (Cal.).
11. Preparatory drawing for a Playhouse in Cleveland (Oh.).

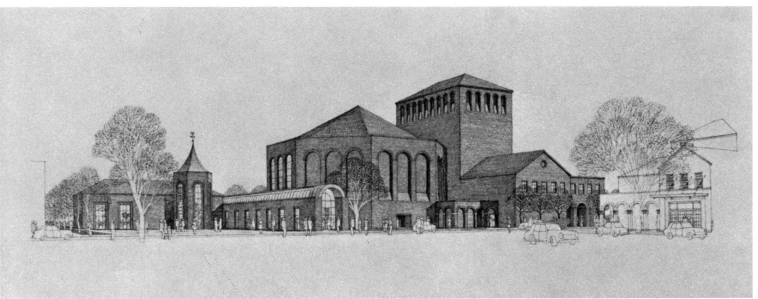

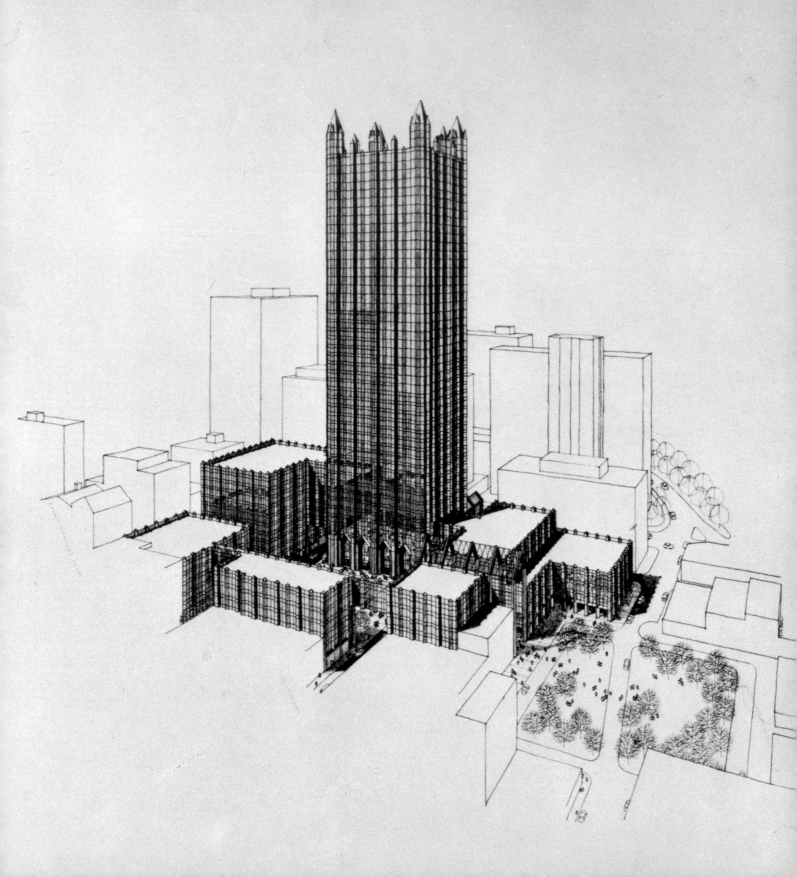

12. Project for the "PPG Industries, Inc." skyscraper in Pittsburgh (Penn.).

13. Project for the "AT&T Building" in New York City (N.Y.).

The craft of Mario Ridolfi

Francesco Cellini, Claudio D'Amato

If the effort marking the departure of today's architectural culture from the droughts of the Modern Movement and the International Style has its unifying datum in the generalized reconsideration of the entire historic inheritance, then it presents neither an alignment of the results nor their homologation through the realization of a unitary language.

Since totalizing and ideological interpretations have ended, each architect turns to history through the optical correction furnished by the conscious reconsideration of his own context, of the traditions of his own country.

The culture of "place" which characterized the end of the 1960's and the beginning of the 1970's has facilitated this process.

The reconquest of the general takes place in the presence of a second dialectic term, the detail, defined as a process of slow sedimentation.

Now, the conscience of history tends to coincide with that process which must be tried out if one is to take possession of one's inheritance.

The figurative choices characterizing the new revelations necessarily carry with them, as in every movement, the "rediscovery" of one's fathers.

The new mentors will be those who, with the weight of their authority, will make the new positions legitimate, and they will be different for different generations and different countries.

Thus, even in the sphere of so-called Post-Modernism, the figures of the fathers stand out on the horizon: in their diversity, they return to live the different motivations with which Anglo-Saxon and Latin cultures rediscover history.

How far can this reasoning be applied to Mario Ridolfi? In this case, the answer is complicated: in trying to formulate a possible hypothesis, we shall also try to clarify implicitly some peculiar features that distinguish Italy's presence on the international scene.

Mario Ridolfi has always followed his profession with coherence, apparently not worrying about the uproars that his work, through good and bad, provoked: he didn't worry about them during his greatest professional success, and doesn't now that he has retired to the Marmore. His rule is made up of several unbreakable principles of work: professional honesty, adherence to the program and to its scrupulous interpretation, the overcoming of difficulties, attention to detail, control of everything liable to improvement, the descriptive anxiety of the project which, even before being built, is already "all" represented on drawing paper.

Much has been written about Mario Ridolfi, especially recently. A few months ago, a conference was held on his work, and many up-to-date and fascinating hypotheses were reformulated, some concerning the real intentions of the artist and his attitudes.

It is nevertheless worthwhile to print a quotation by Ridolfi from a 1943 issue of the magazine *Stile*. The architect's words point up well even today the difficulties in labeling him, and in forcing him into improbable roles: "... My inclination is to penetrate problems deeply, to know the materials in order to put them to good use. The severity of my upbring-ing in the early years of my life, the search for quality and not quantity in my production have contributed to making me an individual who perhaps seems outside his time, but who is really certain of not losing touch with his time."

In the refusal of all intellectualistic manners and sophisms lies one of the principal keys for understanding the ground Ridolfi proposes in code to whoever wants to understand it, to understand architecture with him.

Ridolfi is one of the few masters without a school: many architects copied him during the years of his professional success, but it was always a case of particular aspects of his work: from time to time, typology, the prefabricated solution, the decorative motif. Many have copied him in Terni, where the master plan elaborated by Ridolfi and Frankl favored this diffused "Ridolfism," like Ridolfi's following building tradition. But even in this case, the central nucleus of that elaboration has remained on the exterior.

The students of the new generations cannot have known him, since he never taught at the university, and magazines have stopped publishing him.

Ridolfi's incapacity to or desire not to systematize his work theoretically has surely contributed to this. But we feel that the reasons for it are to be found elsewhere.

Paolo Portoghesi has singled out well some of these in his "Presence of Ridolfi" (*Controspazio*, n. 1, 1974), in writing about the real contradictions which provoked and accompanied the birth of the Modern Movement, and before its conventional and reductive hagiography: "The whole meaning of Ridolfi's investigation probably lies in his having taken those contradictions upon himself, without the comfort of a critical atmosphere capable of understanding him..." In this inattention of criticism, and in this imposed isolation lies one of the explanations for the difficulty in placing Mario Ridolfi today among the precursors of a new architectural age.

Another reason, closely related to the one above, is to be found in Ridolfi's aesthetic program, based on the recovery of expressiveness and meaning in an architecture seen as the reinterpretation of the collective patrimony of history: never an abstract and ideological history, but a concrete history of the solutions which from time to time have made the realization of architectural space tangible. In this conscious program of re-appropriation and overcoming, there is another explanation for the general difficulty in recognizing Ridolfi as head of a school. Ridolfi is not copied because he is difficult to copy, because the understanding of his work continually refers to something other than itself, requires a complex intellectual effort, and the recognition and acceptance of an entire figurative patrimony. In the article quoted above, Portoghesi continues: "I think that among the real terms of reference of the Italian tradition of modern art, Ridolfi today constitutes a resting point with which the new generations and new tendencies will have to come to terms if their aspiration to concreteness, to the Sachlichkeit, is not just sentimental recollection." And just as history for Ridolfi is always the history of solutions, so is his architecture the solution of solutions, conscious and re-elaborated. They are solutions strictly related to a specific region regarding technology and figurative reference. These solutions are characteristic of the professional man and authentic artist, who moves with nonchalance among aulic and "popular" references.

In these barely-mentioned reasons is a partial response to the question of why Ridolfi's teaching reappears as topical. The latest message is found in the residences of the Marmore: a building program where the small number of square metres constructed is inversely proportional to the richness of the results. In the Marmore cycle, several themes come to our attention: planning through unity and the central space; the articulation and quality of invented building techniques; decoration; the cognitive inclination of the project expressed through the drawing (not drawn architecture, but the drawing of architecture). Our hypothesis will be articulated with special reference to the graphic work of Mario Ridolfi.

Ridolfi's drawings

Even at an inexpert glance, his drawings seem to present various characteristics not common to the abundant graphic production of the past few years; these characteristics are:
– descriptive and representative rigor realized through the almost exclusive use of orthogonal projections;
– the extraordinary, almost indecipherable complexity, due to the presence of various scales and various moments of representation;
– the substantial indefiniteness and opening up, even in the most beautiful drawings; shown in part by their singular compiling or reflections and additions, paper upon paper and metres of adhesive tape;
– the almost constant written comment, not only numerical and descriptive, but often self-critical and ironic, like a lucid and detached counterpoint to the dramatic quality of the elaborations. One gets the impression of an uncommon coherence between the aesthetic finalities of Mario Ridolfi's architecture and his graphic work (which seems obvious, but isn't completely); and also a shocking analogy between the toil of the process of drawing, and the toil of the design process itself (at least what can be deduced from the analysis of the developments – *viae crucis* – of the design.)

Finally, an analysis of the toil between definition and indefiniteness, between the aulic stability of the form and the prosaic instability of the detail, between the investigation of the geometric and tridimensional absolute (central plans) and the indulgence in variation and dissonance.

The theme of the central plan

The figurative unity, the same physical identity of the architecture of Mario Ridolfi is often resolved in the compact and geometrically determined aggregate usually called an "organism with a central plan;" but we don't want to use a term which calls to mind a glossary or manual.

1. Project for an Agip motel in Settebagni (Rome), 1968 (together with Volfango Frankl).

2. Lina House, Marmore (Terni), 1966.

Centrality in this case is never, in fact, the result of calculation, artifice, or the objective of a program, but is always the subtle mediation (sometimes the fleeting balance) among different stimuli, tensions, memories.

Thus, there co-exist: naturalistic inspiration in the harsh and irrevocable geometry of glass, enlivened by the luminous reflections and changing nuances of the tones or in the rigorous and spontaneous soft articulation of the lobes of a leaf or the petals of a flower; the culture of history, the attention given to the expressionist polycentric structures of the Luckhardt brothers and Bruno Taut; the love of the built tradition, of the solid tectonic unity of the farmhouse of Umbria, Latium, or Tuscany, and of the immense patrimony of that "deviance" from the architectural norm, the vernacular.

Order, in this architecture, permits disorder; the drawing reveals the overbearing quality of the material; the general structure guarantees the liveliness and irregularity of the parts; think of the "Casa Lina," of that wall so wisely and regularly articulated, so insistently described by horizontal courses, and yet so brutally natural, corroded stone, raw material; think of that pyramidal roof, Euclidean structure, ideal floors, faces, arrises, that barely contain the irrepressible irregularity and variable tonality of the traditional terracotta tiles.

In the memory of the architect, there are often ideas, abandoned and then recovered, ghosts and shadows which come back to life; this is a phenomenon common to the investigations of many artists.

If, though, we go deeper and better observe the themes of these presences, we get an idea of the extraordinary vitality of Mario Ridolfi's profession, and an idea of the complexity of his activity. We realize that he isn't interested so much in the central plan itself as in a certain type of plan (pentagonal, polycentric, lobed) and in several types of aggregation and growth (i.e., the spiral).

And one central structure certainly isn't like another: the ambiguous odd polygons of scarce and laborious symmetries don't have the same value as the tedious clarity of even ones; the sense of ordered but mysterious growth suggested by a lobed, polycentric, or spiraled structure isn't equal to the obsessive clarity of a rigid structure. One isn't the same as the other at least in the hypothesis of architectural logic in which a conflict is desired between the idea of regularity and the perception of its opposite, in the hypothesis of a building impressed on the mind for its firmness and also giving the impression of a diaphanous concretion of crystal, or at most giving the sensation (Agip Tower) of its own imminent collapse.

But exactly this conflict between thought and image, between logical structure and perception, between architecture and nature, seems to be the objective of Mario Ridolfi's pursuit.

Looking in retrospect at the dramatic expressionist and romantic work of Mario Ridolfi, the resulting fact is precisely this balance between empirical methodology and the tendency towards a logical-synthetic order.

It matters little that this balance is achieved through a tortuous and difficult road, which appears above all to originate in far-off academic sources and rationalist training.

Thus, while we verify the impossibility of placing Ridolfi in the Modern Movement, we can see in him an illumination of problems of method (empirical or synthetic-logical); of that debate which (even if it appears a bit dated today) was and remains one of the discriminant foundations of architectural criticism and thought.

The role of drawing for Ridolfi

A second theme immediately comes up if we question the sense (specific role) of the drawing. In times like the present, we could easily contrast the supposed professional seriousness, rigor, and instrumentality of Ridolfi's drawing with the unrestraint of the fad of the drawing.

Even though we don't share similar moralisms regarding an area of research recently discovered and still to be explored, there is no reason to mistake Mario Ridolfi's drawing for a pure, axiomatically perfect (a prototype) professional work. The drawings are in fact too hermetic to accomplish credibly that enjoyment of communication to the client and building site which marks the professional product. On the other hand, these paradoxical cryptograms of an exasperated working drawing exclude a "different" interpretation. They are neither liberating raids on drawing, nor the verification of some architectural hypotheses in the spaces evoked more or less on drawing paper.

They are profoundly introverted drawings. In fact, they require a careful deciphering more than a reading, almost an indelicate and embarrassing intrusion into the creative process.

The knowledge of their "private character" makes the apparent incongruity of their beauty show up; that is, their absolute and meticolous perfection of line and tone, of light effects and maniacal descriptiveness.

The obsessive realism of Mario Ridolfi's drawings, realized with so much academic propriety, need an explanation.

We realize that Mario Ridolfi doesn't undertake a project unless he does it in the understanding of the material processes that architecture implies, above all the building process. We also understand that he doesn't undertake a project without attempting to evoke the processes following construction-use, time, aging. The drawing remains the testimony and principal means of this sort of evocation or divination of the concrete.

And along with one theme of pure Ridolfian philosophy, the necessity to avoid an overly restricting definition of the supposed "profession" of the architect, other general themes come up: the relationship between artistic planning and the building hypothesis, and more generally, the relationships between project and the real.

These themes seem to be of pressing reality at a time when the generality of positions oscillates between extremes: on the one hand, a kind of disdainful refusal of real building (experienced as a second moment, a muddy contradiction of the

3-4. Preparatory drawings for the Lina House, Marmore (Terni), 1966.

5. Briganti House, Terni, 1975: detail of the iron staircase.

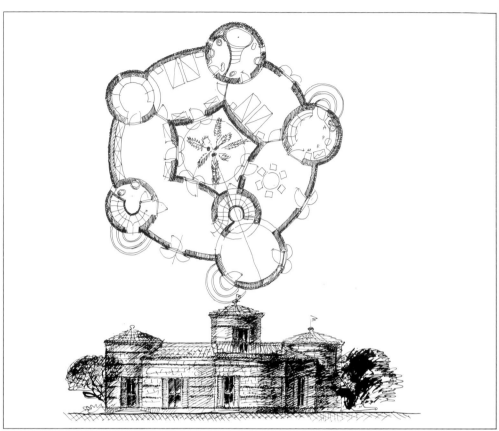

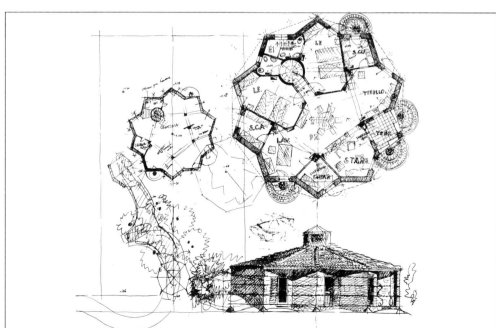

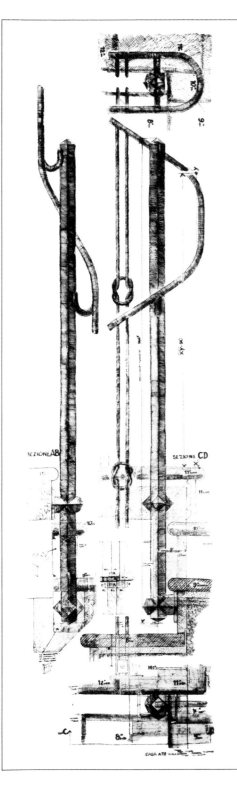

purity of drawing ideas, necessary but not essential to the idea); on the other hand, the total immersion in the required problematics, those of technology, etc. (experienced as a moralistic alternative to individual creativity), at a time when any tension towards the concrete ends up confined in a symbol, in an attempt, in the shaded and redundant world of ideology.

Craftsmanship and detail
One last theme comes up in the analysis of Mario Ridolfi's work, that of craftsmanship. This work hangs over the critical fortune of our architect with all the meanings of backwardness and regret which are characteristic of it: Mario Ridolfi and the lost paradise; "The abacus of technological delay." In defending Ridolfi, it is easy to demonstrate the weakness of this accusation regarding recent production objectively and necessarily situated in a backward productive sphere. But it is better to defend, (or better, understand) Ridolfi's lesson, and try to avoid thinking of the term craftsmanship as just a world of Roman vaults, wood frames, roof tiles, "sponga" stone, bricks, trowels, picks, wheelbarrows, etc.
We have already understood how Ridolfi succeeds, in the sphere of craftsmanship, in deeply understanding the constructive datum in the project, the real. And this miracle appears unrepeatable with regard to rather advanced complex technological systems, and is, in effect, a bit mysterious for everyone.
A balance between that lost dimension and this one, still to be conquered, seems totally unproposable and even reactionary to us, until we admit that not every aspect of the world of craftsmanship must be considered surpassed.
Going over the craftsman's world of Mario Ridolfi's production, we realize (and only here does a real comparison with any other type of craftsmanship make sense) that what we call technology, a term that defines an absolute and immanent universe, is now presented with a surprising historical continuity. Just as if, in place of values given or at least experienced as objective and almost absolute, there is a simultaneous whole of the modes of production and historic building solutions, made coherent only by personal experience and material knowledge.
Just as if in the way of building a window we did not find the tormented co-existence of present solutions with those of the eighteenth, nineteenth centuries, etc.; these solutions are given and known in their constructive logic and in their own formal meaning and their own force of references, emotions, meanings, and memories.
And we get the feeling that the choice of the artisan and the architect loses all evolutionary inhibitions at this point, but tends to work on this entire historical repertoire with the unconstrained coldness of the highwayman: taking what is useful from everyone. And so history enters even into Mario Ridolfi's architecture, not only through the intentional and determined charge of general figurative references, but also through the humble road of the concrete building experience. And so we see why signs,

historical elements and forms, "candelabre," friezes, wrought-iron knots, etc. appear so naturally in this architecture.
Thus, for Mario Ridolfi, the ability to travel the road towards the reappropriation and use of the immense collective stock of constructive and formal knowledge (so provokingly nonchalant with respect to Post-Modern intellectualisms, and so far from neo-academic indifference), seems to prove that in the myth of technology there is nothing but the projection of a knowledge manqué.

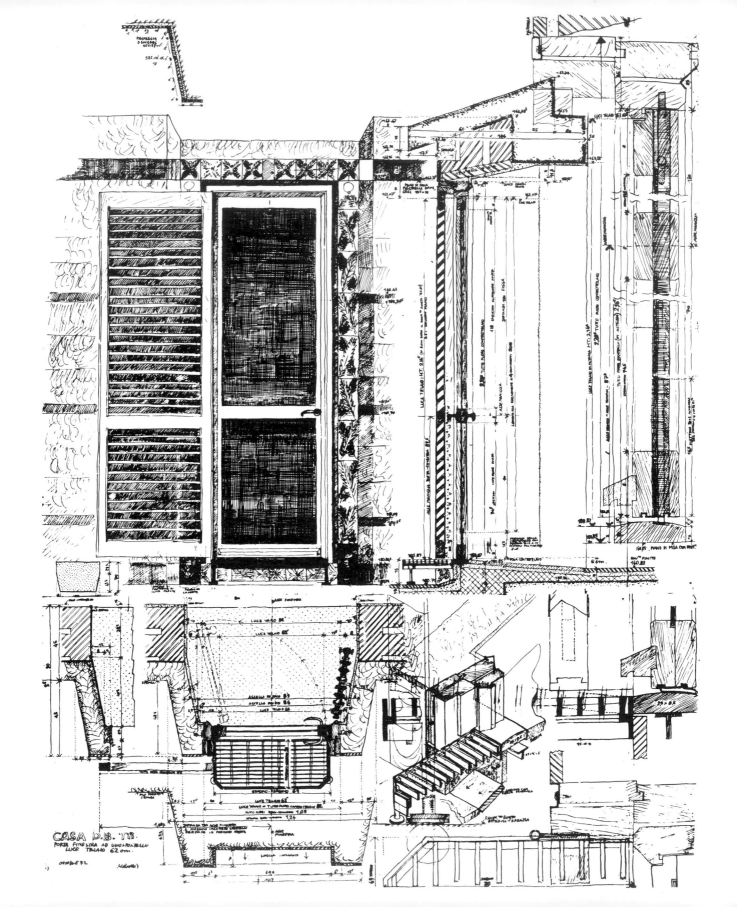

CASA D.B. '73
PORTA FINESTRA AD UNO SPORTELLO
LUCE TELAIO 62 cm.

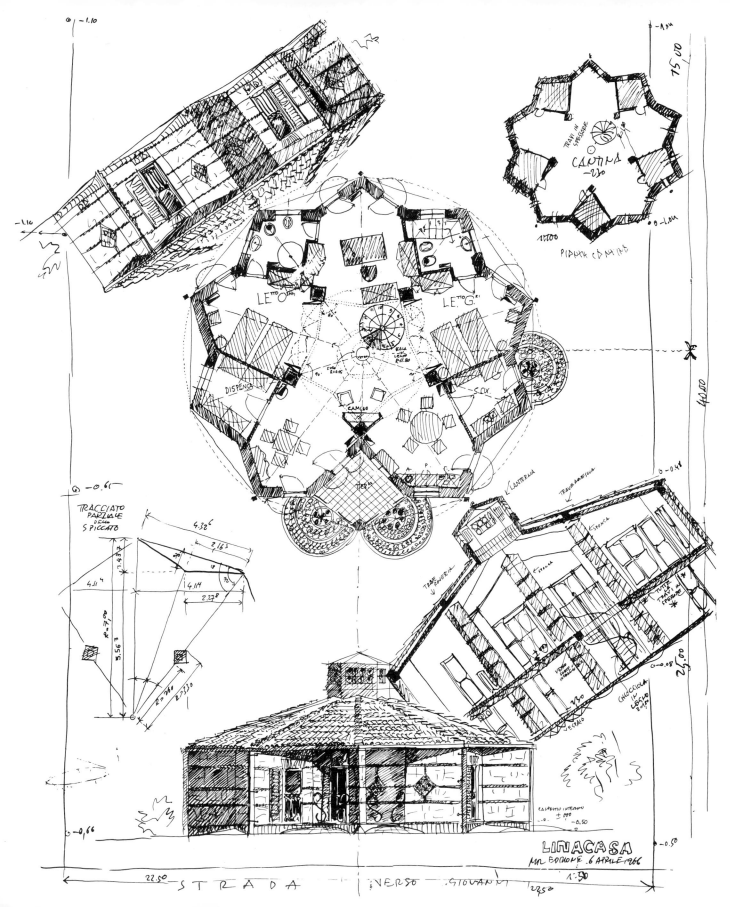

CANTINA
-250

PIANTA CANTINA

LE TTO

LE TTO G.

DISPENSA

S.C.

CAMINO

TERR

TRACCIATO
PARZIALE
DELLO
SPICCATO

4.32

2.16

4.14

4.14

2.27

5.56

LANTERNA

STRADA VERSO GIOVANNI

LINACASA
MR BORDONE 6 APRILE 1966
1:50

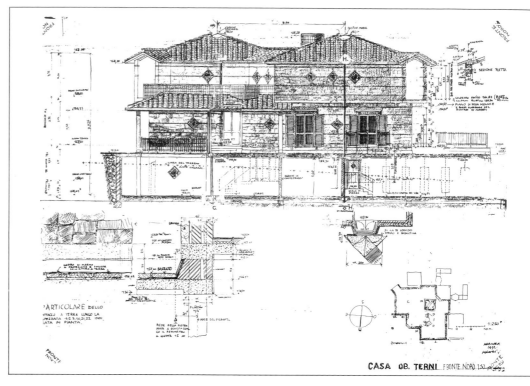

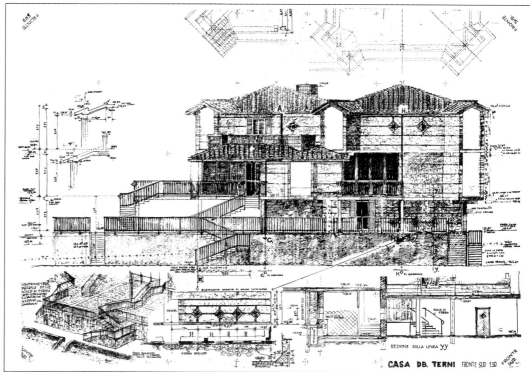

10. Lana House, Terni, 1974: preparatory drawing for the staircase in the living-room.
11. De Bonis House, Terni, 1972: preparatory drawings for a window.

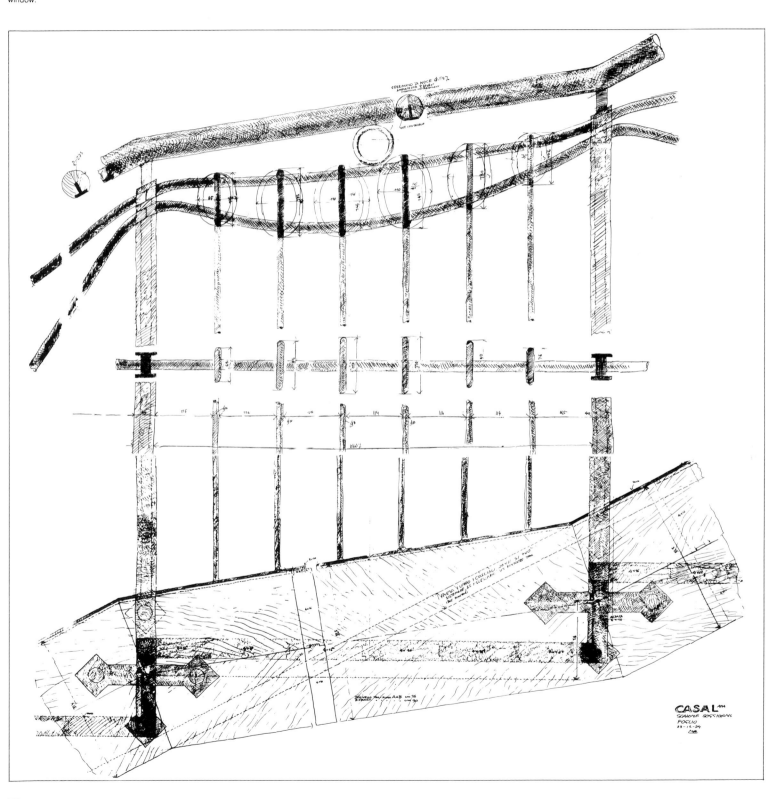

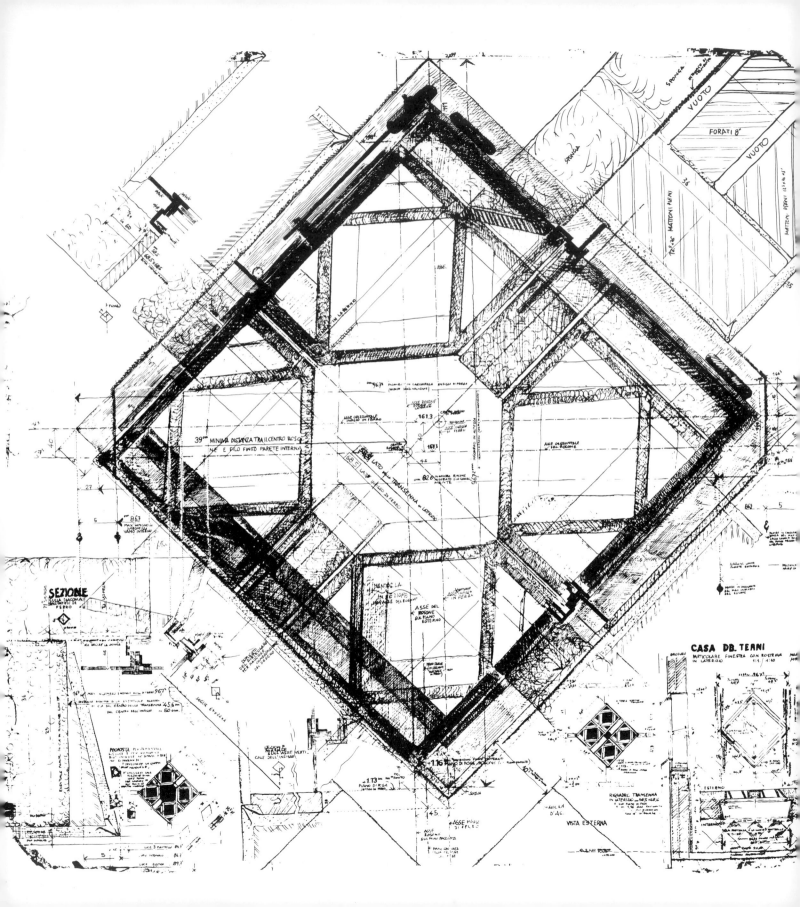

Participants

Architektengroep VDL

1-4. Housing, Purmerend (Holland), 1978: general plan and views.

Professional outfit with office in Amsterdam.
The following work there as architect designers:

Ben Loerakker
The Hague (Holland) 1931.
Degree at the Academie van Baunkunst of Amsterdam in 1965.
Has worked professionally since 1968 and in the VDL since 1975.

Kees Rijnboutt
Amsterdam (Holland) 1939.
Degree at the Technische Hogeschool of Delft in 1964.
From '64 to '75 was managing director of the Amsterdam Municipal.
Council housing department. Joined the VDL in '75.

Hans Ruijssenaars
Amersfoort (Holland) 1944.
Degree at the University of Delft in '69.
Attained his Master of Architecture at the University of Pennsylvania under the guidance of Louis I. Kahn in 1970.
Part of the VDL since '71.

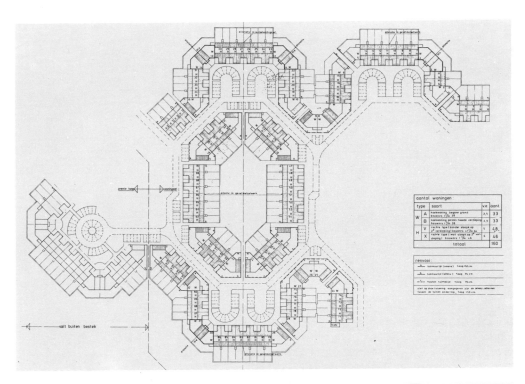

In the designing of buildings and their environs, to live in and to work in, we are consciously searching for a place in the middle of (not on the edge, or outside, let alone above) all the other participants in this process.
We are not searching for a bizarre situation which is suited for a bizarre expression. We desire this middle position as it keeps us abreast of what one could call "the expression of the cultural and social mainstream."
This desired, pragmatic approach demands permanent searching of the means which give answers to the needs and goals formed in society today. Vincent Scully pointed out in *The Shingle Style Today* that: "like lyric poetry, single family houses most openly mirror the character and feeling of their architects and so most directly mirror the influence of those architects upon each other. In them, history can be seen being made at individual heat, where new architects wrestle with their precursors in order to find a way to begin and room to operate for themselves."
Much architecture after the Second World War was experienced by its users as being cold and unapproachable. The purely functional building has often not been able to symbolize the small celebrations of daily life which occur in a building, even if, in a certain manner, that was their intention. With the 1920's example of factories and grain silos an optimistic expectation from and through the expanding possibilities of industrialization shared precedence with the social concerns for more light, air and room. That this has become the "International Style" must mean that these goals have in some respects been met. This same International Style, however, through dry repetition, is being worn down to the bare symbolism of "organised anonymity."
The reaction to this period, from its lack of satisfying symbols and at times alienating nature, is now producing a general nostalgic trend which encompasses everything from "Back to Nature" to "Historicism."
Our attitude in the making of buildings is that we don't backtrack but rather look ahead with the feeling of being a part of a long tradition of formgivers to buildings and their surroundings; moving forward with an awareness of the past. Therefore the Renaissance has no less place than the Modern

Movement and vice-versa.
The present tables of architectural streams, in which the relation to other crafts, to civic ideas, and to historic minutiae is tried to be encompassed, speak for themselves.
Although these works in the so-called Post Modern age generate and receive much publicity, in our eyes they are not achieving many of their self-proclaimed goals. They distract the attention and carry no more weight in the development of architecture or theory than the emperor's new clothes.
It has been and will be the goal to determine the significance of the individual in correlation to society through the design of buildings and on a larger scale, the landscape and the public space.

Andrew Batey
Mark Mack

5. Project for Pavillon at Napa Valley (U.S.A.), 1979.

6-7. Project for an underaround house at Napa Valley (U.S.A.), 1979, perspective view, section and plan.

They have worked together since 1976 and have their studio in San Francisco (Cal.).

Andrew Batey
Marced (Cal. - U.S.A.) 1944.
He attained his Master of Architecture at Cambridge University in 1972.

Mark Mack
Judeburg (Austria) 1949.
Degree in Architecture at the Graz Polytechnic.

Batey & Mack have focused their attention on purifying the architecture of a transitional and confused era. This purification ritual has been acted out many times after the effulgence of stylistic extravagance in classical, Romanesque, Renaissance and Neo-classical periods. Their neo-primitivist philosophy is translated through houses in rural contexts, and it is more sympathetic to European neo-rationalism and neo-classicism than the American Post-Modernism with its suburban language of symbolic substitutions and "gargoyly" eclecticism. The architecture finds its tranquility in the archaic assessment of primitive and vernacular shelter. The rigor and simple virtuosity found in Greek and Roman types, growing out of a structural fuctionalism with integral decor, has inspired these houses. This primitivism is conservative in its reaching back to a well-mastered building technology, progressive in promoting a utopian purism, intellectual in its reduction of architectural principles, and emotional in its rugged natural form tied to its site condition.
The insubstantial artificial building materials which have produced the Post-Modern aesthetic suits the confused language of lowered expectations and applied ornament. This has increased the distance between the natural environment and the built artefact. The structural vernacular combined with the desire to fit the building into the landscape reinforces the notion of permanence, and counters the vicissitudes of fleeting trendiness now rampant in architecture.
The plans reflect a typological rather than specific use of space which, over time, allows more flexibility in spatial arrangements than tailored high-tech solutions. Delight is provided by straightforward perception of the substance of the building fabric rather than manipulations of the surface and pyrotechnics of color and layers.
It is the ruins of Pompeii, the classicism of Schinkel and Asplund, the archotypal austerity of Loos and Barragan, rather than Las Vegas, that inspire us.

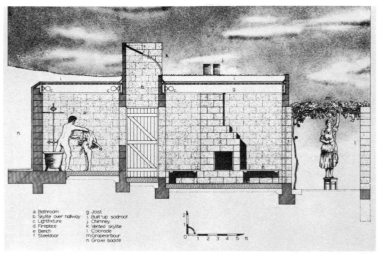

a. Bathroom
b. Skylite over hallway
c. Lightfixture
d. Fireplace
e. Bench
f. Steeldoor
g. Joist
i. Built up sodroof
j. Chimney
k. Vented skylite
l. Colonade
m. Grapearbour
n. Gravel backfil

8. Project for avilion at Napa Valley (U.S.A.), 1979: elevation and plan.

9. Project for Gulf of Mexico Villa (Tex.), 1980: elevation and plan.

10. Project for Underground House, Napa Valley (U.S.A.), 1979: elevation and plan.

11. Project for Courtyard House at Napa Valley (U.S.A.), 1980: elevation and plan.

12. Bowles House (Cal.), 1973: elevation and plan.

8

9

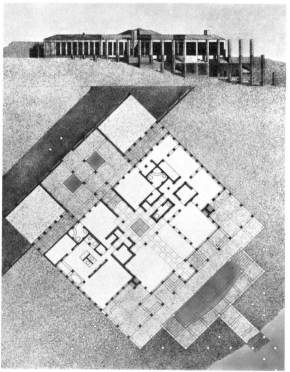

10

11

Thomas Hall Beeby

Oak Park (Ill. – USA) 1941
Master of Architecture at Yale University in 1965.
Professional studio in Chicago, Ill., since 1971 (Hammond Beeby and Babka)
Associate Professor at the Illinois Institute of Technology since 1978.

A city is the expression of the cultural aspirations of a people revealed through the eyes of her architects. America was a land of immigrants, heir to a rich European peasant culture. Each arriving group clustered in enclaves, isolated by language in an alien wilderness. They built in the manner of their origins, transformed eventually by the necessity of climate and material. However the American Dream drove them away from their culture as they aspired to assume the role of an absent aristocracy. Sentiment tied them to an ancient, anti-authoritarian folk tradition but social aspiration drove them towards Classicism, the architecture of authentic taste. This dichotomy of intentions is most clearly seen in Chicago, the most American of cities.

Two resultant conceptual positions became evident. The first, employed by Sullivan, was to return to peasant craft tradition and build on pragmatic imperative softened by an elaborate ornament grounded in the abstraction of nature. The resultant form was representative of a classless Democracy, forming an idealized City of Truth. The counter position was taken by Burham at the Columbian Exposition where European taste was employed by an ambitious society to establish the legitimacy of high culture in America through classical form. The imagery of the Worlds Fair became the basis for the City of Beauty, opposing the City of Truth as the controlling image of American culture.

Mies introduced an architecture based on a transformed European society to an American City. He adopted a philosophy which supported the morality of the craft position of Sullivan but utilized the abstracted classical forms of Burnham. This coalition of local attitudes has dominated the architects of Chicago for the last forty years, but never really satisfied the people. Younger architects in recent years have opposed the cultural arrogance inherent in Modernism. History has become a desire, ironically at the moment when Chicago finally has an authentic past of its own, as a result of two hundred years of building. The City of Truth and the City of Beauty can join at last through the inspired use of history and flower into an American architecture which reflects the desires of the people completely.

13. Project for townhouse (House of Poliphilus), for the Kelly Gallery of Chicago (Ill.), 1977.

14. Beasley House, 1979.

15. "The house of Virgil awaiting the return of the Golden Age," 1976.

16. "Garden of the Moon," Cooper Hewitt Museum, New York City (N.Y.), 1979.

17-20. Walker Art Center, New York City (N.Y.), drawings from the "Classical City" series, 1980.

21. "The house of Virgil awaiting the return of the Golden Age," 1976.

Georgia Benamo
Christian de Portzamparc

They have worked together in Paris since 1969.

Georgia Benamo
Theatre director, has worked in Italy at the Teatro della Scala and at
the civic theatres of Turin, Genoa and Rome.

Christian de Portzamparc
Paris 1942.
Graduated in 1967 from the Ecole Supérieure des Beaux-Arts in
Paris.

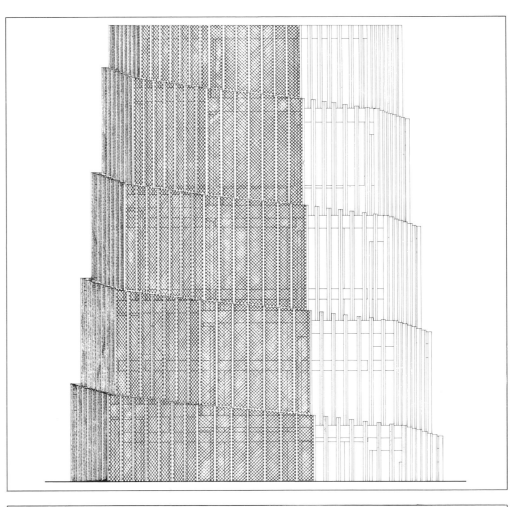

The fact that the most formidable "stylistic" revolution in the history of architecture, which was what took place in the twenties, at the same time started a world-wide process of conceptual and material disintegration, made us pursue for many years one and the same basic idea, project after project: build urban space. The logic of the building as an object must be overthrown, for it is based on the metaphor of the machine and simple internal requirements, and this fascination for technological objects, which are indifferent to the place, to the soil, is out of place. What this means for us is that the facade was not an exhibition of function, the interpretation of an aesthetic sign or 'divertissement', but for the most part the wall to a public space, a sort of vast open-air interior, a continuous wall pierced by two kinds of openings: those of the dwellings — the windows; those of the city — the city's other spaces. It seemed that all the construction we dreamt up could be achieved on this limitless ground, surrounded by towers, in this place that appears to be a caricature of all that is most absurd about urban renewal. It would only have been possible, according to unanimous opinion, to build two towers, perhaps a building, but definitely never a space, a street or a square. Architectural language, architectural "style;" each project works out for us its specific rules depending on to what extent it is based on knowledge, typologies, vernacular elements. But there must always be a little bit of new formulation, this sweet evolution that is life-giving.
Christian de Portzamparc

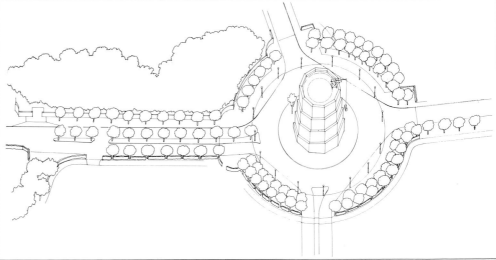

We are condemned so often to speaking, not building, so what is "new" in what we have to say is immediately inserted into the finished project and involves the future of architecture, and that of society as well. We are roused, enlivened by keeping these two threads in hand at the same time, no longer having to choose between conventionality and babbling. The range of our work must be valued in accordance with new rules: the evident need for change has brought us to a new debate on the role of the architect: role, and not function. Improvement in quality does not depend on the use of exceptional financial resources, but on the effectiveness of overall forecasts: this discipline and sense of morality is what is new: it is a continuous contrast between the coordinated layouts that our eye recognizes (Architecture) and the real, unsymbolical conspiracy of what is inconvenient, ugly and miserably poor. The vivid awareness of this new grammar and the common criterion that studies and gives order to streets, buildings and dwellings, now frees our soul and gives us a feeling of great joy.
Georgia Benamo

24. C. de Portzamparc, Château d'eau at
Marne-la Vallée (France), 1971-1974.

25-28. "Rue des hautes formes," Paris
(France), 1976-1979: general views and ground
and standard floor plans.

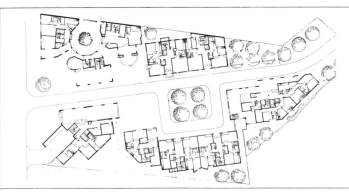

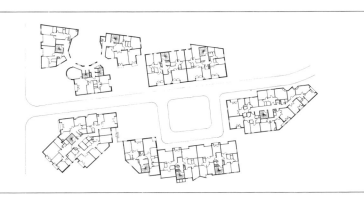

Francisco Javier Biurrun Salanueva

Pamplona (Spain) 1946.
Degree at the University of Barcelona in 1969.
Works professionally in Navarre.
Has taught Applied Arts at the School of Pamplona since 1973.

Project for the sensitivization of the emptiness, the cavity, the silence from which the *Une* concept is taken, (in euskera, space, point, instant)
ACTION 1...Month: March 1980
Site: Aniz-Navarra
Object: sphaeristerium
acquire the image of the rebound wall
acquire the orientation of the rebound wall — 132° N-S
acquire the space 10/10/40 metres
ACTION 2... Month: June 1980
Site: Venice
exhibit the image of the rebound wall
exhibit the orientation of the rebound wall — 132° N-S
exhibit the space 10/10/40 metres
SPHAERISTERIUM: space horizontally bounded by a line whose further end links up with one wall (the rebound one) and then another (on the left)
— PLACE FOR GAMES, MEETINGS, COMMUNICATION, HISTORY, MAN, TIME
— MONUMENT TO ABSENCE, EMPTINESS, THE CAVITY NATURE — SPACE PROJECT
Before the Cromlech Man's loss of spatial sensibility, the recovery of this sensibility, starting from the poetry of absence, of a SPACE which debates between NATURE and MAN.
SPHAERISTERIUM

29-30. House at Ibero, Navarre (Spain), 1976.

John Blatteau

Philadelphia (Penn. - USA) 1943.
Graduated in Architecture at the University of Pennsylvania in 1971.
Works professionally at the Ewing Cole Cherry Parsky studio in Philadelphia.
Taught at the University of Pennsylvania until 1976. At present is Lecturer in Design at Drexel University.

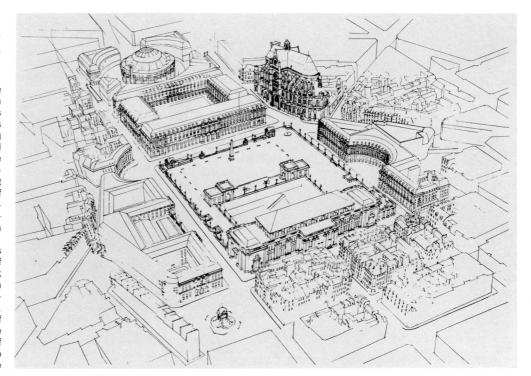

Implicit within the theme of "The Presence of the Past" is a recognition of the importance of an academic tradition in architecture. The past has substance. It is an intellectual reality surrounding us with ideas. It is also a physical reality surrounding us with buildings. These intellectual and physical realities, the ideas and buildings of the past, are fundamental to the make-up of this academic tradition in architecture. Combined with an independent sense of beauty, they have inspired generations of great architecture. The common thread which underlies both these realities and the academic tradition, from the earliest western cultures to our own time is the language of classical architecture.

Classical architecture has canonized its past. Its forms carry with them the accumulated meaning of the centuries. While the treatises and the built work define the rules for the use of these forms, each succeeding generation gives them a different connotation and adds to the potential for their use. Classical architecture has given to us a legacy of professionalism and scholarship which allows the ordinary architect to attain at least a measure of success. At the same time, it allows the genius to use the language as a means and not an end. The great strength of the language of classical architecture is its ability to provide for creative work within a frame of reference, and to extend its use and add to its meaning.

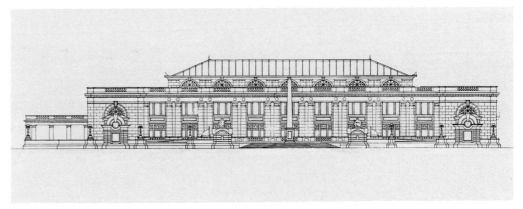

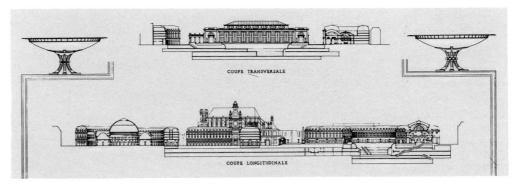

33-35. Competition entry for the layout of Les Halles area in Paris (France), 1979: perspective view, main elevation and sections.

BAYONNE HOSPITAL
PROPOSED
ADDITIONS AND RENOVATIONS

MCMLXXIX

36-37. Re-structuring and enlargement of Bayonne Hospital (N.J.), 1979.

38-39. Project for Mount Pleasant House in Philadelphia (Penn.), 1976: elevation, section and ground floor plan.

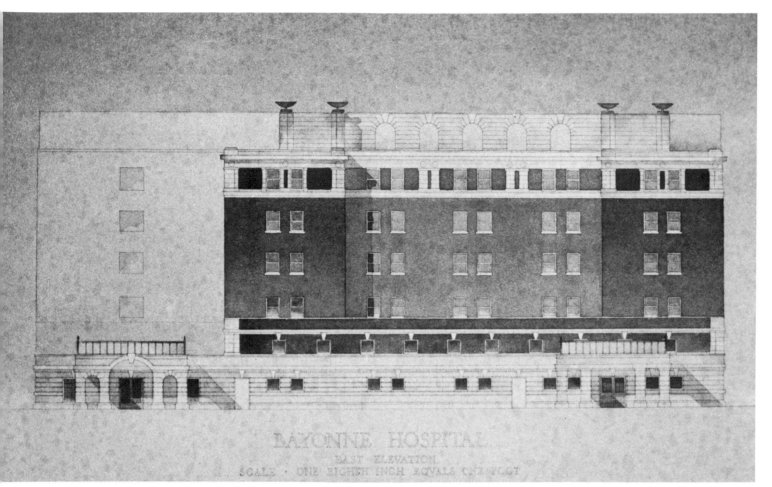

BAYONNE HOSPITAL
EAST ELEVATION
SCALE · ONE EIGHTH INCH EQUALS ONE FOOT

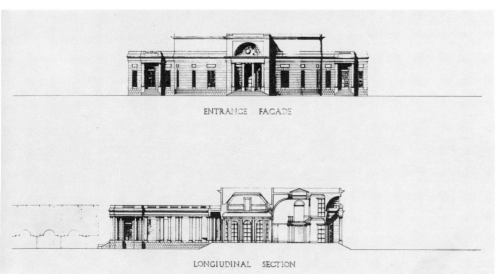

ENTRANCE FACADE

LONGIUDINAL SECTION

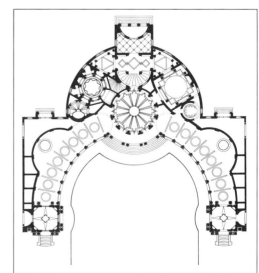

Barcelona (Spain) 1939.
Degree in Architecture at the University of Barcelona.
In '63 he founded the Taller de Arquitectura, a mixed design group which has the following members:
Anna Bofill, Ramon Collado, Emilio Bofill, Serena Vergano, Peter Hodgkinson, Hilario Pareja, Salvator Clotas, M.D. Rocamorra, J.M. Rocias, J. Jansana, Xavier Llistasella, Bernard Torchinsky, Xavier Grau, Omar Migliore, J.P. Carniaux, Thierry Recevsky, Patrick Genard, Patrick Dillon.
As well as working professionally in Spain, Bofill and Taller also work in France and Algeria.

The Taller de Arquitectura of Barcelona is a team of people directed by Ricardo Bofill, who work mainly in architectural and town planning.

After some houses built in Barcelona and designed in 1962 and 1963, the first great social housing plan was the "Barrio Gaudì" in Reus area, Tarragona, of 1964. With this plan the Taller de Arquitectura started a long period of work and research on the habitat in the urban environment with a view to proposing an architectural language appropriate to the Mediterranean area, as an alternative to the rationalist modern language imported by Anglo-Saxon culture. Through this the Taller defends local architecture which respects, establishes and expresses the specificity of the place and attacks the principles of the so-called "international" architecture.

This kind of language, worked on between 1964 and 1975, is always trying to define itself, alters, revolves, changes, develops; as a logical-mathematical game it enriches itself with images and meanings, revolutionary contents and musical poetics to become afterwards such a powerful mechanism for the creation of spaces as to go beyond the possibilities of comprehension and adjustment to building techniques and to today's technology.

The main research topics in this first phase of the work of the Taller de Arquitectura are:
— Symbolic-cultural images;
— Qualities and characteristics of habitat designed taking into account the individual and collective behaviour of its inhabitants;
— the logico-mathematico-geometrical generation of spatial fabrics, where the constructed entity and the void are the positive and the negative of an environmental wholeness.

The projects exemplifying this period are, inter alia: the "Barrio Gaudì" in Reus area (Tarragona); "la Città nello Spazio," the "Plexus," the "Xanadu," "la Muraglia Rossa" in Calpe (Alicante), the "Walden 7" and "la Fabrica" in San Just Desvern (Barcelona), "Petite Cathédrale," "la Maison d'Abraxas" and others in Paris.

In a second work phase, from 1975 up to now, the Taller de Arquitectura has been developing, above all, projects on a different dimensional scale, being much closer to urban planning than to the architecture of buildings, operating in or near urban centres of historical cities, designing new centres.

In this way the influence of the learned language of architecture and of historical planimetries has imposed itself and taken the place of the former patterns of population clusters typical of the Mediterranean area.

Among these lay-outs of towns and parts of town,

there is also the design of buildings that surround urban spaces and that work as examples for the successive interventions of other architects, within the general proposed plan.

There is a desire to bring back to life the architecture of the past, high-quality architecture, noble and cultural and to adopt it to the present systems of building technology; to make the town-planning scheme Baroque and to prefabricate the Renaissance.

Faced with the barbarity of development speculation which has destroyed the equilibrium of the urban landscape, the tendency is to adopt the rules of divine proportions from the design of the panel to the composition of the façade right up to the modelling of urban void.

After the chaos caused by "unrestricted" urbanization, citizens need to find again equilibrium in open public spaces to alleviate the isolation brought about by the grinding routine of work and by the closed family system.

There are no strict rules, the field of formal possibilities is immense (within the limits of building technology), therefore the eclecticism is not only possible, but almost natural. Without falling into the anecdotal which may lead to "collage," the impetus

is towards a Pythagorean rigour guaranteed by the use of a strict geometry. A great formal purity is maintained; something which gathers together the different historical languages and those elaborated during the first phase of the Taller de Arquitectura. The use of Baroque planimetries in the design of urban spaces is an immediate consequence of the necessity to insert volumetric masses and urban voids in already existing urban fabrics. Need for flexibility, for adjusting to pre-existing structures, for creating "double" structures which enclose completely different voids.

These formal rules imply a strong socio-cultural meaning; palaces, no longer assigned to the nobility, become houses of ordinary people; urban voids, cleared of traffic, become collective spaces where every individual and all the people together can identify themselves again with their town, their quarter, their culture.

The projects corresponding to this second phase are, inter alia, "*le Jardin des Halles*," "le Lac," and "le Viaduc" (St. Quentin en Yvelines, Paris), Abraxas Palace and the Theatre (Marne la Vallée, Paris); "Gasteizberry" (Vitoria), "Castro Novo" (Bilbao), "Sta. Maria de Gallecs" (Barcelona), "Antigona" (Montpellier, France).

41. "Parc de la Marca Hispanica," monument to Catalonia, Le
Perthus (Franco-Spanish border), 1974-1976.
42. "Can Massoni," Gerona (Spain), 1977.
43. "Walden 7," residential and commercial complex, Barcelona
(Spain), 1970-1975.

44-45. "La Fabbrica:" restructuring of an old cement factory for the headquarters of the Taller de Arquitectura, in the "Walden 7" area, Barcelona (Spain), 1970-1975.

46. "Il Palazzo:" project for a residential complex at Marne-la Vallée (France), 1978: main elevation.

47. Project for linear agricultural village at Abadla (Algeria), 1979-1980: general plan.

48. Project for circular agricultural village at Abadla (Algeria), 1978-1979.

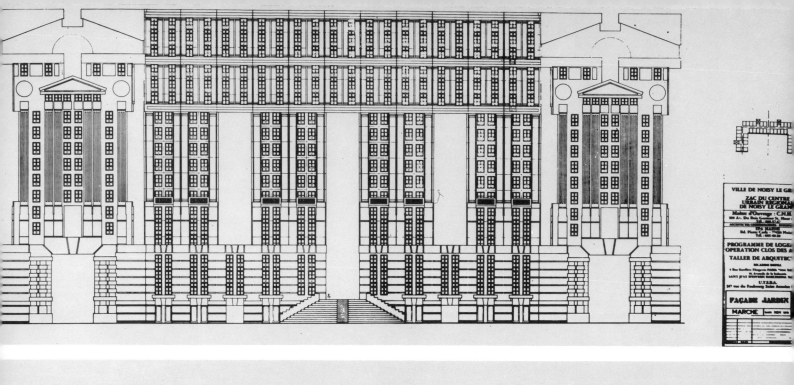

VILLE DE NOISY LE GR...
ZAC DU CENTRE
URBAIN REGIONAL
DE NOISY LE GRAN...

Maître d'Ouvrage : C.N.H....

ARCHITECTE ...
IPA MARNE
Bd. Pierre C...

PROGRAMME DE LOGE...
OPÉRATION CLOS DES A...

TALLER DE ARQUITEC...
RICARDO BOFILL
...

U.P.B.A.
27 rue du Faubourg Saint Antoine...

FAÇADE JARDIN

MARCHE

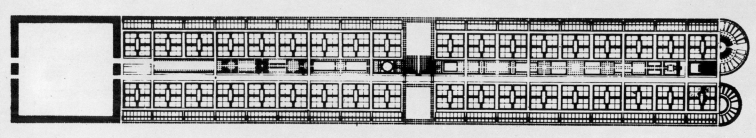

PLAN DE MASSE POUR UNE VILLE DE 1000 LOGEMENTS ET SES ÉQUIPEMENTS

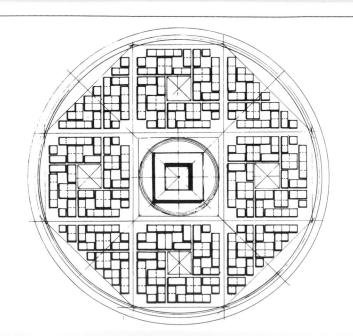

Pep Bonet
Christian Cirici

They are part of the Studio PER, which they founded in 1965 together with Lluis Clotet and Oscar Tusquets.
In '72 the Studio PER set up the "Ediciones de diseño," a small industry for the construction of furniture and building components.

Pep Bonet
Barcelona (Spain) 1941.
Graduated from the ETSA of Barcelona in 1965.
Taught from '75 to '78 in the IIIrd course of planning at the Escuela Superior de Arquitectura in Barcelona.

Cristian Cirici
Barcelona (Spain) 1941.
Graduated from the ETSA of Barcelona in 1965.
Taught from '75 to '78 in the IIIrd course of planning at the Escuela Superior de Arquitectura in Barcelona.

An architecture to be built, the subject and the transgression ot its rules, the economy of means
Over the years of our professional experience, certain constants have emerged which, in a certain sense, define the way in which we like to deal with the problems facing us. Some of these constants derive from the characteristics of projects which we had the opportunity of carrying out: generally small works for clients who normally demand the greatest economy.

We like to build and we are aware that our work acquires its true value only when we build. We treat projects as means and we constantly find ourselves designing the best contributions for the worst projects.

The first problem of our work is to find out the model which embodies our general attitude to the project. Our experience has helped us to know when to eliminate inadequate models rather than to create a definite way of seeing things.

We would be very pleased to have the opportunity of repeating the models in similar situations and correct the mistakes; but chance has not yet presented itself.

Still more we like to adjust to pre-existing reality. We enjoy removing the obstacles which, in some way, stand in the way of a theory, rather than establishing a theory of our own. It is when we face obstacles that we find the best supporting points to go on with our work.

We wouldn't know what to do in the desert.

So it happens that we very often reach the perversion of inventing some transgressions of rules, a system of designing which offers the greatest formal freedom and which enables us to tackle any subject with the greatest efficacy.

We don't like waste, since it betrays ignorance. We like things in moderation as with food. We look for the efficacy of each element, that sensation by which everything has neither too much nor too little of anything.

We believe that beauty can arise from efficacy and it is this belief which enables us to take advantage of an age of constraints like the one in which we happen to have to live, and to derive from that most of our formal repertoire.

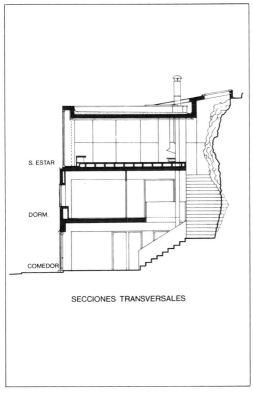

S. ESTAR

DORM.

COMEDOR

SECCIONES TRANSVERSALES

49-51. Casa Frances, Isle of Minorca (Spain), 1977: exterior, detail of interior staircase and section.

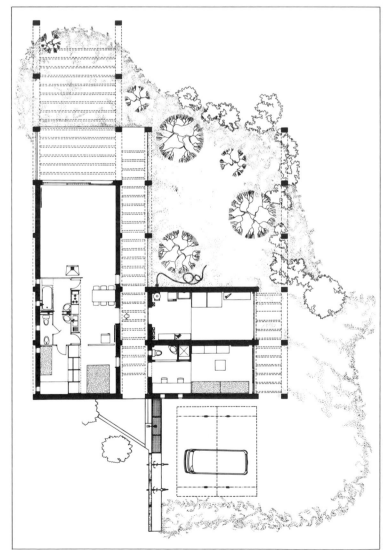

Manlio Brusatin

Castelfranco Veneto (Treviso) 1943.
Graduated from the Faculty of Architecture in Venice in 1970, where he taught for a short period before passing permanently to teaching at the Faculty of Letters and Philosophy of Venice.
He has often been published in magazines and periodicals; he has written pieces for the Einaudi *Encyclopedia* and the book *Venezia nel Settecento* (Einaudi, Turin, 1980). He lives and works at Asolo (Treviso).

One is taught how to discern the layout in the grounds of a house that had disappeared several hundred years ago.

If you like travelling around the countryside in your region or in other areas, you might end up looking for a house, a palace, a villa or a church, whose existence is mentioned by an old book; instead it has disappeared for natural reasons or because of man's neglect. You will not find out much by asking around, for human memory fades away even in yarns — some of grandfather's tales or great-grandfather's sentences can at the most cover a century, which is already a great deal, but that is all.

Let us suppose that the thing you are looking for has been erased from human memory and all that you have is a rare written testimony to the effect that house had really existed and disappeared: it is more a problem of *where* than *when*.

This situation really befell the author, along with L. Krier and M. Scolari, during an architectural tour of the Veneto.

It was spring and inside a wall (still in good condition) a meadow reached as far as the eye could see. There was no trace of ruins or remains amidst the green expanse, which had overwhelmed the monument, but an overriding feeling of having found something brought us all to a thoughtful stop at the edge of the meadow, as though at a loss when faced by a tomb levelled by time and devoured by grass. What should we do?

For a while we stood there aimlessly, then a peasant came out from behind a tree and approached us, asking rather brusquely what we were looking for. One thing fascinates peasants: their fields may be concealing a treasure and they are convinced that some story or yarn might bring it to light.

We replied that we were looking for an ancient house that had long ago been situated in this very meadow but had now disappeared.

The peasant's face lit up cunningly and he answered that the house could still be seen.

You can imagine our amazement. Nevertheless the peasant confidently accompanied us into the field and the layout of the house gradually appeared to us, drawn on the grass. The grass had grown slightly lower where the walls had been; its colour was different, a lighter green. The design was clearly marked: the meadow had given back the house. No one has ever thought of seeing a design in this way. How can one conceive the layout if not by thinking of being able to walk inside the walls? But the house, lost for many hundreds of years, appeared beneath our eyes and marked itself out under our footsteps — the real great, green, silent house.

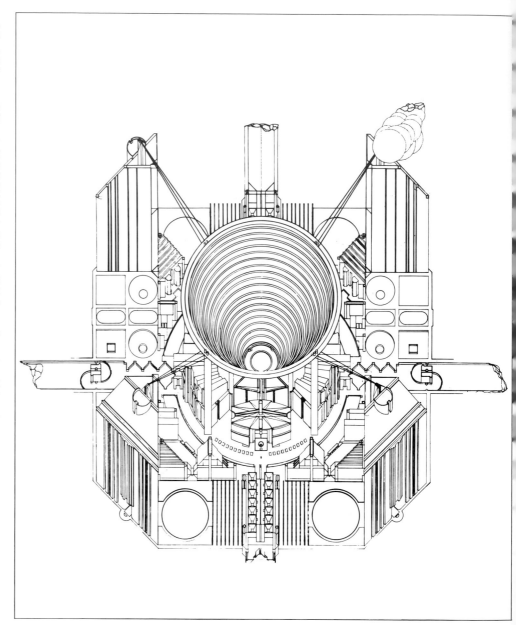

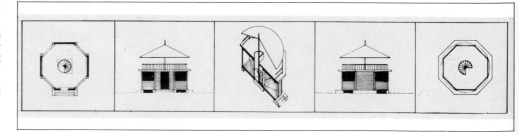

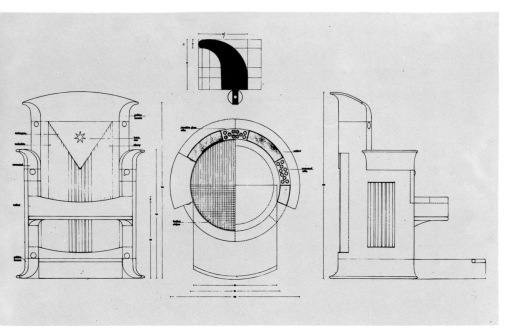

57. Project for a suburban temple (degree thesis), 1970.
58. Project for a "pensatoio" at Asolo, could be carried out, 1977.
59. Throne for King Hussein of Jordan (not carried out), 1977.
60. Duse Chair for the Café at Asolo (Treviso), of which two copies were made, 1975.

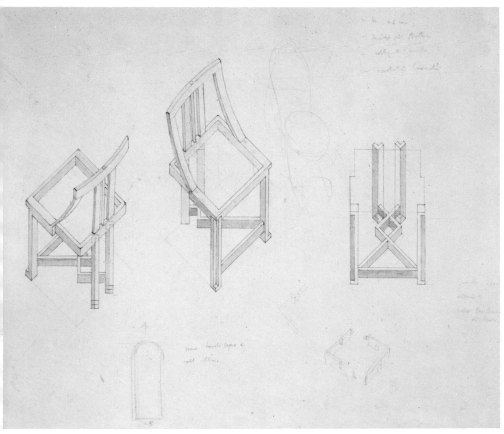

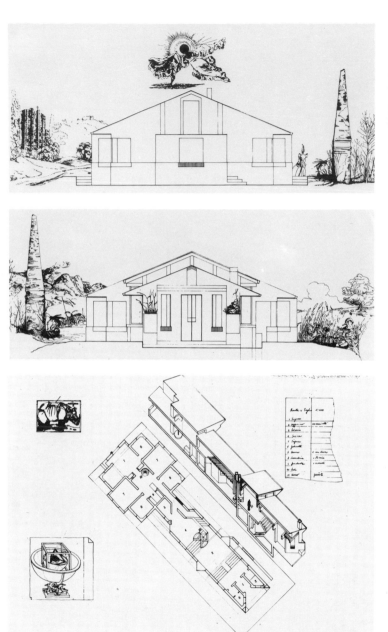

61-66. Casa Conz, Asolo (Treviso), 1974: front, rear, plan, axionometric vertical section; view of the work during construction: the chimney, the main elevation and the roof trusses.

Jean-Pierre Buffi

Florence 1937.
Graduated in 1963 at Florence with Libera and Quaroni.
Teaches at the Ecole Nationale des Beaux-Arts in Paris Up-6 Raucourier.

Materials for planning

There is something worrying about the projects and research that we have been carrying out in these last few years.

— The research into the materials for the project inside the historical laboratory which is the city. This re-reading of architecture and urban forms is what supports every project.

— The city considered as a place that accumulates systems of reference, models and archetypes. In this sense every project is the check on certain spatial models and on a series of images that link up again with images of the city that were already in existence (the close-packed city = the walled city) and of architecture. They are part of our culture, our memory — an itinerary through history which includes its "own" history.

— Each planning operation tends to repropose order as opposed to the disruptive disorder and loss of identity of the contemporary city's urban spaces, and so it becomes part of a system where public precedes private space. In this way monumental buildings represent the necessity of architecture's presence wherein the rule allows the infringement but not chaos, and where effects and emotions are still possibilities.

— The necessity of building as the sole possibility of verifying the insertion of what is manufactured into the urban reality, no longer just a drawing belonging to a piece of paper, but a confrontation with the constructed city and its materials, forms and dimensions.

67. Casa Lusena in Milan, 1973 (with A. Magnaghi): (a) axionometrics and (b) east elevation.

68-70. Competition for the French Institute of Culture in Lisbon (Portugal), 1979 (with F. Genovese): Avenue Bivar façade; Rue Candido elevation; ground floor plan. First prize, under construction.

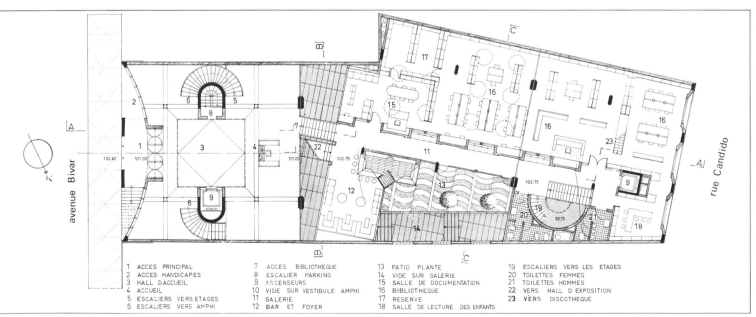

1 ACCES PRINCIPAL
2 ACCES HANDICAPES
3 HALL D'ACCUEIL
4 ACCUEIL
5 ESCALIERS VERS ETAGES
6 ESCALIERS VERS AMPHI
7 ACCES BIBLIOTHEQUE
8 ESCALIER PARKING
9 ASCENSEURS
10 VIDE SUR VESTIBULE AMPHI
11 GALERIE
12 BAR ET FOYER
13 PATIO PLANTE
14 VIDE SUR GALERIE
15 SALLE DE DOCUMENTATION
16 BIBLIOTHEQUE
17 RESERVE
18 SALLE DE LECTURE DES ENFANTS
19 ESCALIERS VERS LES ETAGES
20 TOILETTES FEMMES
21 TOILETTES HOMMES
22 VERS HALL D EXPOSITION
23 VERS DISCOTHEQUE

Francesco Cellini

Rome 1944.
Graduated from the Faculty of Architecture of Rome in 1969.
Has been teaching since '71 in the courses of Architectural Planning at the Planning Institute of the Rome Faculty of Architecture. Writes for *Controspazio* magazine.
Lives and works in Rome.

The modern house

Not much time has passed since, as children, we left ajar the door of what we thought was the forbidden room.

With dazzled eyes, and happy in our transgression, we showed our friends the contents of our pockets: a shell, a piece of glass, a stone; the large and ordered world of the house refused them. We began to despise this world, and loved the objects. More attentive this time, we reopened the door, and tried to understand; beneath that dazzling ceiling, so blue and changeable, we thought we found the answer to our secret thoughts.

Squinting, we saw the old stones in the huge room, and they seemed to be the complete and wise realization of our moral tensions, the verification and moral guarantee of the scorn and intolerance we began to feel for our teachers. But we turned back, certain of our future, and we became adults in the large, ordered world of the house, until we found the unfillable void of the lack of humanity behind the proud clarity and unrelenting moral rigor of domestic ideas.

We went out again from the forbidden door; no longer ignorant, and this time without joy or pride, but fearful and grieved; to save our lives.

Starting to walk, we learned that everything around us is testimony to a former life, a pain, a pleasure, an idea; that everything around us is a whole of meanings and messages, not always happy and serene, but often dramatic and atrocious; we understood that every stone around us has a shred of skin or a drop of blood on it, and that each stone continues to live, and that each one solves a problem.

And although knowing we were different, with little hope, with our senses almost completely blunted by now, we tried to use these stones, to live outside the house.

On the other hand, there are no walls and ceiling, the horizon is lost to view, in light or darkness, while we see the large, ordered world: all there, behind us, behind the door left ajar, in that pathetic white square house, bleached by the sun.

71-73. Houses for the Aleph Co-op, Ciampino (Rome), 1972-1977 (with F. Marchioni): general views of one residential unit.

74-75. National Competition for the Theatre of Forlì 1977: general
perspective wiews, detail of the central passage.

76-77. National Competition for the Theatre of Udine 1973: detail of
the tree-like load-bearing structures, elevations and general
sections.

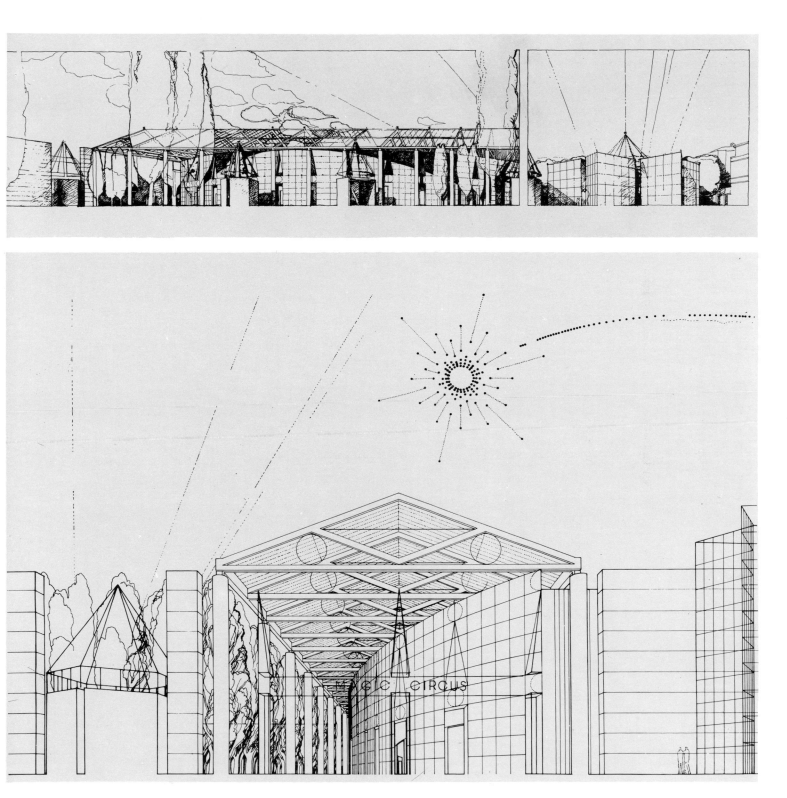

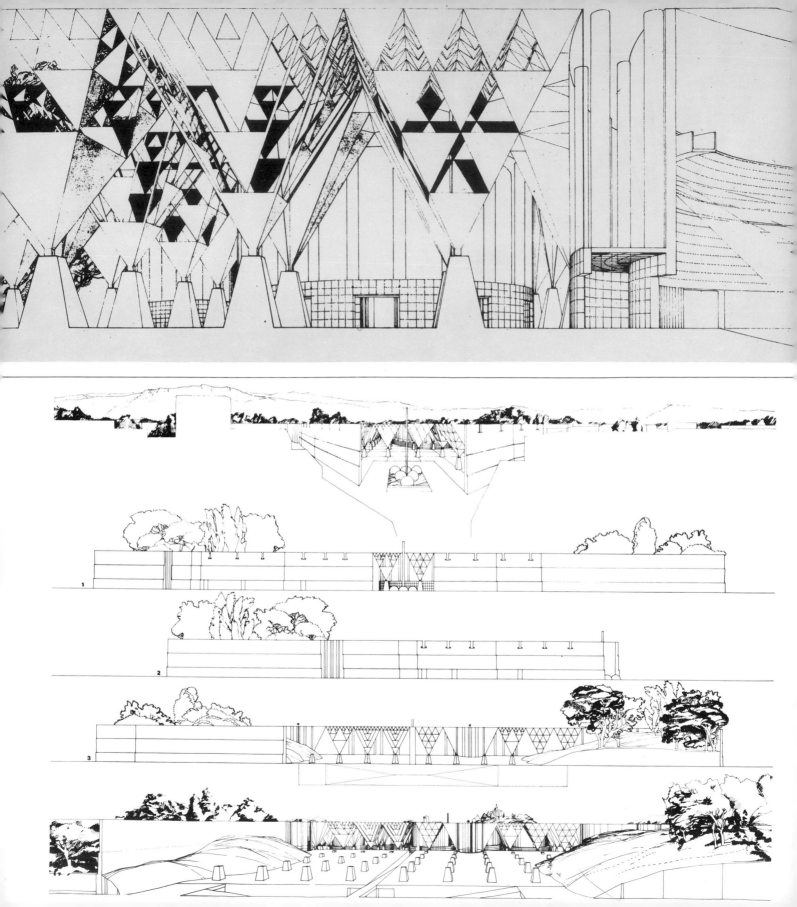

Luis Clotet
Oscar Tusquets

They are part of the Studio PER which they founded in 1965 together with Pep Bonet and Christian Cirici. In '72 the Studio PER set up the "Ediciones de Diseño," a small industry for the construction of furniture and building components.

Luis Clotet
Barcelona (Spain) 1941.
Graduated from the ETSA of Barcelona in 1965.
Taught from '75 to '77 in the Ist course of planning at the Escuela Tecnica Superior de Arquitectura in Barcelona.

Oscar Tusquets
Barcelona (Spain) 1941.
Graduated from the ETSA of Barcelona in 1965.
Taught from '75 to '77 in the Ist course of planning at the Escuela Tecnica Superior de Arquitectura in Barcelona.

Recycling versus the model, the particular versus the general, the anecdote versus the theory, ambiguity versus clarity, the figurative versus the abstract.

The three works we exhibit at the Biennale are examples of one of the most conscious features of our work. The problems were all alike, the programmes were simple, the volumes were little, the landscape surroundings very beautiful and little altered, the creation of the new building conditioned by already existing structures.

Despite this, the solutions to each case have been of a very different nature.

Casa Regas is modern in style, attached to the ruins of a traditional popular building. Two independent languages which operate by contrast. The "belvedere" of the house itself is an element independent of the main building, not only because of distance but also because of the architectonic style which directly goes back to the traditional architecture of gardens, pergolas, gazebos ...

The House of Pantelleria is the enlargement of a "damuso," typical building of the isle. An enlargement which gives to the structure an air of an old ruin: the additions have made what was already there for centuries older still.

The Balsa is a small building placed in an old water deposit so smoothly shaped as to make it appear that the stony walls are all one with the foundations of the project.

In short, not much trust in the autonomous values of the discipline of architectonic styles.

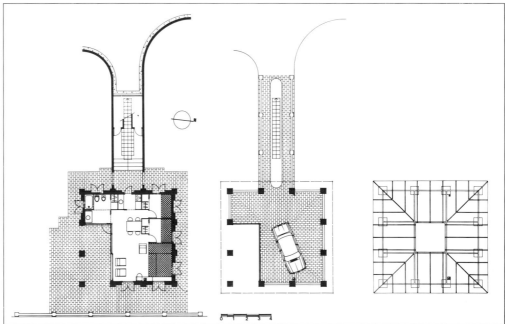

78-80. Belvedere Georgina, Llofriu, Gerona (Spain), 1972, view of the main axis, plans of the various levels, view from the road.
81-83. House at Pantelleria (Island of Pantelleria), 1973-1975: general views.

Jo Coenen

Heerlen (Holland) 1949.
Graduated from the University of Eindhoven in 1975.
In 1978 taught at the Maastricht Academy of Architecture.
Lives and works in Eindhoven.

The revaluation of regional architecture
"the most universal and the most human works of art are those, bearing a most unambiguous feature of their native country."
Jaques Maritain, "Art et scolastique," 1919.
In my opinion the Cosmopolitanism of the Modern Movement has made us "wanderers" in the darkness and put us on a dead-end trail.
With the propaganda for a "new and better" style an élite, semi-intellectual and abstract language of architecture was employed. This new language however, being used only by a small, selected group of "gastronomers," has started a life of its own.
Only a few architects did succeed in expressing the peculiarity of their region, or in getting to the roots of the cultural inheritance of their generation. The solutions of most architects grew more and more artificial and superficial; (exceptional, ingenious tricks, jokes of style or nostalgic references); ageless cultural and emotional consciousness was set aside. To my understanding this is bound to fail because the fundamentals are typically those of the modern instant-society, overflowing with superficial materialism and hollow pragmatism.
Contrary to the above I think it to be appropriate to search for region-bound aspects, principles that dared the teeth of time. Too easily the Modern Movement depicted as antiquated — in its struggle with academic eclecticism — older principles for city planning and architecture.
Born and bred in the south of the Netherlands I have strong ties with a mostly Catholic cultural inheritance, contrasting with the Calvinistic north — finding its roots in a civilization that dates from the times of the ancient Romans, Carlovingians, and Burgundians, in a region between the Rhine and the Meuse, between Cologne-Aachen and Maastricht-Liége.
The Middle-Ages, in particular, having generated an exemplary modest attitude of the masters-craftsmen, cooperating in guilds, still set for me a lively example.
"zu erfinden, zu beschliessen
bleibe Künstler oft allein;
Deines Wirkens zu geniessen
eile freudig zum Verein."
Goethe, Wilhelm Meisters Wanderjahre.
A friendly monumentalism, security, tranquillity and equilibrium, lucidity and serene order are the main themes of my work, whether concerning a small country cottage or a metropolitan building.

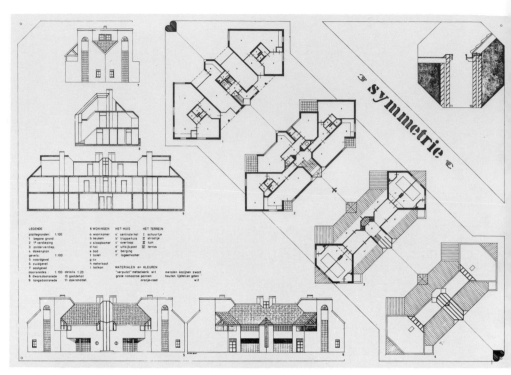

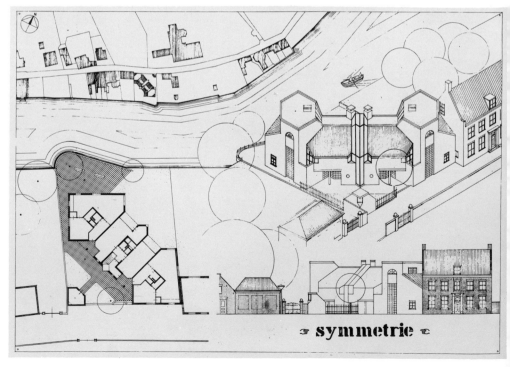

86. Project for the Weena district of Rotterdam (Holland), 1977: view of the main street.

87. Project for the Appeals Court at Berlin-Tiergarten (West Germany), 1978: general overhead view.

88. Studies of residential buildings.

89. Competition for the enlargement of the Chamber of Deputies at The Hague (Holland), 1978.

86

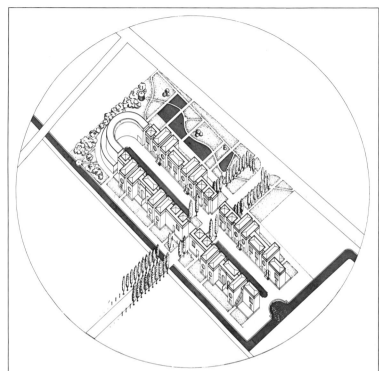

88

87

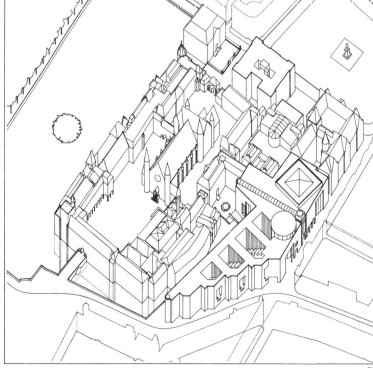

89

Stuart Cohen

Chicago (Ill. - USA) 1942.
Master of Architecture at Cornell University in 1967.
Professional studio in Chicago.
At present is Assistant Professor of Architecture at the University of
Illinois, Chicago Circle.

I do not believe in original art. Everything I make is made from those things I already know. What I think about my work, how I view it, and how I feel it relates to the theme of this exhibit, "The Presence of the Past" has been said before, so my statement is made from previous sets of words. It has not occurred to me how to better reformulate them.
"Tradition is a matter of much wider significance. It cannot be inherited, and if you want it you must obtain it by great labor. It involves, in the first place, the historical sense ... and the historical sense involves a perception, not only of the pastness of the past, but of its presence ... No poet, no artist of any art, has his complete meaning alone. His significance, his appreciation is the appreciation of his relation to the dead poets and artists ... What happens when a new work of art is created is something that happens simultaneously to all works of art which preceded it. The existing monuments form an ideal order among themselves, which is modified by the introduction of the new (the really new) work of art among them ... Whoever has approved this idea of order ... will not find it preposterous that the past should be altered by the present as much as the present is directed by the past. And the poet who is aware of this will be aware of great difficulties and responsibilities."
T.S. Eliot, Tradition and the Individual Talent

"Each man's lifework is also a work in a series extending beyond him in either or both directions depending upon his position in the track he occupies ... By this view, the great differences between artists are not so much those of talent as of entrance and position in sequence ... talent itself is only a relatively common predisposition for visual order, without a wide range of differentiation. Times and opportunities differ more than the degree of talent."
George Kubler, The Shape of Time

90. Townhouse project for the Kelly Gallery of Chicago (Ill.), 1978.
91-92. Project for Tudor House at Elgin (Ill.), 1979: views of the model.

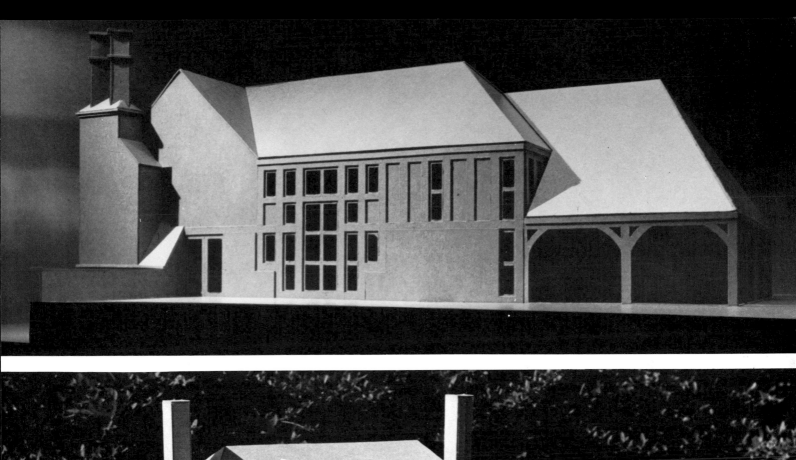

93-94. Mackenbach House, Itasca (Ill.), 1980: living-room interior, detail of the entrance.
95. Addition to Gourguechon House, 1979-1980.

Guillermo Vazquez Consuegra

Seville (Spain) 1945.
Graduated from the Escuela Tecnica Superior de Arquitectura of Seville in 1972.
From '72 to '75 was the professor in charge of the course of Elements of Composition at the ETSAS.
Works professionally in Seville.

Interest linked to historical circumstances have brought Seville to the exportation of typical forms, masks from the daily carnival in which some people think to live.

Nowadays we speak about the type, a logical proposition originating from a history that prefigures the present. Typical forms and type are two opposing concepts.

One is favoured by the ill-disguised interests of speculators of every kind, while the other brings to life the hope of finding reality, a city developing at a rhythm that is dictated by the daily ascent of a tradition that has not been reduced to behavioural patterns or obscure formal positions, but is in a constant tension, handing on to history a present of a reconsidered past.

Knowing about houses with patios or "corrales de vecinos," "cierros" or balconies, galleries, roofs with terraces or belvederes, walls with windows and metal staircases, bouganvilles, orange-flowers and silences, means making proper nouns of elements whose material achievement is always a new adventure, a new creation. This profound knowledge of figurative nature is an opportunity for abstraction toward the comprehension, beyond the form, of the concept that can be rediscovered with a new language.

On the other hand, the abstract substance of the Modern Movement shows us the capacity of language for the figuration of concepts over and above their use as simple signs of modernity.

The work presented here has not been developed from rigid theories, but more by conceiving architecture as a hope for a reality dialectically committed to the contents offered by the study of history and of the city.

The contemporary consideration of the traditional city as a bearer of autonomous material that is suitable for conceptual abstraction, and in the Modern Movement's second thoughts about history, the delicate formulation of an abstract nature suitable for the portrayal fo new concepts, convinces us of the possibility of handling these premises in a simultaneous and dialectic fashion.

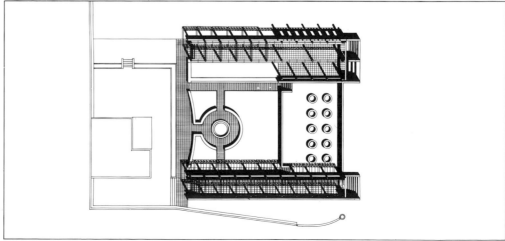

96-99. Garden of the "Esperanza Macarena" farm-house, Olivares, Seville (Spain), 1975-1977: general views, details and plan.

Nicoletta Cosentino

Rome 1944.
Graduated from the Faculty of Architecture of Rome in 1969.
Lives and works in Rome.

A considerable amount of my work is based on the feelings and impressions exercised by places; natural situations undoubtedly have the most charm: there the relationship between architecture and nature is direct — one element is changeable, cyclical, biological, and its opposite, a definite, immobile, unchangeable object. The history of architecture is basically the product of ever-different interpretations of this relationship. My hypothesis aims to try and make the artificial object participate in the cycle of life, insert itself into the flow of time.

The modification and aging that traditional building materials undergo under the atmosphere's action are a phenomenon within architecture which diminishes its artificial dimension in favour of its biological one, which is emphasized and enlarged by natural external factors such as light, atmospheric phenomena, the appearance and colour of the plants which all act on the object and modify it continually.

This is exactly why it is necessary to see a work of architecture directly in order to understand it: a photographic reproduction is never sufficient. The series of natural, environmental and historical factors, which are an integral part of the building, or building complex, can then be clearly observed.

The phenomenon which most strikes one is perhaps the importance of a place's light; the cold, crystalline light and the transparent atmosphere of some days in Paris, for instance, when every roof-tile and chimney-pot is perfectly visible, clearly explains the motive and meaning of that kind of architectural design; while the ever soft atmosphere of Rome and its bright light are inseparable from the use of plaster, colour and volumes.

The links that each architectural work establishes with its surroundings can still be perceived immediately, be they natural or artificial, until a unity of a superior order is created; just think of Palladio's villas and their relationship with the Veneto countryside, or the Gothic cathedrals and the villages that surround them.

All this interlaces nature indissolubly with history, and forms our field of work.

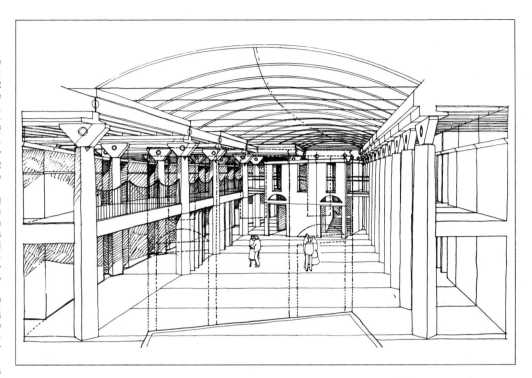

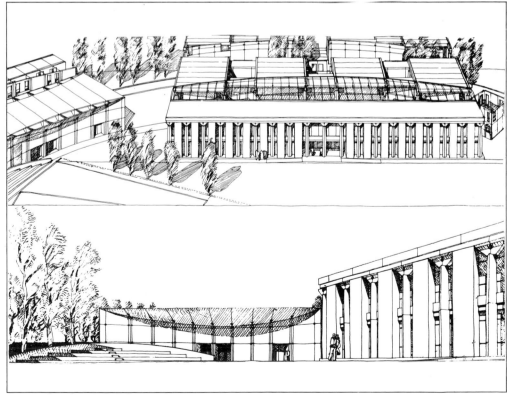

100-101. National Competition for the Agricultural Technical Institute at Maccarese (Rome), 1980: Internal view looking at the staircases, general view.

102. Project for country dwelling, 1978.

103-104. National Competition for Piazza Stamira in Ancona, 1978: temporary structures for free time, the bar-restaurant.

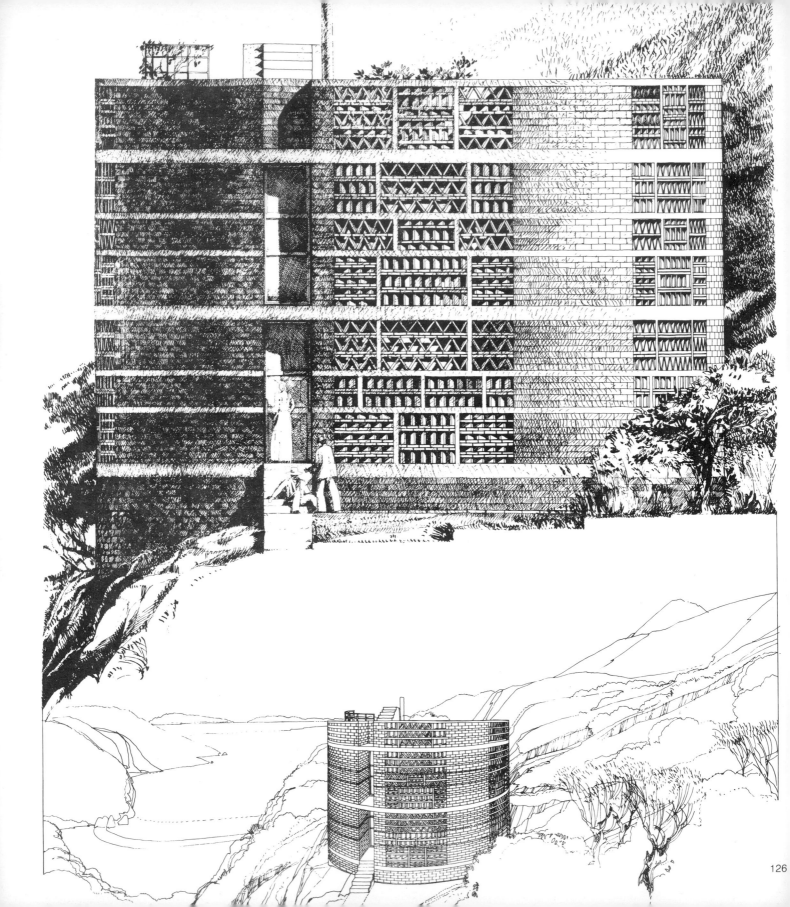

Maurice Culot

Seville (Spain) 1943.
He graduated in architecture at La Cambre (Brussels) in 1968.
He was Director of the Section d'Architecture at the same University until 1979, when the Belgian Ministry of National Education suspended him along with half the teaching staff. He now teaches at the new "Ecole pour la reconstruction de la ville européenne."
He is the Director of the Archives of Modern Architecture in Brussels and is responsible for the publications and magazine.

Contre-projects

Since it was founded in 1968 the Archives of Modern Architecture has carried without charge more than one hundred counter-projects in response to the requests of citizens' committees of Brussels who are fighting against private and public speculators.

These counter-projects throw up two main problems: the first is that of tackling the structure of industrial production of the built space, the second is that of re-creating the philosophical instruments of architecture.

After more than ten years of activity in collaboration with the Atelier of Town Research and Action (A.R.A.U.) directed by the sociologist René Schoonbrodt, we have come to the conclusion that urban struggles must be based on the image of the traditional town and not on the image of utopias such as the Modernist and industrial one developed by the International Meetings of Modern Architecture.

Let's sum up the political reasoning which is at the bottom of our conviction: financial monopolies need considerable management skills in order to answer the problems posed by the contemporary industrial process, which is remarkably fragmentary, since it is incessantly in search of occasions to reduce production costs. It follows, as a corollary, that the important structures of bureaucratic control, vital for the functioning of this planetary-scale system grow up in towns and thus benefit from the external economies linked to this site, from the free availability of facilities and from the urban environment itself which, thanks to its concentration, is a place of innovations. The town appears, therefore, as an indispensable element to the working of industry, and it is, thanks to this, that the economical power gets stronger at the expense of the cultural and political ones. It is possible, therefore, to state that urban struggles when directed against the appropriation of the town by monopolies, coincide with the struggles of workers.

Consequently, the problem of urban layout cannot be dealt with without taking into account urban struggles. And since we are not facing the structure of industrial production like "desperados," we try to take a forceful line and, for this purpose, to get people together with the attainment of precise objects in view. But it is pointless to say to people that the town is a means of development (hence a revolutionary instrument) if we do not specify what kind of town we are talking about. Experience shows that a town endowed with the greatest strength of persuasion, capable of getting public consent, is a normal town, the traditional European town with its subdivision into complex districts, squares and streets.

The stake is, therefore, much more aesthetic: it is a

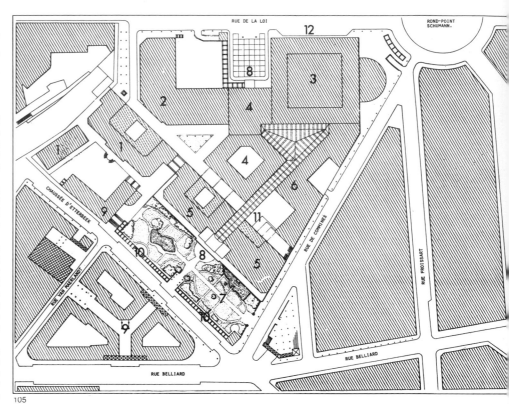

105

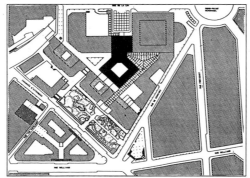

106

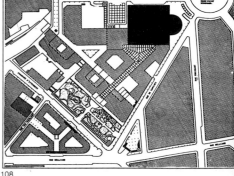

108

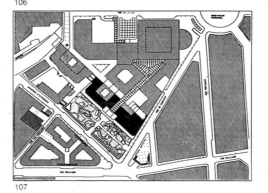

107

109

128

110-113. Suggestion for restructuring the area
between Rue de la Loi and Rue Belliard
in Brussels (Belgium), 1979: the "rue publique,"
the access from Rue de Commines, the access
from the Residence Palace, the Park.

110

112

111

113

and prompt struggles against industrial repression. To Leon Krier's work on the organization of the town in complex districts we owe the revelation that the concept of mobility — keystone of industrial town-planning — is not a factor of progress but rather of alienation. It is thanks to this discovery that we have given up the superficial slogan, the leit-motif of left-wing claims, embodied by the priority given to public transport.

We realized that this priority given to public transport — which is being analyzed by economic and political authorities more and more seriously — will be, once put into practice, just as fatal to towns as urban motorways were. Krier showed how the demands of the popular districts of Brussels, to live in their own districts, is a claim which finds its foundation in the real history of European towns.

Our social and economic problems have reinforced the architectonic truths that Krier repeats time and time again. So the vertical window can be not only classic, but also democratic, an intelligent solution to energy problems, to the usual way of living, to the economy of construction, to the logic of natural materials.

In this way our town project becomes part not only of the struggle of the workers but also of the rejection of large scale town and energy solutions (from the systematic use of concrete and other non traditional and "energy consuming" materials, such as glass and aluminium, up to the corollary of this waste: the "nuclear" and its police-like apparatus). A French magazine recently threw out a warning to Leon Krier concerning his project for Les Halles of Paris: "Be careful Krier, you are repeating yourself, you are not creating any longer." However this magazine, run by intelligent people, does not think of addressing itself to the thousands of streets and squares of European towns still preserved from destruction, in order to make them note that they are out-of-date, that they are always the same; it does not think any longer of encouraging experiments directed to the improvement of the human race.

Those who are committed to town struggles in Brussels, Palermo or Luxemburg have never considered Leon Krier's works as a result of a superior intellectual game or as one of the aspects of Post-Modernist fashion; they have never imagined that Leon Krier's drawings might prefigure reality and logically never asked him to carry out his projects. In the popular districts of Brussels, where they were on show, Krier's projects were understood, as they should be, as a demonstration, a reflection of the consent to the global project and of the legitimate aspirations of the inhabitants, as an efficacious weapon for anti-industrial resistance. In Krier's projects there is no sign of authoritarianism; the only people who accuse Krier of fascism are those who collaborate and prostitute themselves in the field of an alluring Post-Modernism which is taking over from the successive fashions of modern architecture.

Only those who devote themselves to the destructive games of fashion and chance can be surprised at the prominent position held by Leon Krier in the Pantheon of the urban struggles in Brussels.

matter of fighting to maintain that instrument of freedom which is the town and to develop, to the maximum, its benefits in favour of the workers, that is of the victims of an advanced industrial society. But our work on the town does not satisfy only a political plan. People rightly miss the beauty and the perfection of old towns and also know that the traditional town is far less expensive — in financial and social terms — than the experiments and fan-

tasies of modern town-planning and architecture: experiments which have revealed their repressive character and have inevitably engendered waste. The "zoning" law keeps up with the strengthening of social control, with the deterioration of social communication and local solidarity.

We owe largely to Leon Krier the chance we had to specify and embody in a global town project everything we learnt and developed in our daily

Hermann Czech

Vienna (Austria) 1936.
He studied at the Technische Hochschule of Vienna, where he graduated in 1959.
He has been teaching since '74 at the Academy of Applied Arts of Vienna.
His studio is in Vienna.

Architecture can be representative and moving; it can represent a desired society other than the existing one and move us to bring it about. It can implement freedom and self-realization — both directly, as a concrete object (without necessarily including elements of variability or owner-built components), and figuratively, as expression (without necessarily exhibiting decipherable codes or quotes). It must incorporate, in its essence, the external, the superficial that surrounds us; in its unity, all possible multiplicities. What basic attitude is necessary to achieve this? First of all an attitude of intellectuality, of consciousness; further a sense for the irregular and absurd, that which breaks away from contemporary precepts: the attitude of mannerism.

But this standpoint is simply a method of grasping a portion of reality. (Intellectualism as an empty husk or irregularity as mere scenery have already begun to define themselves as the boredom of coming years.)

Mannerism is the conceptual approach to accept reality at the level required at a particular time; it grants the frankness and imagination which is necessary to set even alien processes in motion and to tolerate them without giving voice to the disingenuous fiction that architecture has given up its claim to create an expression; to be open yet defined, poor yet comfortable.

(From: *Mannerism and Participation,* Vienna, 1977)

117. Project for a family house at Schwechat (Austria), 1977.

118. Dicopa Management offices, Vienna (Austria), 1974.

119. Addition to Villa Pflaum, Altenberg (Austria), 1977-1979.

120. Project for an Art Gallery in Vienna (Austria), 1971.

121. Project for the restructuring of a discotheque in Vienna (Austria), 1974.

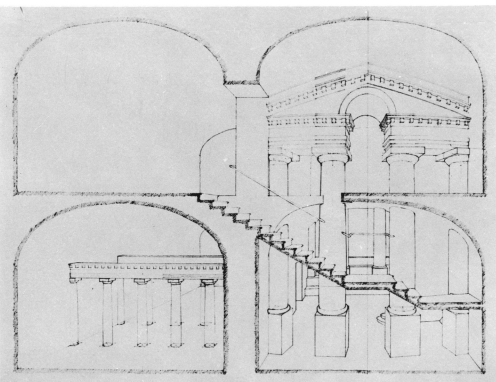

Claudio D'Amato

Bari 1944.
He graduated from the Faculty of Architecture in Rome in 1971.
He has been teaching since '71 in the courses of Architectural Composition at the Institute of Planning in the Rome Faculty of Architecture.
He writes for *Controspazio* magazine.
He lives and works in Rome.

18 Brumaire 1980

Today, it is again necessary to travel over the tortuous and uneven paths of Parnassus.

It is necessary that each individual confront that walk, it is not enough only to have heard of it.

The goal moves continually, and we are forced each time to trace a new, ever different map.

In this process of transformation, the only help to be found is in those who traveled that road before us: "... in times of crisis, men evoke with anguish the ghosts of the past, so as to use them for themselves; they borrow their names, passwords of battle and customs in order to represent the new scene of history under this old and venerable disguise and with these borrowed phrases."

The question is: how far are we allowed to ask for loans from the past? How far can we wear the costumes of Filippo and Maso, of Palladio and Bernini? How far can we speak with phrases borrowed from them?

A technical answer and a question of style: "... the beginner who has learned a new language translates it constantly into his mother tongue, but can not possess its spirit and express himself freely, except when he moves within it without reminiscences, forgetting his own original language."

Another question: modern or post-modern?

The answer lies in the facts: the return to history is the self-knowledge, the deepening of one's own work, the articulation of the expressive datum, the answer to the separateness and parcelling of knowledge, a reaction to the harsh verification of the realized hypotheses of the International Style.

Implicit and natural answer:

The Modern Movement is dead; the question at hand is another: how far will the resurrection of the dead exalt the new ideas? And how far, on the other hand, will the past be parodied?

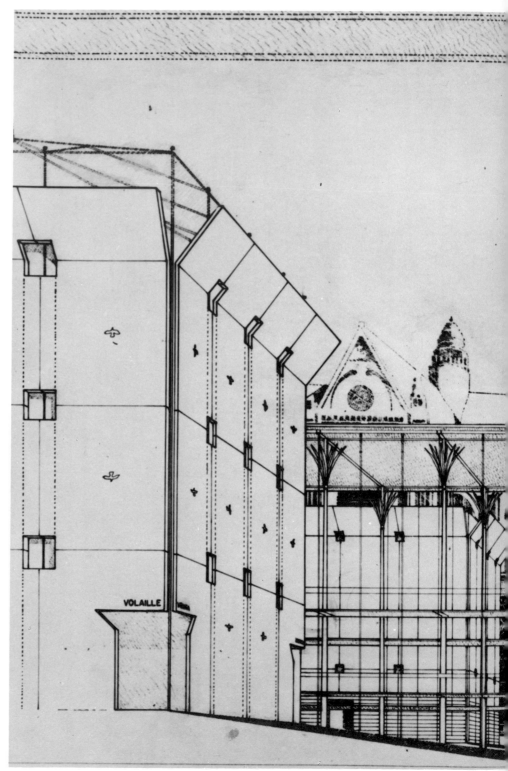

122. Competition entry for the layout of Les Halles in Paris (France), 1979 (with Francesco Cellini).

123-125. Studies for related central plans. Experiences from the
Fifth Course of Architectural Composition at the Planning Institute of
the Rome Faculty of Architecture, under Prof. Salvatore Dierna:
projects for public facilites in the new town centre of Latina
(students: S. Caira, V. Sica; M. Corsetti, P. Mazzocchi; D.
Cardamone, G. Scalise).

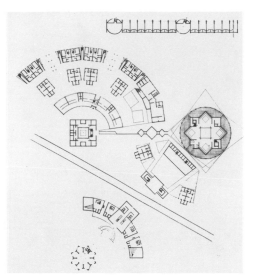

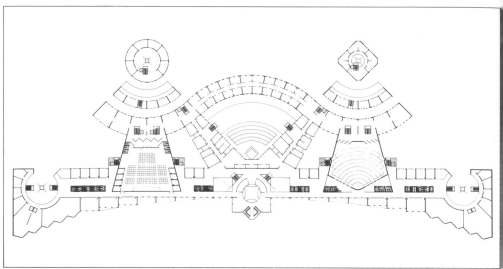

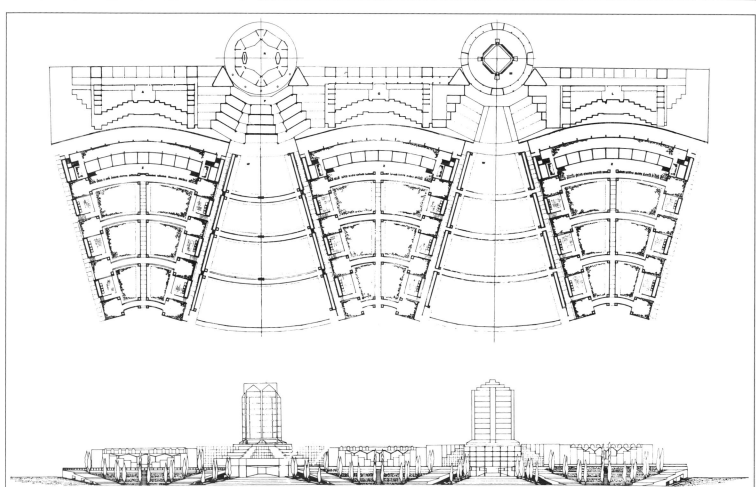

Costantino Dardi

Cervignano del Friuli (Udine) 1936.
Graduated from the Faculty of Architecture in Venice in 1962.
Professor of Architectural Composition at the Faculty of Architecture in Rome.
Lives and works in Rome.

Despite half a century of removing, architecture speaks and builds the city, it writes and is read mainly within the urban framework through the character of its facades. The facade is the meeting plane between interior articulation and urban dimension, a filter and a diaphragm that shields what is private and public, and relates them.
Even if the values of shape of architecture are recorded in its section and its becoming a meaningful form and a profound structure of its type, moment of recognition intersected by questions and motivations on one side, and spatial inventions on the other, the role of internal/external filter is performed by the facade. Against the institutional character of the vertical order of the column the rationalist *fenêtre en longeur* has proposed the image of a nullified system in the superimposed stratification of the horizontal elements.
People have resorted to the fragility of the cut-out piece of paper too often; instead the filter needs a thickness that shields the affective and anthropological dimension, the psychological values of the interior compared to the exterior. Light is the instrument that gives depth to this restlessness. The historicity of architecture is also the historicity of the light that passes over its surfaces: it is the historicity of the meeting and modulation between the Platonic solid matter and the light; the sharp, absolute light that cuts and shapes planes and volumes in a Neoclassical temple, a Renaissance palace or a Rationalist villa; the ambiguous, vibrant light of a Mannerist church, a Baroque square, a Medieval street. In their relationship with history and nature, European and American culture display a specular and symmetrical attitude: while the past is so deeply injected into European culture that it need not consider operating explicit quotes, American culture expresses a continuous desire for roots, for demonstrating the historicity of its workings exactly because it possesses no history; while the natural dimension, especially in the form of large spaces, has an anthropological presence in American culture, European civilizations observe the landscape with anxiety and populate it with obscure forces and mysterious messages.
In these last years I have done a lot of work on the theme of plots, the binary frameworks in an alternating modulus contrasted with the emergent polarity of the volumes of architectural objects: but in the end I have discovered that the facade designed for the *Strada Novissima* could be interpreted as an operation of autobiographical recovery; on the one hand, the rupture, the breaking up, the discovery of the cavity, light as a solution giving continuity to the compact stone masses of the first projects (the Vidali house at Cervignano di Friuli, or the Museum of the Resistance in Trieste, or the rice mill at S. Sabba); on the other, the question of rationality and order, the geometry subtended to the plan, the clean edges, the

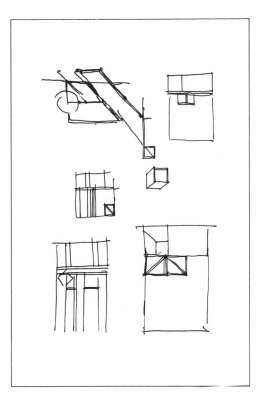

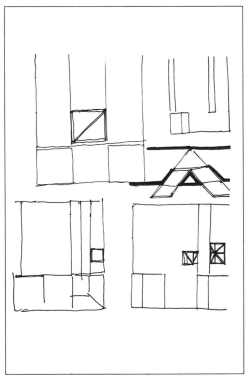

polished surfaces of the primary objects (the theatre at Udine or the landscape across the straits of Messina). Among these elements, among the two lines of work appears the theme of the spatial gantry; the technology of light structures up against the problems of architectural composition.
Behind the facade, the exhibition has been organized on long tables on which the projects and drawings have been set out: *reading as writing.*
The drawing of architecture is an extraordinary instrument and a means of communication; nevertheless it refers to a distant reality — architecture that has been or is about to be built.
Architectural elements that are drawn, painted, displayed, printed, reproduced or exhibited too often bring the research to a close as soon as a valid result has been achieved inside the universe of representation.
Architecture is not represented: it is presented, it is.

126-133. Preparatory sketches for the façade in the rope factories at the Arsenale, 1980.

134. Casa Vidali, Cervignano del Friuli (Udine), 1962: details of the façade.

135. National Competition for a Museum of the Resistance in the Rice-mill of S. Sabba in Trieste, 1966: details of the model.

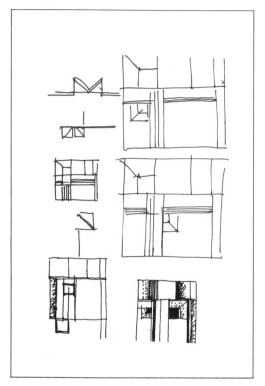

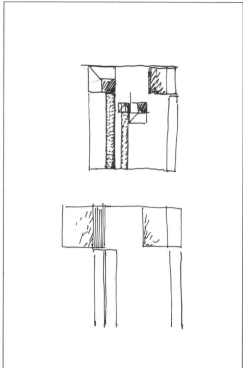

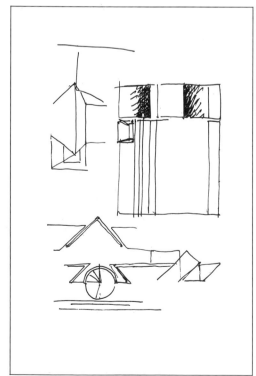

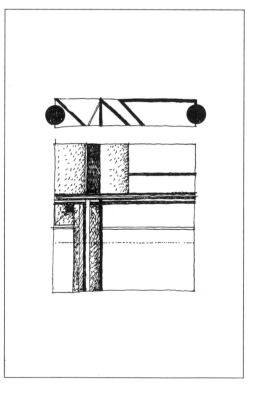

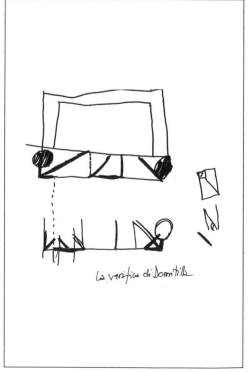

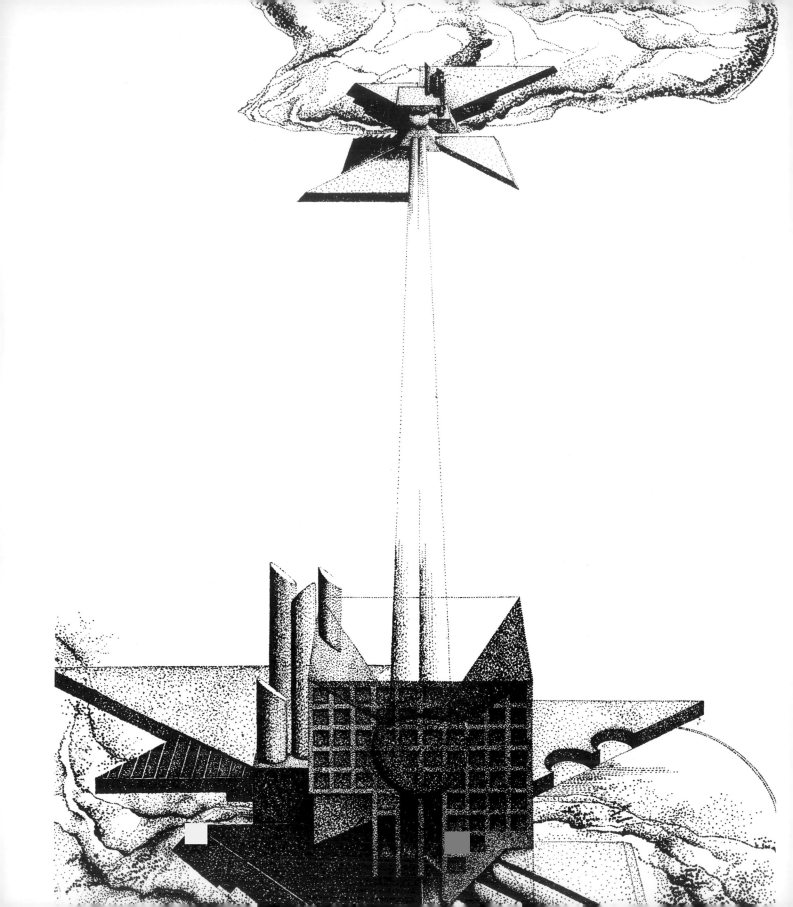

136. International Competition for the crossing of the straits of Messina, 1969: aerial view.

137. Competition for the new Theatre of Udine, 1974: overhead and perspective view.

138-139. Layout of the "Architecture Project" at the XVI Milan Triennale, 1979: preparatory sketches.

140. "Architecture as agricultural design," 1978: sketch for a territorial hypothesis.

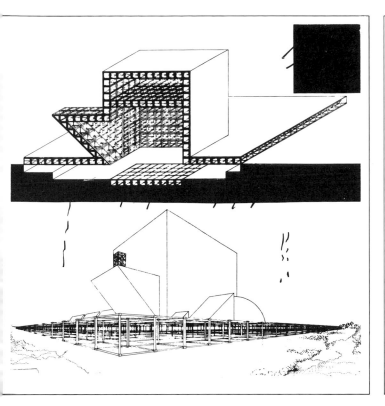

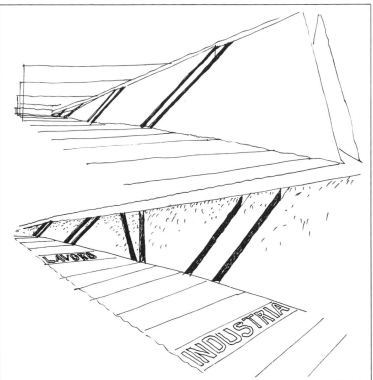

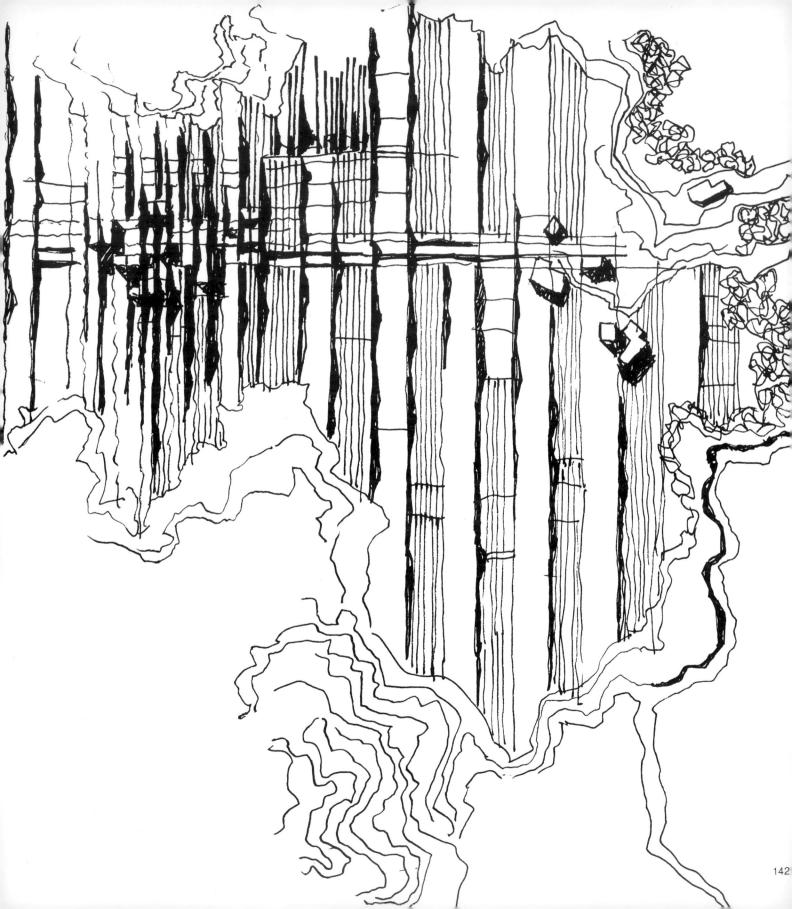

Giangiacomo D'Ardria

Rome 1940.
He graduated from the Faculty of Architecture of Rome in 1967.
He teaches in the courses of Composition at the Institute of Planning of the Rome Faculty.
He has a studio in Rome together with Giancarlo Mainini.

Project for the development of a hypothetical fluvial town in the province of Venice

This project was worked out for the Biennale of Venice as the synthesis of some architectural ideas and themes that have been the subject of my work over these last few years and the object of discussion with my friends Dario Passi and Giancarlo Mainini, with whom I work.

The houses and public buildings are situated in a hypothetical area that has been lucky enough to escape the anonymous and bureaucratic proceedings of the post-war town-planning schemes; they are on the banks of a river that is about to flow into the town, linked by small bridges which can be crossed on bicycles.

The highly essential urban lay-out has the sole aim of fixing the position of the project's themes and the urban images that result from their simple links.

The residential architecture is the starting-point for the project work, based on archetypes that are common to our provincial towns (houses around courtyards and in rows, small mansions), stripped of all their distributive and linguistic complications and brought back to their essential forms. This simplifying process, which is applied to all the components of the type, aims to return the original identity to the architectural functions and solutions. The materials used are typical of residential architecture, like painted plaster, cement blocks and bricks. On the opposite bank stretches a big square paved with lightly hued granite, which comes right down in steps to the water's edge, around which the public buildings have been placed. In this case the archetypes are the civic tower, the market, the news-stand, the monument and the flagstaff.

The civic character of these buildings is suggested by their uniqueness and by the materials used for facing and finishing. It is underlined by the humble, almost familiar aspect of its monumental forms.

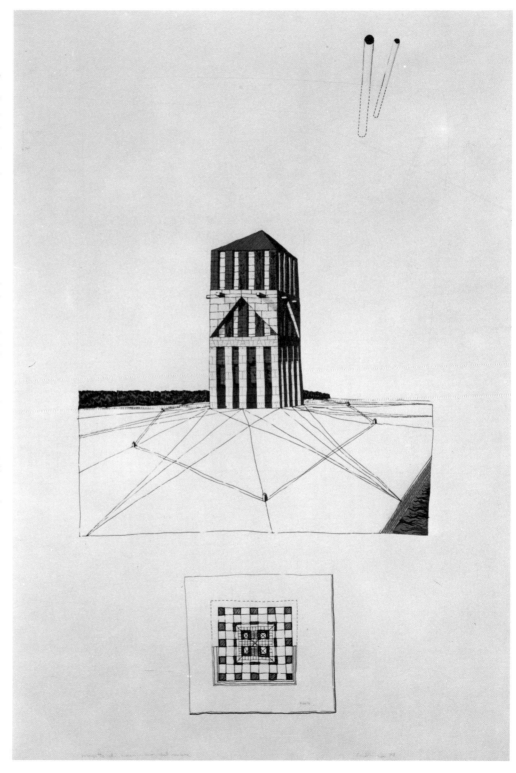

141. Studies for towers, 1979.

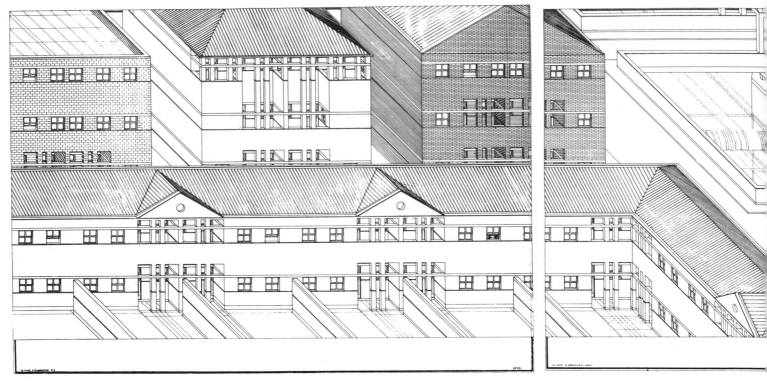

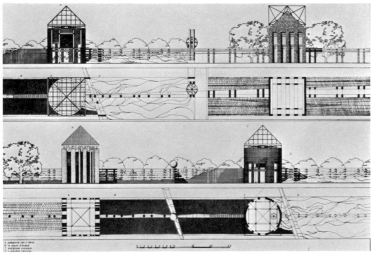

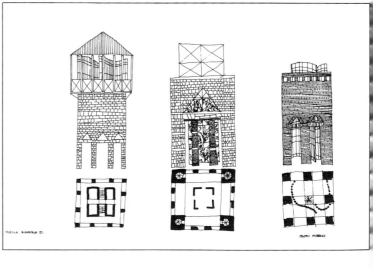

142-144. Project for the layout of a hypothetical river city in the Veneto province, 1980: the courtyard, palace, bridges, embankment, the small public building.

145. Competition for the layout of Piazza Stamira in Ancona, 1978: the pavilions in the garden (with Dario Passi).

146. Public buildings.

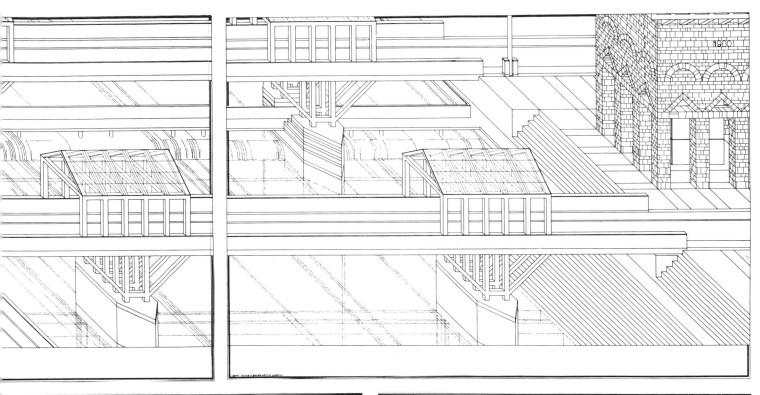

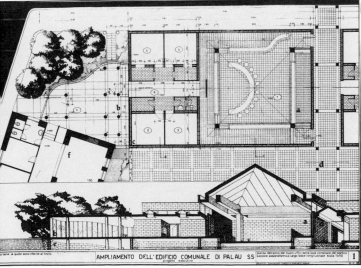

AMPLIAMENTO DELL'EDIFICIO COMUNALE DI PALAU SS
progetto esecutivo

1

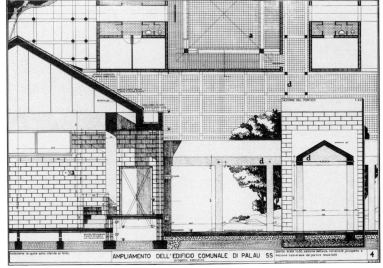

AMPLIAMENTO DELL'EDIFICIO COMUNALE DI PALAU SS
progetto esecutivo

4

147-148. Project for the enlargement of Palau
Town Hall (Sassari), 1976-1979 (with Giancarlo
Mainini).

Jeremy Dixon

Bishop's Stortford (Essex – England) 1939.
Graduated from the AA School of Architecture in London in 1964.
Teaches at the Architectural Association in London.
Studio in London.

This exhibit is arranged to document a personal way of working, by illustrating in parallel with each project various sources and historical references that may have influenced the design.

Perhaps the most difficult stage in the design of a project is the first move, which has to hold in embryo as yet unexplored possibilities, that can be realised as the scheme develops. For me, the most productive starting points come out of an understanding of the particularity of the place in which the project is sited; place, in the sense that includes the historical context and development of local types as well as the position and shape of the site itself. Out of this analysis come chance discoveries, accidental relationships that direct a scheme towards unexpected territory, while at the same time ensuring a layering of references and signs that relate back to the context. This combination of reasoned analysis, intuition and concern for historical memories does not correspond with the major concerns of the Modern Movement, and leads in some senses to each project needing a fresh start, derived from particular circumstances. However, it is possible to distinguish between a total rejection of the Modern Movement and its incorporation into one's list of references as one further historical style.

Within this kind of approach there are obvious dangers of sentimentality and pastiche, but I would like to think that one is able to remain sensitive to the inheritance of a situation and at the same time to employ strong geometry and forms, radical analysis of the brief, and all the other powerful tools of design.

The housing "infill" in St. Mark's Road in London has as an underlying concern the traditional and understood elements (the street or square of houses) of residential London, which differs so fundamentally, as a historically unfortified and loosely organised city, from European counterparts with their dense city blocks and tradition of apartment living. By contrast, the Northampton pyramid, a symbolic building on an open site, is concerned with large scale composition in relation to the landscape, and uses English landscape techniques, with their mixture of formal and picturesque devices, amongst other references.

This pair of projects incidentally illustrates another aspect of appropriateness, the degree of monumentality and symbolism that different building types and situations can carry.

All the projects illustrated are in England.

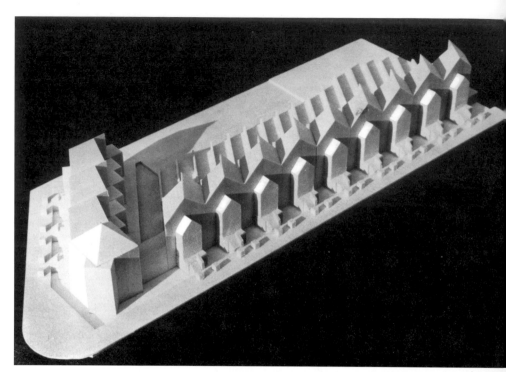

149. Residential buildings in St. Mark's Road, London (England), 1975-1979: model of the block.

150. House for a joiner to build for himself, Essex (England), 1978.

151. Residential buldings on St. Mark's Road, London (England), 1975-1979: street frontage.

152. Project for a House on an axis, Buckinghamshire (England), 1974.

153. Housing project for Millbank, London (England), 1975.

Paolo Farina

Milan, 1949.
Degree in Architecture at the Faculty of Architecture of Milan
Polytechnic in 1974.
Has been teaching there since 1974. Has written essays and articles
for architectural magazines.

In his 1714 *Lettre à l'Académie*, François de
Salignac de la Motte-Fénelon wrote "Notre langue
manque d'un grand nombre de mots et de phrases:
il me semble même qu'on l'a gênée et appauvrie,
depuis environs cent ans, en voulant le purifier."
The remark appears in the "Projet pour enricher la
langue" – one of the short chapters that makes up
the *Lettre*, written to sum up his reflections on
language, rhetoric, history and the "querelle des
anciens et des modernes." The torture and impoverishment of the language which have been
achieved under the pretext of purification, to the
advantage of a would-be revolution of production
methods, have become the trademark of most of
what has gone on in modern architecture over the
last fifty years. Not only did Fénelon suggest that no
words should be lost, but also that new ones
should be acquired, elaborated and "authorized;"
he sought synonyms and took an interest in foreign
terms when it was a case of making up for specific
deficiencies.

The "thoughts" about a project for the torre dei
Gorani area which were developed during the
"Galateo in Città/atto II" seminar (Milan, Faculty of
Architecture, May 1980) have their limit in only being notes for a possible chapter in a larger "Projet
d'enricher la langue." In Milan an intermittent "Neo-
classical" tradition, as regards tension and quality,
has arbitrarily overshadowed and eliminated the
material contexts and even the memory of a less
renowned urban civilization which developed and
spread a complex, flexible, strict and good-natured
language between the 17th and 18th centuries,
which ranged from the typology to the urban landscape, from the monument to the building fabric.
Even after the "rappel à l'ordre" wielded by the
"dictators of taste" on the 19th century Decorating
Commission, this was one of the most important
and familiar components in the city's appearance,
the expression of a calculated mixture of novelty
and facility which was aware of architecture's flat-
tering nature – an art which, as Guarini says, "does
not want to disgust the senses for any reason." The
work on the building screen, the contamination of
preceding traditions – from Gothic to Mannerism –
the attention to the European dialogue, the dialectic
relationship between the surfaces and the cornices,
which join the elements in an accentuated verticalism, the planimetric modulation and articulation
are some of the mechanisms of this language that
have been investigated in the "thoughts."

154-160. Thoughts on a project for the area of the Gorani tower in
Milan, 1980:"vegetable archaeology," the sequence of public space
between the Terme and the Verziere, the plan of the Verziere
colonnade, the corner of Via Gorani, studies for views of dwellings.

161. Ideas for a "Teatro del Mondo."

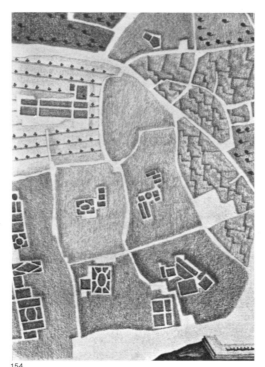

154

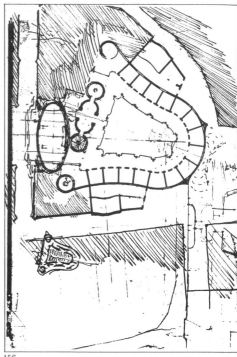

156

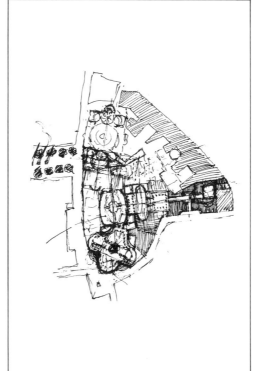

155

157

148

158

160

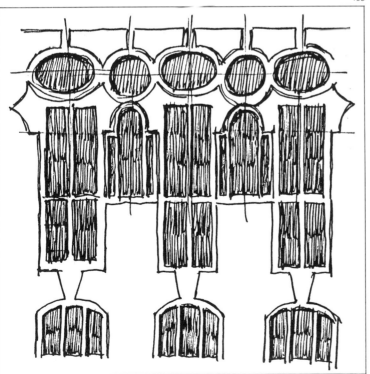

159

161

149

Terry Farrel

Manchester (England) 1938.
First Class Honours Degree at the University School of Architecture at Durham in 1961.
Master in Architecture and Master in City Planning at the University of Pennsylvania in 1964.
Has worked professionally since 1965 in the Farrel/Grimshaw Partnership.

Roots and Learning from History

Ancestor-tracing can be a stimulating return journey with the excitement of discovery the motivation; mentally it's a cross between fishing and detective work – whilst emotionally it can be closer to a demanding psychoanalysis. But for us westerners the paths to our roots are so well preserved and documented, that ancestor-tracing can be more like comfy return trips to the old folks back home.

The Modern Movement essentially had a firmer belief in the future than the present and the pioneering paths to the future were full of moral zeal, discomfort, and rigorous self-denial. By contrast, to relax back into the present and acknowledge the rear window view of history offers a journey full of the warm comfort of familiarity. It's a relief to get back in touch with our roots where human form predominates in columns and arches and where our senses, particularly our eyes, are the controlling criteria for what we create.

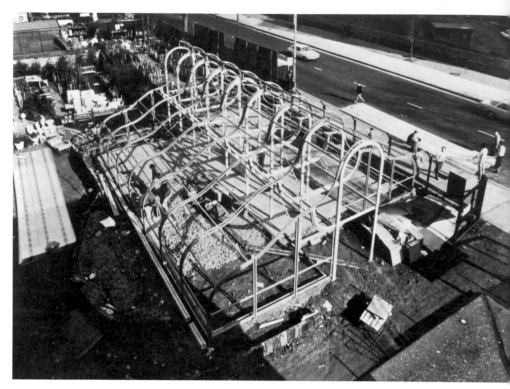

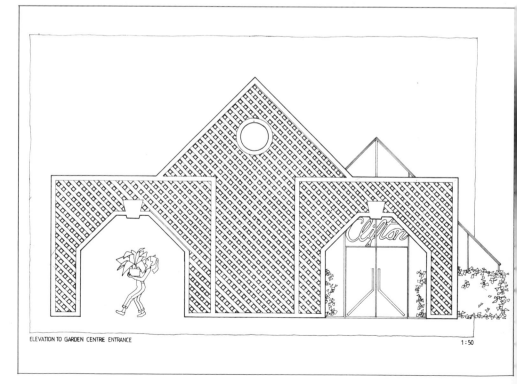

ELEVATION TO GARDEN CENTRE ENTRANCE 1:50

162. Clifton Greenhouse, London (England).
163. Clifton Garden House, London (England).

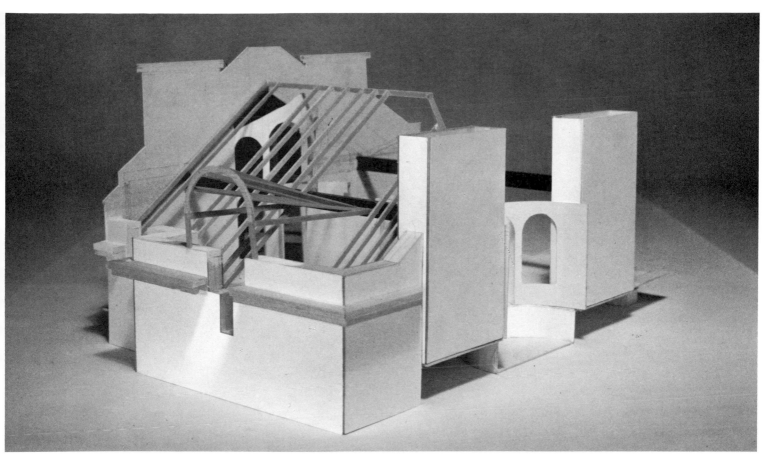

164-166. Jencks House, general model and axionometrics.

151

Friday

Group founded in 1970, studio in Philadelphia (Penn — USA).

Frank Mallas
Elisabeth, New Jersey 1943.
Bachelor of Architecture at the Cooper Union in 1966.

Donald R. Matzkin
Philadelphia, Penn. 1940.
Bachelor of Architecture at Cornell University in 1963.

David S. Slovic
Chicago, Ill. 1941.
Master of Architecture at the University of Pennsylvania.

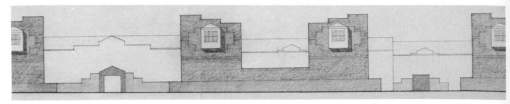

The *unity of plural references* functions for us as a paradigm, a tool used in the investigation of the history of architecture.

By *references* we understand all of the available possibilities to bring into the present the appropriate sign of history.

By *plural* we understand the polyvalent levels of knowledge, both accumulated and experienced.

By *unity* we understand the rational use of the relationship between cultural, historical references and the multiplicity of their meanings.

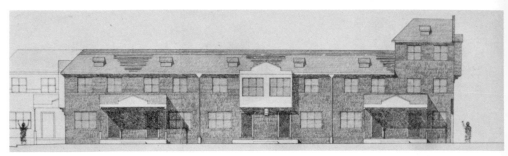

This notion contributes to the development of ideas and the transformation of modes of representation. The architectural project, from its concept to its realization, uses the reference in relation to the needs and questions of the present. In our work, we elaborate a specific and accessible language answering to the community yet addressing theoretical concerns.

We recombined the colonial style elements from a historical neighborhood in a different use, modifying the traditional brick pattern to gain new meaning for a symbolic front facade. The community social room of this building recalls a living room complete with chandelier, fireplace, bay window, and oriental carpet. (See *Old Pine Community Center*).

We reproduced, in large scale, a 1940's kitchen pattern in the dining room floor of a center for the elderly to create a new, but familiar, image. (See *Grays Ferry Citizens Center*).

We exaggerated the scale and reversed the order of the traditional building colors to help identify a new center as a neighborhood landmark. (See *Lancaster Neighborhood Center*).

Knowing how to look and to read a sign; knowing how to understand and interpret a symbol, reveals a language used to give meaning. The history of architecture functions for us as a sign to convey specific meanings. The past is a vocabulary with which to invent and communicate new propositions. (See *Sign Language*).

167-168. Market Street family house, Philadelphia (Pa.), 1979.
169. Old Pine Comunity Center, Philadelphia (Pa.), 1978.
170. Student Center at Temple University, Philadelphia (Pa.), 1979.
171. Grays Ferry Comunity Center, Philadelphia (Pa.), 1979.

Frank O. Gehry

Toronto (Canada) 1929.
Bachelor of Architecture at the University of Southern California in 1954.
From '72 to '79 he taught in the Universities of Houston, Los Angeles, Southern California and Harvard.
Since '62 he has been head of Frank O. Gehry Associates Inc. with an office in Santa Monica, Cal.

The facade I conceived for the Venice Exhibition is made of rough studs framed in the traditional way that mass housing is provided in California. It is intended to be a kind of perspective drawing made from a very basic and very meaningful material to the architecture of my region. Of course this building technique has been used for centuries in regions of the world where wood is available and is, therefore, even more meaningful. It has touched and will continue to touch many lives.

In my own recent working with simple wood frame construction I have been exploring the idea of using the rough carpentry techniques as the finished product. I have been interested in the kind of immediacy that creates.

It is a compelling idea for me to work in the area of making an architectural statement, creating a spirited space, something beautiful, maybe using the simplest of available building techniques with the hope that good architecture would be available for a larger use.

In making this wood frame drawing for the exhibition I have used the traditional diagonal bracing techniques for stiffening a frame to draw perspective lines which incorporate the window of the exhibition building located in the outside wall of my designated space.

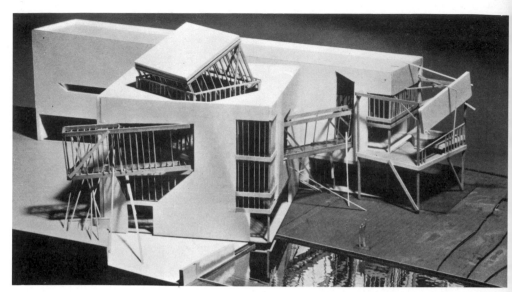

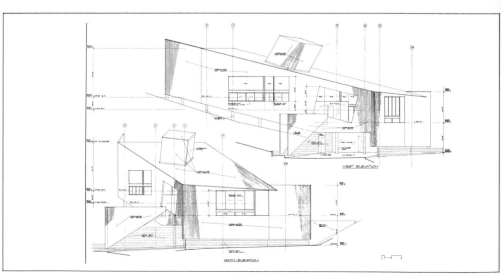

172-173. Familian Residence, Los Angeles (Cal.): general model.
174-175. Wagner Residence, Los Angeles (Cal.): south and west elevations and view.

176. Mid-Atlantic Toyota Offices, Baltimore (Maryland): interior.
177. Study for a house in California: model.
178. Loyola Law School, Los Angeles (Cal.), detail of the model.

Michael Gold

London 1939.
Diploma at the Architectural Association of London in 1964.
He teaches at the AA of London (Unit 5).
Has worked professionally since 1966, lives and works in London.

History of architecture and other histories in relation to design
In the "Dublin" project (1975) the basic motive was to revive something of the sumptuous, exotic, and fabulous, and to present it in the context of a public authority housing competition as an immediate practical possibility.

And so, Gothic architecture in Venice was brought to the docklands of Dublin...

Since then, I have tried to find other techniques for opening these aspects of history to modern architecture, techniques which are less susceptible to the thin theatricality and general air of quaintness which historicism brings to contemporary design.

In more recent work ("Millbank" 1976/7 and "Jerusalem" 1980) history as "An account, *without reference to time*, of a set of natural phenomena..." has been explored.

In "Millbank," natural elements — the changing skies, flows and tides of the river, tilts of the earth — are reflected in mirrors, refracted in prismatic glasses. Rocks, gems, crystals, cosmic geometries, star forms, comets, collisions and explosions, are invoked.

In "Jerusalem," fabulous layers of history are evident in the place, and become motives in planning, and motifs in superficial form. Seams of precious stone embedded in rough, and smooth, polished rock appear on the buildings. A long sloping avenue with a line of diamond shaped stones along it structures a plan to mark a boundary between east and west Jerusalem, in the area already known as "the Seam."

In all these projects, impressions arising from all levels of experience of context, the momentary, incidental, and personal, as well as the more general and common, play equal part in an initially indiscriminate process of association in design.

At one level, such a process may seem arbitrary, even irrelevant, to design in an often fiercely contested social context.

But ideally, the result would be the perfect crystallisation, as in a dream, of everything pertinent to the context, the moment. And the architecture, like a dream, contemporary, timeless, and irreproachable.

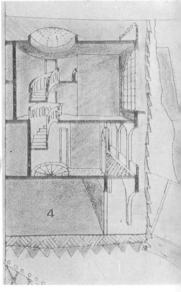

180-181. Competition for public buildings at City Quay, Dublin (Ireland), 1976: elevation and perspective section (with M. Masheder).

182-185. Project for the "gate" to Mecca (Saudi Arabia), 1979, (for Alimgradridra Associates): detail, elevation and section.

179. Entry for the Millbank housing project in London (England), 1976: overhead view of the tower area (with M. Masheder).

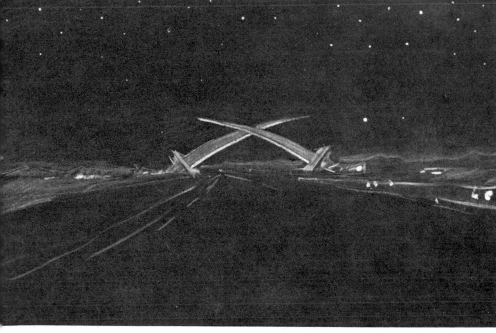

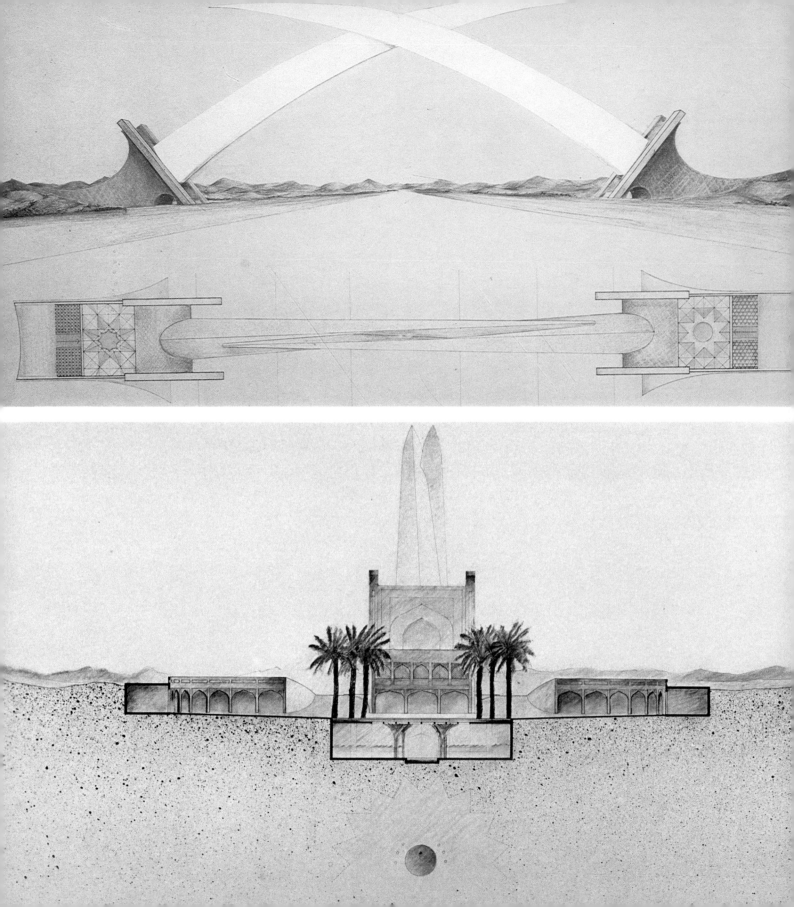

Burkhard Grashorn

Oldenburg (Germany) 1940.
Studied at the Hochschule für Bildende Künste (HPK) of Berlin and at the University of Rome.
Lives and works in Dortmund; teaches Composition and Theory of Architecture at the Chair of Prof. J. P. Kleihues at the University of Dortmund.

On the threshold to the solution of the puzzle

Architecture is a kind of uproar, but has run down to become impotent and weak. There is only the utopia of the legalized social garbage, a utopia of social uninhabitability, subsidized by the State — State architecture.

Viewed in the light of this interpretation of social architecture the architect must be "antisocial," whether he likes it or not. Only through this can he be a political figure. He must therefore fight for his right of free expression. If this right is given to him as a present then he might as well pack up and go home. For architecture has been for 5000 years a vision of the world, which at times has been achieved through an exhaustive struggle of strained will. The seers have sold themselves these days; the poets have grown fat. These people have lost their farsightedness, in the lack of which we turn deaf ears to present life. The international situation is developing fast and the causes of war are growing.

The past has no future, as long as traditional architecture has given nothing but free admittance to a museum of picturesque impressions: a helpless tottering in the grammar of styles instead of searching among the historical monuments for the millions of positive dreams which are pressing to be realized. The time has not yet come, when people would team up with the architect to build a wall, a beautiful square or a tower which leads heaven to earth. His work would be theirs, because in this case he would be in the position to realize the wishes of the masses. The people as well as the architect would be happy. That is the genuine solution of the conflict between existence and essence, the solved puzzle of history, the significance of architecture of the highest attainable standard.

That is why architecture has to remain in uproar so that we don't lose sight of this ultimate goal. These wishes and dreams, incised, inscribed, carved and painted in the past will, in the transition to the future, lead to unrest and fighting. The world is already vibrating.

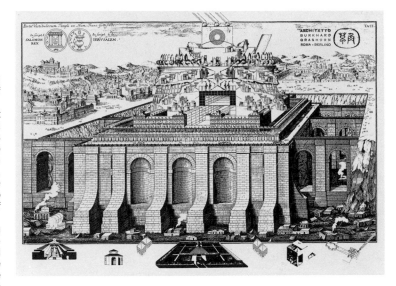

186. Collage for the history of architecture, 1978.

187-1980. Competition for the Bürgerweide in Bremen (West Germany), 1979: elevations and views of the model.

191. Competition for the Teerhof in Bremen (West Germany), 1978: overhead view.

192. Siedlung at Hagen (West Germany), 1974: plans.

193. Project for the Wallraf-Richartz Museum in Cologne (West Germany), 1975: section.

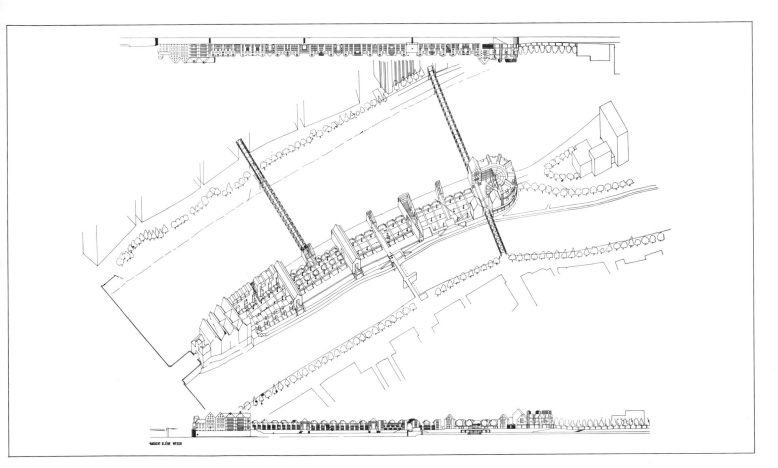

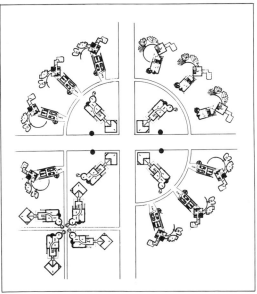

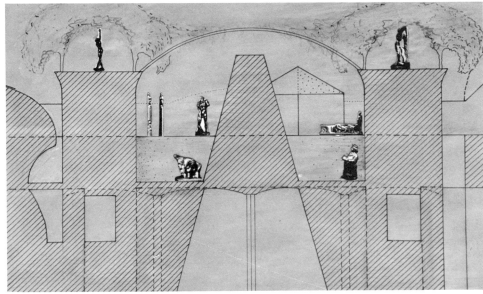

Studio GRAU

The Roman Group of Urban Architects (G.R.A.U.) was formed in 1964.
The studio serves as a general point of reference for the cultural and professional activity carried out by its members singularly or in little groups.
Regular members of the studio are:
Alessandro Anselmi, 1934;
Paola Chiatante, 1939;
Gabriella Colucci, 1936;
Anna Di Noto, 1939;
Pierluigi Eroli, 1936;
Federico Genovese, 1934;
Roberto Mariotti, 1937;
Massimo Martini, 1937;
Pino Milani, 1937;
Francesco Montuori, 1937;
Patrizia Nicolosi, 1944;
Gianpietro Patrizi, 1936;
Franco Pierluisi, 1936;
Corrado Placidi, 1936.
The painter Franco Mulas (Rome 1938) and the sculptor Enzo Rosato (Taranto 1940) exhibit with GRAU.

Sixteen Years Later
Sixteen years have passed since GRAU, in its projects, separated itself from the Modern Movement and from the cultural officialism supporting it; this was a few years before it undertook a theoretical reconstruction in its writings of the architectural discipline within Marxist methodology.
The opportunity to participate in the First International Exhibition of Architecture, organized by the Venice Biennale, is a favorable occasion for determining the pros and cons of the situation, from the particular viewpoint of the course of our experiences.

Some unrenounceable issues
We have been given the opportunity to repropose some theoretical points that have progressively characterized our activity, not for an act of mere "re-attribution," but, and this matters to us, to fully claim an ideological dimension of artistic work: as a factor always significant in itself; particularly in this phase, characterized by the impact of our break with the Modern Movement and by our attempts to reconstruct a new, higher order of human work.
The stages leading to our radical consciousness begin with the recognition of the language of architecture as an autonomous language. Through the re-acquisition of meaningful categories like geometry, the number, and the original theorization of the plastic module and the aggregative law as

the dialectic structure of the project; until the problem of meaning and symbol as the spatial metaphor of history, and finally of the toil and hopes of the time, and for us, of the class struggle.
In the sphere of this problem, as a consequence of the liveliest trends of modern Marxism, the discovery of the historical real as the eternal present of testimonies: logical antecedents of the figurative act and the project; the discovery of nature-history as the uneliminable dialectic context of the work. The objective, and finally, the ground itself for daily work, in weaving new bonds and in establishing new references, the re-creation of a renewed, real unity among all the figurative arts.

How the theoretical picture is articulated
The richness and complexity of this theoretical picture, interwoven well into the experience of the projects, have, we think, let us go basically unharmed through both the difficulties of a reduced and marginal professionalism (which we share with the majority of young Italian architects), and through the artificial paradises of so-called drawn architecture.
Going unharmed does not mean not paying a price at least with regard to formal equilibrium; in the same way we can notice having had excessive faith in and having given too much attention to the single organism, the single building, understood above all in its strict and tangible building limits; just as we learn from the excesses of monumentalism, from the excesses of articulation and plastic development, from the almost programmatic detachment from the immediate physical surroundings.
It is true that at the same time, the rationalist neo-academy attempted to renew its own figurative and ideological stock with the invention of the so-called planning on a large urban scale, the last desperate shore before absolute silence and the death of art. But it is equally true that the problem certainly isn't that of keeping our distance constantly from the Modern Movement and from the International Style, but rather that of establishing, if at all, our position within the thematics defined as Post-Modern; contributing, if this definition is not just a convenient label, to the definition of its outlines and historical identity.
We therefore see these as the principal consequences of our attempting these balances, at least

on questions of the organism, of nature-history, of the city:
1. The concept of the isotropy of space is specified in that of polycentrism, which now fully invests the composite process with its qualities, in a notion of figurativism that could be called planetary. As a result, the concept of "limit" relative to the architectural organism is presented not only literally, and well beyond the physical limit of the wall mass; this walled box loses its characteristics as the homogeneous place of homogeneous events, or the pure sequence of solids and voids. The plastic module and the aggregative law inevitably take on new value, stretched to accomplish new spatial-temporal tasks; in succession even fully experimented elements like geometric bodies (symmetry-horizon-spatial triaxiality etc.), the methods of representation (central perspective-upsetting in the horizontal plane), the phenomena of gravitation around a projective center, the free signs of a naturalistic character.
2. The concept of nature is articulated and extends to all geographic expression, whether constructed, agricultural, or uncultivated, with a first overwhelming identification with a tree, a rock, and a hand-made article, and a subsequent, no less overwhelming investigation into their specificity, classifications, analogies, rules, and so on.
The concept of history is enriched by the qualities derived from the preceding point as a sequence of historical layers (nature-history). And from this point of view, the new appears obviously only as a conscious transformation of pre-existing surroundings, almost a continual restoration that today inevitably tends to assume the value of a moral and material indemnity for the human race. From this standpoint, the concept of historical antecedent, recognized as having a disruptive function with regard to the Modern Movement and the International Style, is delimited more appropriately within the semantic balance of the work, taking care that its only literary values don't characterize the meanings and symbols of the work itself.
3. Finally, the problem of the city can arise, as extension, but not physical or dimensional, but of composite architectural categories, when the logic of the project has been settled upon, (control of the drawing-delimitation of functional problems — semantic closing...) with the assumption of history and nature as the sole referents of the figurative act:

transfiguration of the old into the new, the sacredness of daily life, the idealization of the history of the histories of collectivity, the Socialist indemnity for the human race.

And on the other side of the issue of the city, the rediscovery of the "ornato" as the guarantor of ever-growing values to the ends of "the representation of space," and as the possibility of an architecture as a loose and re-echoing whole where the closed form-open form, centrality-laterality dilemma subsides. "Ornato" as the link and symbol of the relationship with history and nature, as composite category which, including all preceding ones, sets them out for the new tasks of restructuring human work.

GRAU

GRAU has always been the mysterious object of the present figurative panorama. This is true somewhat because of the radicalism of its positions, and also because of the different credit given to its elaborations. Thus, the monolithic quality and unanimity which appeared to outsiders and which we've never taken the trouble to explain, have been interpreted as the effect of purely moralistic positions. The fact is that the issues at stake (detachment from and constructive struggle against the Modern Movement) left little space for the maturation of very different figurative and ideological positions. Moreover, it was our deliberate intention not to found a simple current or figurative school as an avant-garde for a deliberate and necessary delimitation of the figurative repertoire adopted in opposition to other existing schools and currents, and in this case to those derived from the language of rationalism. The principal objective was that of refounding the entire architectural discipline and the consequent renewed ideological dimension of artistic work.

It could be said, paradoxically, that all Post-Modern experiences (with the exception of L. Kahn) have already been accomplished by GRAU, and that, nevertheless, GRAU constitutes an incoherent sequence of lucid coherences. And so in order to understand, to orient ourselves, to polemicize within this important although contradictory phenomenon defined as Post-Modern, we have no other road to follow than that of our own history, and not in monolithic or unanimistic terms. This is not yet a history written by critics, but an open history of languages which, in the design process must find their own identity and brightness.

And so, having confirmed a common reference to the theoretical picture and to its successive developments, and conscious of the present state of things, for us, both individually and as a group, GRAU today must exist.

Franco Mulas and Enzo Rosato

We have requested several works from the painter Franco Mulas and the sculptor Enzo Rosato which we feel help us in defining the problems of the representatitivity of space. The motives for this choice go well beyond our more than once mutually verified cultural affinities, and our common tendency to work for the renewal and expressive unity of the figurative arts. In particular, it was surprising how each of us arrived independently at a working out of products incredibly alike in the very transparency of their meanings.

Enzo Rosato, trained in the school of Leoncillo, re-acquired the world of the human figure first through the acquisition of geometric thematics, understood as instruments of new rationality, and then through the courageous re-visitation of handicraft products such as vases and plates, seen as instruments for recovering nature-history (for him, his childhood in Grottaglie) and the confirmation of ceramics as a total expressive means (yet another non-conformist link to Leoncillo's work).

Franco Mulas' artistic development is well-known to critics, and we will not attempt a summary of it here. When he abandoned the themes of the so-called commitment (the social struggles of 1968, the condition of the artist, etc).), he hit the center of two objectives which included and went beyond them, significantly for us also regarding the debate taking place in architecture. First, he went back to the figurative and ideological roots of the Modern Movement, placing the mythic figure of Mondrian at the center of criticism. He gave relevance and value to this criticism, centering his attention on the series of "Trees" which, in their almost didactic process, demonstrate absolutely clearly the logical reasons for Modernist thematics. Secondly, on his way towards the reconquest of a nature-history (and of a new pictorial space) he measured and repainted, in the long tradition of painters, precisely one of these pictures ("The Red Tree"). And he did this going backwards, symbolically, almost as a counter-demonstration, running the same course as in the series by Mondrian.

More generally, our relationship with Mulas and Rosato became useful for us in that it prevented GRAU from having an image of self-sufficiency in today's vast but ambiguous panorama of experiences extending from drawn architecture to behavioral thematics. Almost symmetrically for these two artists, it was a question of verifying the role of one's identity within a sector, that of architecture, in full ideological and figurative expansion. In practice, it was a question of verifying what was happening once it was decided to articulate the facade as a pagan columbarium and enter an interior space not mechanically following formal laws, but rather presenting itself as a self-sufficient and closed space. The facade, therefore, as immediate carrier of the most disruptive symbologies: the break with surrounding history; the opening towards other histories, other lives, other forms of life; the making sacred of one's testimony as men and artists; the refusal to reduce architecture to pure "facade" and pure "scenography."

At the moment this short piece is being written, we don't yet know what the final solution will look like, at least with regard to the spaces beyond the facade. Enzo Rosato has woven the history of his "Vases" with the spatial development of the hemispheric niches and the initials of the authors. Now, he tends to arrange his sculptures more freely in the so-called interior: a naturalness of relationships and a dense interweaving of small things, sign of a rediscovered faith that we specifically called before the reconquest of the "ornato." Franco Mulas has resolved the problem of the representational plane both through the quality of his painting and the mechanism of serializing that connects the four pictures, or "Mondrian's Red Tree." This serializing, this development, this process of almost cinematographic restitution of a rediscovered pictorial nature, and the symbols and meanings that appear obviously from them now tend, like Rosato's sculptures, to go beyond, to accomplish new tasks together with architecture: to find, to prefigure higher orders of the logic, limits, and quiet of artistic work.

The works are in progess.

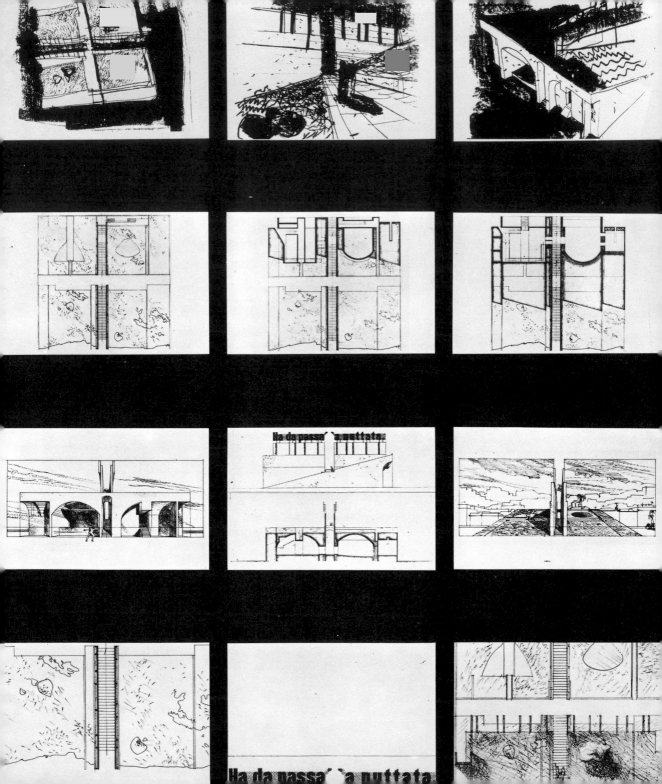

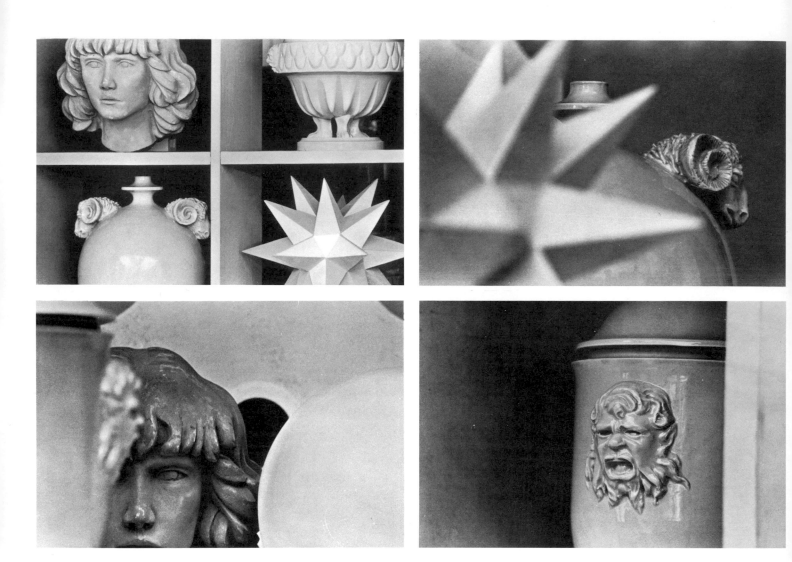

Michael Graves

Indianapolis (Indiana - USA) 1934.
Bachelor of Science in Architecture at the University of Cincinnati in 1958, Master of Architecture at Harvard University in 1959. Prix de Rome in 1960: two years' study at the American Academy of Rome. Lives and works in Princeton (New Jersey).
He is Professor of Architecture at the Princeton University School of Architecture and Urban Planning.

If we were to consider that the language of architecture has, as its primary interest, the metaphorical representation of man and landscape, we will probably be able to use that basically simple language in a way which can express not only simple ideas but also more complex and poetic ones.

Architecture before the turn of the last century was more conscious of itself as a language than that which we generally regard as Modernism. If the abstractions which are inherent in the basic assumptions of the Modern Movement are seen to be derived from a series of influences which surround architecture, they are, I would suggest, however, not primarily germane to architecture as a language. Modern architecture, as we know it through its insistence on upsetting the existing former state of the art, is generally based in part in undermining figural references in favour of non-figural or abstract geometries.

The components of architecture, which we know to be derived not only from pragmatic necessity but also from symbolic sources, constitute a select group of particular elements.

Those elements are within or germane to architectural culture and, though they are used metaphorically by other disciplines, they are primarily ours. These elements are simple in nature: walls, columns, ceiling, floors, doors, windows.

By saying that we can label such elements as these, we are also saying that they are by necessity representational, or even figural. I assume that the figural qualities of these elements and the base that they characterize or configure are derived from the assumption of our own bodily presence relative to them. I think it would be fair to say that the vast majority of modern architecture as we know it, though employing elements such as walls, floors, and ceilings, would first see these elements as abstract planes and solids rather than as grounded in a representational (i.e. man-landscape) mode. If the standard language of architecture sees the floor as the ground plane, it cannot see that same plane as a pure, abstract, geometrical element.

Yet at the same time that one is interested in making a more figural basis for the reading, communication, and action that takes place within an architectural composition, one should also be aware that the composition cannot be so literal that only one reading or likeness is available. Rather the composition must also be capable of a range of readings.

One has attempted to describe the anthropomorphic bias or relationship between man himself and the frontal or face-to-face confrontation with the plane of the facade. While the face of any building is not a literal representation of man, it does, however, share quite basic similarities. It, like

170

Fargo – Moorhead
Cultural Bridge

201. Project for Kalko House, Green Brook (N.J.), 1978: the sitting-room.

202. Warehouse conversion, Princeton (N.J.), 1977: Solarium.
203. Sunar furniture showroom, New York City (N.Y.), 1979: mura[l]
in the entrance vestibule.

us, is weighted or rooted in the ground by its ba[se]
or leg. In turn, the facade has a center
body/heart, which can be read or understood [as]
the piano nobile, the ground again. And finally, li[ke]
the human body, it has, at its uppermost level, [its]
own head or attic storey. We have as a culture al[so]
located particular activities appropriate to levels [of]
privacy relative to this tripartite configuration [of]
base, body and head. While the base of t[he]
building quite naturally is given over to the mo[re]
communal or commercial aspects of the buildin[g,]
the body of the building contains the semi-priva[te]
habitation or the social realm, and the attic sto[rey,]
furthest from the street or ground, allows t[he]
greatest privacy simply by its separation from t[he]
base.

we have, in our particular Biennale facade, co[n]
sciously attempted both to suggest protection at t[he]
door and threshold and to frame them, for it is t[he]
role of the facade not only to establish the bou[n]
dary between outside and in, but also, by virtue [of]
the door, to provide the axis of penetration of t[he]
facadal boundary

We have, in turn, located an enlarged sconce pr[o]
jecting from the facade, as a representation of t[he]
middle ground or piano nobile. The sconce has [a]
variety of possible readings by virtue of [its]
somewhat ambiguous formal characteristics. [Its]
projected form offers a measure of protection f[or]
the entrance below. It can also, in its thrust out fro[m]
the facade, be seen as borrowing space from t[he]
street and therefore acting somewhat like [a]
balcony. And finally it offers, at the uppermo[st]
horizontal surface, a ground upon which I hav[e]
placed an allegorical "first house." This replica [of]
first inhabitation is again a reminder of the triparti[te]
organization of the building and, in detail, sugges[ts]
the head or eye of our particular facade at the att[ic]
storey.

We have further attempted to reinforce the hiera[r]
chical elements of the facade by polychromatic a[s]
sociations. The green framing columns of the ent[ry]
are a somewhat literal representation of the lan[d]
scape and might be seen as suggesting one[s]
entrance into the garden or paradise. The centr[al]
figure, colored terra-cotta, is also a natur[al]
reference in that its original derivation comes fro[m]
an earthen souce. Finally, the flanking shin of t[he]
remainder of the facade is represented as lig[ht]
ochre which is based on the similar travertine a[nd]
limestone surfacing prevalent in Italy.

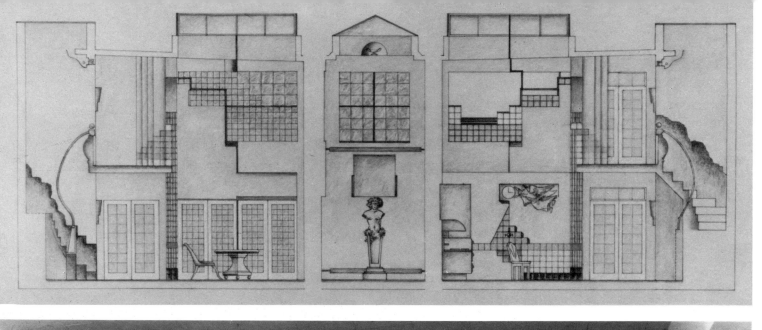

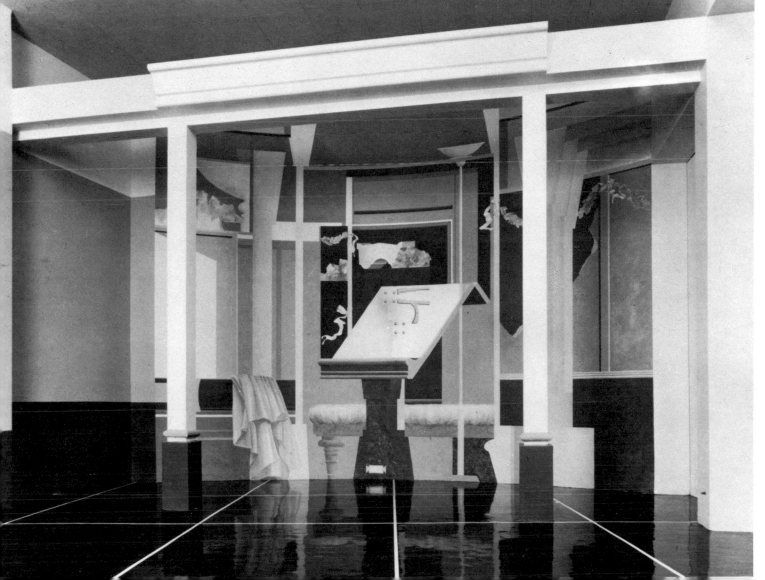

204. Building for public facilities at Portland (Me.), 1979: view from the park.

205. Project for a house in Aspen (Col.), 1978: general view of the model.

Allan Greenberg

Johannesburg (South Africa) 1938.
Bachelor of Architecture at the University of Witwatersrand (Johannesburg) in 1960. Master of Architecture at Yale University in 1965.
Lives and works in New Haven (Connecticut).
Taught at Yale and Princeton Universities from 1968 to 1978.

The meaning of the past
The meaning of our architectural past is more complicated than simply duplicating or distorting the forms bequeathed to us by history. As a tradition, it is the vehicle through which we embody our systems of social, political, and religious norms. This is accomplished by means of typologies of buildings which are continuously modified, as circumstances in society change. These building types provide a range of expressive and functional solutions to architectural problems.

It is the role of the architect to aid in the realization of society's aspirations by designing buildings which express the meaning and significance of the institutions they house. Architectural forms should facilitate, therefore, both the communication and the expression of these meanings. The most highly developed language of form available to us for this purpose is the classical language of architecture. Since antiquity, generations of architects have worked with the elements, grammar and meanings of classical architecture and adapted it to the needs of widely differing cultures, climates, and functions. The use of precedent enabled both the architect and the client to incorporate the aesthetic and functional experience of the past into new solutions. For the great architects, this was liberating as it enabled them to master and expand the boundaries of the tradition; for the average practitioner, it provides a canon to design competent buildings, such as the great Georgian squares of London, Edinburgh and Boston. The buildings should complement, rather than contrast, with the extant architectural tradition. The legacy of the past challenges us to create a fitting architecture for our times.

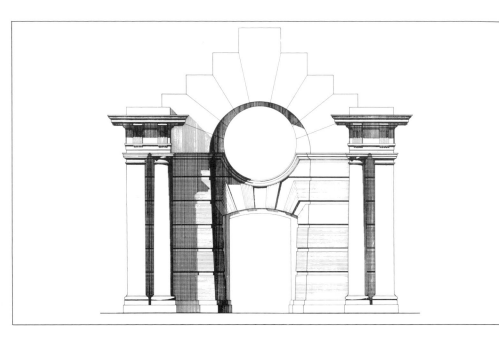

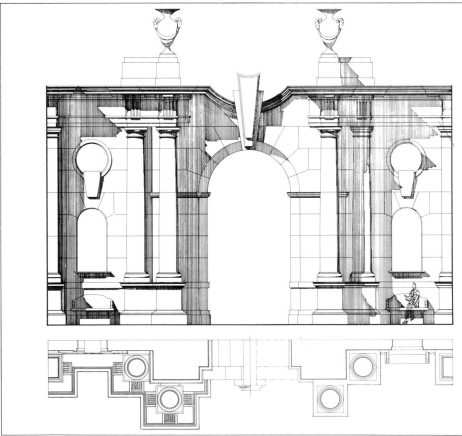

206-210. Project for Mid-Block Park, Manhattan, New York City (N.Y.), 1979: gateways at 50th Streets and 49th overhead view, view down alley, sections and plan.

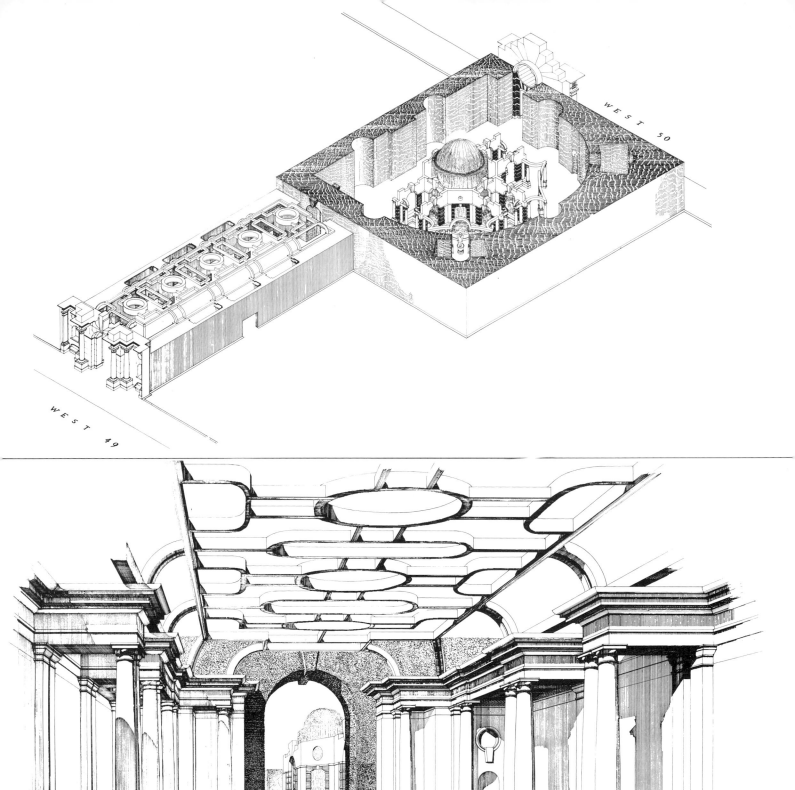

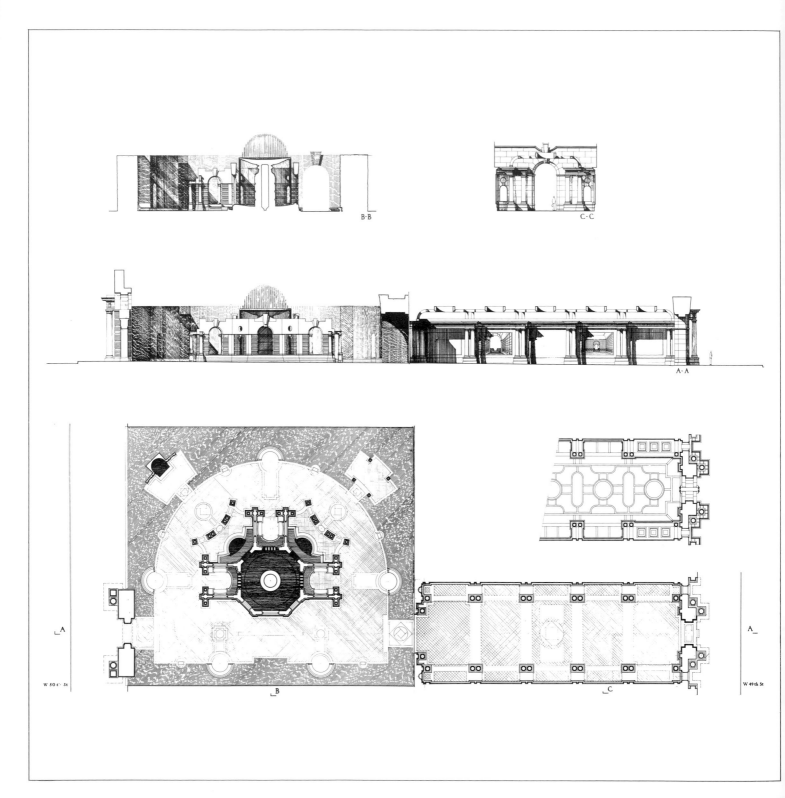

B-B

C-C

A-A

A

W 50 th St

B

C

W 49 th St

A

178

211. Façade study for "Best Supermarkets" competition.
212. Study for Law Courts at Alexandria (Virginia), 1976.

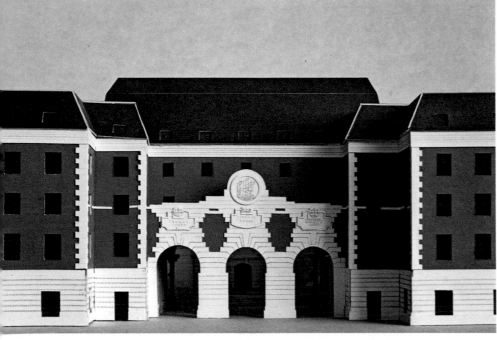

Giuseppe Grossi
Bruno Minardi

Have worked in a studio in Ravenna since 1970.

Giuseppe Grossi
Pieve di Cento (Udine) 1944.
Degree in Architecture at the University Institute of Architecture in Venice in 1970.

Bruno Minardi
Ravenna 1946.
Degree in Architecture at the University Institute of Architecture in Venice in 1970. Has been an Assistant Professor there since 1974.

When considered separately, architectural designing for historical centres or for areas with historical traditions, presents similar general problems, which are different for their peculiarity.

If we consider the surrounding space not as a background for architecture, but as a component of architecture itself, we can say that the choosing and the defining of a building type is detached from the analysis of the city and at the same time it is something we have to compare to it by taking into account its own components seen from the point of view of the city and history.

The building type proposed, which can be generalized and used elsewhere, is not a contingent element, but it is basic in decision making while its architectural specification determines the extent of its necessity in the relationship with the place where it is located.

Therefore type choice is the first answer to the problem to be faced, their first conceptual definition; while architectural factors such as quality, dimensions, quantity, distribution, interior-exterior relations, construction materials and colours are a further and necessary specification of the answer and a demonstration of its close link with the future of a city, of a country, of any defined place.

Two kinds of choices are pointed out: on the one hand they refer to the architectural and, more generally, cultural background in which we operate; on the other hand, they refer to changes suggested by an increasing knowledge of the city and its architectural features.

In conclusion we can say that the whole planning act is directed to clarify the initial choice, the landmark of which is the purpose of expressing a typology in necessary architectural terms avoiding unfounded contaminations and clarifying the logical meaning of the formal units; thus the rigour of the method and the clarity that formal creation must reach in connection with its own aesthetic aims, gain a basic importance.

214. Fountain house, 1977.

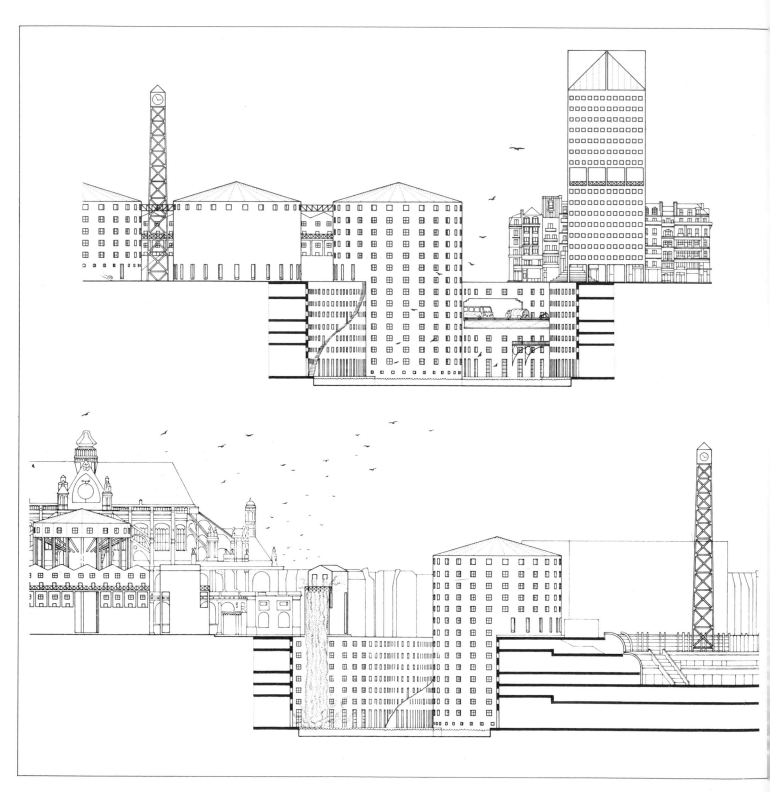

Antoine Grumbach

Oran (Algeria) 1942.
Has taught at the University of Vincennes (1969), the Ecole
Supérieure des Beaux-Arts at Paris, in the Unité Pedagogique n. 6
(1969/78), the Ecole Nationale des Ponts et Chaussées (1971/74),
the University of Essex (1972), Princeton University (1979) and the
I.A.U.S. - New York (1979).
Lives and works in Paris.

The City-Palimpsest
Architecture and the art of memory
The art of building time
Building cities on cities
Atlas of urban forms
Rhetoric of minor composition
Addition
Transformation
Combination
Substitution
Shifting
Rites of foundation and recovery of places'
poetic potential
Collage versus eclecticism
Pure and Impure
Long-lasting
Materials and the grasp of time
For incestuous city-architecture relationships.

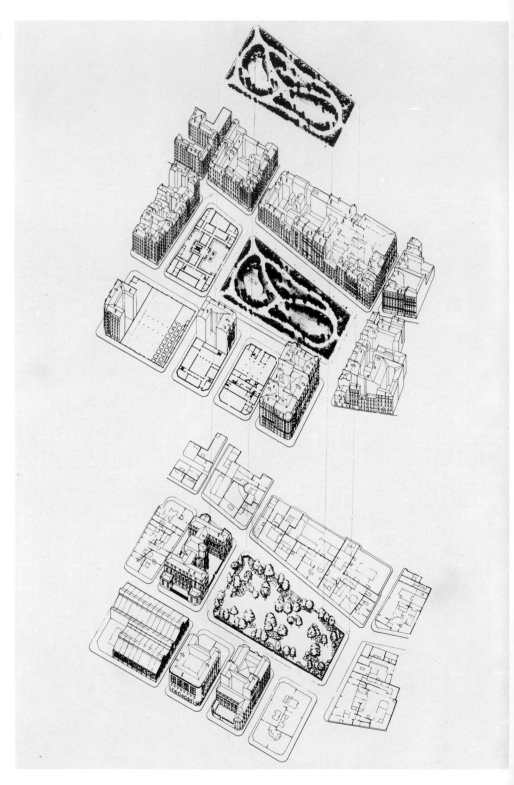

217. From "Atlas of urban forms": Temple Square, Paris IIIe
(France), 1978.

218. "The city on the city," Milan, 1979.

219-220. "Mare et Cascades" sector, Paris XXᵉ (France): overhead view of Rue de Mélnilmontand; overhead view of Rue des Pyrénées.

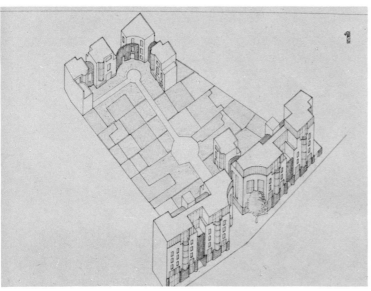

Heinz Hilmer
Christoph Sattler

They live and work in Munich, where they have had a studio since 1974.

Heinz Hilmer
Münster (Westphalia - Germany) 1936.
Diploma at the Technischehochschule of Munich in 1963.

Christoph Sattler
Munich (Germany) 1938.
Diploma at the Technischehochschule in '63.
Master of Science at the Illinois Institute of Technology (Chicago) in 1965.

In Greek mythology the goddess of memory is Mnemosyne, mother of the nine muses.
Architecture is new Gestalt out of memory.
The primary interest in Architecture is how it *is*, not how it was developed.
Architecture is impacted by the progress of technology, but not improved.
In Architecture the problem of form is constant, as well as remaining undefined.
Architecture has to do with taste.
"Taste is a faculty, to judge of an object or a form of imagination by approval or disapproval, without any interests.
The object of such an approval is named beautiful."
(I. Kant, "Kritik der Urteilskraft")

224-225. Herter House, Munich (West Germany), 1977-1980.

226-228. Public residential building at Karlsruhe (West Germany),
1975-1980: two views of the kindergarten; general view.

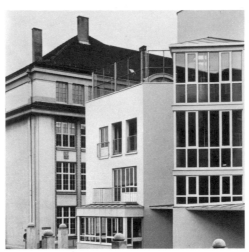

Vienna, (Austria) 1934.
Graduated from the Faculty of Architecture of the Academy of Fine Arts of Vienna in 1956.
Graduate Studies at the Illinois Institute of Technology (1958/59) and at the University of California (College of Environmental Design, 1959/60), Master of Architecture at the University of California 1960).
Has worked professionally in Vienna and in Düsseldorf since 1964.
Has edited researches and essays on R.M. Schindler and the pueblos of the North America indians; he is a correspondent for many international magazines and periodicals.

"The presence of the Past" is apparent in my contribution in a manifold way. It is an architecture of memories, memories not only in the sense of architectural history, but memories of one's cultural heritage and of one's personal past — manifesting themselves in quotations, transformations and metaphors. My work of today incorporates — consciously — the presence of the past in terms of a continued (sometimes fragmentary) re-elaboration of earlier work and ideas. I am concerned as much with history as with my own history.

Almost as a countermove to what would suggest itself, I decided to do my facade in the "street" as a presence of the past as found in the "corderia" — the columns.

Both the facade — as applied sheet — and the column are matter of concern in my work. I could have transplanted some of my storefronts right to the exhibition site both in terms of scale and also of intent — they are not just facades but built manifestos, incorporating in a nutshell an approach, an attitude. As I have done this so often (in real streets), I rather decided to continue (the past) on the idea of the columns (continuing the already existing columns). A column — as Loos has clearly understood — presents itself. It is a structural element which has become absolute architecture. Bernini in San Ambrogio, Loos in Chicago, my predelíction for the garden and my concern with the — sometimes menacing — presence of the past in terms of archaeological fragments is my selection here. I would have many more "columns" to fill the more than 300 meters of the magnificent colonnades of the corderia of the Arsenale in Venice.

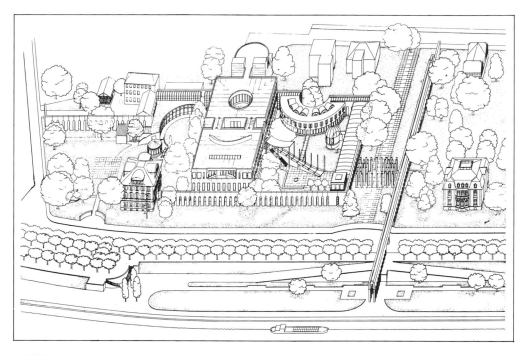

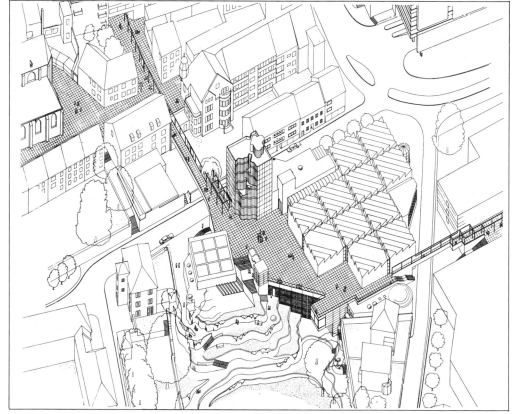

29. Project for Handicrafts Museum in Frankfurt (West Germany), 1980.

30. Municipal Museum, Moenchengladbach (West Germany), 1972-1980.

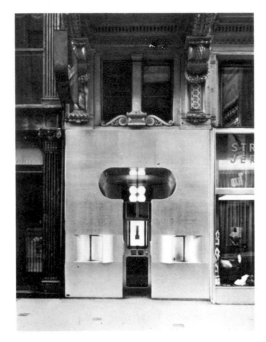

233-234. Skyscrapers, 1958.

235. Skyscraper (Rolls Royce radiator on Wall Street), 1966.

236. Venice Biennale, 1972: columns-palm.
237. Travel agency, Vienna (Austria), 1978: columns-palm.

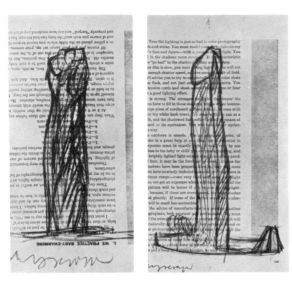

238. Nymphenburg (Vienna), Reception Hall: adaptation of part of
the old building.
239. Marble table for the Siemens general administration office,
Munich (West Germany), 1975.
240. Archaeological reconstruction, 1969.

241. Travel agent's in Vienna (Austria), 1978: columns.
242. Museum of Glass and Ceramics, Teheran (Iran), 1978.
243. Set of "Comedy of seduction," Vienna (Austria), 1980.

238

239

240

242

241

243

Arata Isozaki

Oita (Japan) 1931.
Degree at the Faculty of Architecture of Tokyo in 1954.
Worked in the studio of Kenzo Tange from '54 to '63.
Has taught in Japan and in the USA (Rhode Island School of Design
and Columbia University).
Lives in Tokyo, where he has had a studio since '63.

The facade presented here represents a typical house facade located in a traditional Japanese street.

The main body of the house was set back from the street itself, being screened by a high timber fence. Visitors would enter through a gate to find a garden path conducting them to the house. This resembles the process of approach to traditional European town buildings where entrance through an arcade leads to an inner court, off which were the entrances of the individual units. In Japan, however, there is a difference, in that there is no tradition of collective housing, and the enclosed space belonged only to one town house.

Consequently in this presentation it is intended that the visitor enters by a gate to find a garden path. The exhibition space behind is not a room, or any interior space, but an outdoor garden. To symbolize this concept the floor is covered with gravel. A loquacious facade could diminish the effect and invite confusion.

The facade was usually composed of the minimum of elements so as to signify the minimum expression of meaning.

The facade generally indicates to the street the existence of a house behind, and so, leaving this facade understated results in counterposing intentions, such as ostentation/concealment, manifestation/eliminitation, loquaciousness/silence, sense/no sense, and thereby demonstrates the contradiction that it is.

Thus once existed in Japan an important manner of Japanese life, the perception of subtle nuances amid such a contradiction. Such a feature should be retained in the composition of this facade.

This facade has two openings; one is tall and narrow while the other is square and slightly raised from the floor. The openings are just large enough to let people slip or crawl through, squeezing them both psychologically and physically as they pass. This pressure represents an etiquette required of the entrant as he penetrates the boundary to another world behind the facade, thus forcing him to change his state of mind which includes the manner of his physical behaviour.

In the past we had many examples of entrance/exits which forced people to stoop as they passed through. Kuguri-do was a secondary opening used as a service entrance which was set beside the large formal entrance of a town house, and nijiri-guchi was the entrance to the tea ceremony house. To enter through nijiri-guchi even the noblest guest must crawl, just like a dog, without his swords.

In this exhibit the openings are partially concealed by two planes which lean against the facade. This device is a gesture which, although it almost refuses entry, does permit access. Such a manner was evident in the town house of Japan in hiyoke, a sunshade constructed of wooden battens or bamboo meshwork, and in noren, a shop-curtain hung

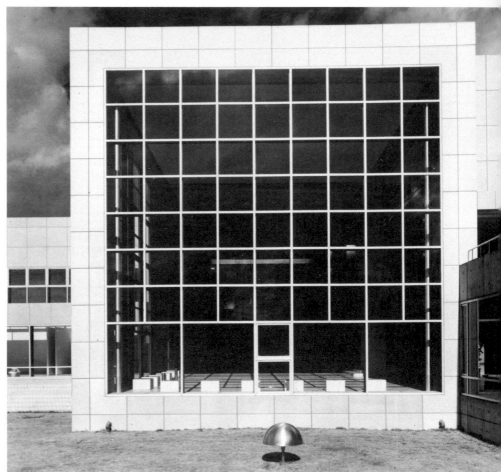

over the entrance.

These openings represent the same device, that of almost refusing entry as, according to the special terminology, they are entrance. Similarly the whole presentation of this facade could not but be expressed as only facade.

244. Country Clubhouse,
Fujimi (Japan), 1972-1974,
aerial view.

245. Museum of Fine Arts,
Gunma (Japan), 1970-1974: front
view.

246. Y House (Japan), 1972-
1975: part of the exterior.

247. Central Library,
Kitakyushu (Japan), 1973-
1975: interior detail.

248. Kj House (Kapan), 1974-
1977: front view.

249. H House (Japan), 1976:
front view.

246

248

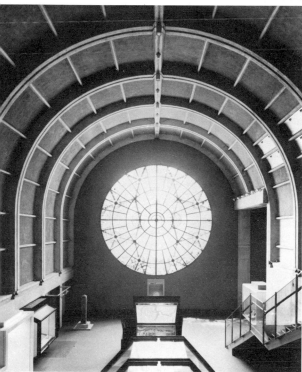

247

249

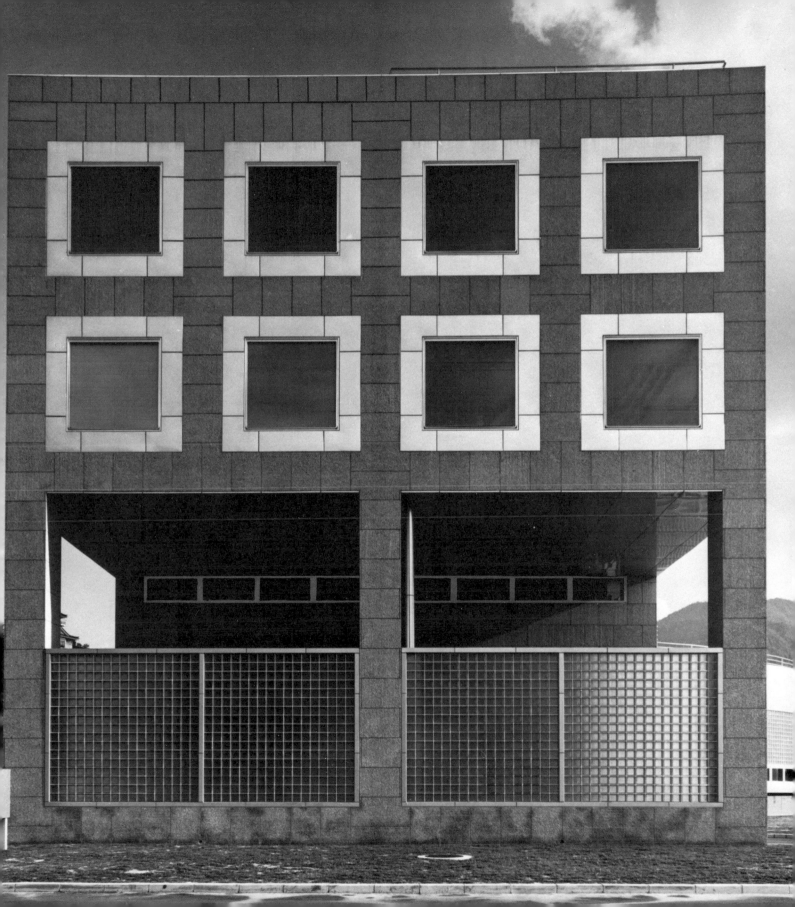

Helmut Jahn

Nuremberg (West Germany) 1940.
Degree at the Technische Hochschule of Munich in 1965.
Has lived in the United States (Chicago) since 1966.
Diploma at the Illinois Institute of Technology in 1967.
Has worked with Murphy Associates of Chicago since 1967, where
he has been in charge of planning and design since '73.

In a time when the direction of Architecture is the subject of a great theoretical debate the relationship to the past has emerged as a polemic issue.

We see our work as an appropriate and innovative recomposition of classic and modern principles of the building arts.

Rather than using formal quotations as orthodox duplications of a historic style, we seek conceptual relationships to the principles of history and architecture like:
— response of a building to site and to context
— entry and procession
— spatiality
— ornamentation
— symbolic associations of historic forms.

We synthesize these goals with intentions peculiar to a client, program, economics, efficiency and amenities of use and operation, and the possibilities of our age and its technology.

Any denial of those implications of the present would prove as mistaken as the disregard of the qualities of History, Context and Ornament once shown by the Modern Movement. The synthesis of these influences surpasses any attempt to either use only geometry or historic recall as a generator of form in Architecture.

By going beyond mere "styling" and technology and paying attention to human amenities, we are also aware of Architecture's most significant human goals and expand beyond the narrow pursuit of Architecture's present pursuit of styles and abstract forms.

This is a theory of Architecture as practical Art, produced within current constraints and by current methods. The fundamental language — as a response to our practice — is very strongly rooted in the idea of making a building along those often divergent determinators. It is a pragmatic mix of Reality and Idea content, along a process directed towards building architecture which conforms to the reality of the present and respects history, wherever relevant and appropriate.

By avoiding historicism of the revivalist kind as a mere pastiche, we try to suggest how we can build for a future that honors its past, while above all expressing the truth of our contemporary condition through a new architectural Typology.

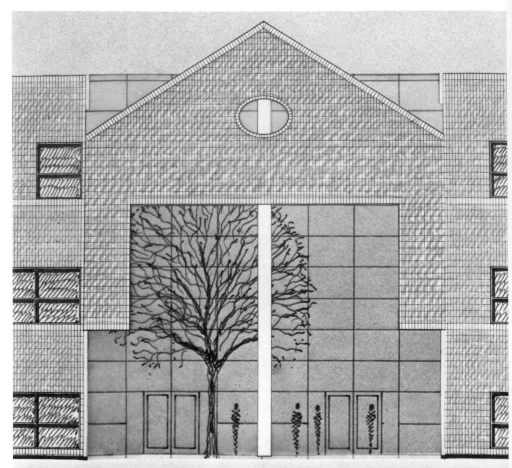

254. Project for Agricultural Engineering Sciences Building at the University of Illinois (Ill.); detail of the elevation.

255. State Illinois Center, Chicago (Ill.): general view of the model.

256-257. Chicago Board of Trade addition, Chicago (Ill.):
perspective section and general view of the model.
258. One South Wacker, Chicago (Ill.): general view of the model.
259. Northwestern Terminal, Chicago (Ill.): general view of the model.

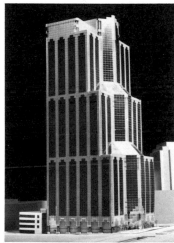

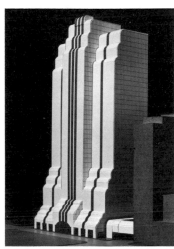

Jan & Jon

Have worked together since 1970.

Jan G. Digerud
Oslo (Norway) 1938.
Master of Architecture at Yale University in 1965.
Has been Associate Professor at the Oslo School of Architecture since 1968.

Jon Lundberg
Oslo (Norway) 1933.
Diploma at the Technischen Hoschule of Graz (Austria).
He was Associate Professor at the Oslo School of Architecture from 1958 to 1969 and since '69 has been professor and director of its Planning Department.

Some remarks on aedicular systems of composition
Works by Jan Digerud & Jon Lundberg, arch. mnal
"... a temple to receive the statute of a deity – a sort of architectural canopy in the form of a rudimentary temple – or, to use the classical word, pediment. It was also used for the shrines – again miniature temples – .... I suspect it (the aedicule) is practically as old as architecture itself, and as widespread."
John Summerson (1949).

"Cubism is the plastic expression of a new spirit engendered by the philosophical conception of the tangible world as *inside man*, rather than that of man as part of the tangible world." *Daniel-Henry Kahnweiler (1948).*

The work of an architect is simply a way of representing the world by creating places capable of inspiring human affairs. Architecture is not the copying of nature but the invention of emblems which signify it. Inventions in architecture as in music, are often variations on some recognizable, hence ordering device, – *a tema*.

While our interest in cubistic spatial relationship is our *method*, the aedicule ("little building") is our *medium*. This easily recognizable symbol of gable-ended roof supported on corner columns has remained fairly constant during the development of architecture all over the world. Fig. 4,5. It is the purpose of our contribution to show how we in certain projects have proceeded from a general historic "type" to particular solutions.

We are working with the knowledge of its ability to reconcile various scales within a single context. It responds to the human need for security, protection and ceremonial transformation of everyday behaviour. We are particularly interested in using it when confronting the problem of conflicting scales e.g. the singular act of entry into public domain. The three-dimensional aedicula permits spaces to nest in each other.

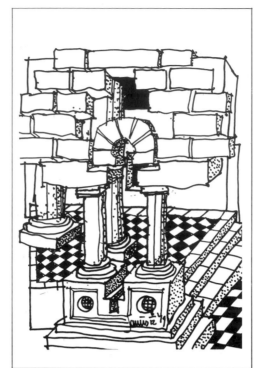

260

263

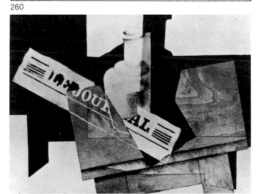

261

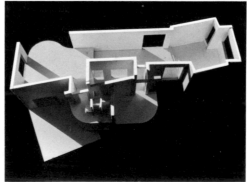

262

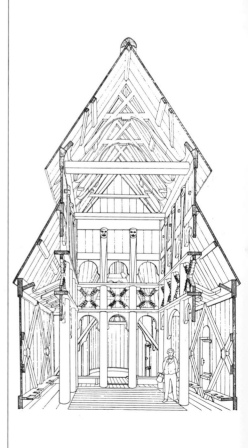

264

260. Image of "little building," drawing by Jan Digerud, 1979.

261. "Le Journal," Juan Gris, 1916, Norton Gallery and School of Art, Florida.

262. Jon Lundberg's house, Oslo (Norway), 1977: view of the model without its roof.

263. Heddal Stavechurch, Telemark (Norway), 1248: external view.

264. Burgund Stavechurch, Laerdal (Norway), 1150: perspective section.

265. "The singular act of entry:" Wencke Myhre House, Oslo (Norway), 1977: detail of the entrance.

266. Competition entry for planning 200 family units, Sannergt. 14, Oslo (Norway), 1974: overhead view (first prize).

267. "The aedicular motif:" "Mountain Cabin," 1977: model.

268. Wencke Myhre House, Oslo (Norway), 1977: canopy.

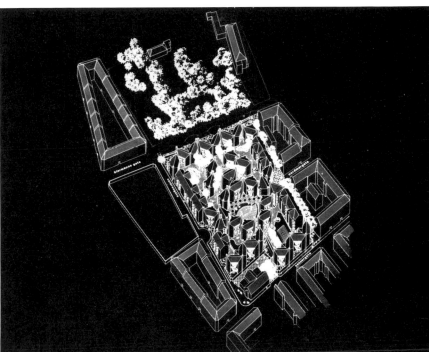

St. Albans (G.B.) 1939.
Diploma at the Architectural Association School of Architecture in 1963.
Worked with Cross, Dixon, Gold and Sansom from 1973 to 1977.
He has had his own studio since 1977. He is Senior Tutor in the Department of Environmental Design at the Royal College of Art in London.

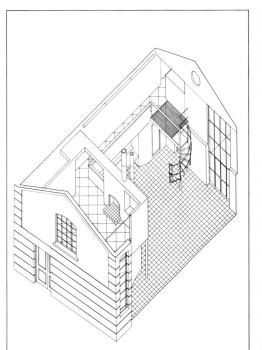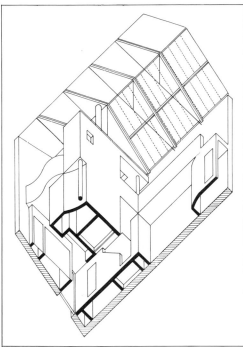

For any living architect born before 1910, whose formative years had been spent in an industrial city, who later might have subscribed to an avant-garde position, the last decade would have been most troubling, traumatic even. At the end of his professional life the strongest and most extreme polemic would appear to be a return to the very forms his life's work had been dedicated to overthrow. My own generation, born at the end of the 1930s, was carried along in the swell of this reformist enthusiasm with no complete memory of the apparently archaic and repressive world our fathers and grandfathers had dedicated their architecture to change. (A would-be reformist and even moralistic ethic has always been central to modern architecture in England.)

For the same reasons the questioning of these zealously held ideals and the inspiration of a broader view of history has been more available and in a sense less heretical. To this end my exhibit includes work whose shared concerns are addressed to the typological and autonomous ideas of architecture, as opposed to invoking the superficies of historical styles. Firstly on the small scale by the transformation and adaptation of existing structures by the dialectical inclusion of new components — Studio House, Chelsea, Studio Office. The valuing of type has given the idea of conversion new meaning opposing the taxidermist mentality that had characterized it previously. Secondly on the larger scale of the existing urban fabric, by the reinterpretation of the given forms of the street, square and avenue; the terraced house or crescent with their complementary fronts and backs — competition entires for Bristol Docks 1979 and Millbank 1977.

The almshouse or court typology is presented in the Old Person's Home at Cranford Lane, and the villa typology is proposed in my entry for the Schinken-Chiku Competition — both represent precise forms that had previously been associated with social stigma and subsequently discounted by the reformist mentality of the modernists. And finally I include my entry for the Irish Prime Minister's House competition that raised the dormant issues of architectural composition and symbolic representation associated with a head of government.

Suspended between the memory of a not-forgotten past and an unwanted present that promises nothing for the future, Architecture must urgently re-establish its own language at all its levels of meaning and subtlety.

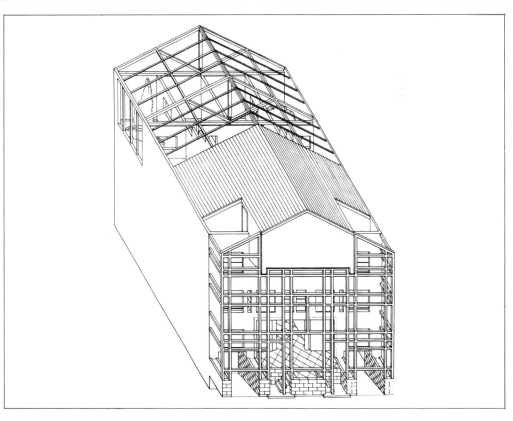

269-270. Studio house in Chelsea, London (England), 1975-1977: axionometric vertical sections.

271. Project for Urban Villas: overhead view.

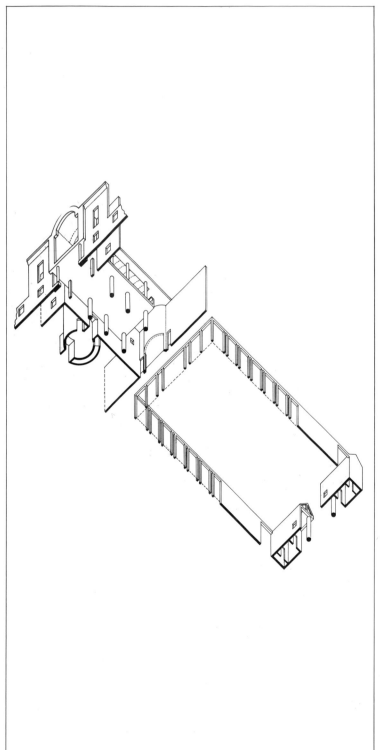

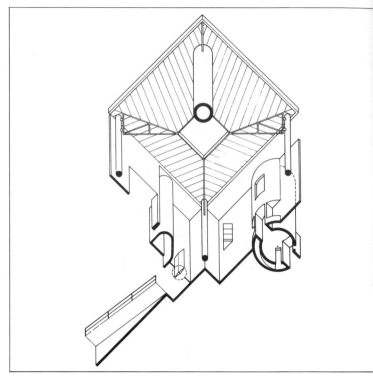

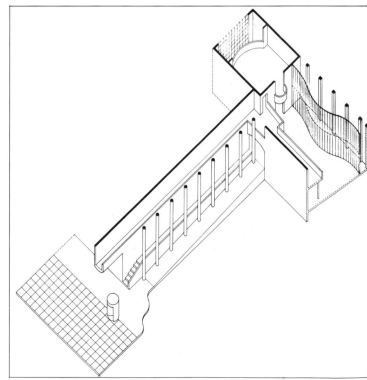

Haejew, Korea, 1937.
Graduated in Architecture from Waseda University (Japan) in 1962.
Has worked in the studios of Kenzo Tange and Ichiro Kawahara.
Has taught since 1971 at the school of Architecture at the University of Kumamoto.
He has been head of the "Yasufumi Kijima + YAS and Urbanists" studio since 1970.

Con-sein, hay sont

I wish to understand architecture in concrete terms without converting it into abstractions. But I like the implicit rather than the explicit. I prefer perception to conception. Architecture does not need such things as rhetoric and metaphors. Each individual human being has a definite idea of what he considers beautiful. In my opinion, it is easier to coexist with others when I myself am isolated. I establish my own sphere of activity when I demonstrate to myself the differences between me and others. I consider this kind of mixed coexistence — Con-sein, hay sont (in Japanese, Kon Zay Hei Son) — a correct interpretation. I am not bound to other people, but both parties recognize each other. And this mosaic coexistence manifests itself in my buildings. Each part of a building should have its own innate life. Substantiating the boundaries among these various parts is architectural design. For this reason I have great interest in architectural styles and the design and decorative elements included in them. Ornamentation has a highly individual life of its own. At a glance it would seem that I introduce ornaments and ornamental patterns in an attempt to fill up the cultural gap, but I would like to use it to better effect for the sake of coexistence on a non-heroic, human scale. No matter how abstract they may be, ornamental patterns are generally rooted deeply in a given cultural tradition. If the decoration expresses only one tradition, the building becomes no more than a revivalist's device for evoking historical associations. I believe that everyone should have his own history; then he might rearrange the world histories according to his own contacts with them. A sequence in a personal history doesn't coincide chronologically with the actual time. In my history Greek could be after the Gothic or Mussulman. There might be Renaissance and Art Nouveau side by side, and Byzantine should be close to us. Now we have lost the numerous brilliant idols who had been dominated by a single idealism.

275-276. Structure in Shirakawa Parke, Kumanoto (Japan) 1980.

Joseph-Paul Kleihues

Westfalen (West Germany) 1933.
Hauptdiplom at the Technische Universitaet.
Has worked professionally since 1962.
He has been professor of Architectural Theory and Planning at the University of Dortmund since 1973.
Since 1979 has been Director of the "Internationalen Bauausstellung" which will be held in Berlin in 1984.

The Presence of the Past in Architecture and Urban Design, as a constant with a continually changing covering, is above all obligated to the principle of hope. It is believable only in contradiction to Chaos and Superficiality; against fashionable Monday Architecture and technocratic pragmatism, which negate the past as well as the future.

The Presence of the Past in texts, drawings, and built houses and cities has the opportunity to mark new goals as anti-symbols.

The commercialization of these symbols, which is in the meantime the rampant business with the past, leads easily into embarrassment and cynicism.

The "Post-Modern," which Jencks patronizes in such a magnanimous and carefree way, and launches as an "ism," may sublimate Venturi; in epigonal reply the long degenerated degenerates further into the abstruse. Poetry, which tries to affirm itself through the past, will only manage where not adaptation but opposition is made clear.

Since Ferguson, the English Architectural historian, wrote in 1858 his, in that time, much acclaimed handbook of architecture, the use of historical experiences and accomplishments in Architecture has led to a new dimension of Architectural theory. One speaks about architecture as Language, while the theory of Ferguson was that there were two different Arts of Architecture: one phonetic and one technical.

Following his philosophy of Architectural thinking, the Phonetics of Architecture correspond to a deep spiritual/intellectual need of men to communicate; with image and Architectural language.

As such a language, Historicism, the eclecticism of the 19th century, had its special merits: the Presence of the Past as an instrument of meaning, as weapon, literature, smoke-screen, embarrassment, art, kitsch, avantgarde and backbencherism. Sources of form and reference were striven for at the point in time which brought the awakening of Mass Society, which correspondend to the most differing structures of culture and society, and which tried to comply with, according to comprehension and the intent to communicate, the most varied experiences and expectations.

That the Historicism which was fashionable at the time obviously granted itself particularly good prospects to be understood on the basis of the historically justified formal repertoire, was the starting point and perceptual source for Ferguson and in a certain way it was a theoretical anticipation of the semantic and semiotic theories of our time. With Ferguson, one is not speaking of Foutenelle's conception of perfection, an artistic demand in which historical interpretation and aesthetic judgement in Humanism and during the Renaissance converge.

Contrary to the "architecture parlante" of the

283. Project for the Landesgalerie, Düsseldorf (West Germany),
1975: general view of the model and perspective view.

284. Project for Park Lenné, (West Germany), 1976: perspective
view.

285-287. Headquarters of the Berlin Street Cleaning Service, Berlin
(West Germany), 1975-1978: drawing of façade and roofing detail;
views of the elevation.

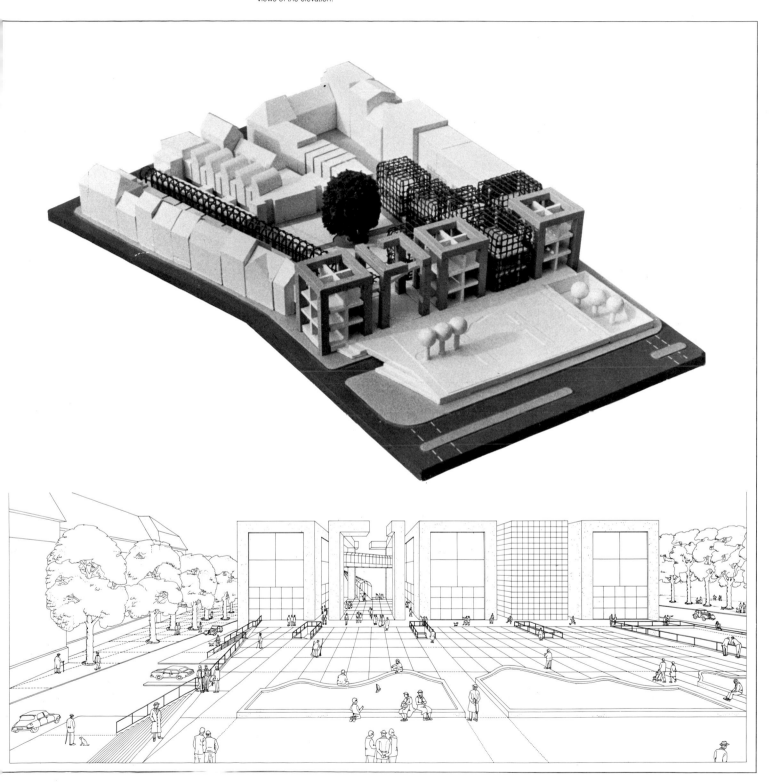

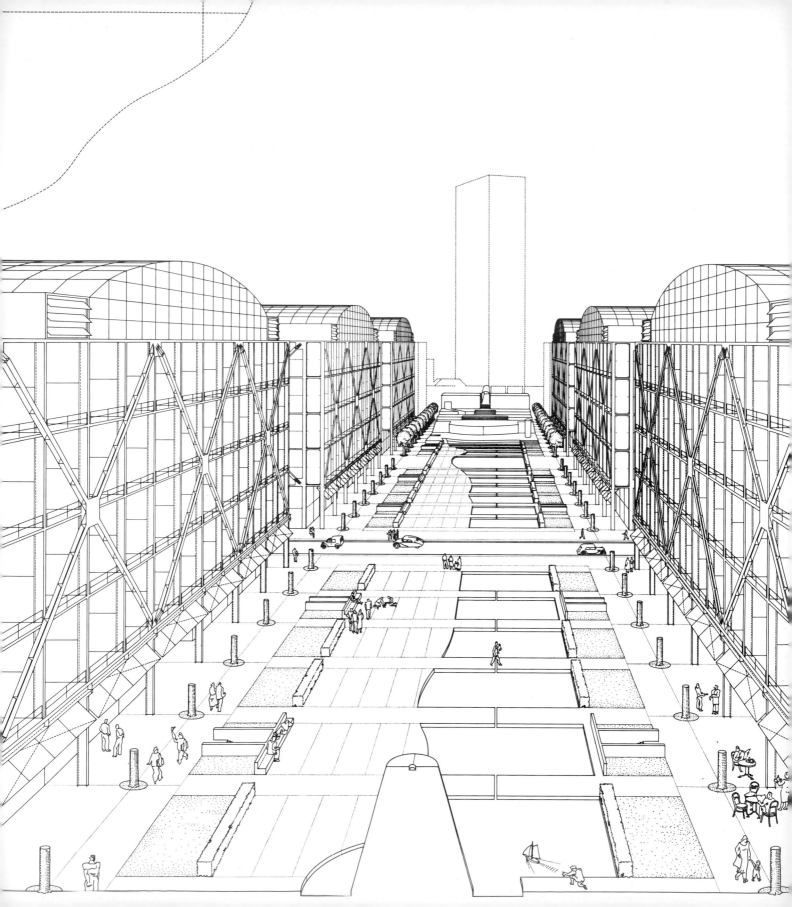

French Architecture of the Revolution, the speaking Architecture of Eclecticism stands out by way of further complexity. The power of form evocation in the way it was used by Boulleé would be supplemented, just as would be the literary originality and the immediately conceivable contexts of Ledoux's Architecture through the conscious injection of historical quotes, which expand the language of Architecture and Urban Design less through their formal aesthetic quality than because of their origin.

So it developed in the Architecture of the Past; an Architecture which to a great extent requires the preconception of the Observer, at just the moment in which the Metropolis, the Industrial Revolution, and Mass Society set an indication of the path towards anonymity; in a time in which a reverberating manifesto would be composed. While Bettina von Arnim lovingly engaged herself in writing, Pugin composed his Architectural Catechism of the Gothic, Ruskin and his follower Morris preached the Art of Craftsmanship and the World of Well Being, and the garden architect Paxton built his pure construction of glass and iron. Labrouste, on the other hand, tried to synthesize the past and the future.

But, in this sense, Schinkel had predated him with his Bauakademie, which was a built ambivalence of everyday experience and artistic perfection.

In comparison, the repeating of "Learning from Las Vegas" endangers itself in the world of the Artificial, just as Rationalism is not secure if it does not allow itself to bring things into discussion in Architecture which withdraw themselves as images or copies from any rational formalization and interpretation.

And this is the insecurity to which our work is fortunately condemned; that Architecture, sentenced to Speaking, doesn't allow itself to be verbally defined.

The striving for the Conventional, which is experienced in the increasing exertion of the Past, will change as little about it as the rational and realistic tendencies will be able to. Only the Past which anticipates is timeless.

OMA
Rem Koolhaas
Elia Zenghelis

The "Office for Metropolitan Architecture" (OMA) — has existed since 1975.
Rem Koolhaas and Elia Zenghelis are its partners, with Madelon Vriesendorp and Zoe Zenghelis.

Rem Koolhaas
Holland, 1944.
Studied Architecture at the AA, London, until 1972.
Visiting Fellow at the Institute for Architecture and Urban Studies, New York, since 1973.
Published *Delirious New York, A Retroactive Manifesto for Manhattan* in 1978.
Now lives and works in London.

Elia Zenghelis
Athens 1938.
Studied at the AA, London; was an associate of Douglas Stephen & Partners.
Has taught at the AA since 1964. Is now Visiting Professor at Princeton University School of Architecture.

Our "New Sobriety"
"... The plan is of primary importance, because on the floor are performed all the activities of the human occupants..."
That formulation by Raymond Hood defines a "functionalist" architecture not obsessed by form, but one that imagines and establishes on the "floor" (= the surface of the earth) patterns of human activity in unprecedented juxtapositions and catalytic combinations.
OMA has been concerned with the preservation and revision of this tradition of so-called functionalism — exemplified by Leonidov, Melnikov, the "Berlin" Mies, the Wright of Broadacre City, the Hood of Rockefeller Center — that was a campaign of territorial conquest for the programmatic imagination so that architecture could intervene directly in the formulation of the *contents* of a culture based on the givens of density, technology and definitive social instability.
Recent architecture has abandoned such claims.
Procrustes was the robber who made his victims fit his bed by stretching or lopping them.
In the "new" historicist and typological architectures, culture will be at the mercy of a cruel Procrustean arsenal that will censure certain "modern" activities with the excuse that there is no room for them, while other programs will be revived artificially simply because they fit the forms and types that have been resurrected.
In spite of the relentless criticisms concentrated on the insignificant episode of bastardized Modernism — it is essentially uncritical: it can only endorse the past.
OMA shows two projects here whose involvement with the past is more complicated.
The first is an intervention in a medieval Fortress — (that had lost much of its authenticity through a series of restorations à la Viollet-le-Duc) — the second a project for the renovation of a pure Panopticon, one of three ever built.
Both the Fortress and the Panopticon had to be equipped for their continuing operation in the 21st century: the Fortress with an extension of the Dutch Parliament that would proclaim the conquest of a former Royal Palace by democratic institutions, the Prison with a series of programmatic revisions that would adapt it to recent ideology.
In such situations, both historicist and typological

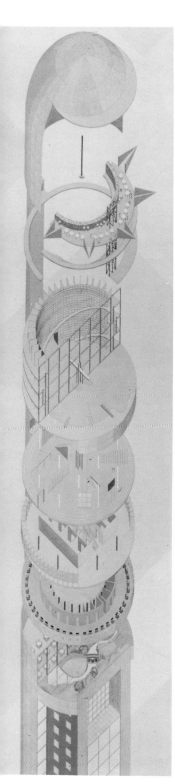

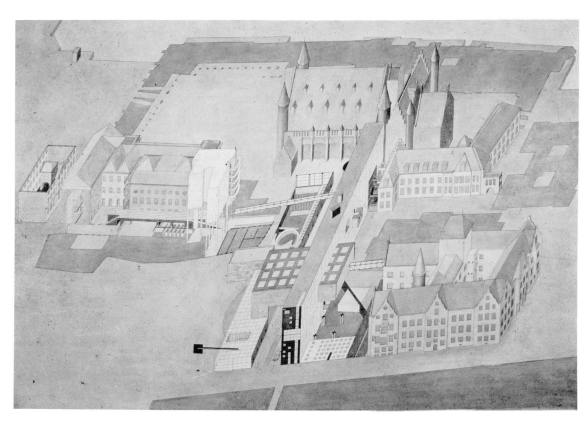

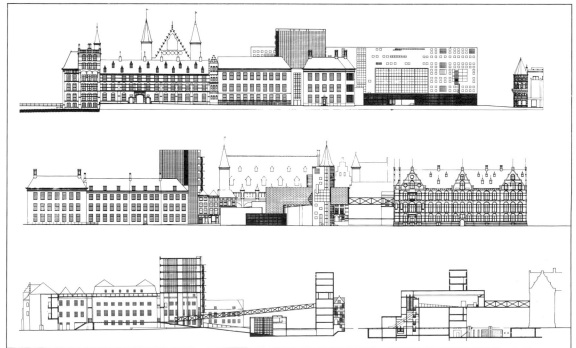

292. Hotel Sphinx, exploded axionometric of the Head, 1975.

293-294. Expansion of the parliament in The Hague, competition entry axionometric, sections and elevations.

doctrine would represent artificial and unacceptable obstructions in a process of continuous cultural transformation that is desirable.

Only through the concrete projection of these revisions, and their embodiment in tangible modernity, can the weight of the past be made tolerable.

The significance of these two projects is in the way past and modernity are related and made to coexist.

Otherwise, the wholesale desertion of the camp of utilitarian architecture opens an exhilarating prospect: that the field of modernity will be abandoned to create a condition where newness will be rare, invention unusual, imagination shocking, interpretation subversive, and modernity once more exotic... an era of a new sobriety.

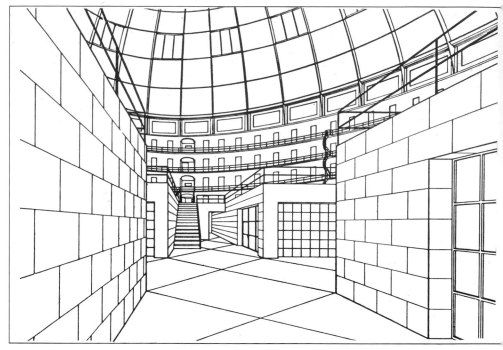

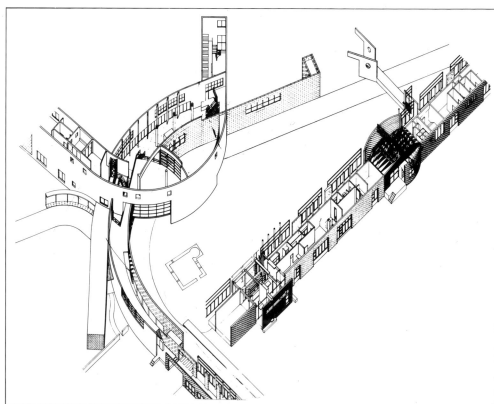

Luxembourg 1946.
Worked with James Stirling from '68 to '70, and with Joseph P. Kleihues from '71 to '73.
He taught from '73 to '77 at the Architectural Association of London; Cornell University (Ithaca, N.Y.); the Royal College of Art of London and Princeton University.
Edited the books *J. Stirling. Building and Projects* (Stuttgart, 1974) and *Rational Architecture* (Brussels, 1978).
He lives and works in London.

*The reconstruction of the European city
or the anti-industrial resistance as a global project*
The fact that I could persuade Maurice Culot and his assistants to display their work in the exhibition space, which was put at my disposal by the Bienhale takes on a significance which surpasses personal friendship at the limits of any international côterie. We wish to draw the attention to the existence of a movement of convergence of theoretical reflection on a European level. We wish to define and explain further a movement in which intellectuals who engage in the urban struggles at a daily level and others who develop a project for the city on the basis of a personal reflection on architecture and on the city, pursue pedagogical work in the context of social and cultural preoccupations, outside any spirit of artistic avant-garde. This convergence has nothing in common with the publicity campaign orchestrated yesterday by the C.I.A.M. Instead it formulates the means necessary to escape the trap of fragmentation (which all avant-garde experiments have consciously or unconsciously in common in an industrial civilization) t situates itself within the framework of a specific project for urban democracy.
My own work in the last ten years has been to elaborate a global strategy for the reconstruction of the European city.
I am therefore not interested in methods of construction or of planning, which will tomorrow be revolutionized by innovations of production or marketing. I am not interested in those ideas which are consumable like industrial gadgets. I am above all not interested in a critique which is without a project, or a historiography which is without a vision.
The kind of order I am interested in is not the one which compels people to change their habits according to the interests of insurance companies, or fire brigade unions; the production techniques I am nterested in are not the ones which will be thrown overboard every five years by innovations on the building market or of any artistic avant-garde.
The destructions which now ravage the European cities cannot be stopped by fragmented interventions. Only a global project for reconstruction could in time make it possible to save a millennial culture of cities. For the moment I see no progress anywhere, and the current enthusiasm for architecture (as demonstrated by an increasing number of exhibitions, publications, schools, etc.) by its very fragmentary and episodical nature, ignores or even glorifies the holocaust which is ravaging our cities.
Maurice Culot had warned me several years ago that a responsible architect cannot possibly build today. I then had to experience myself that involvement in fragmentary battles to build this or that is

not only useless but distracts from the most urgent work, which is the one of the reconstruction of a global theory.
Considering the magnitude of destruction and the theoretical confusion which agitates the most enlightened professionals I understood that building today can only mean a greater or smaller degree of collaboration in this process of self-destruction of civilized society.
We find ourselves in a war and a movement of resistance cannot be organised in the battlefield. Strategic thinking is not carried forward in the trenches.
If a project of resistance is to have any chance, then it needs a rigorous strategy and the intimate knowledge of all those tactical movements which can bring about victory. This is the work in which I am engaged.
My theoretical work consists of a written and a drawn part. What is written, is always demonstrated in the drawings and what I draw always finds its explanation and foundation in written texts.
Each project that I have done is a manifesto about a particular tactic of reconstruction, either on the scale of architecture and building, or on the scale of the entire city. All these projects lead me to formulate very simple theses which are the basis of all reconstruction work.
A city can only be reconstructed in the form of streets, squares and urban quarters.
The quarters must integrate all functions of urban life in areas which cannot exceed 35 ha and 15,000 inhabitants.
The streets and squares must present a familiar character.
Their measures and proportions must be those of the best and most beautiful pre-industrial cities.
Simplicity must be the goal of a however complex urban topography.

The city must be articulated into public and domestic spaces.
Monuments and urban fabric,
Classical architecture and vernacular building,
squares and streets.
And in that hierarchy.
The projects done at the Archives d'Architecture Moderne under the direction of Maurice Culot show that these theses are fully applicable in the day-to-day urban struggles and that it is possible to ally the great majority of the citizens around a "common sense" which is not dictated by industrial mass-media but which is still profoundly rooted in the surviving traces and the overwhelming memory of the pre-industrial European cities.

297-302. Project for the reconstruction of the city of Bremen (West Germany), 1980: riverfront; general view; view of the music house; the new St. Martini Square; the promenade along the Weser; St. Martini Square.

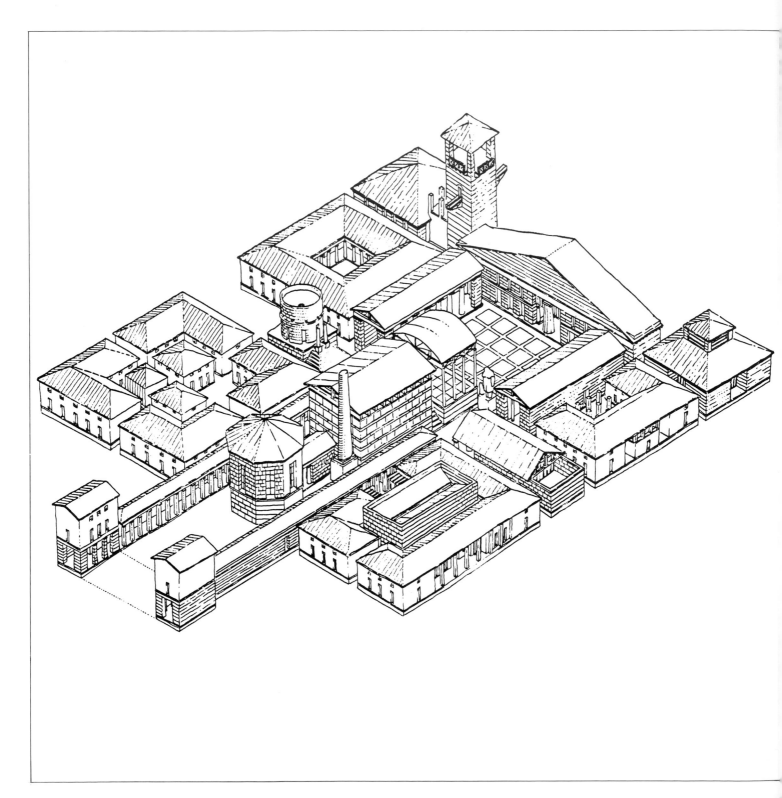

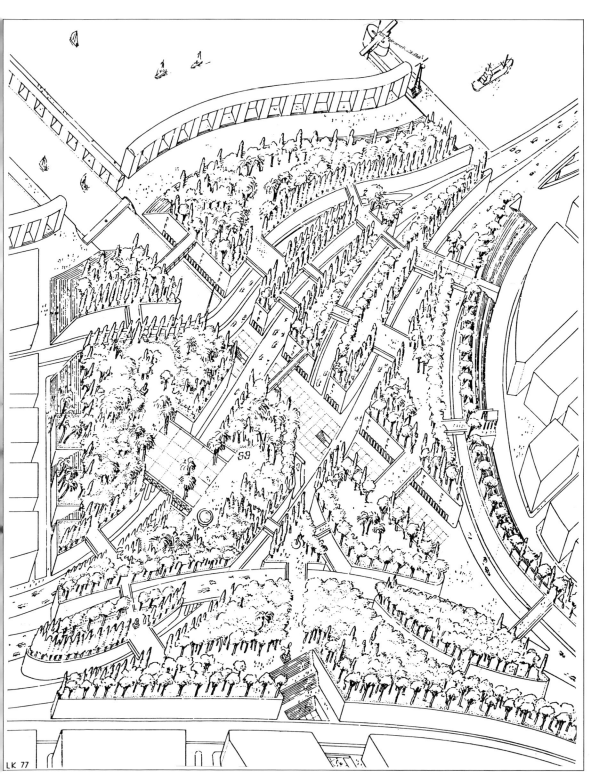

304. Project for Athens-Piraeus motorway intersection and the two north and south quarters, Athens (Greece): general overhead view of the project which restores the green space in the motorway intersections to the city.

LK 77

Eugene Kupper

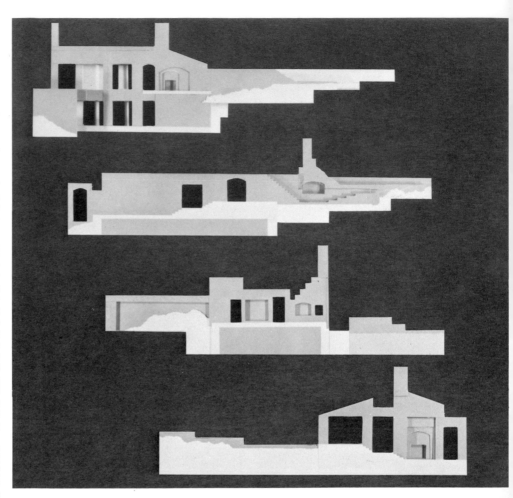

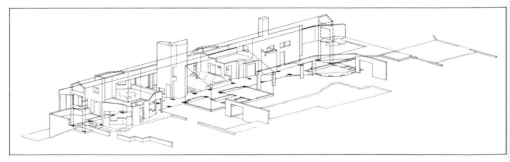

Oakland (Cal. - USA) 1939.
Took part in the "Works" studio with Craig Hodgetts, Peter De-Bretteville and Keith Godard. At present is working professionally in Los Angeles.
He has been Associate Professor of Architecture and Urban Design at UCLA since 1969.

The history of culture is written in architecture, substantiated in always repeated, always changing forms. The colonnade that reciprocated our presence projects us into its own realm. The realm of the colonnade is a cultural idea, rendered in physical form. The realms of room and street are not just invented design solutions, they are embodiments of a continuous discourse within architecture. The City of Towers appropriates the elevator and steel cage construction, and architecture elicits a richer cultural history — Manhattan. The stable structure of the architectural concept invites the interpretive possibility of the architectural medium.

The historical presence of the past immerses us in the form and sense of human events. Style and character — marks by which we define social attitudes and ethical motives — are accentuated by historical awareness. We fill our imagination with images of societies distant or past; overwhelmed by nostalgia, we embrace or reject those images as appropriate to the making of our world. History is the record of powerful emotions and astonishing deeds. With skill of narration and editorial juxtaposition, the historian can stop us in our tracks and cause us to evaluate all of our present actions and decisions in the light of the age of the Cathedral Builders of Christian Piety or the era of Dazzling Innovation and Finesse by which the Baroque is known to us. History is a method that is assured of frustrating our desire, even as it kindles it.

The archetypal presence of the past is the irreducible core of architecture. When we build house and city we summarize the existence and meaning of the past in that place. To make the smallest action within the realm of architecture is to uncover the vital relationships between Place, Culture, and Architectural Work. Historical dialogue is inevitable, but to make a line on the ground — axial or surrounding — is a primordial act, beginning in the unconscious, exposed to the rhetorical variations of millenia, and always new. The history of architecture should speak of the geneology of that line and its projection into wall, roof, street and city. The gathering places of public life and the tranquil protections for individual reverie are born of these basic existential and architectural forms. Landscape and city form rely upon where our walls are placed — what is outside and what is inside. The archetypal presence of wall to floor, floor to city, is the reference within which history is granted the replenished vigor of the immediate.

305. Project for Washburn House, Berkeley (Cal.), 1979: studies for the walls.

306-307. Project for Nilsson House, 1976-1979: studies of the colonnades and the walls.

Jean-Marc Lamuniere

Rome 1925.
Graduated in Architecture from the Faculty of Architecture of Florence University in 1951.
Has had a studio in Geneva since 1953.
Joined up in 1980 with Gérard Kupper, George van Bogaert, Alain Poncet and Patrick Schwarz.
Has been Professor of Theory and Planning in Architecture and Urban Studies at the Federal Polytechnic of Lausanne (Department of Architecture) since 1973, and since 1971 he has taught "Analysis of the Urban Environment" at the School of Architecture of Geneva University.

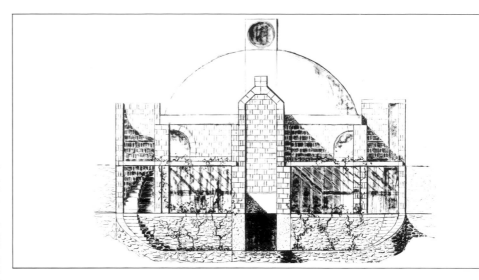

If architectural history is to be used again as an essential part of the architectural composition process, one must be conscious of all the "language breaks" the Modern Movement has provoked, with the perfidy of its innocence, in the collective memory of our communities. These ruptures were not only felt by the general public but, by a rightful movement of pendulum, by the architect himself. The latter, presumably freed from the heavy paternity of history, has lost the control of formal signs and meanings. His work has thus emptied itself of the references that were most necessary for a fruitful production of meaning if not of those ambitious and culturalistic connotations applied to modern painting and sculpture. In this context we might, as a hypothesis, suggest that modern architecture has sometimes acted as true metalinguistics for the "happy few" and, most frequently, like a mere and vulgar denotative system, without ever denouncing new (and old) processes, imposed by the industrial age, for the production and use of its privileged spaces.

But architectural history, taken in fragments or as a whole, could not possibly, nowadays, be manipulated by a rational methodology, unless one aims towards a reduction of the role of the critic-historian or else simply towards a new nemesis. On one hand architectural history must recompose itself and thus again be handled (aside from the contents and the production of architecture) on the systems of significance from which it originally came and which it re-creates through renewed reading.

On the other hand, the diachrony: "Formal expression-historical determinism" is an entwining rather than overlapping relationship, leaving some spaces in-between as witnesses of the heavy permanence of form within the unconscious. "It is not the contents that are unconscious but rather the forms: in other words, it is the symbolic function itself "(Barthes)." Last, and above all, no history can ever equal the scope of living experience. The architect must feed more, as a natural process, on the sources of his own origins, of his own wanderings, the sources of his apprenticeship, of his own environment and of the environment he creates for the living of others (this reconquest of the notion of space dear to Portoghesi), as well as the sources of the "Other" through whom the desire for an architecture can exist. This desire being itself "articulated as a system of significance" (Lagan).

Architectural design represents the "desire of this object of desire" which is the space of the Other. And this desire is (rather more than by history) woven with the discontinuous and broken tales that

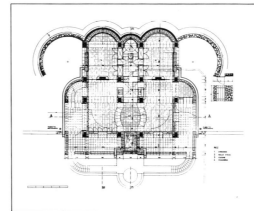

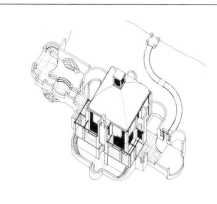

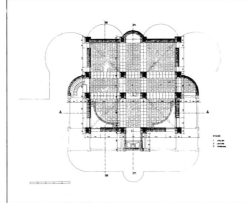

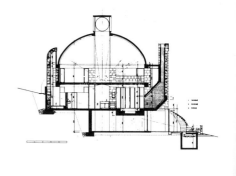

dream and memory associate "in absentia" (De Saussure) with the project, aside from the selective process, for the pleasure of one (The Author) and the enjoyment of the other. The new critical thought, dealing with the relationship between the

history of architecture and architectural design, has to go through an explicit process of these associative relations which have, since Delacroix determined that a work is, in itself, critic and critique, a work.

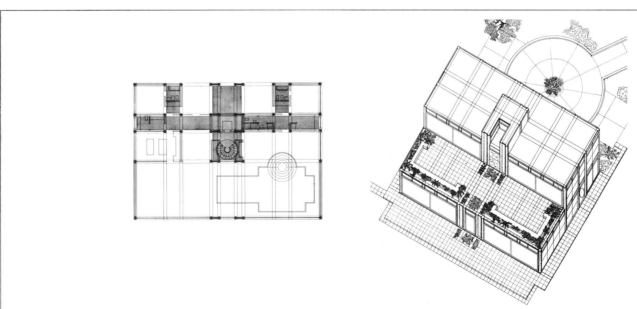

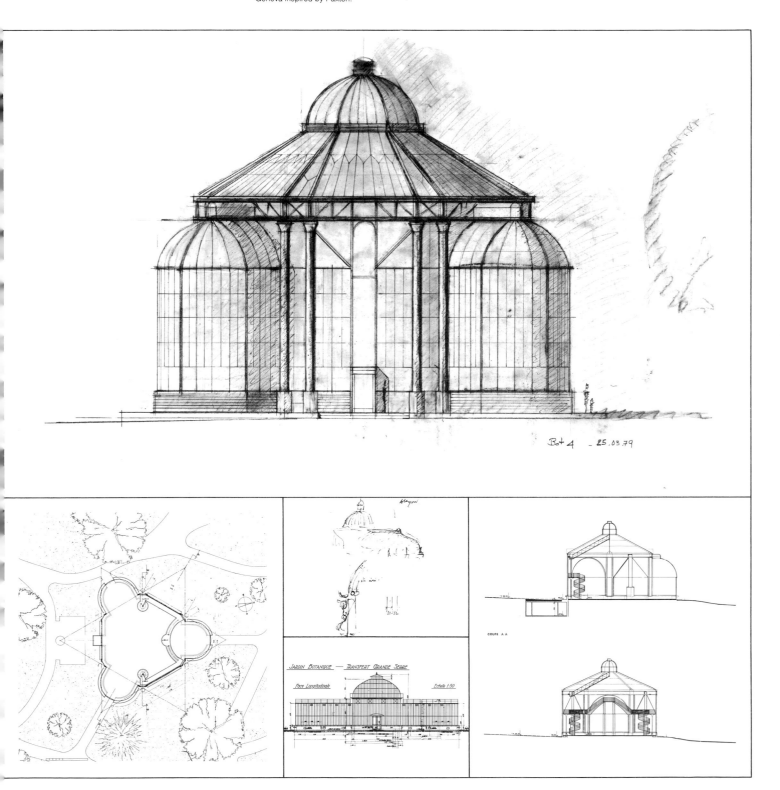

318-319. Project for a greenhouse in the Botanical Gardens of Geneva (Switzerland), 1979: elevation and ground floor plan.

320. Sketch by J. M. Lamunière: the Kibble greenhouse in Glasgow.

321. Elevation of the old greenhouse in the Botanical Gardens of Geneva inspired by Paxton.

322. Project for a greenhouse in the Botanical Gardens of Geneva: transversal sections.

Yves Lepere

Walhain (Belgium) 1942.
Degree at the High School of Architecture at Tournai and Master of Architecture at the University of Pennsylvania.
Teaches at the Università Cattolica and is Visiting Professor at the University of Pennsylvania.
He is professionally associated with Catherine Lagache and Joseph Polet.

Chez Palladio,
The window is formed by a roof, a gable,
a lintel, balusters... a threshold.
Each of these elements takes its form and weight
from mouldings, flutings and projections
of its own.
The sun's rays are picked up and
project shadows that reinforce
the compositional elements: thus
the roof, the gable, the mouldings, the balusters...
the threshold is emphasized by a succession
of lines that repeat the original form.
Well beyond justified or justifiable
practical or functional considerations,
the different components turn out to be enlarged.
The "window," normally considered
a "compositional" element, finds in itself
all the basic principles of the idea of "living:"
the window is decorated by emphasizing the details
that stimulate the very notion of "living,"
the window implicitly seeks to enrich
the idea of "living."
In it is contained that magic power of telling a tale
all on its own, almost without our knowing it.
It suggests that we build a world in the world
where past and present intermingle
in the instant that is experience.
In celebrating the occurence of the window,
Palladio is questioning.
In celebrating insistently an architectural element
he illuminates this perpetual present
by stimulating its latent potential.
And if the conditions change, the phenomenon
persists.

323. Drawings carrled our for brick walls.

324. Building with offices, boardrooms and conference halls for the Catholic University of Louvain at Louvain-la Neuve (Belgium), 1976.

Rodolfo Machado
Jorge Silvetti

Have worked together since 1969. Studio in Boston, Mass. USA.

Rodolfo Machado
Argentina 1942.
Degree in Architecture at the University of Buenos Aires in 1966.
Master of Architecture at the University of California, Berkeley, in 1969.
Has taught as an Assistant Professor at the University of Berkeley, Cal., and at Carnegie-Mellon University.
At present is Director of the Department of Architecture at the Rhode Island School of Design, where he teaches Architectural Theory and Planning.

Jorge Silvetti
Argentina 1942.
Degree in Architecture at the University of Buenos Aires in 1966.
Master of Architecture at the University of California, Berkeley, in 1969.
Has taught as an Assistant Professor at the University of Berkeley, Cal., and at Carnegie-Mellon University.
At present is Associate Professor of Architecture at the Graduate School of Design at Harvard University.

The current controversy about the "presence of the past" in architecture needs clarification, as there are many interpretations that confuse some current stylistic manifestations with more fundamental issues of what is the production of architecture.

All this controversy is related to figurative choices, where "the presence of the past" can be checked literally. However, most of these literal figurative changes resemble in tone and in modes and effects the typical avant-garde operation of "inversion" as an opposition to what had previously happened. As most of Modern Architecture's ideological tenets seemed to have been exhausted in the '60s, the continuity of the "modern" stand had to resort blatantly to history in order to assure continuity. These manifestations contain all the avant-garde ingredients; and as such they contain also its quick self-demise, as they soon become the prey of modern society's most peculiar trait: the consumption of symbols.

Against these literal, avant-garde operations, we would like to present a more solid premise. Rather than attempting a critique through inversion with its consequences of shock, controversy and alienation of both artist and public, and the assured final, quick collapse into kitsch, we would like to see a critique of the present state of architecture based on the more solid and general notions about the production of forms, the production of meaning. From this perspective, the idea of the "presence of the past" is at its foundations and it is an inevitable beginning: for we are what we know, and forms come from forms. The act of production is then, inevitably, one of transformation of the known, and it is only through this that mutations may occur, and eventual novelty result.

Our stand is then not "stylistic;" for better or worse, the present problems cannot be solved as a matter of style. We would like to discuss through our projects more fundamental principles, independent of style, against which architectural performance should be checked, a test that only history can substantiate. Thus the controversy about modern architecture is suspended, and whatever in it is valuable is incorporated into our own "historical resources."

26. "The steps of Providence," 1979: general lan.

327-328. "The steps of Providence," 1979: "Woods-Gerry Steps."

329-332. "The steps of Providence," 1979: façade, Waterman Street Entrance and the Pool, the Garden Steps, Frazier Terrace.

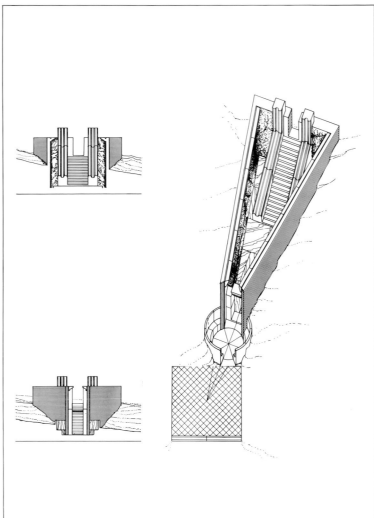

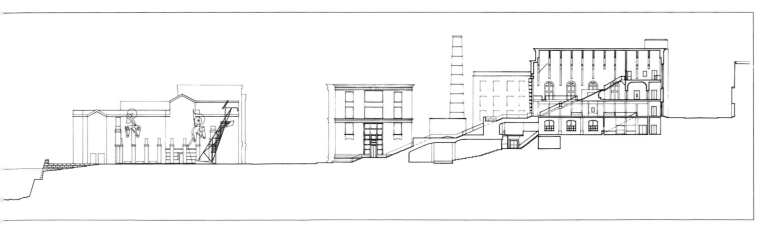

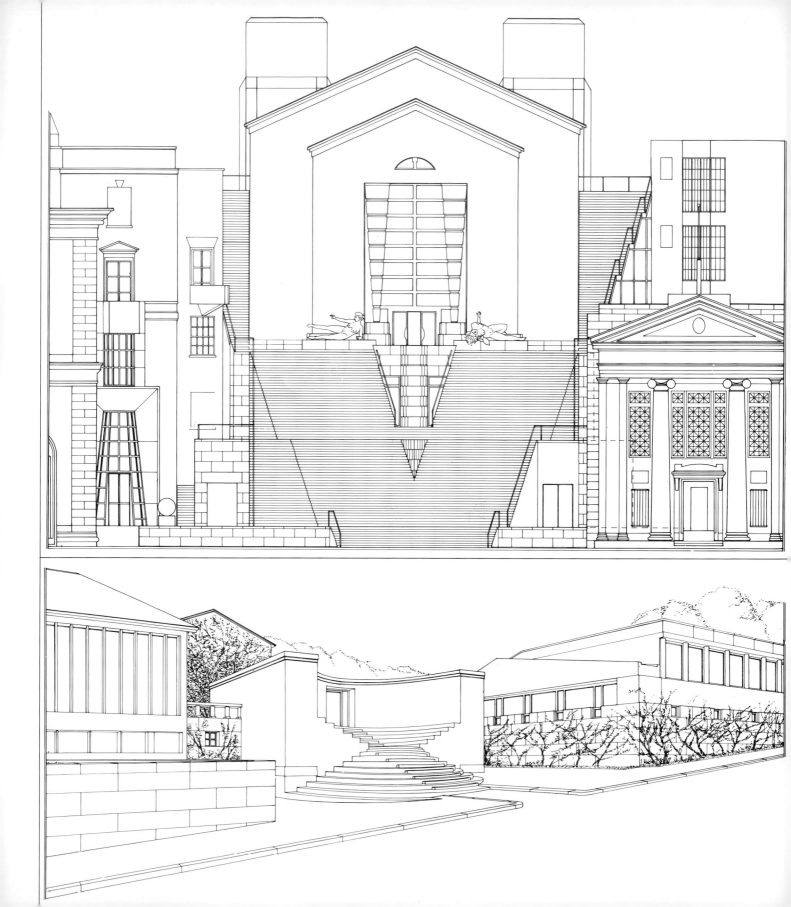

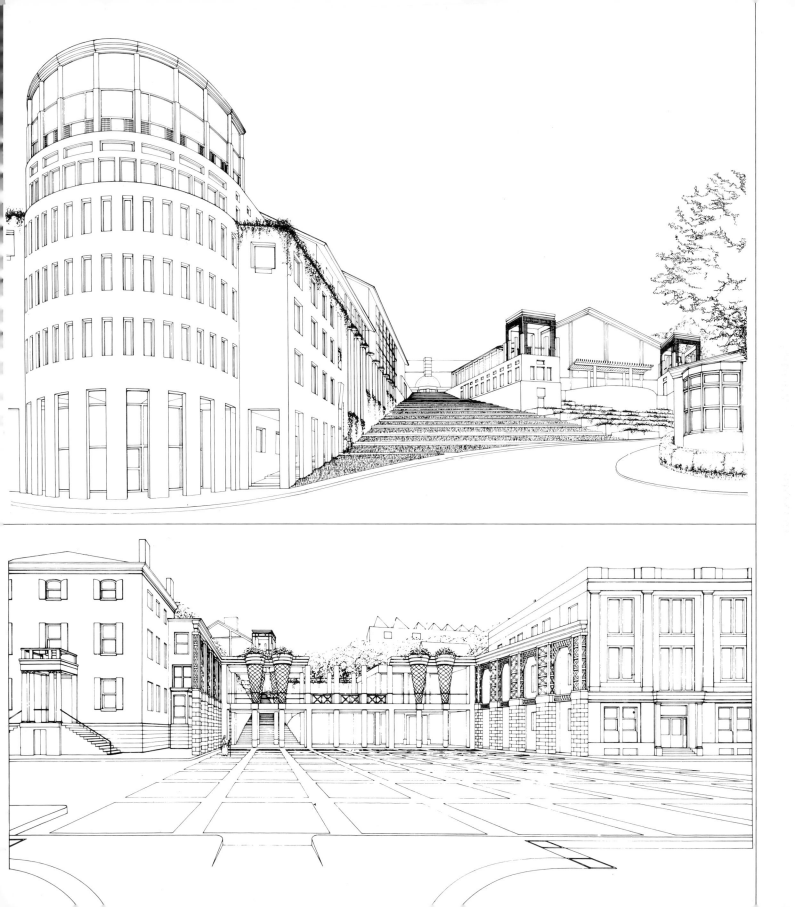

Fernando Montes

Quinteros (Chile) 1941.
Architect D.P.L.G. Lives and works in Paris.
After architectural studies in Chile and Germany, worked in Paris, and in Berlin with Sh. Woods and G. Candilis. Has taught Architecture since 1972, first at Strasbourg and then at the Ecole Supérieure des Beaux-Arts of Paris, in the Unité Pedagogique n. 6.
In 1980 he has been invited as a professor to the Royal College of Art in London and to the "Ecole pour la reconstruction de la Ville Européenne" in Brussels. He is the author of *La maison de verre*, Adita, G.A. Tokyo 1978 and *Mallet Stevens*, Archives de l'Architecture Moderne, 1980.

An Art Bureau in Venice

A tribute

Two months ago Roland Barthes died in an accident.
This project is dedicated to him. That is even more my intention seeing as how his works are one of its sources of direct inspiration.

A programme

An Art Bureau in Venice, i.e., a public setup destined to be used as a temporary place of work for artists of different disciplines, a well as a space for exhibitions of their products.

An intention

Over the centuries the Public Building has visibly been the subject par excellence for Architecture and, in every case, has caused the Architect to be sought after.
So it should not be surprising if it is admitted that the public building is what it is, on the condition that it should bear the expense of the social ritual. Thus Architecture and Culture come together naturally in the Public Building.
Nowadays we witness a double, alarming phenomenon, seeing as how the discrepancy between architecture and culture keeps on increasing. On one hand the public facilities, which by now are required to be the primary source of public buildings, are becoming ever more banal due to the lack of a developed social code, ending up, for better or for worse, in offices or shops.
On the other hand, the city, changing under the blows of modern architecture's bulldozers and savage expansion, appears less and less capable of supporting the dialogue between the public building and its urban framework.
In order to avoid "le degré zéro qui hurle et le chaos qui se déplace," as Ernest Bloch says, the public building must absolutely rediscover its means of expression alongside the reconstruction of public spaces like streets and squares.

A layout

In the preface to "Sade, Fourier, Loyola," Roland Barthes calls these three reformers "logothetes" — founders of a language.
It is not here a question of "natural" languages of communication, but of "artificial," circumstantial languages like that of architecture. Our authors resort to three similar operations to get there.
First operation: self-isolation. Sade shuts his libertines up in a castle or a convent; Fourier commands the decadence of libraries; Loyola demands a retreat.

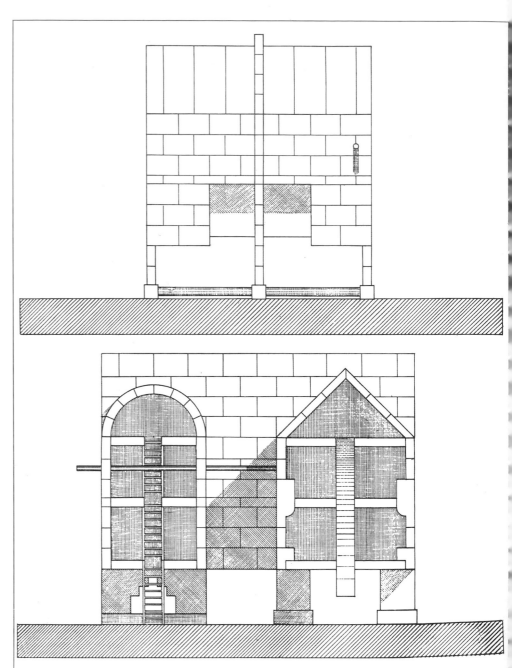

Second operation: articulation; Sade breaks pleasure down into positions, episodes, figures, etc.; Fourier divides man into 1620 fixed passions; Loyola prescribes exercises in 4 increasing phases.
Third operation: order. The erotic sequences, be they eudaemonistic or mystical, must refer to a superior order, one that is no longer syntax, but metre.
We shall revive these three authors' three proposals, which will be transformed for the occasion into:
1 - the definition of limits and passages
2 - the break-down of the phases of artistic work
3 - the linkage of sequences and the departure from fixed basic structures.

334. Project for twin houses at Saint-Louis, Haut-Rhin (France), 1978: perspective view, longitudinal and side elevations.

335-336. Project for an estate of 150 flats at Cergy Pontoise (France), 1978: general view of the model, longitudinal section and general plan.

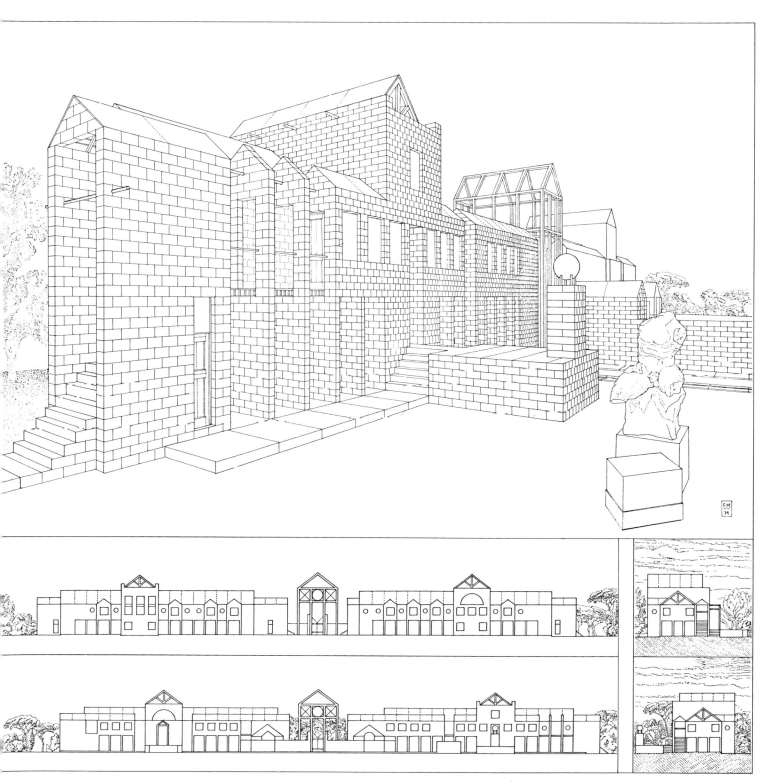

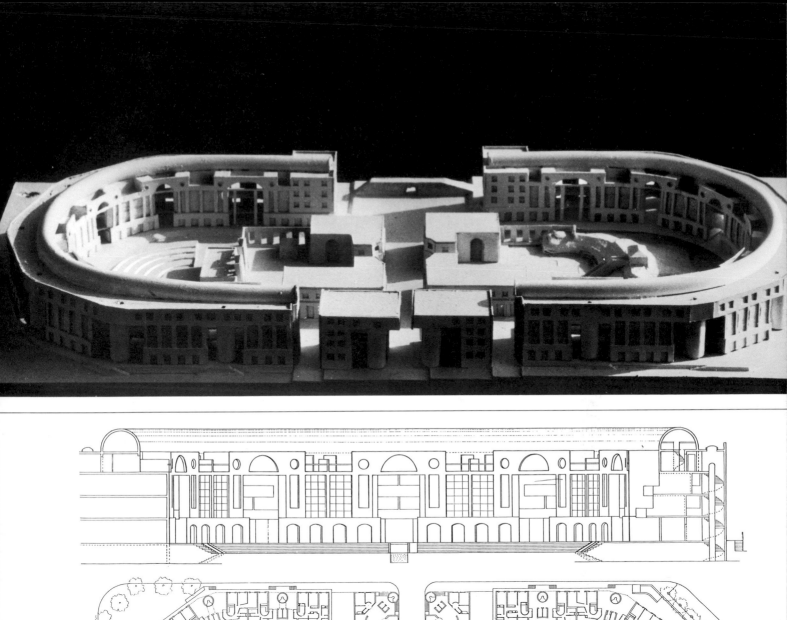
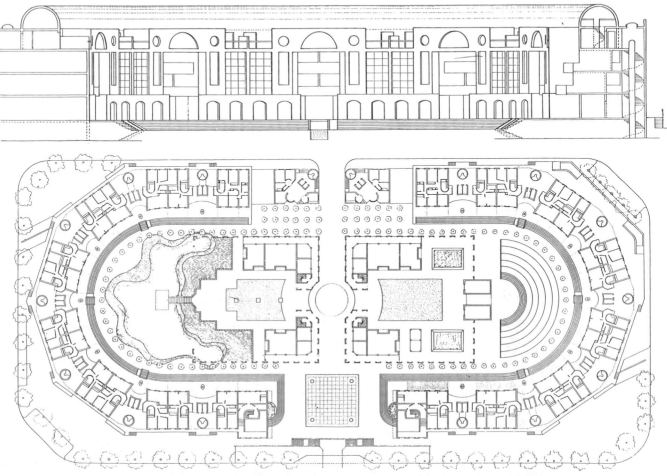

Bristol (Virginia - USA) 1939.
Master of Architecture at Yale University in 1963.
Has his studio at Atlanta, Georgia.
Has taught in the Universities of Auburn, Clemson, Louisiana and in the Georgia Institute of Technology.
Is at present Lecturer and Design Critic at the Mississippi State University.

Regional classicism exists throughout the southern United States drawing for inspiration from generations of European models, resulting in very few successful interpretations. Dealing with this dominant southern conservatism that is deeply rooted in historic references and romantic memories of imagery has had major impact on this office's product. The reality of architectural imagery understood and appreciated by the majority has also influenced the direction of many design initiatives.
Earlier in many projects of the '60s and early '70s, a real effort to deal with these southern images began with restoration/renovation projects; it continues today in the new projects.
Through most of these projects there has been a constant intent to create memory for the user through the use of image and spirit. In 1965, a project responding to the needs of children with varying degrees of mental handicaps, dealt with the abilities of these children to comprehend space and place; regional themes of architectural layforms dominated the massing and character of the Center. Aspects of imagery resulted in 1976 with the Newton House which has deliberate borrowings from Venturi and Rauch's Tucker House as well as less specific memories of the past... color, texture, scale and symbols.
Later projects and sketches continue to deal with this response to generations of architectural history and to a degree forms of classicism, as the exhibited sketches might indicate.

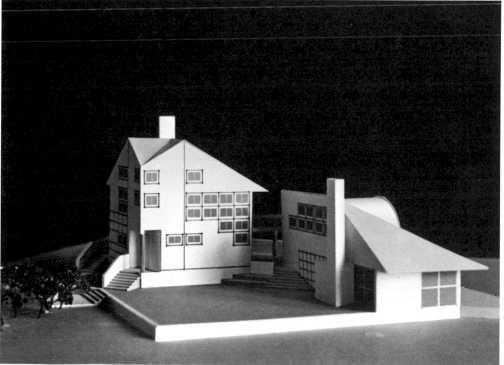

37. Project for Brewer House, Atlanta (Georgia), 1980: view of the model.
38. Project for Inman House, Highlands (N.C.), 1979: view of the model.
39. Newton House, Griffin (Ga.), 1979.

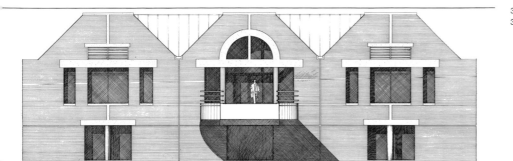

340. First study for the Dundee Mills offices, Griffin (Ga.), 1976.
341. Dundee Mills offices, Griffin (Ga.), 1976: elevation and view.

Charles W. Moore

Bachelor of Architecture at the University of Michigan in 1947.
He was Chairman of the Department of Architecture of the University
of California at Berkeley from 1962 to 1965; Chairman at Yale
University from 1965 to 1969 and Dean there from 1969 to 1971.
He was Professor at Yale University from 1971 to 1974 and has
been so since 1974 at U.C.L.A.
Up till 1965 he worked professionally in association with D. Lyndon,
W. Turnbull, D. Whitaker; from 1965 to 1970 with W. Turnbull and
from 1970 to 1975 was the sole head of Moore Associates. Since
1975 he has been head of Moore Crover Harper.

"The past" lies in everyone's memory and imagination. It is the places we have visited or lived in or
read about or imagined. For decades we have
been told that the normal urgent human interest in
all this is "nostalgia," a rather cheap emotion that
has no place in architecture, which must purge
itself of all that, to become a formal philosophical
"statement" by the architect, and that if the possible
inhabitants of the architecture do not respond to
either its "rational" or its "functional" qualities, then
we architects will soon commence their
"education" so they indeed eventually want what
we are providing.

That presumption, mercifully, is collapsing. There is
finally stirring the realization that buildings are
brought alive by the investment of human care and
energy and love and that to have enough of all
these the buildings need to be able to receive the
investment not just of their architects, but of
everybody else concerned, too, especially their inhabitants. Buildings thus energized are not going to
be designed in private by an architect communing
with himself; they will be given their shape by him
(or her) allright — that is a learned capacity. But
their images, and direction, and content will have to
come mostly from people's memories and imagina-
tions and will therefore embrace the Past, individual
and collective, historic and imaginary. Buildings
cannot any longer stand free of human energies
and recall: they must absorb and embody them.

342. Competion entry for Best. Supermarkets, detail of "The forest."

343. Barn in Maryland, 1979.

344. Housing for the Armed Forces Reserve Center, Norwich
(Conn.), 1978.

242

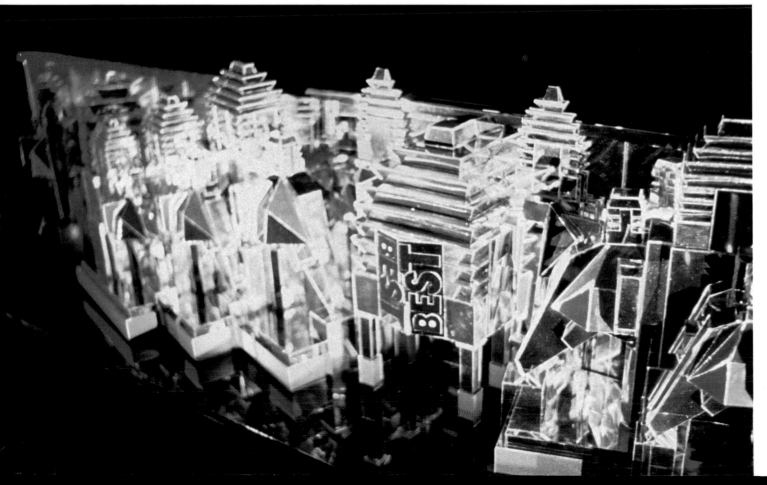

349-350. "Piazza d'Italia," New Orleans (Lou.), 1975-1978.
351. Rodes House, Los Angeles (Cal.), 1979.
352. House in South Carolina, 1980.

Monta Mozuna (Kikoh)

353. Heaven phase: T House, Wakayama (Japan), 1976.
354-355. Zen Temple, Eisho-Ji, Tokyo (Japan), 1979: general view interior view.
356. Mirror-Hall, Y House, Saitama (Japan), 1980.

Okkaidd, Kushiro City (Japan) 1941.
Studied at Kobe University, where he was also a professor from 1965 to 1977.
He has been head of the Monta Mozuna Kikoh Architects Studio in Tokyo since 1977.

The seven messages of Amitabha to Maitreya
An idea of mankind has created the cosmic architecture that has evolved since the time, four billion, thirty million years ago, when Amitabha, whose teachings can still be heard today, entered Nirvana, and will continue to evolve until the reincarnation of Maitreya to rescue mankind, forty-six billion, seventy million years later.

Amitabha's deep meditation and Maitreya's power of actualization result in the materialization of the spirit, or essence; the Energy of ideation of the universe's invisible structures become world images of the columns sustaining the Earth, a myriad stars, the planeto-terrestrial globe, the world's platform, the dome of the skies and a map of the starred heavens. It can thus be said that architecture possesses certain mythological elements, albeit as undercurrents, borrowed from the Earth's primitive ocean, global eruptions, the moon's attraction, the sun's combustion, the planetary system, a knowledge of the orientation of the stars. One may want to recall Eliade's and Semper's four architectural elements.

Rather than saying the correspondence between architecture and the cosmos originates from the memory layer in mankind's braincell, one might say it results from synopsis send-outs on the part of both of them.

Obviously, as the image of the universe changes, so does that of architecture. There is hardly any need to cite, as examples, the Platonian universe of the Renaissance or the Baroque elliptical universe. Leaving aside the question of Utopia and anti-Utopia, if Vitruvius, Plato, Lao-tzu, Kūkai, Alberti, St. Ignatius, the priests Genshin, Campanella, Garnier, and Le Corbusier have felt the influence on mankind's brain cell of Amitabha's faculty of ideation and Maitreya's power of actualization, then there should be no need to deny the same for the architect megalomaniac, Monta Mozuna.

The seven new messages of architecture's cosmology, made up of the universe, the body and architecture, are derived from the sixteen laws of meditation from Amitabha's Land of Perfect Bliss, taken from the Kanmuryojū sutra.

The first message (Heaven and Earth):
It is the topological space of Heaven and Earth, stemming from the fourth meditation of the Kanmuryojū sutra, the conceptualization of Mother Earth.

The second message (Mirror Images):
According to the Kagenkyo, the universe is comparable to an infinite number of worlds resulting from a myriad self-reflections in an unlimited number of mirrors. It is Amitabha himself.

The third message (Mandala):
It also derives from Amitabha's seventh meditation, the Meditation on the suigyoku, according to which the body, the spirit and architecture constitute the myriad layers of the nested universe. They are, in a word, the mandalas of the Taizo world.

The fourth message (The Cosmic Heritage):
Nebulae and planets constitute the cosmic heritage; theyu are the universe's consciousness.

The fifth message (Yin and Yang):
Often mentioned in the sacred Buddhist scriptures, the Yin-Yang universe is the medium through which Amitabha transmits his messages to Maitreya.

The sixth message (Effect):

It is a symbolic structure of a conception of urba architecture derived from Amitabha's meditation the lotus position.

The seventh message (The Universal Ovum Ovoid):
It is the beginning of a new world, with new li coming forth, constituting the memory for th future; it is the manifestation of Maitreya.

24

Gerd Neumann

Berlin 1935.
Graduated in 1961 from the Technische Universität of Berlin.
He was Assistant Professor at the same university in 1964-1965.
Lives and works in Berlin.

Thing-Myths - a second dimension of history
Let's not talk about a new conception of history. We can't rely on it. Let us rather think about experiencing the loss of history in the products of the Modern Movement when we try to understand our new historicism.
Thesis:
Most of us are conscious of history as a series of epochal events.
More subconsciously, however, we experience a second, more mythical dimension of history in objects, where things not only "have a history" but also "are history." Habitual use tends to concentrate historicity in things, to preserve their historical character in forms: thing-myths, in which certainty and familiarity are condensed into the quality we also know as "home." We feel the loss of this past in the objects more keenly than the forgetting or the loss of the historic bygones.
Hence the yearning for the ancient, the traditional and time-honoured forms.
Hence the plea for continuity and historical identity.
Hence also the rush for substitutes and the revelling in museum consumption.
However, behind this there still remains the vital need for conservation: not mere conservative preservation but the "re-erection of the past in the present," a creative nurturing. To preserve creatively in such a manner is, however, only possible in the interpenetration of "renewal" and "innovation." Only within this dialectic of "imitation" and "invention" (mimesis and fiction) can we grasp genuine "architectural poetry" (or: "poetics of space").
This approach releases the qualitative assessment of architectural form from the narrowness of a simple functional-aesthetic purposefulness as a purely environmental phenomenon for orientation, stimulation, identification, etc. Real aesthetics match the emotional quality of obvious beauty and adequacy with intelligible beauty. Consequently dealing with a historic inventory must necessarily lead to more than a merely formal "adaption;" for the old forms also confront us again with the old orders. Again and again they demand an answer to the question: What is architecture?
All this becomes especially evident when "building in a historic context" and here once again in the "self disclosure" of the house, the facade:
facades as mirrors of the peculiarities of a specific place, facades as an analogous interpretation of context, facades as elements of manifold whole, facades as manifest witnesses of assent or dissent.

I have selected several projects for the historic districts of Lübeck and Spandau to illustrate this. Lübeck, one of the large Hanseatic cities on the German Baltic coast, manifests continuity in its existent Gothic, Renaissance, Baroque and Classicist buildings. The traditional gable house determines the basic theme which in turn calls for a topical nowadays variation. Spandau, a once fortified town on the river Havel at the outskirts of Berlin, on the other hand has lost its identity through war damage and uncontrolled growth. Here we are confronted with the task of redetermining the spirit of the place and of harmonising structural discrepancies.

357-365. Studies for transformations in sequence of the people's house in the Grand Place, Brussels (Belgium), 1979.

360

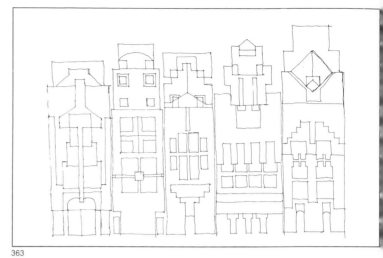

363

361

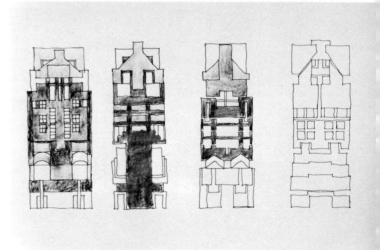

364

362

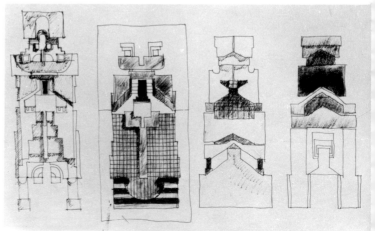

365

What I have presented here is a project for a competition and five degree theses by my students at the Faculty in Palermo. In the exhibition the projects have been inserted onto a map of the city at a scale of 1:2000.

First of all I must admit that this city has influenced me much more than I would have liked to believe up till now, naturally in its architecture, and especially in the people with whom I have worked and who are mentioned further on; however it is in its overall effect that this "maimed city" shows a virulence, which is softened elsewhere by compromises that are more toned down, while here the phenomena appear as signs of heightened dispute. It is thus to this city that I owe my present conviction about the misery of contemporary architecture, not so much (or to a lesser extent) because of the inconsistency and triviality of its forms as because it represents a systematic method of social and environmental destruction, so much so that ecologists should consider it a pollution no less dangerous than the others. Thanks to this city — seriously speaking and without the slightest sarcasm — I have not managed to take refuge in the peace of Total Conservation. I am indebted to it for having forced me to refine an "ars memoriae" like that of Scopas, the Greek poet, whom Cicero mentions, one that is elaborate enough to permit me to deal with what is buried beneath the fallen roofs.

Working in a disaster necessitates the refining of one's own skills.

Then I am more convinced than ever that the present conservation syndrome is derived from an unavowed conviction about the ugliness of modern buildings. So what we have to change is modern architecture and the only task left to our generation is to make this hope live.

So, while laying out these projects on the map of the city for the Biennale, we — Marcella Aprile, Adriana Bisconti, Franco Castagnetti, Roberto Collovà, Teresa La Rocca, Fabio Lombardo, myself, the students and my friend Italo Rota — realized that our proposals were realistic. The students merit particular applause in that they have brilliantly overcome the examination of forgetting the empty ideological indoctrination received at university and have given concrete proof of their ability to work at "rebuilding the city". Up till now we had emphasized the difficulty of doing the projects, joking with the students about the comments others would have made about the anti-modern aspects of their drawings, and we had savoured the pleasure of seeing them finished.

Now we are finally convinced that they have a political significance because of their realism and their attractive popularity.

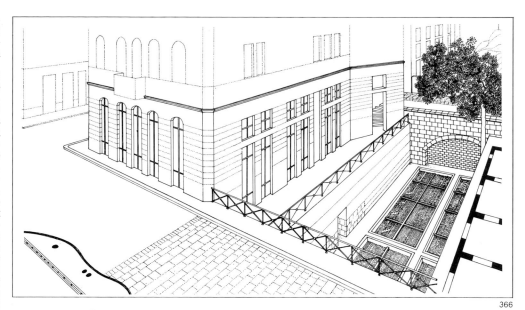

366

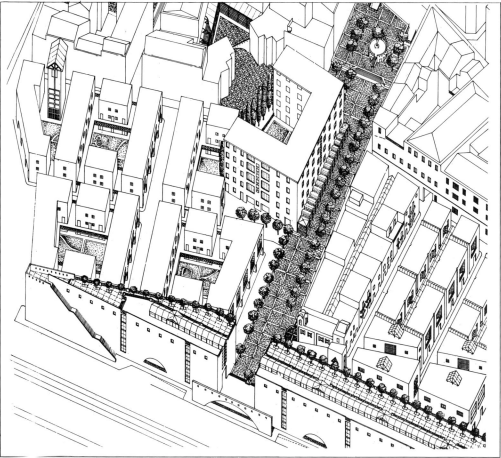

367

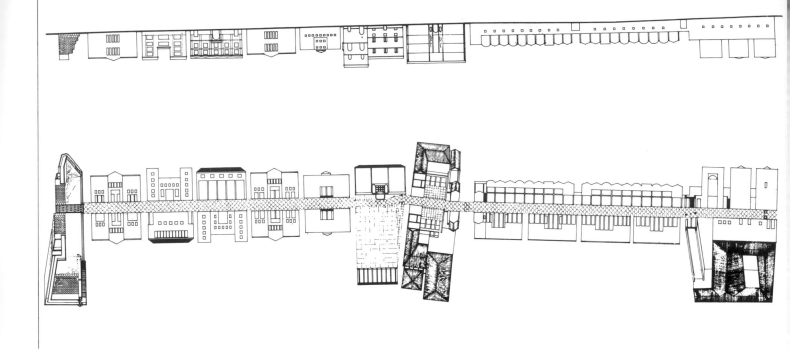

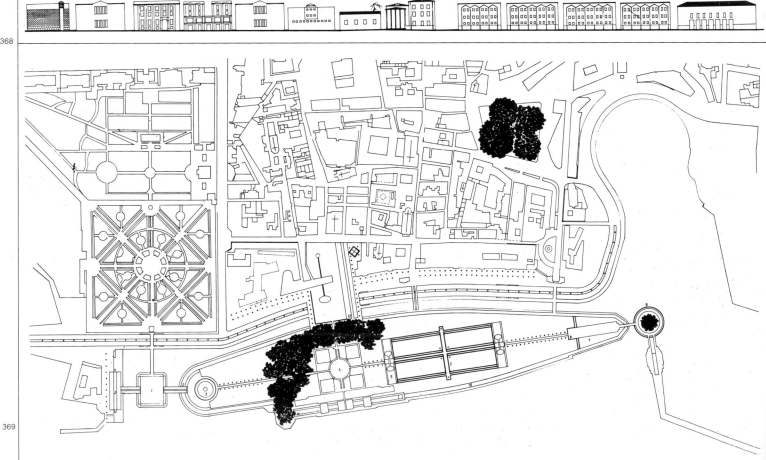

366. "Broadway": nine projects on the railway cutting, Palermo, 1979: view of the café with the tub of water (thesis by B. Asaro, A. Alì, A. Molino; supervisors R. Collovà, T. La Rocca). The projects along the cutting once occupied by the railway, which cuts diagonally across the orthogonal grid of the nineteenth-century city, propose the transformation of the first two floors and levels under the buildings lining the railway into space for the public.

367. "The Borgo in the city": reconstruction of a destroyed district (Castello S. Pietro), Palermo, 1979: overhead view near the Cala (thesis by P. Campana, P. Guzzone, F. Pernice; supervisor A. Bisconti).
All that is left in this district near the sea is ruins and the old outline of the roads. The reconstruction bears in mind the popular tradition of his district by proposing a framework whose functions are mixed with the characteristics of the traditional city.

368. "A sweet disembowelment": project for the renovation of thirteen blocks in via Alloro, Palermo, 1979: elevation of the internal street (thesis by G. Di Grigoli, I. Venti; supervisors M. Aprile, F. Castagnetti).
The cutting of a route that is almost an alleyway introduces a structural correction to the dimension and typology of these blocks, making it possible for them to be habitable again. There is a façade at both ends of the block.

369. "The island": a project for the sea front, Palermo, 1979: general plan (thesis by O. Amara; supervisor F. Lombardo).
What was once a fine place for a walk was transformed after the war into a tip for the rubble from the bombed city. This terrain won from the sea has had no history since then. The project proposes its transformation into an island for free time, separating it from the mainland with a canal dug at the edge of the ancient perimeter to the old city.

370. "Museum and surroundings": a project between the Cassaro and the Gran Cancelliere, Palermo, 1979: general overhead view (thesis by V. Graci, F. Jacopelli, C. Mannino, V. Ognibene; supervisor F. Lombardo). An empty space caused by the destruction of the last war has been left between two eighteenth-century buildings on one of the city's oldest streets. Other functions can be organized around the Museum which will enhance the proposal of repairing this important part of the oldest city centre.

371. "Urban villa": project for the competition for the IRFIS head office near Villa Lampedusa, Palermo, 1979: perspective view (Pierluigi Nicolin, Marcella Aprile, Adriana Bisconti, Roberto Collovà, Franco Castagnetti, Teresa La Rocca, Italo Rota). A competition requires the offices of a public bank to be put beside the Favorita park. Behind is the city built by Mafia speculation and in front is the Pellegrino mountain and the ruins of the Leopard villa. The project introduces a long wall between one element and the other — a taste of "Architecture at the limit..."

370

371

Richard B. Oliver

San Diego (Cal. - USA) 1942.
Master of Architecture at Yale University in 1967.
Lives and works in New York.
Has taught at the Universities of Austin and Los Angeles.

"What is learnt from others becomes really our own, sinks deep, and is never forgotten, nay, it is by seizing on this clue that we proceed forward, and get further and further in enlarging the principles and improving the practice of our art. Study, therefore, the great works of the great masters. Study.. those masters... consider them as models which you are to imitate, and at the same time as rivals with whom you are to contend."
(Sir Joshua Reynolds, *Discourses to the Students of the Royal Academy, 1769-1774*)
The projects which my associates and I have designed each attempt to be a specific piece of architecture, rather than a generalized architectural statement, particular to the place in which it is built and to the desires of the person(s) who commissioned the work.
Each project is based upon images which are important to us and to our clients. These images are focused on three issues: the type of project, the traditions of the place in which it is to be built, and the lessons of architectural history including the distant and the near past. The fabric of images for any project, therefore, is diverse and complex, historical and contemporary, formal and metaphorical. Because we incorporate these images as the project and our intuitions suggest, our work is eclectic. As a result, our work is quite varied, especially with regard to style.

GENERAL VIEWS

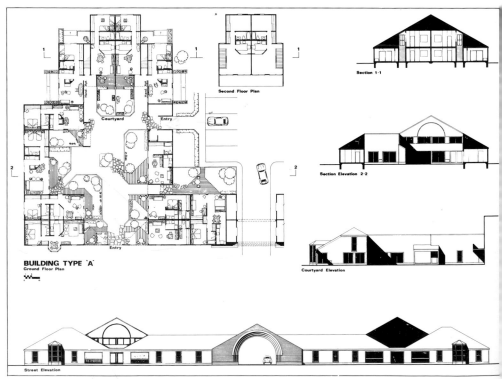

372-373. Competition for St. Joseph's Village, Long Island (N.Y.), 1976: perspective views; plan and sections.

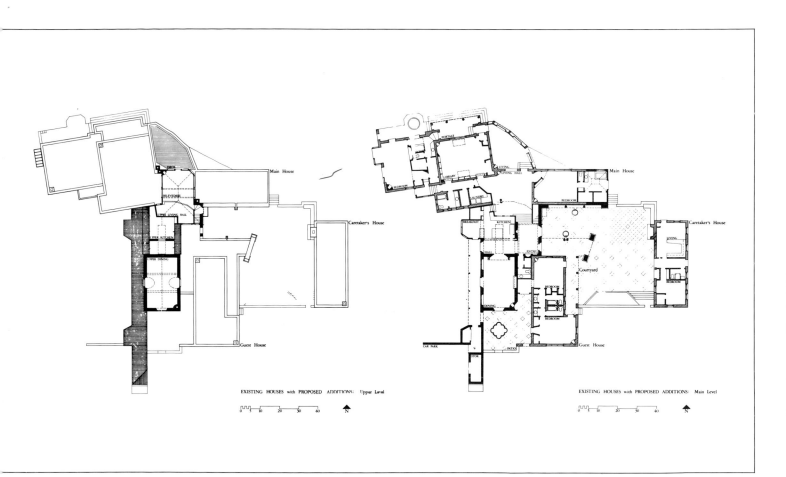

EXISTING HOUSES with PROPOSED ADDITIONS: Upper Level

0 5 10 20 30 40 N

EXISTING HOUSES with PROPOSED ADDITIONS: Main Level

0 5 10 20 30 40 N

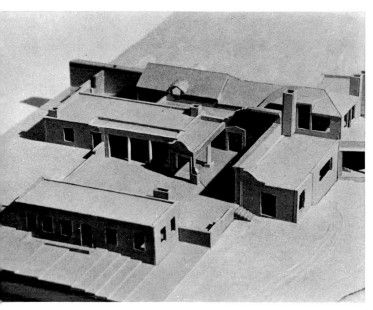

Luciano Patetta

377-378. National competition for the Theatre of Forlì, 1975-1978 general view of the model and longitudinal section.
379. Project for a villa at San Colombano al Lambro (Milan), 1976.
380. Project for the Diocesan Museum in the San Eustorgio complex in Milan, 1980: general elevation.

Milan 1935.
Graduated from Milan Polytechnic in 1961.
Has been Professor of History of Architecture at the Faculty of Architecture at Milan Polytechnic since 1971.
Wrote for *Controspazio* magazine from 1969 to 1976.
Has published many articles and is the author of *The Architecture of Eclecticism* (Milan, 1978).
Lives in Milan, where he has his studio.

These latest projects of mine, which seem rather nostalgic and retro, can probably be brought in line with the symptoms of general reflux that can now be observed almost everywhere.

Furthermore, one could check what their relevance, if any, is with regards to Post-Modernism. This is done by someone who understands Post-Modernism to be a movement (even if it is based only on the highly obvious refusal of the ideological dogma and the orthodoxy of the Modern Movement), rather than our complex, but "natural," present condition, whose contradictory theories must be compared by singling out the interesting and valuable contributions, and perhaps giving less weight to the neo-Neoclassical and metaphysical experiences, even though they are sometimes of a remarkable standard. It seems to me that right up to now the debate has carefully avoided this; instead it has alternated sarcasm with the banality of a check on the theoretical solidity of Post-Modernism and what is presumed to be its role in opposition.

My latest projects are the result of a crisis of a personal kind which I do not feel like comparing directly with others'.

While studying and interpreting in the last few years the historical development and the formation of the city of Milan, I ended up by finding I was less and less interested in theorizing about the city's construction, in classifying it and in conducting typological research. Even the language of the Modern Movement, which I had believed for a long time to be a logical, comprehensive and irreversible system, paled. Nowadays I look at the works of the great masters of the 20s and 30s as mere admirable expressions of an ideal beauty and of a stylistic tension that is sometimes extraordinary. What on the other hand now seem to me ever more worth reflecting on are the subjects that were overlooked or schematized by the Modern Movement: the seemingly casual muddle of different functions in the urban framework (such as the productive and the residential), the characterization of secondary elements both in the city and in its buildings; the originality of each solution, the characteristics of a rational approach that has not been reduced to the elementary, as can be found in some craftsmen's workshops and in rural buildings, the richness of detail, and so on. I have been promising myself for some time to face up with an open mind to the problems of decoration, colour and materials in construction. The squalor of our suburbs is based not only on the ludicrous urban setup, but also on the absence of "tone" in their architecture, something that can be compared with the absence of "timbre" in music: an impoverishment. It is not easy for me to give a precise definition of "tone" without getting back to some fragments still in existence of the suburbs of the last

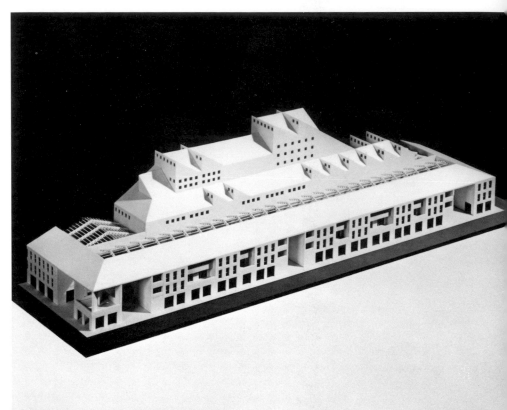

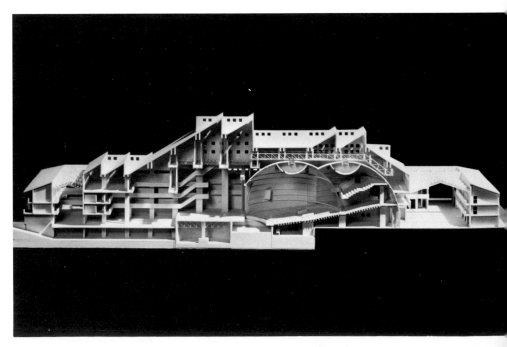

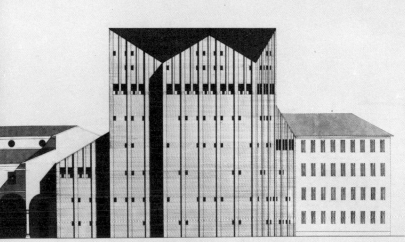

museo diocesano   corso di pt. ticinese

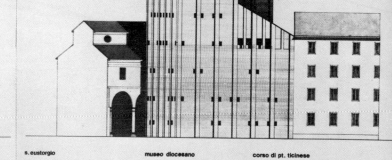

s. eustorgio   museo diocesano   corso di pt. ticinese

381. Project for the restructuring of a barrack block in Milan, 1980: dwellings and handicrafts workshops.

382-384. Project for double houses in Lombardy, 1980: elevations general plan.

century, to their streets and courtyards, to that way of conceiving architecture that did without fanfares, but did not neglect attributes such as creativity and characterization.

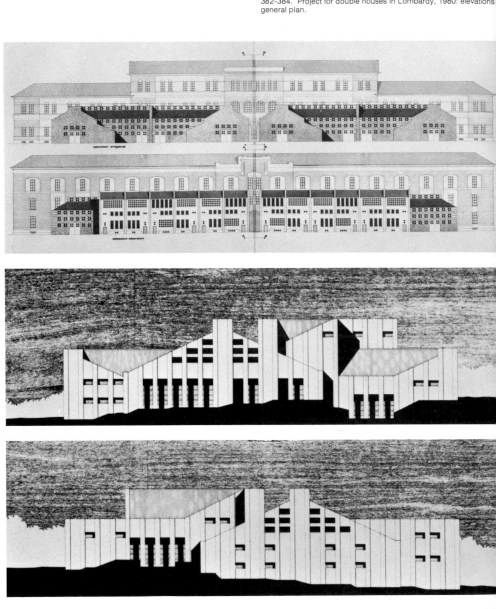

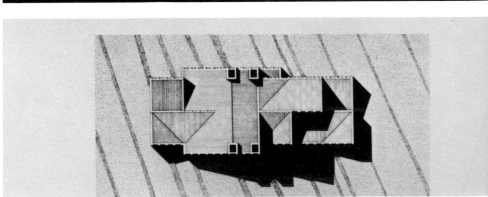

Herbert Pfeiffer

Stuttgart - Bad Connstatt 1935.
Got his diploma at the Tecnische Hoschschule of Stuttgart in 1961.
Has carried out teaching and planning activities at the University of
Dortmund since 1969. Since 1976 has also worked free-lance.

Reflections on my work

The starting point of my work is to be found in my critical attitude towards "International Style" and Utilitarianism, which are both the result of functonalism and "New Building."

Economic Empiricism or Utilitarianism did away with the autonomy of architecture and caused the question of architectural form to disappear completely behind the extra-architectural criteria of an optimalized functional frame.

The "International Style" led to an impoverishment of the architectural style, since local and regional characteristic features of architecture were given up in favour of this technocratic and functional conseption of architecture. The historic and regional relationship of architecture was given up.

From an economical point of view this did not even bring advantages, because the rationalized methods of craftsmanship are more favourable for the size of projects I am dealing with than industrial or semi-industrial construction.

Out of this conclusion I deduce the justification to try and realize in my work a historical and regional relationship.

As I live and work in the cultural landscape of the Province of Münster, a rural region in Northrhine-Westphalia, this relationship is quite clear.

It is a historically grown brick architecture of waterside castles, farmsteads and small rural towns with their magnificent environment of trees, avenues and canals, which determine the appearance of this landscape.

The outstanding historical architect of this area is the Baroque architect Johann Conrad Schlaun (1695 - 1773) who was active almost exclusively in the province of Münster. He succeeded in developing the traditional anonymous architecture to a certain perfection.

His example for many architects can be traced as far as into the thirties of this century. Then came the abrupt end of this continuous development. The lack of imagination of the post-war years, coupled with the diversity of materials offered by the building market threatens to destroy the specific characteristics of this landscape with its towns and farmsteads.

385-386. Kleffmann Farmhouse, Lüdinghausen-Westrup (West Germany), 1977-1979: drawing of south front, view from north.

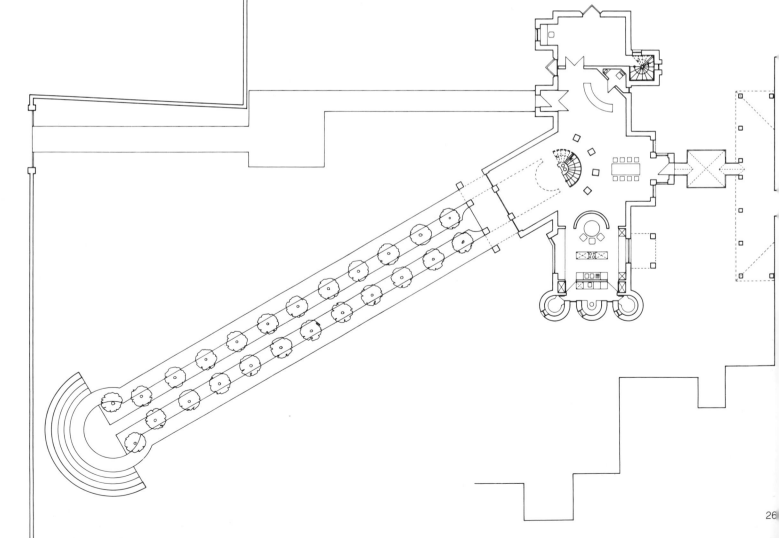

87-388. Project for Dalhoff House at Lüdinghausen (West
Germany), 1979: view of model from south and ground floor plan.

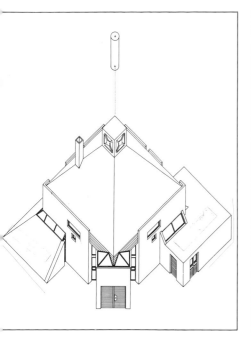

389-391. Pfeiffer House, Lüdinghausen (West Germany), 1975-
1979: axionometric view, central internal area, external view from
north.

Boris Podrecca

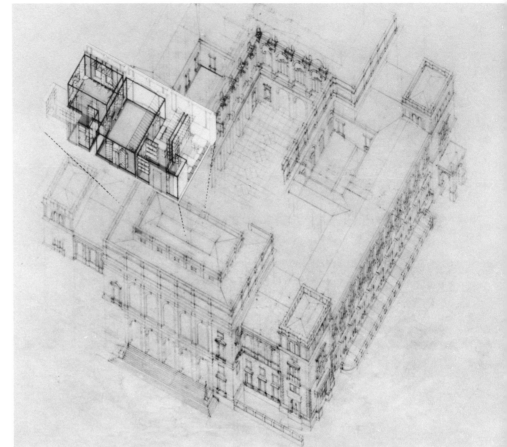

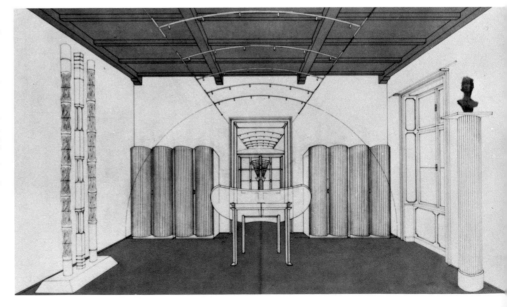

Belgrade (Yugoslavia) 1940.
Got his diploma at the Technische Hochschule in Vienna in 1968.
Taught at the University of Munich from 1974 to 1979 and has been teaching since then at the University of Vienna.
Lives and works in Vienna.

Architectural Needs

There are two ways of approach: one, the need of fulfilment (the purpose); the other, the need of desire — the inspiration, and I shall handle the latter. Here I make the difference between two fundamental basic themes, which prejudge the aspect of architecture.

The theme of the transmitted idea of building elements, which is constant and has no causal relation. The other theme of the situation, location, or the character of the environment, where one builds. The theme of the building idea has its roots in the artificial. The other one from the situation which is connected with its nature.

The building idea offers me a scale, how to handle and solve architectural problems. They are immanent in architecture and a priori present, however, lacking the immediate social implication. These elements do not just follow a rational ideology, or a physical or an applicable possibility, they are rather exchangeable, variable or can just exist out of a mood.

This is because their base is artificial, and independent if born out of an emotional or intellectual point of view. Were it not like that, the roundstone of the framework of the roof of Sakarra, which follows naturalistically the law of logic of the wooden round beam, they would have to be abolished in architecture.

If one element of this chain leaves its lawful place of its application (use), to change into a simple metaphorical or into a sensational component, then architecture only fulfills the necessities of the current taste.

Besides the physical structure and the image aspect of building, I am interested in the atmosphere a space generates, the non-physical components of architecture. The precisation of light, the "color" of light, the temperature and the balance of the space, etc. — are themes which have always been a part of the building, which from the rational point of view it is difficult to be turn into objects and have escaped into the partial and the circumference.

The theme of the situation (place or milieu) belongs to nature, and is — seen a posteriori — always adhoc. Only a subjective filter can offer a balance between the mechanism of these two groups of themes to be melted into the building work. In this instance architecture can be objectivised.

The more intensive the individual grip is, the further its influence will grow into a larger spectrum.

392. Alteration of a wing of the building by Teophil Hansen in the Ringstrasse for the "Oréal de Paris" office, Vienna, (Austria), 1979: general overhead view.

393. Alteration of the office of the Institute of Opinion Research, Vienna (Austria), 1979: perspective view of the central space.

394. Alteration of a wing of the building by Teophil Hansen in the Ringstrasse for the "Oréal de Paris" office, Vienna (Austria): view of the interior.

395-397. Alteration of the office of the Institute of Opinion Research, Vienna (Austria), 1979: internal views.

394

396

395

397

398. Four-family house, Acropoli (Cosenza), 1979-1980: general perspective and site views.

399. Housing project at Kiefersfelden (West Germany), 1980: perspective drawings and view.

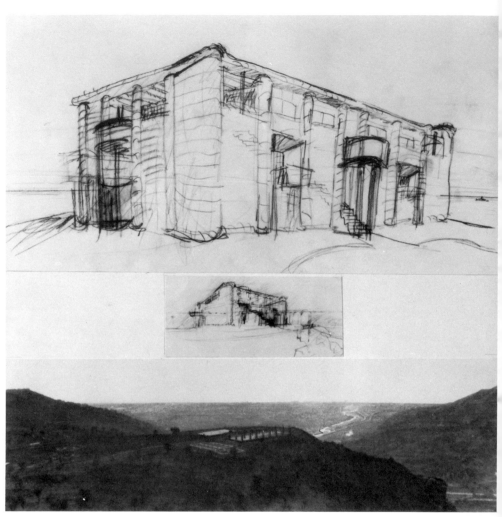

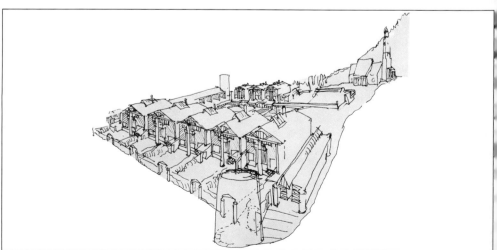

Franco Purini
Laura Thermes

They live in Rome, where they have had their studio since 1966.

Franco Purini
Isola del Liri (Frosinone) 1941.
Graduated from the Rome Faculty of Architecture in 1971. Has had a long career in planning in national and international competitions, at the same time developing research into design in architecture.
He is the Professor in charge of Architectural Composition at the Reggio Calabria State University Institute of Architecture.
Has written many articles, and the books *Luogo e progetto* (Rome, 1976), *Alcune forme della casa* (Rome, 1979), *L'architettura didattica* (Reggio Calabria, 1980).
He writes for *Controspazio* magazine.

Laura Thermes
Rome 1943.
Graduated from the Rome Faculty of Architecture in 1971.
Has taught in the courses of Architectural Composition at the Planning Institute of the Rome Faculty of Architecture.
Has taken part in many national and international competitions.
Writes for *Controspazio* magazine.

Rome-Venice, a single landscape.
Our project for a facade of the Strada Novissima basically constitutes a reflection of the cities of Venice and Rome considered as myths capable of multiplying their urban identity into infinite individual elements in possession of a common memory that often, and with much ambiguity, likes to transform itself with the desire of denying its very self, bedecking itself with the coquetry of not knowing 'where it is."

So we have superimposed them from their real locations in order to join up again somewhere imaginary where the interlacing of reality and memory would be explicit and the city's game of "hide and seek" would at least be more closely observed, if not unmasked.

This game obviously has some rules: the quote must be allusive, consisting in the revelation of the areas of superimposition in the two names evoked, that is, the dash that joins them rather than any similarity in their roots; the architectural elements chosen should be the least personalized ones exactly because only these carry the greatest number of indirect relationships; the references to historical architecture must be overcome by a sort of remote "antecedence" produced by models forced to recede into indistinctness by their extreme distance in time.

The existence of an interior to the facade, that is, its composition as a main front or a rear enclosing two small observatories, has after all permitted the simulation of the presence of a building, an isolated house inserted into a landscape capable of being the landscape common to the two cities.

The project reflects the fact that it has been planned by two people: in fact the number two appears in the composition as the figurative theme par excellence.

Only the tree trunk which organizes the main front seems to want to have a discussion verging between the resentful and the threatening on the "history of nature as a function of architecture:" but the roots and cut-off branches, as we know, make the most beautiful foundations and the most exquisite capitals. The trunk had better remember that...

Naturally what we are saying about this project is perhaps not the most real of the many possibilities:

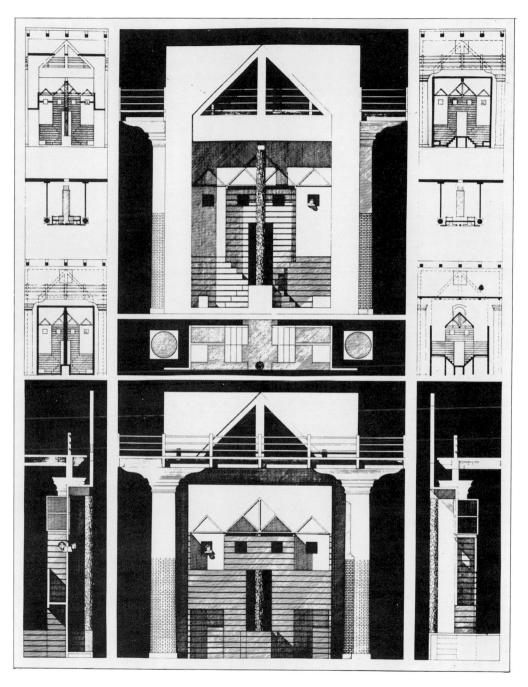

we are left with the satisfaction of having played pleasantly inside a consideration of architecture as "something that smiles."

405. Franco Purini: "After modern architecture," etching on zinc, 1977.

406

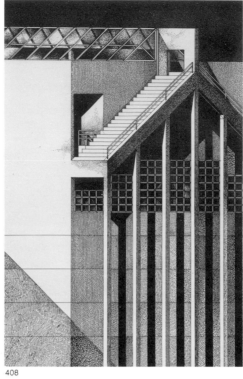

408

410

407

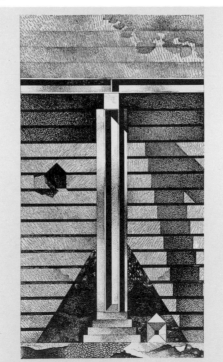

409

411

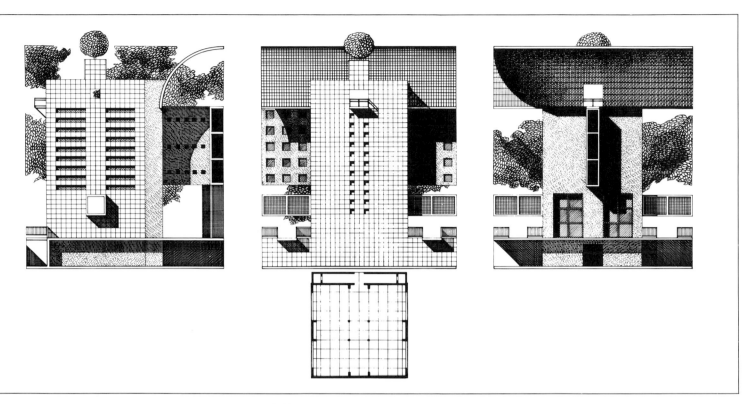

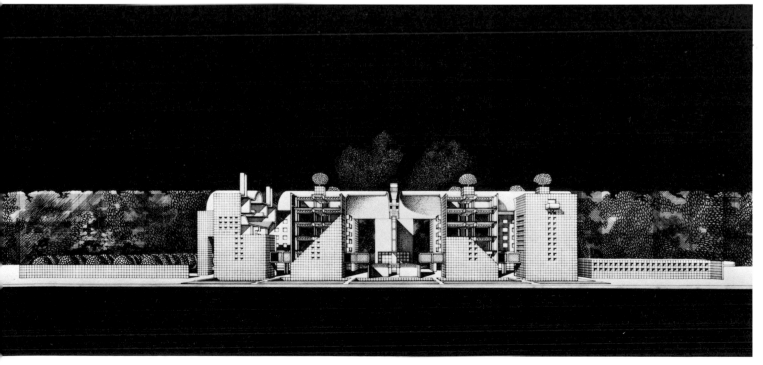

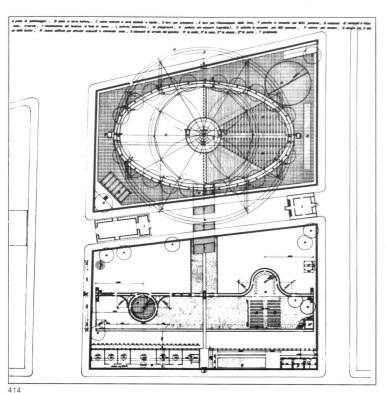

414

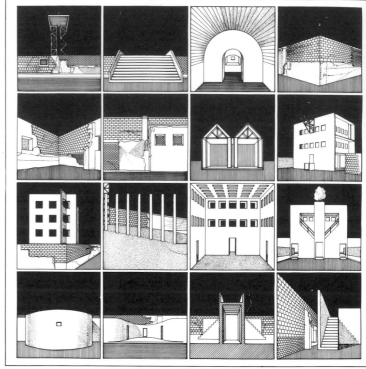

415

416

417

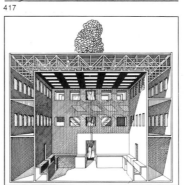

418

419

420

Bruno Reichlin
Fabio Reinhardt

Have worked together since 1970.

Bruno Reichlin
Lucerne 1941.
Got his diploma at the Federal Polytechnic School of Zurich in 1967.
Was assistant to the Chair of History of Architecture at the Faculty of
Florence from 1969 to 1970. Was assistant to Aldo Rossi at the
Zurich Polytechnic from 1972 to 1974.
At present does teaching and research at the Institute of the History
and Theory of Architecture at Zurich Polytechnic.

Fabio Reinhardt
Bellinzona, 1942
Got his diploma at the Federal Polytechnic School of Zurich in 1969.
Assistant to Aldo Rossi at the Zurich Polytechnic from 1972 to 1974;
assistant to Dolf Schnebli from 1974 to 1975; to Mario Campi from
1975 to 1977. Has taught Planning at the Technical High School of
Lugano-Trevano since 1974.

A Position

What is new must be produced by manipulating the system and an order that has been given us.
In used things the "bricoleur" notices the presence of a silent interlocutor, an accomplice.
Secrecy and richness portend behind what has already been done.
The "bricoleur" selects, fixes and composes; he plays around cunningly with the limits of the imagination, with predilections and phobias — sometimes blindness helps to get the work accomplished as much as the certainty of the guiding idea.
What has already been done resists — the technician's trained eye discovers the connections and distinguishes the pieces.
Each piece has values that should be taken more or less into account — an anomalous knowledge is put into action: Bouvarque and Tebusco are carried away in the vortexes of meaning.

A Condition

Visiting the museum, handling beloved objects.
Living in the reverberation of acquired values, the Elysian Fields of Architecture, now that the Great Critic has impetuously taken the subject of legitimation to pieces.
It falls on the world scene and is reborn in the theatre of Architecture.
Everything is a parody of everything else.
Architecture fashions its masks from a heap of signs stripped of their usefulness — it attempts the grave tones that once moved the public. But the public has no wish to know that the dying king has a wife and children who await him for dinner after the performance, and goes away. Does it not like make-believe? It depends at this point on the objects and how the architect-healer thinks and hopes: does he want architecture to be made by everyone or by no one?
Now the performances are family ones: exhibitions, congresses, books and magazines: both the performers and the audience are architects.
Many projects are sentenced to the limbo of paper.
It cannot last.

21. Casa Sartori, Riveo (Ticino, Switzerland), 1975-1977.

22. Project for a house at Vezio (Ticino, Switzerland), 1975: elevation and sections.

423-424. Casa Tonini, Torricella (Ticino, Switzerland), 1972-1974: central internal area; external view.

425. Restoration of the church of San Carlo, Piano di Peccia
Ticino, Switzerland), 1971-1980: the altar.
426. Restoration of the Community Hall, Sornico (Ticino,
Switzerland), 1974-1975: the table of the Justice of the Peace.

Aldo Rossi

Milan, 1931.
Graduated from the Faculty of Architecture of Milan Polytechnic in 1959.
Wrote for *Casabella-Continuità* magazine, edited by Ernesto Nathan Rogers, from 1959 to 1964.
Has taught at the Faculty of Architecture of Milan Polytechnic and at the Federal Polytechnic in Zurich.
Has held the chair of Architectural Composition at the Venice University Institute of Architecture since 1975.
Has written, among other things: "L'Architettura della città," published in 1964, and a collection of essays from '56 to '72 in the volume *Scritti scelti sull'Architettura e la città*.

The constructed works or projects

I am looking at these constructed works and latest projects: a school, a cemetery, a theatre, which is like saying life, death, imagination. The occasion of the works and their connection is casual, but the ambiguousness of the event is always decisive. The theatre is situated between the house of infancy and the house of death as a place that is purely for performances, and memory and foreboding belong to the two houses in an indifferent way.

Thus architecture takes its identity from unchanging things, as long as they are not inside the things themselves; in the sense that every window is the window of an artist and of every man, it is always an opening from which to lean out and look. It is like childish letters that go "Tell me what you see from your window;" and this is what architecture will be in reality, a witness.

The tumulus and the palace, the school and the cemetery, the dwelling and the library, all these forecast one event; and perhaps the event can change in the telling, but only the tangible signs by which it is transmitted are what we can still call history and, in the end, project.

For me the life of the building has nothing to do with what is called "the examination of the project" during construction. Great architects like Alberti and Filarete can be recognized by fragments; the temple of Malatesta, the column and the Venetian plinth represent the dizziness of architecture and its abandonment. If I look at the photograph of children running around in the courtyard at Fagnano Olona, I think this school is like all the others: but it is certain that the architect can in a manner of speaking programme the action, the scene fixed in different situations, and can try to seal the relationship between the building and its site.

In this way the building, constructed work or project, also has a relationship with the city and with technique. In the "theatre of the world," or Venetian theatre, I built a machine with the materials at hand, which was to settle in Venice; what I saw as materials were water and boats, iron and wood, and everything they could add to the city in some way.

So the works and projects are elements, fragments of a general design, a long research or history of things, and illuminations that keep all this company.

427-428. Extension to the Cemetery at Modena, 1973-1980 (with G. Braghieri): view of the burial ground; drawing of the project.

429. The "Teatro del Mondo" built for the
Theatre and Architecture Sectors of the Venice
Biennale, 1979: roof interior.

430-432. Primary school, Fagnano Olona
(Varese), 1974-1977: the arcade; the steps to
the entrance; the central block.

433. Project for the competition for the Students' Hall of Residence, Chieti, 1977.

434-436. Studies for the competition for the new town centre of Florence, 1977.

LANDESBIBLIOTHEK KARLSRUHE   323874

ANSICHT NORD   M. 1: 100

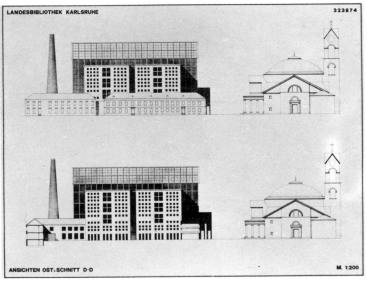

LANDESBIBLIOTHEK KARLSRUHE   323874

ANSICHTEN OST·SCHNITT D-D   M. 1:200

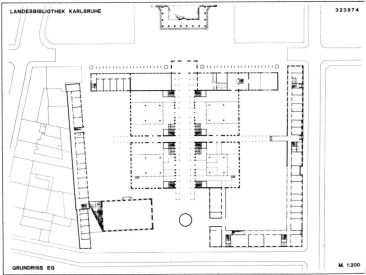

LANDESBIBLIOTHEK KARLSRUHE   323874

GRUNDRISS EG   M. 1:200

Novi Ligure, 1943.
Graduated in Architecture at the Polytechnic of Milan in 1969.
Has taught at the universities of Milan, Palermo, Cooper Union,
Cornell and UCLA. Has taught Drawing and Surveying at the Univer-
sity Institute of Architecture in Venice since 1973.
Has written for *Controspazio* and *Lotus* and at present is editor of the
"Franco Angeli" series on architecture.
His works have recently been collected in a general catalogue edited
by the "Centro DI" in Florence and in one produced by the I.A.U.S.
in New York.
Lives and works in Milan.

A painter might find himself wrestling with the
problems of architecture or an architect might do
the same with painting. What is certain, though, is
that two such different and specific techniques cannot be confused. Those caught up in this mess
know just how pitiless they can be to people who
do not know how to use them adequately.
Architecture should be compared with architecture,
painting with painting.
In this façade project I have chosen to build
something *representative*: the axionometric image.
Since I am a painter interested in the problems of
representing architecture, this façade could only
conceal its own pictorial image.

40. "Gas Station Inn," 1975, watercolour, 13 x 18 cm.

441. "Monument," 1977, watercolour, 18 x 25.5 cm.
442. "Buried architecture," 1978, watercolour, 13 x 18 cm.
443. "Project," 1978, watercolour, 16.3 x 23.5 cm.
444. "The Bridge of the Honest Woman," 1979, watercolour, 15 x 20 cm.

445. "Heliotherapic baths in the Atlantic," 1977, watercolour, 51 x 36 cm.
446. "Architecture of the limit," 1978, watercolour, 15 x 20 cm.
447. "The meeting," 1976, watercolour, 15 x 20 cm.

441

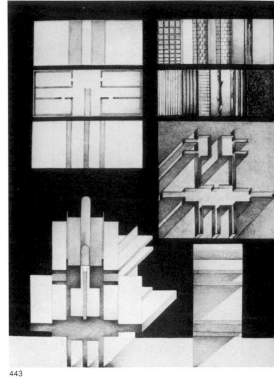

443

442

444

Thomas Gordon Smith

Oakland (Cal. - USA) 1948.
Master of Architecture at the University of California in 1971. Has taught History of Architecture at the College of Marin in Kentfield, California.
Rome Prize in 1980: is resident at the American Academy in Rome.

In my buildings I am working to achieve a synthesis of form, function, and symbolic content. I admire architects who have achieved a fusion of these considerations in their work and I feel a close kinship with them. For the past ten years I have been particularly drawn to the work of the Roman Baroque architect, Francesco Borromini. Borromini's accomplishment represents at once the most stimulating and the most challenging model for the synthesis which I want to achieve.

In all of his buildings Borromini was challenged by functional constraints which spurred him to devise brilliantly logical solutions. Adversity as a stimulant to genius is a trait of many great artists, and Borromini proved this himself time and time again. I believe that Borromini's buildings convey emotional content and that their meaning is deepened because he believed in the inseparability of formal, functional and iconographical solutions. Borromini was capable of orchestrating the intuitive, literal, and symbolic meanings associated with the elements of architecture to accomplish this depth. He possessed an innate sensitivity to the meaning inherent in the elements of architecture which he strengthened with his thorough knowledge of the sophisticated syntax which had been elaborated for the classical elements of architecture in theoretical writings since Vitruvius. Borromini articulated abstract ideas in his buildings by integrating sculptural and symbolic forms. Although he knew the canonical meanings of his architectonic and symbolic forms, Borromini often contradicted the meaning of his prototypes. This step left him free to create new meanings which extended tradition and made his architecture appropriate to his age and accessible to his peers.

I feel a sense of continuity with the efforts of Borromini and many other architects. Although I am deeply interested in architectural history, I object to the current emphasis on the word the "past." I have no interest in the "past;" it is too remote and unapproachable. I am passionate, however, about the elements of architecture which have been available to architects throughout history and I am excited by the opportunity to design buildings with this wide vocabulary which solve today's problems and convey spiritual content. From my point of view, our current challenge is to extend the meaning of the elements of architecture and iconography for appropriate expression today. I have no doubt that the experience of modern architecture and culture will enrich the product.

The building in which I am achieving my goal for the synthesis of form, function, and symbolic content is a hypothetical project for a church in Rome, the Oratory of St. Jean Viannay, the patron of parish priests. A priest served as a surrogate patron for the building and I chose a site adjacent to the Borrominian Revival convent and chapel of St. Filippo Neri on the Via Giulia. The ideal form of the centrally planned church is resolved with the irregular site. The spherical volume of the church is segmented by three axes which originate in aediculae. The aediculae are dedicated to St. Jean Viannay, and his personal patrons: the Virgin and St. John the Baptist. They define the places for three aspects of the priest's ministry and are oriented toward the goal of each. The main axis, which runs north-south, begins at the sacristy door, from which the priest enters the church. The door is surmounted by a statue of the Virgin which is oriented toward the altar, and beyond to a chapel for the reservation of the Eucharist. The aedicula to the right of the altar is for preaching and contains a statue of St. Jean Viannay which faces the vestibule, the entrance for the congregation. The aedicula to the left of the altar provides access to the confessionals. A statue of St. John the Baptist is placed over the door, and faces the baptismal font located in the courtyard. The plan is organized to accommodate and emphasize the ministry of the priest to his community in his traditional roles as priest, prophet, and king.

A Star of David is inscribed on the floor of the church. It defines the axes and symbolically conveys a historical and theological reality about the Church. The Star of David is an ancient symbol of Judaism and stands for the Synagogue.

Within each of the triangles of the star a mosaic medallion represents one of the six virtues of the Virgin at the time of the Annunciation, the moment the Law was fulfilled and the Virgin became the first tabernacle of Christ. From that instant, she represents Eclesia, the Church, and supplants the Synagogue.

The cylindrical wall of the church rises from this foundation to support the half sphere of the dome. Tuscan pilasters and entablatures of grey-green tufa articulate the wall and define the aediculae. Doric columns support the more refined entablature above the altar and symbols of the sacrifice of the Eucharist are placed in the metopes.

A baldacchino hovers within the outer shell of the church. It is composed of serpentine Corinthian columns which spring from pluvinated pedestals to support the interwoven ribs of a vault. Pairs of these columns demark the three aediculae from which the axes of the church originate. Each pair of columns is textured with the bark of the tree which symbolized the human quality required for the ministry which it accomodates. Corinthian capitals are composed of the leaves, fruit, and flowers of each tree and are tied with the skin of an associated animal.

The baldacchino represents the presence of God's grace in the world and its resilient forms convey the intangibility of spiritual energy. This is expressed on a perceptual level by the ambiguity of directional movement. The torqued columns seem to strive upward, which contradicts the impression gained from the pluvinated pedestals which bulge in response to a force greater than gravity. On a more literal level, I employed the Corinthian order because of its traditional association with "lofty" applications. The symbols of plants and animals convey more precise ideas about abstract qualities than the

architectonic elements connote by themselves. Through this theoretical design for a church, I have sought to give expression to the symbolic content inherent in architectural forms. I look forward to applying the concepts which I have developed in this project to an actual church and I want to extend this potential of architecture to enrich all types of secular buildings.

451. Tuscan House and
Laurentian House, Livermore
(Cal.), 1979: view from south.

452. Project for Long House at
Carson City (Nev.), 1978: view
from south.

287

Robert A.M Stern

454. Project for Shaker Village, Pleasant Hill (Ky.), 1979: plans on three levels, section, elevations.

Born in 1939
Bachelor of Architecture at Columbia University in 1960 and Master of Architecture in 1965 at Yale University, where he studied under Louis I. Kahn and Vincent Scully.
As well as being Professor of Planning at Columbia University, he also teaches in some of the most important universities in the U.S.A., such as Yale, the Rhode Island School of Design and the University of Pennsylvania.
He has published many articles and books.
Among the most important are: *New directions in American Architecture* (New York, 1969); *George Howe: toward a Modern American Architecture* (New Haven, 1975).
Lives and works in New York City.

"We didn't need sound. We had faces...." Gloria Swanson as Norma Desmond, extolling the methods of the silent film in Billy Wilder's film, *Sunset Boulevard* (1951).

The single most positive aspect of the current exploration of traditional values in contemporary architecture is the recuperation of the concept of the facade. No longer, as in the canonical modernism of the past 70 years, is the facade merely a representation of the syntactical aspects of architecture: that is, the building's plan and section — or merely a revelation of the processes of its own production. The facade has been unbound and its blindfold and gag untied. Like the silent faces, the facade offers revelations of things as they are, while representing things as one might want them to be.

Our proposal for "La Strada Novissima" is a discussion of the reality and illusion of the past. The past is treated both as recent past — addressing the work of our office, and as distant past — addressing the history of architecture. The elements of the facade connect these two levels, while also addressing the pavilion's location in a street of ambiguous scale and in a coastal city that was once a great sea power. Thus the abstracted curtain/columns with their suggestion of a proscenium not only tell of a "show" of office work that lies within ready to be seen by the audience at La Biennale but also of a more enduring drama acted out by players upon a stage of infinite dimensions. While the "show" is a reality in the present, the greater drama is a constantly changing flow of illusions, interpreted differently at different times by different people. Noble among the players in this shadow play is the Greek temple, an abstraction of which appears as a void upon the silent face of the figure that stands before the curtain of history. This image — at once literal and abstract — inhabits the new street, a Venetian trader dressed in gold and red damask before a backdrop of maritime colors. Yet the temple, like the over-scaled moulding which adorns the proscenium above it, refers also to office projects that have marked important stages in our stylistic direction: the former refers to the Best Products facade of 1979 and the latter to the Lang House of 1975.

The illusions of the past become the reality of the present on the interior where the temple form becomes more explicit and is used as a framework to display the work. The threshold of this transition is a void, rusticated column, an icon from another recent project, the house at Llewellyn Park, emphasizing the importance of entering the past in order to fully experience the richness of which the present is capable.

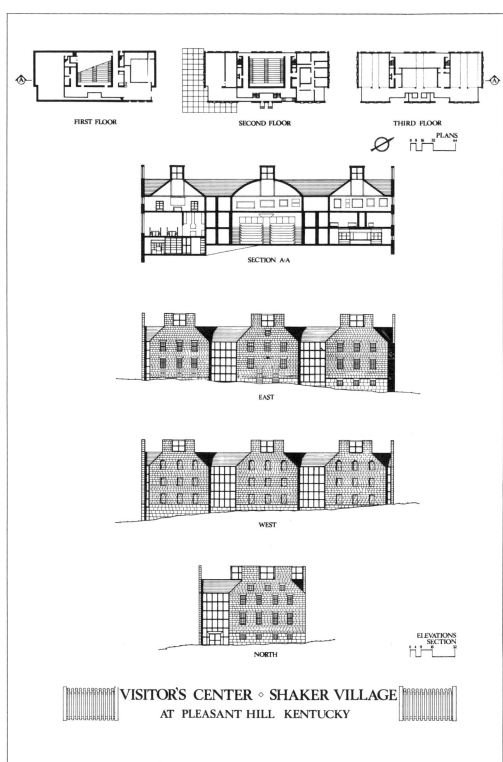

FIRST FLOOR SECOND FLOOR THIRD FLOOR

PLANS

SECTION A·A

EAST

WEST

NORTH

ELEVATIONS
SECTION

VISITOR'S CENTER ◇ SHAKER VILLAGE
AT PLEASANT HILL KENTUCKY

455. Lang House, Washington (Conn.), 1973.

456. Bourke House, Greenwich (Conn.), 1974.

457. Residence, Eastern Long Island, East Hampton (N.Y.), 1976: detail of the swimming-pool.

458-459. Ehrman House, Armonk (N.Y.), 1975: general views.

460-462. Project of a prototype façade for Best Products Inc. supermarkets, 1980: view, study of the façade and perspective detail of the model.

463. New Community Centre, Quail Valley (Tex.), 1976.
464. Purnell development, comprising house and buildings for breeding, Waller (Tex.), 1977.
465. Project for YMCA offices, Houston (Texas), 1979.

Group founded in 1972. Studio in Houston, Texas.

John Joseph Gasbarian
Alexandria (Egypt) 1946.
Bachelor of Architecture at Rice University in 1972.
Associated Professor at Rice University.

Danny Marc Samuels
Memphis (Tenn.) 1947.
Bachelor of Architecture at Rice University in 1971.
Has taught at Rice University and at the University of Houston.

Robert Howard Timme
Houston (Tex.) 1945.
Master of Architecture at Rice University in 1971.
Associated Professor at the University of Houston.

The universality of order allows people, generations apart, to experience, comprehend and share the same intrinsic spatial "senses." Time does change, however, the extrinsic meanings of the components that are ordered.

The work of Taft Architects has been concerned with investigations of generic order and the expression of that order in the development of design. Design parties are synthesized and explored for their formal logic and structure. These investigations are conducted apart from any considerations of functional determinism. The formal structures of the solutions and the relationships of elements within those structures are then evaluated in terms of their responsiveness to the context and program. What often occurs is an interaction of the formal systems which evolve first into a hybrid party, and then into an elaborated design.

The stronger the "sense" imparted by the formal clarity, the greater the range of visual contrast and extrinsic meanings of architectural forms that can exist and be understood in the developed design. Such architectural elements will, through this "sense" of the formal order, assume extrinsic meanings that were never associated with them in the past.

Thus the past is seen as a language whose order allows for a constant rediscovery of complex meanings within individual words. Our method has been to understand this language of order and elements in a generalized sense, enabling description and comparison of basic diagrams which accommodate design intentions. Such diagrams can acquire a richness as they respond to visual and programmatic problems on a complex variety of scales.

Through this development, the basic abstract formal order, though given variety by circumstantial and specific design modifications, will maintain a sense of clarity, which, it must be said, is the basis of architecture as it moves from a conceptual process to reality.

It is within the built presence of this reality, today's reality, that future generations will discover their own perceptual understanding, their own "presence of the past."

Has its office in Paris. Its members are:

David Bigelman
Havana (Cuba) 1943.
Graduated from the Catholic University of America in Washington.
Worked with Ricardo Porro from 1971 to 1973.
Teaches at the Ecole Supérieure des Beaux-Arts in Paris, in Unité Pédagogique n. 8.

Jean Pierre Feugas
Batna (Algeria) 1944.
Architect D.L.P.G.
Taught at the Institute of Architecture and Urban Planning at the University of Constantine (Algeria) from 1974 to 1977.

Bernard Huet
Quinton (Vietnam) 1932.
Architect D.L.P.G.
Master in Architecture at the University of Pennsylvania with Louis Kahn.
Professor at the Ecole Supérieure des Beaux-Arts in Paris, where he is chairman of the board of directors.
He was head writer for L'Architecture d'Aujourd'hui from 1973 to 1977.
Has been a consultant to U.N.E.S.C.O. since 1978.

Bernard Leroy
Paris 1949.
Architect D.L.P.G.
Has taught at the Ecole Supérieure des Beaux-Arts, in the Unité Pédagogique at Strasbourg, since 1977.

Serge Santelli
Paris 1944.
Architect D.L.P.G.
Got his Master in Architecture and Urban Planning at Pennsylvania University with Louis Kahn.
After teaching at Penn State University (USA) and at the Institute Technologique d'Art, d'Architecture et d'Urbanisme of Tunis, he is now Professor at the Ecole Supérieure de Beaux-Arts, Unité Pédagogique n. 8, in Paris.

Our projects take on the inheritance of architectural and urban types produced by History and blend in the essential and permanent value of archetypes (such as the Door, the Wall, or the Temple) which are part of our collective memory and enable us to give back sense to our towns.
They recover and restore existing traces by revealing the structures written down on the land-register or by bringing up to date their symbolic potential.
By respecting and conserving all the outlets transmitted by the history of places, they also assume a physical continuity within the urban structure.
As urban fragments they are clearly bounded and defined by a boundary that marks a new limit to urban development and ensures the transition into the countryside.
Faced with the disintegrating and pointillist landscape of towers, parking-lots and haphazard patches of green that make up our modern conglomerations, they insert themselves in a clear and simple urban layout — an orthogonal and rational mesh that forms blocks — where the Streets, Squares, Arcades, Alignments and Perspectives are elementary types shown up in their formal specification.

They participate in and respect a certain number of urban and spatial rules (like what Haussmann prescribed) that guarantee a certain degree of urban homogeneity in which the urban aspect is more important than each architect's individual contribution. They decline grand architectural complexes, favouring an urban composition of elements that conforms with a town's historical development.
The civic areas and public buildings form

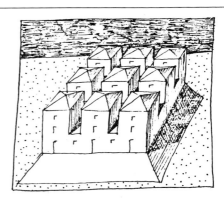

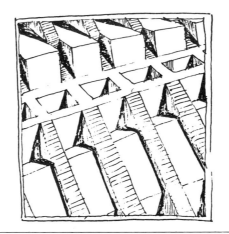

meaningful monumental groups that mark out the urban structure and give it a hierarchy; they create a strong monumental element that permits an obvious identification. Together with the town parks and gardens — pieces of nature, vegetable microcosms — they make up the spatial picture of town life whose formal character and visual situation give them a marked semantic value and exclude all architectural exhibitionism and eclecticism.

Their formal statute, which is written down in their inhabitants' urban consciousness, and the fundamental appearance of the space that bounds them, legible and mineral, must give them the character of sectors of a city on an urban scale.
Lastly, the use of formal and traditional conventions in construction and of typologies that have been recognized and experienced by everyone will enable ordinary collective architecture to reach the sublime heights of the great, classic works.

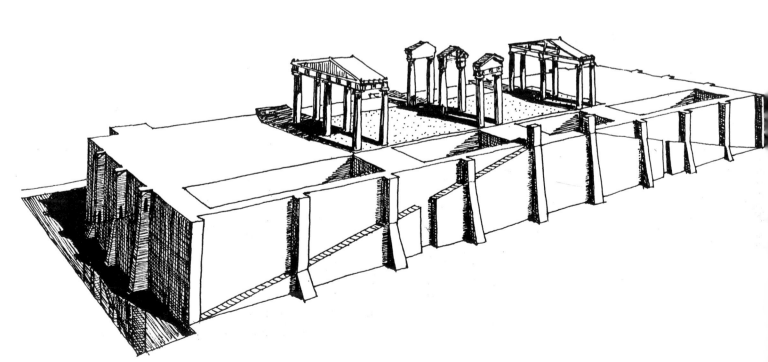

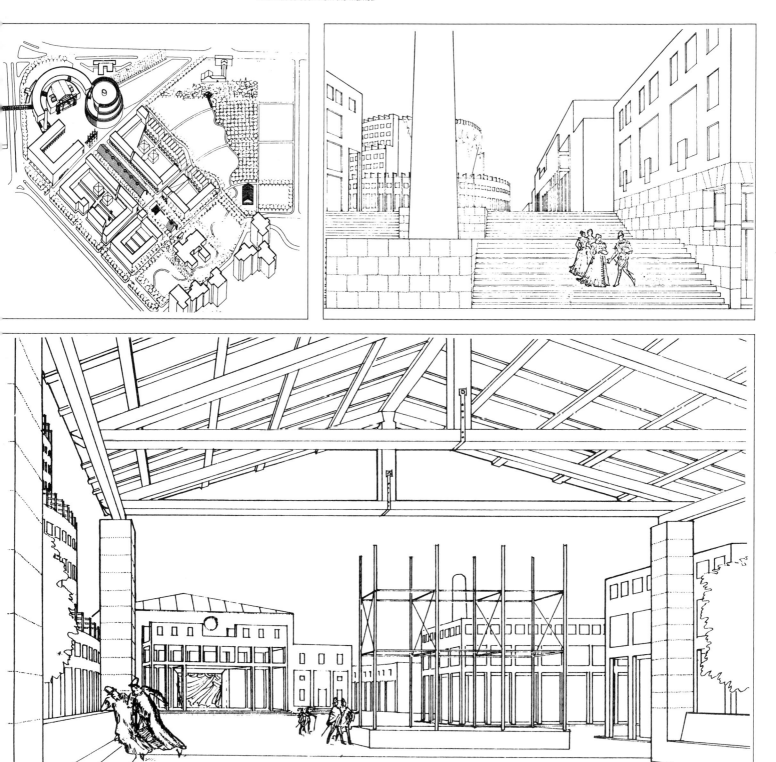

467-468. Project for the layout of the old Halles de la Villette, Paris (France), 1976: study sketches.

469-471. Competition for the layout of the "Croix Rouge" sector in Reims (France), 1978: general overhead view; partial view of the colonnades, the Château d'eau, the theatre and the young people's house; the Chateau d'eau, the theatre, the tribune and the colonnades seen from the market.

Quinlan Terry

London 1937.
Diploma from the Architectural Association of London.
Went to study in Rome and the Middle East from 1962 to 1972.
Has taught at the Universities of Oxford, Cambridge, London, Edinburgh, Stockholm and Barcelona.
Worked for two years with Raymond Erith, until the latter's death in 1973.
Has been head of the Erith & Terry studio since then.
Lives and works at Dedham, Colchester (Essex).

There are many ways in which contemporary architects have tried to get over the crises of the Modern Movement. Their results depend on the degree to which they consider the Modern Movement a good thing. I have never seen any good in it and therefore look for inspiration to a more natural and stable world before Modernism began. Such a world existed in England from Inigo Jones until Soane, and such a world never really ceased to exist in Italy for 2500 years from Greco-Roman times until the beginning of this century. Whereas it was revived from time to time in England; it survived all the time in Italy.

In Italy, more than anywhere else, the knowledge and application of traditional classical building was understood, practised and admired by all sections of society; and it was in such surroundings that Andrea Palladio lived and worked. He was a practical builder with a vast working knowledge of the monuments of Imperial Rome; and he had a rare ability to express the simple needs of his own day in a way that was direct, beautiful and classical. He was therefore able to bridge the centuries with masterly skill and ease; and therein lies the way forward for us today.

The time has come to abandon useless innovations and seek inspiration in the wisdom and experience of our predecessors. The needs and desires of man have changed little over the centuries, the climate still dictates the same principles of detail and craftsmanship; the modern materials have proved inferior — and rapid changes in taste have done nothing to produce a better style than the time honoured classical.

Alas, this age has only just begun to see where it went wrong. The fact that here in Italy there is an exhibition devoted to the rediscovery of these skills is a hopeful sign. We have not the natural nor stable world around us of the Cinquecento, nor the appreciative patrons. But similar obstacles have been overcome by men of conviction before.

472-473. Seven small houses at Frog Meadow, Dedham, Essex (England), 1967-1980: the two rows of elevations that form the street, with the date of construction of each building.

474-477. Seven small houses at Frog Meadow, Dedham, Essex (England), 1967-1980: elevations and floor plans of houses nos. 1, 2, 3, 4 and 5.

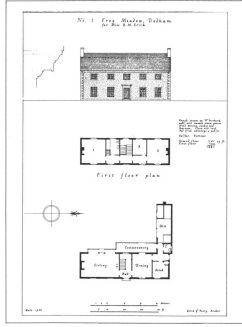

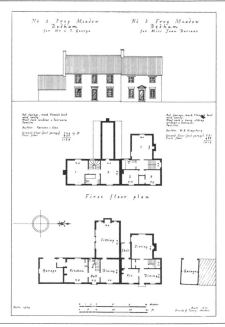

478-480. Seven small houses at Frog Meadow, Dedham, Essex (England), 1967-1980: elevations, sections and details of the front doors to houses nos. 3, 4 and 6.

481. Seven small houses at Frog Meadow, Dedham, Essex (England), 1967-1980: general plan.

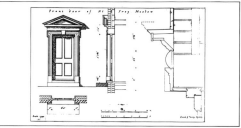

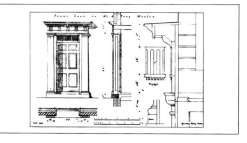

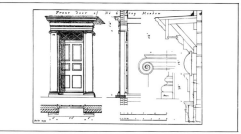

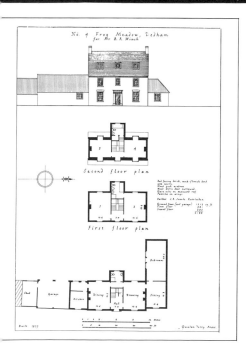

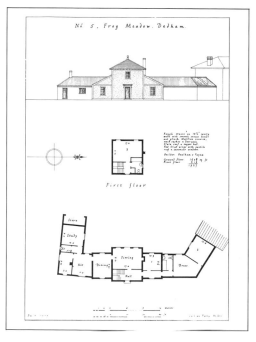

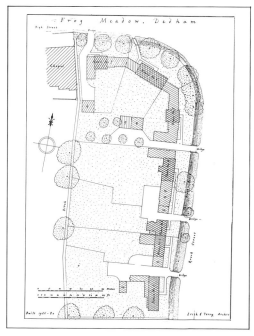

482-483. House at Kings Walden Bury, Hertfordshire (England), 1969-1971: general view porticoes on the south elevation and façade towards the park.

484. Waverton House, Moreton-in-Marsh, Gloucester (England), 1979: elevations, plans and sections.

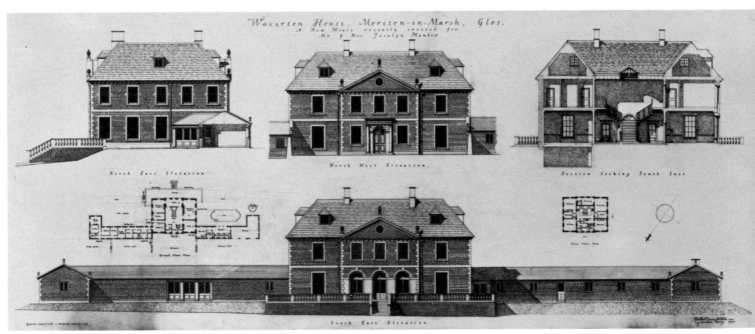

485-486. Rustic Hut, West Green, Hampshire (England), 1973-
1980 (one of the ten garden buildings designed for West Green):
general view, sections and plan.

487-488. Column at West Green, Hampshire (England), 1976: view
and drawing of the elevation.

485

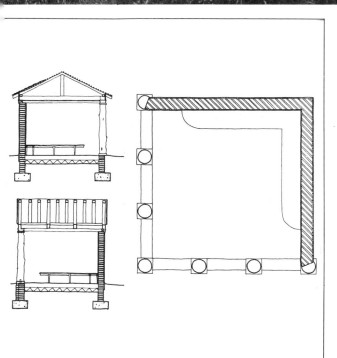

486

487

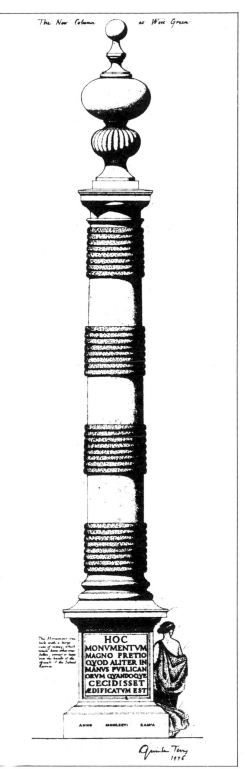

The New Column at West Green

HOC
MONVMENTVM
MAGNO PRETIO
QVOD ALITER IN
MANVS PVBLICAN
ORVM QVANDOQVE
CECIDISSET
ÆDIFICATVM EST

488

Heinz Tesar

Innsbruck 1939.
Got his diploma from the Vienna Academy of Fine Arts in 1965.
Has worked free-lance since 1975.
Lives and works in Vienna.

Fragment to characterization and type

It's a question of an architecture that is committed to *formulation* and to *naturalness*. By formulation I mean the linguistically precise graphic designation of a thing in the terseness of its imagery and in its brittleness, in the inexorability of the thing itself. It is the laying down of the necessarily important lines — hence drawing in a literal sense. What has developed during the times are all natural *and* artificial substances, called naturalness.

The interrelation of *individuality* and *type* becomes visible in a work of architecture. The tension that the two notions generate by themselves and in relation to one another is the point of departure for the architectural statement. In 1973 I noted that building is important for me when its motivation and expression are to be found in the I-we duality, whereby it is not a matter of the one-sided assertion of the notion but of realizing the polarity in architecture. Starting with studies of the head, man, soft monuments, and petrifaction I have arrived in the development of my work at the theory of *homotypes*, which on the level of objects represent a vocabulary of fundamental architectural forms — an expansion of the range of *historical* archetypes. I remember a remark in this connection by Peter Behrens for whom typological art represented the highest objective of all artistic activity. A complete awareness of the casual necessities of the object and its context is a prerequisite in the development of a type. In this respect Rodin observed that everything that an artist creates must involuntarily be touched by his emotion. This comment is not to be misinterpreted as a summons to expressionism but as an irrevocable factor in the interrelationship of individuality and type in architecture.

In formulating the object that is to be formed I use as means the drawing, to be exact the watercolor drawing. This drawing contains the discovery and retention of the idea, the memory of an object, as well as being an accompaniment to and means of comparison with the building process. I think we will arrive at an architecture that is a slow, quiet, characterizing language that in its simplicity will be understandable and in its many-layeredness of timeless validity. An architecture that is a designation of the particular circumstances and the characterization of the *place*, the *time*, the *way and means* and the *motive*.

489. Extension and renovation of the parish church, Unternberg/Lungau (Austria), 1976-1979: portal.

490. Parish centre, Leopoldskron (Austria), 1978-1980: general overhead view.

491-492. Riendenthal House, southern Weinviertel (Austria), 1974-1980: view from the hillside and general axionometric view.

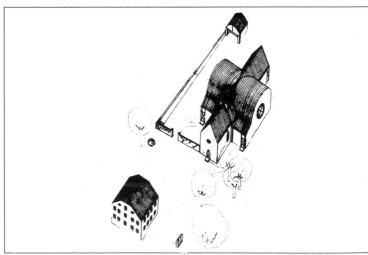

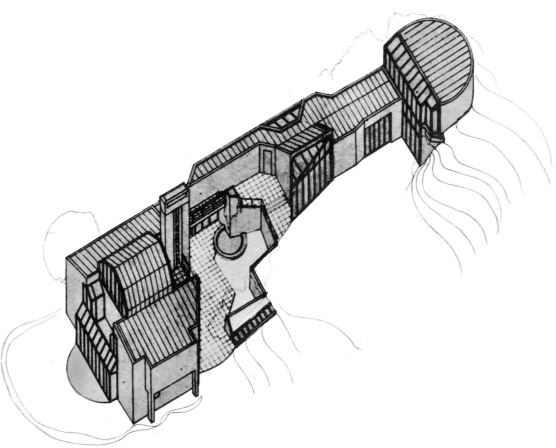

Stanley Tigermann

Chicago 1930.
Master of Architecture at Yale University. Has taught at the principal American universities as a Visiting Lecturer. Coordinated the exhibitions "Chicago Architects" and "Chicago Seven Architects in Residence" for 1980 at the American Academy in Rome.
Lives and works in Chicago.

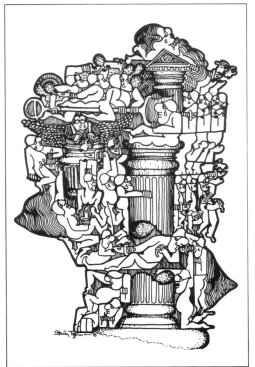

The architectural battle lines of the 1980's are rapidly being drawn as this critical Orwellian decade begins. On the one hand, European intellectualism has been shored up by Neo-Rationalist, Neo-Marxist and Neo-Platonist prejudices. The pretender-descendent of egalitarian Modernism, Europe's post-functionalist champions include: Aldo Rossi, Carlo Aymonino, Rafael Moneo, Leon and Robert Krier and Mathias Ungers. Theoretician/dialecticians include: Manfredo Tafuri, Francesco Dal Co, Giorgio Ciucci and Manieri-Elia, while among the antecedent figures are: Gide, Proust, Ortega y Gasset, Mies van der Rohe and Hilbersheimer. The signs of this movement are silent, hermetic, intrinsic and elitist. A primary concern of the architecture of this movement seems to be the subject of death, or perhaps more clearly stated, the absence of life. The foundations underpinning this movement are abstract, general and ideal, while the body of the work and supporting polemics are self-consciously utopian, normative and innaccessible.

On the other hand, American populism has been sustained by it's own peasant culture come-of-age. The descendent of frontier agrarian values freed from ideological/political motives, contemporary America continues to produce an architecture that is centered on open communication. It's current reporters include: Robert Venturi, Charles Moore, Frank Gehry, James Wines, Michael Graves and Robert Stern and it has neither theoretician nor dialectician since this architecture is not involved in such idealized concepts as timelessness or perpetuity. Father figures include: Emerson, Thoreau, Jefferson, Sullivan, Wright and Kahn. The signs of this grass roots tradition have always been open, optimistic, extrinsic and emotional. The subject of the architecture of this attitude is life itself, or perhaps more clearly stated, the absence of perfection. The interests underlying this commitment are particularized and idiosyncratic, thus they are human. The intention of the narrative component of this work is accessibility.

Now I am an American architect and while I was trained in methods couched in the intrinsic language of modern architecture, I have come to believe in a visceral American architecture tied to it's own individuality. Neo-Marxists tell us that they believe in the good of the many. I believe in the good of every single one of us. Neo-Rationalists proclaim the correctness of the European "Hof," or at the very least, the "Seidlungen." I believe in "Greenbelt" and "The City Beautiful." Neo-Platonists support attitudes of Life after Death. I believe in Life, yet I suspect that everything dies, including ideas. The concept of perfection as a state of being inadvertedly supports a sense of inadequacy attached to existence. Since I am tied to the frailty of existence, I am bound to the individual in

496. Library for the Blind and Physically Handicapped, Chicago
III.), 1975-1978: view of east elevation.
497. Hot dog house, Harvard (III.), 1973: view of south elevation.

his imperfect state and thus am I inextricably committed to the irony of existence in its finite condition. I could never again believe in an architecture presented as "The temple to perpetuity" where life is irrelevant in the face of totemic idealizations when I sense that architecture can be in the service of "our struggle."

Architecture, by it's very nature, is optimistic. To build well is to will some thing into existence, and in order to sustain will, it must be rooted in optimism. I find that the Neo-Platonic view placing architecture in the service of perpetuity is skeptical of life's inconsistencies, while presuming to support larger, albeit valuable attitudes about continuity. I am devoted to life, which in the end, terminates. Thus, mine is a commitment that is necessarily ironic and schizophrenic, yet it is inevitably optimistic as well.

498. Daisy House, Porter (Ind.), 1976-1978: external detail.
499. Animal Crackers, Highland Park (Ill.), 1976-1978: view of the elevation.

500. Ukranian Institute of Modern Art. Chicago (Ill.), 1977: view of the elevation.
501. Office of Stanley Tigermann, Chicago (Ill.), 1980: view of the interior.

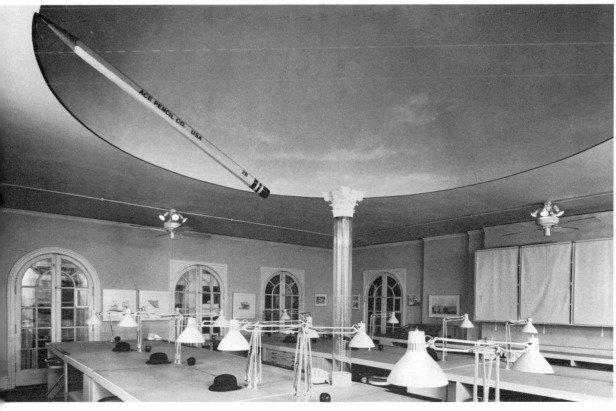

504. "Pensacola" block of flats, Chicago (Ill.), 1979-1982: general perspective view.

505. Project for the Anti-Cruelty Society in Chicago (Ill.), 1977-1980.

Susanna Torre

Bahia Blanca (Argentina) 1944.
Graduated from the University of Buenos Aires in 1967.
Did her specialization at the School of Architecture and Planning of Columbia University.
Was Visiting Professor at some of the most important American universities from 1977 to 1979.
Has been Adjunct Professor at the Columbia University School of Architecture and Planning since 1980.
Organized the "Women in American Architecture" travelling exhibition and its catalogue.
Lives and works in New York.

Between Past and Future

1. I find myself as "He" finds himself in Kafka's parable, staking my ground, clashing in either direction with two powerful forces. The past ("never dead, not even past") does not pull me back but presses forward and it is, contrary to what one would expect, the future which drives me back into the past. In the interval between past and future my presence causes the forces to deflect from their original direction. The resulting diagonal force, whose origin is the clash between past and future but whose end is unknown, marks the place where my own work finds its meaning and direction.

2. These are the theoretical premises:

The exploration of a method of architectural composition that is capable of encompassing proportionally related elements as well as unstable or random architectural relationships.

The development of a critical theory of function that is capable of redefining the Modern Movement's monofunctionalist, mechanistic premise and to embrace all practical, aesthetic, theoretical and symbolic functions.

The formulation of a normative spatial theory that views interior and exterior space, private and public domains and buildings and nature as differentiated components of a continuous spatial matrix.

The elaboration of a prospective urban theory that recognizes two prevalent traditions in the design of American Cities: the ideas of the city as a non-hierarchical network of streets and sidewalks and of the city as garden, with buildings as pavilions.

3. We cannot not know History, but we should not be afraid to create it.

506. Walls of the House of Meanings (collage and ink), 1973.

507. The American City as Garden: redrawing Joseph Smith's plan of the City of Zion (1883), 1979.

508-509. Pension Building Specialty Lounges, Washington (D.C.),
1978: conceptual diagram; view of a bay.

510. Law Office, New York City (N.Y.), 1975: sculpture gallery.
511. Project for the House of two cylinders, 1977.

508

510

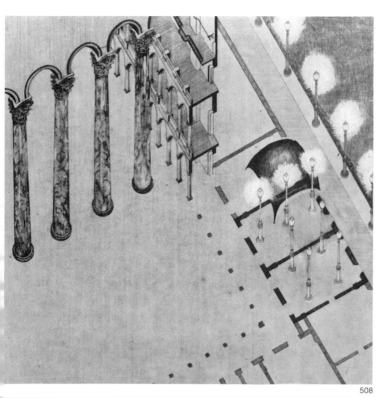

509

511

William Turnbull

514-516. Proposal for cluster units, 1978: plans and perspective views.
517. Zimmermann residence, Fairfax Country (Va.), 1974-1976.
518. Portland Fountain, 1964 (with L. Halprin and Ass.).

New York City (N.Y. - USA) 1935.
Master of Architecture at Princeton University in 1959 under the guidance of Louis I. Kahn.
Worked professionally with Charles Moore and Don Lyndon (MLTW) from 1960 to 1969.
Has had his own studio in San Francisco since 1970.
Has taught at the Architectural Faculty of Stanford University, MIT and the University of Maryland.
Won the Rome Prize in 1980 and has been doing research at the American Academy of Rome.
Won the AIA Honor Awards of 1967 and 1968 together with Moore and Lyndon for the Sea Ranch development.

Architecture in America is undergoing a profound change from the early simplistic guidelines of the Modern Movement through the battlefields of the inclusivists versus the exclusivists to the meanderings of Post Modernism.
We believe architecture is primarily concerned with establishing a "sense of place" whether its inspiration is derived from the idiosyncrasies of the landscape or the pragmatic requirements of an individual client. The role of history and past example in this process varies from direct copy through collage to the world of illusion. Copies, be they the Parthenon of Nashville, Tennessee or another set of Golden Arches, are essentially an intellectual bore, so interest in the past lies in its specific fragments or in its ideas. Collaging of pieces seems to us akin to solving the *New York Times* Sunday crossword puzzles; an achievement of the mind and dazzling display of intellectual agility. However the end result is, like the direct copy, a reheated stew. Far better is an answer which understands the ideas and concepts of the past but refuses the seduction of copying its stylistic vocabulary. For us ideas and references are to be understood and alluded to while the mind enjoys a fresh and unsullied interpretation.
Places are for the specifics of the people who use them; not retreads or bouillabaisses from past architectural triumphs.

512-513. Biloxi Library and Cultural Center, Biloxi (Miss.), 1969: external view; the reading-rooms.

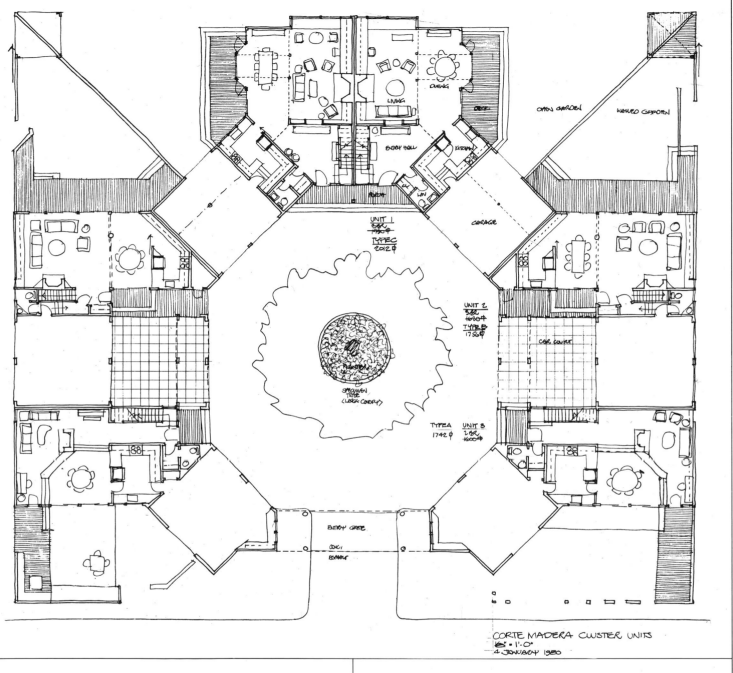

UNIT 1
3 BR
1930 φ
TYPE C
2012 φ

UNIT 2
3 BR
1610 φ
TYPE B
1756 φ

TYPE A
1742 φ

UNIT 3
2 BR
1600 φ

LIVING

DINING

DECK

ENTRY HALL

KITCHEN

FOYER

LON

GARAGE

CAR COURT

OPEN GARDEN

WALLED GARDEN

PLANTER

SPECIMEN TREE
(LARGE CANOPY)

ENTRY GATE

CONC
PAVING

CORTE MADERA CLUSTER UNITS
1/8" = 1'-0"
4 JANUARY 1980

520-521. Project for the Museum in Morsbroich Castle, Leverkusen (West Germany), 1976 (with S. Böhm and P. Dietzsch): general plan and perspective view.

Kaisersesch (West Germany), 1926.
Got his diploma at the Technische Hochschule of Karlsruhe in 1950.
Has been Professor at the Lehrthul für Entwerfen VI of the Berlin Technische Hochschule since 1963.
Was Chairman of the Department of Architecture at Cornell University (Ithaca, N.Y.) from 1969 to 1975.
Has also taught at Harvard University and U.C.L.A.
Lives and works in West Germany and the USA.

Architecture's right to an autonomous language 1979

Architecture nowadays is mostly conceived as an ecological, sociological and technological function. Economical problems like effective usefulness, profitability and economizing, are brought to the forefront by the operators and are declared to be the theme and content of architecture. Attention is given to taking an objective view of the plan's progress and creating standard architectural elements.

However it is useless continuing to discuss architectural problems if it is only a question of satisfying the existing requirements in the most rational way. If that were the case it would be better to abandon the field of architecture to producers who are more capable than anyone else of rationalizing the operational process.

It is equally difficult to derive a formal structural project from mere social conditions, since one cannot trust sufficiently either in the behaviour and habits of a single person's life or in the general public's feelings. In most cases people's good sense has turned out to be a failure as an artistic metre. Social factors naturally influence architecture, but careful analysis of people's habits and customs does not necessarily lead to the choice of an architectural form as well. Any architect who consults a sociologist must realize that the latter will simply exert the right of making a critical analysis and judgement of someone else's creative product, which does not belong to him.

The pretensions of Economy and Sociology are joined by those of Technology. There can be no doubt that the invention of new materials and the arrival of new building methods have enriched the world of construction. This fact, however, must not lead us to overestimate the thinking about construction, which is the case with those who spread the mistaken vision of the engineer as the artist-builder of the future.

When Lissitzky, one of the leaders of Constructivism, claimed there to be a link between the engineer and the architect, asserting that the introduction of new materials and construction methods was enough to make "the opus rise as an independent result," this was certainly a statement comprehensible in the enthusiasm first aroused by the opening of new constructive possibilities. All the same, another architecture cannot be born from the consequences of a material or a logical constructive idea; at best a technical work is born.

I do not deny that economic conditions, sociological requests and constructive requirements have an important part in the carrying out of a building. They are real factors, to which the activity of building is attached. But the overestimation of these factors and the consequent idea that that is

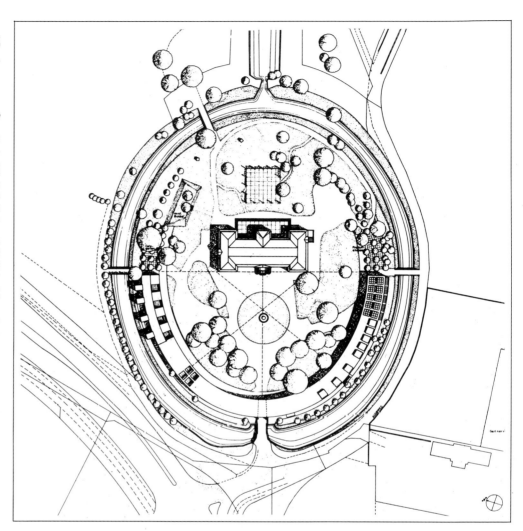

all architecture is for must be rejected. The work's destination does not contain in itself elements of formal choice. The wishes arising from it can only cause modifications in the arrangement, but the practical destination can in no way condition architecture in such a way as to compromise the laws belonging to it. Over and above the laws of construction, the consideration of human necessities and the effective usefulness is the imperative requirement of formal shape, and this is where the architect's spiritual responsibility resides.

The total failure of modern architecture in transmitting the cultural models of our times into formal symbols is proof of the lack of spiritual values and contents.

Since architecture is engaged in a continual process of dialectical tension between creative willpower and intellectual calculation, conception and

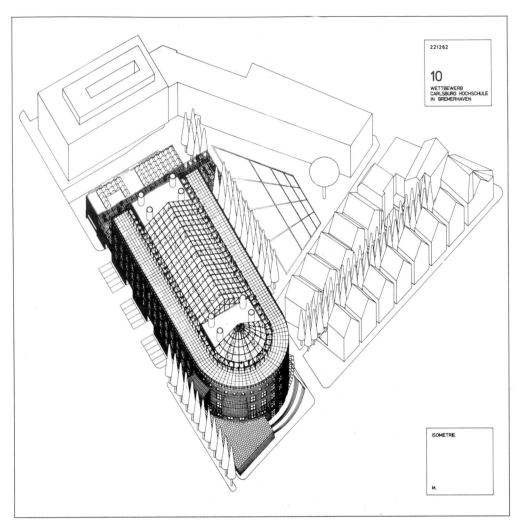

functional acceptance, imagination and reality, every theory tends to distinguish between practical knowledge and experience and intellectual know-how.

Two theories have thus emerged in the debate about the essence of architecture, each unacceptable to the other. The first inserts architecture into a general theory about art as a special field of artistic activity. The second, on the other hand, considers architecture to be autonomous: it has much in common with a general theory about art but in principle is clearly distinguished from it.

The first theory has essentially been in existence since the 16th century and is based on Vasari's work on the "Vite de' più excelenti pittori, scultori ed architettori italiani." Vasari believed that the arts of painting, sculpture and architecture merge in the ability to draw, and they thus had the same origin. The concept of "Beaux Arts," or Fine Arts, came into being as a result.

With the passage of time came the development of principles from the idea of Fine Arts that can be seen in the impartial character of the arts:

— No theory of Beauty should refer to aims of any kind; art should be impartial.

— The Beauty thus conceived should act on all the sensorial perceptions and should stimulate both visual and acoustic reactions.

— The idea of what is beautiful came to be formed as part of a general concept of life centred on the solicitation and investigation of sensorial experiences. Architecture was inserted in this concept of Beauty.

The alternative theory, according to which architecture is an independent art and must thus be considered only in relation to the art of building, is based in general on Kant's "Critique of Judgement." Here, for the first time in the philosophy of art, he distinguishes between the free arts, the "pulchritudo vaga," and the subordinate arts, the "pulchritudo adhaerens." In this way he separates pure art from applied art.

This means that architecture is counted among the subordinate arts, seeing that its existence has an intention and an aim.

This separation has conditioned architectural thinking right up to the present day. This also explains why those who glorify the concept of architecture as "pulchritudo adhaerens" display such a passionate hatred for fine appearances, formal effect and ideal function. One can also understand why the distinction between "pure art" and "art with a purpose" has caused general controversy among architectural theorists, spreading the tendency to consider pure art as an object without any function and disqualifying all activities linked to a purpose like architecture: they are judged to be imperfect and alien to art. Those whose opinion it is that architecture is art are slandered as formalists, individualists and utopians.

The concept of "applied art" became strongest in Germany, under the formula of "art with a purpose" and "functionalism." It has turned into the predominant idea in architecture and has stayed the same to the present day.

Anyway, the basic principles of this concept belong to the average intellectual baggage of every layman who is interested in the subject. They can be summed up in the following points:

— A building is only beautiful if it fulfills its functions in the best possible way.

— A building that fulfills its functions is beautiful as well, and

— An art object derives its form from its function. Thus all art objects, including buildings, are the result of an industrial or artisan production process. They are included in artistic handicrafts and not in art, and the same goes for architecture.

The last axiom was made popular by Semper in his book "Style in technical and tectonic arts." His influential theoretical treatises on material conformity and on the imprint of function on building method form the basic toolkit of modern architecture. They were most accurately reflected in the teaching of the Bauhaus. The professional preparation here was based on the didactic principle that if an object can be designed, then anything can, or, as Gropius put it: "The starting-point for any kind of design be it a chair, a building, a city or even a regional development – should be, as a matter of principle, identical." In this way architecture became no more than a part of the production process. Faced with this declaration of failure for architecture proclaimed by so-called "Modernism," it is worthwhile reproposing the reflection on the original values of architecture. Firmitas, utilitas, venustas, that is, stability of construction, appropriate arrangement of space and external beauty, are on the other hand the three equally important principles with which Vitruvius defined architecture. Any theory that wants to give serious reasons for the overall meaning of architecture is still concerned with these principles. Although different aspects dominated at different times – first the constructive mentality prevailed, then the way of articulating the space, then the formal points of view – it

AXONOMETRIE

nevertheless certain that these three elements: construction, space and form, are the true basic elements of architecture. Their right to autonomy exists independently from the social, political and economic conditions that present themselves now and then.

I would like to pause briefly to consider these three principles and their autonomous meaning in the field of architecture.

Form

Form describes the visual quality of architecture. It is decided by formal laws that are expressed in the building's visible appearance; it takes its vocabulary from the specific law of formal relations and does not depend on external influences. The formal language of architecture is not — as is commonly assumed — a function of empirical conditions in whatever way they present themselves, but it expresses the aesthetic value of architecture as a specific fact. It has its own ratio, and it is only in this way that the concept of rational architecture — which has been much debated in recent times — should be understood. Formal language's means are the laws by which bodies and space are formed. This is the language of architecture, which arouses a marvellous feeling. Architecture's expressive capacity transforms what is useful into something spectacular, that is, into art. With the aid of formal language, functions and constructions are transformed artistically just as sounds are transformed into music, words into literature and colours into paintings. The communication of ideas and experiences by way of the language of form is one of architecture's basic premises.

Space

The concept that a building is suitable for use only if it is employed for its original purpose seems obvious. This theory, however, which seems so evident, has for some time not only been doubted but also, especially in the criticisms of the so-called rationalists, has been the object of the most heated controversy. The real reason for this lies in the fact that even obstinate technocrats and functionalists must gradually realize that spatial conditions cannot be decided with exactitude, and that there is a great variety of types of buildings for which no perfect form can be found. Apart from this, buildings are often used for different purposes than the ones originally foreseen.

Thus doubt keeps on growing: should form be adapted to function or should it be the opposite, function to form?

There are abundant examples in the history of architecture of social and religious institutions which have developed in spaces previously in existence. The British Parliament, for example, where the government and the opposition sit opposite each other, derives from the fact that the first parliamentarians held their sittings in a Medieval choir. The French and German parliamentary systems, on the contrary, are based on the confrontation between the lone orator and his listeners, which corresponds to the form of Greek theatre. Originally the first type of space came from liturgical requirements and the second from those of Greek drama. Neither of the two uses had the

utilizable, but in the sense that its particular dimension expresses itself independently from external constrictions.

Construction

Architecture's third component is construction, "firmitas." What seem like good reasons sustain the supremacy of construction over space and form. The first is that architecture is basically the ability of composing different constructive elements, like walls, supports, ceilings, roofs, etc., into a whole. To this, however, can be added the knowledge that use and function change in the course of time and that for this reason the construction should obey logical and mathematical laws exclusively.

The real debate on the aspect of architecture had already begun in the 19th century and spread to the problem of architecture conceived as the exclusive product of logical constructions and building technique which conformed with the type of material. The debate concerned the idea of

slightest relationship with a functional arrangement for the workings of a parliament. Many examples could be cited so as to demonstrate how different functions from the ones originally foreseen have been transferred into existing spaces and have adapted their forms. Therefore the validity of certain spatial forms does not only depend on the functions, and the building's typology clearly prevails over its functions. The functions adapt themselves to the type of building, which can be conceived as a completely self-sufficient and autonomous project. This means that the creative element in architecture certainly cannot be its function, but rather the idea of the building, the real project, for it is the architectural archetype that defines the building. When it is a question of architectural language the function is secondary; it is simply a means of reaching an end, and not the end in itself. Let's take this formula to its limit: architecture is not dependent on the end, not because it is not

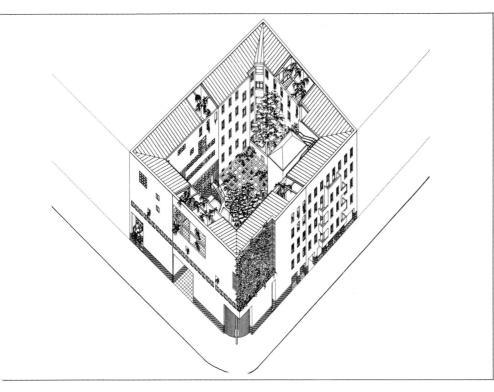

engineering and building ethics that were expressed in concepts like honesty, clarity, cleanliness and genuineness. Adherence to reality was obviously much less important at the beginning of the 18th century, when appearance (which meant appearance of beauty) counted more than reality, and when hypocrisy was highly approved of. Under the influence of the theories and treatises of Kant and Semper a construction was considered true to reality only when its structure and visible appearance corresponded accurately with the building project and with a use of the elements that was in line with the material. This doctrine was gradually dropped after many years of dogmatic domination, and people began to realize that the form of a building contains in itself much more than the correct use of materials or the mathematics of static structures. It was discovered that architecture could be the bearer of spiritual values and that it was capable of expressing emotions just like any other art.

After a long period of doctrinal dependence on the dogmas of modern architecture, what counts nowadays is that architecture should be accepted again as an art. In this way, architecture links up again with its tradition and with its true social mission after a series of deviations, misunderstandings, mistaken interpretations and libels. Like all the other arts, architecture is capable of freeing man's surroundings and existence from grey daily banality and from the vulgarity of reality, it can transcend the constraints of material necessity.

In this way architecture not only contributes to a notable extent in modelling man's surroundings, but also takes on once more its due humanist responsibility.

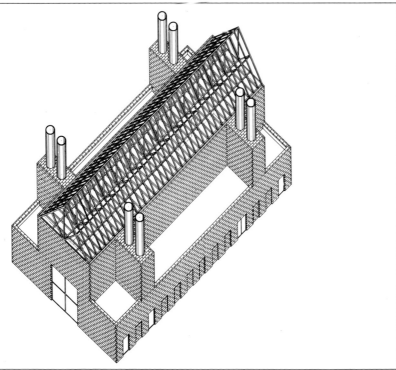

525. Housing project in Berlin-Charlottenburg (West Germany): overhead view.

526. Pumping-house, Berlin-Moabit (West Germany), 1979.

527-529. Project for the competition for the new Badische
Landesbibliothek, Karlsruhe (West Germany), 1979: general
axionometrics, interior perspective view, section and elevation.

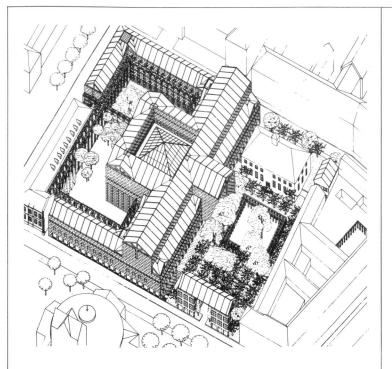

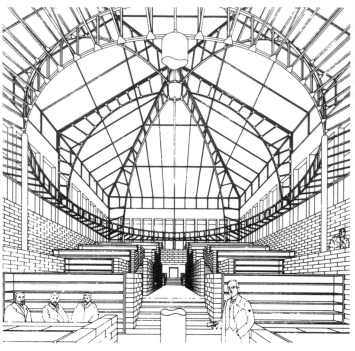

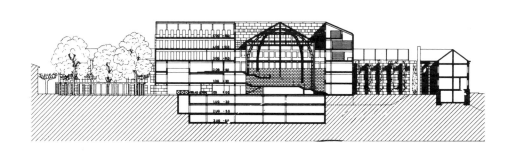

ERBPRINZENSTRASSE

ANSICHT ERBPRINZENSTR

Francesco Venezia

Lauro 1944.
Graduated from the Faculty of Architecture of Naples in 1970.
Has taught at the Planning Institute of the Naples Faculty of Architecture since 1971.
Lives and works in Naples.

The hidden part

Our eyes contain the depth of time.

A place can appear before us in the immobile substance of a petrified sail or in the dazzle of earth-water-air-sail, or reveal itself, monster-like, at the same time with both natures.

Our present is in the places and buildings we know. They are part of the great Machine that we observe so as once again to learn how to work its hidden levers.

An uninterrupted chain of ready-made answers to questions that have already been asked.

A cistern of mysterious sediments.

A plinth of square stone surfacing from a field of grain in Puglia.

An Egyptian obelisk set up over a Roman sarcophagus in the silent Hippodrome at Constantinople.

The expressiveness of what is missing — we would not have the fulfilled felling of a plinth of a platform of a floor (the primary intention of raising a place up), if architecture had not now given us these elements through pilfering — through the disappearance of what weighed them down.

Architecture is sometimes present by virtue of its absence.

The expressiveness of sediments made of sediments — the appeal of architecture's cast-offs: fragments that have mysteriously landed in a place as though left on a beach by a retreating wave.

Architecture is frequently born from cast-offs.

Miscellaneous fragments joined together, mysterious ciphers in familiar texts — ideograms in the verses of Pound, the imprint of the small shell in the concrete of a door at Ronchamp.

The Basilica, at Vicenza.

Galleries of shadow above one another beneath the magister of the sun.

Building fountain beneath the storm — the water falls rhythmically in taut parabolas from the ring of gargoyles.

A monstrous animal crouching in the full moon.

Attractiveness...

Man in time opts for half of the building; the other, the shadowy half, forms and is transformed slowly day by day, season by season...

Historic time and astronomic time intertwine their effects: they are the ever hidden part of architecture.

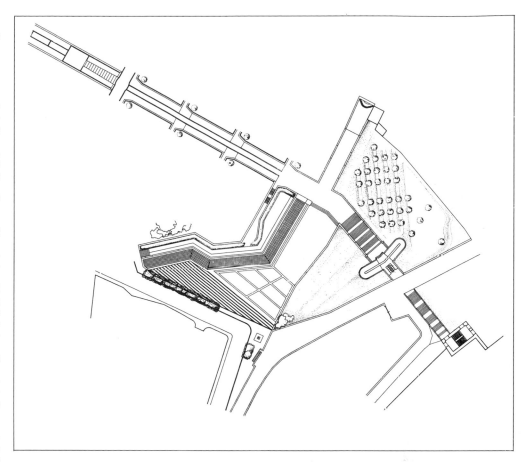

530-535. The square at Lauro (Avellino), 1978: general plan, partial views.

534-536. Project for the Town Hall of Taurano (Avellino), 1980:
plan, elevation and study sketches.

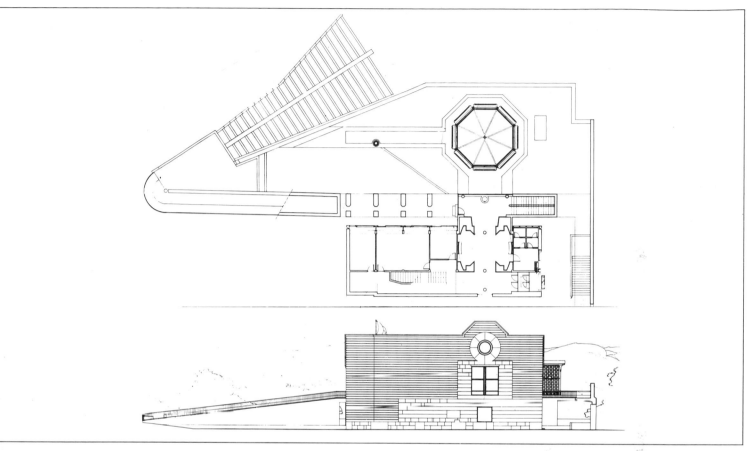

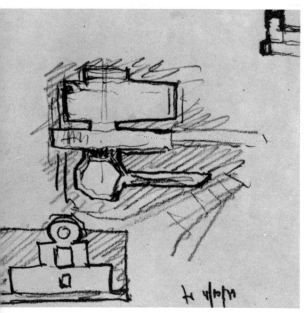

Robert Venturi, John Rauch, Denise Scott Brown

Robert Venturi
Philadelphia (Pa. USA), 1925.
Bachelor of Architecture at Princeton University in 1947 Summa cum laude and Master of Fine Arts in 1950.
Prix de Rome in 1954; three years study at the American Academy of Rome where he was Architect in Residence in 1966.
Taught in the most important American universities such as Yale University.
Member of the Board of Advisors for the Department of Art and Archaeology Princeton University.
He is the author of: *Complexity and Contradiction in Architecture* (N.Y. 1966) and with Denise Scott Brown and Steven Izenour of *Learning from Las Vegas* (Cambridge, 1972).

John Rauch
Philadelphia (Pa. USA), 1930.
Bachelor of Architecture at the University of Pennsylvania in 1957.

Denise Scott Brown
Nkana (Zambia), 1930.
Graduated from the Architectural Association in London (1955) and Master of Architecture at Princeton University in 1965.
Taught in important American universities such as University of Pennsylvania, University of California (Berkley and Santa Barbara), Yale University.
She has written – with Robert Venturi and Steven Izenour – *Learning from Las Vegas* (Cambridge, 1972).

For my teachers at Princeton, John Labatut and Donald Drew Egbert, the past was an important source of ideas and examples which they turned to naturally and easily in their attempt to understand and to teach contemporary architecture. It followed that I as a student, and later we as a firm, since the onset of our careers, have related past and present architecture in our thinking and working.

A brief outline of examples of this involvement would include my first article in the *Architectural Review* in 1953, which dealt with historical context as a factor in the perception of buildings, and used the Campidoglio as its example. *Complexity and Contradiction in Architecture*, published in 1966, relied on historical analogy as a method of criticism and theorizing about architectural form. In *Learning from Las Vegas* (1972) Denise Scott Brown, Steven Izenour, and I used Las Vegas and other historical examples, as vehicles for the study of symbolism in architecture. We analyzed architecture that is based on convention and precedent, illusion and association, and decoration. Since then, we have studied and written about architectural appliqué that recalls history and place, and stands distinct from the structure, function, and form of the building it is on. Our first completed building, the North Penn Valley Nurses' Center, contained an ornamental arch over the entrance and Classical mouldings on the lower windows. In 1961 these decorations were ignored by some critics and highly criticized by others. Since then many of our buildings have contained symbolic elements and some have taken on historical shapes.

537

537. Robert Venturi: Venturi House, Chestnut Hill (Pa.), 1962.
538. Robert Venturi: Project for Meiss House (first version) in Princeton (N.J.), 1962.

538

539

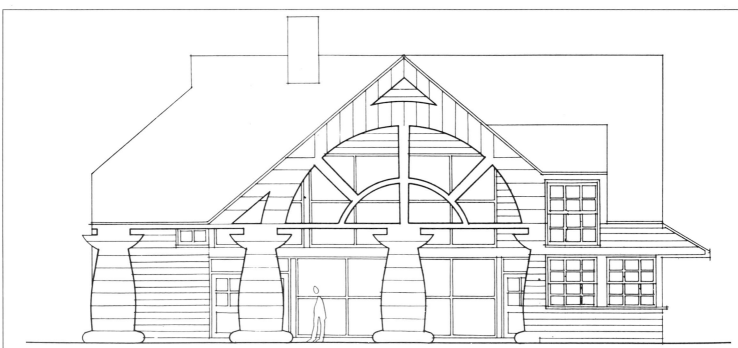

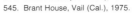

543. Studies for restoration of old center of Jim Thorpe, Philadelphia (Pa), 1979.
544. Brant House (Bermuda), 1975.
545. Brant House, Vail (Cal.), 1975.

Recommended Facade and Storefront Improvements
LOWER HISTORIC DISTRICT STUDY
JIM THORPE, PA.

VENTURI AND RAUCH, ARCHITECTS AND PLANNERS
FEBRUARY 13, 1979

546. Project for a rural house, 1978.
547. Project for County Federal Savings, Stratford (Ct.), 1977.
548. Project for Nichols' Alley, Houston (Tex.), 1978.

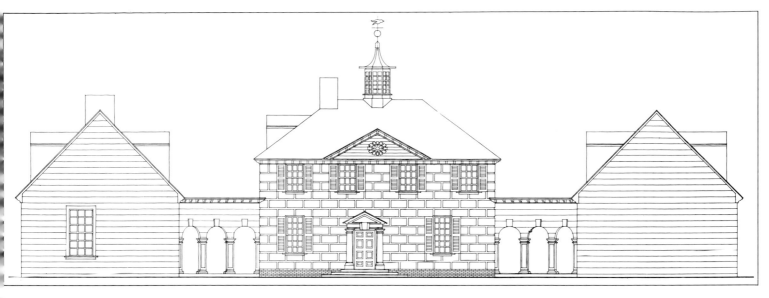

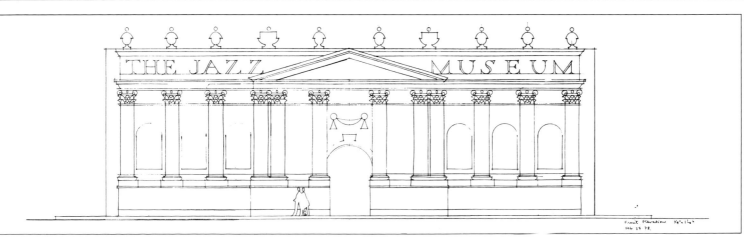

Ante Josip von Kostelac

549. Competition for the Hoechst town hall and people's centre (West Germany), 1979: general axionometrics.

550-551. Project for Stein House at Malchen (West Germany), 1978-80: axionometrics and elevation.

Zagreb (Yugoslavia) 1937.
Obtained his Diplomingenieur at the University of Zagreb in 1962.
Worked in Graz, Karlsruhe and Darmstadt.
Has been Lecturer in Building and Design at the Technische Hochschule of Darmstadt since 1978.

An Architectural self-portrait
"The spirit creates its own body" Adolf Loos.
Technical discipline and a rigorous concept of graphic description were the basis of my formation at the Zagreb University Faculty of Architecture in a historic, Neoclassical, intact city: graphic studies of ancient forms and admiration for the noble architectural ascesis of Mies van der Rohe were the starting points of my architectural consciousness. Even a few years ago it was out of the question for a convinced follower of modern architecture that contemporary life should create its wrapping, free from compromise. In the meantime this pioneering concept, untouched by doubt, gave way to a variegated consciousness.

Functionalism, which we believe to have been dead for some time, preached the fixing of the given function as an expression of architecture; now we know that our relationship with the function is mostly variable, but what distinguishes it is the connection and superimposition of the single functions.

I recognize myself in architecture's historic inheritance, in the traditions of classicism and humanism which have mostly been repressed by modern architecture, especially after 1945.

European culture and the poetic dimension of forms seen as an aesthetic quality are what counts in my work.

"Creative eclecticism" as a starting-point for surrealistic collages: no detail is a new discovery, but the assembly is new. Find novelty in what is familiar! Seek self-expression between experiment and eclecticism.

The grand gesture linked with self-irony and allusions to classical traditions are making headway through the blank stereometry of what is modern (Haus Malchen). This stirs up formal tension that threatens the precepts of what is usual and accepted.

Formal elements of modern classical architecture from the twenties, Bauhaus and Italian Neorationalism as the language of a poetic romantic rationalist.

The richness of formal and poetic invention as contributions to creative communication. Spatial vision checked by Intelligence. The desire for a sparing use of ornament on facades.

The portrayal of nature founded on the polarity of light and material, which shows up as a mutual playing of two partners on an equal level... so that through light, space can be penetrated and light can produce architecture in which man himself can be included.

My works must be seen as a subtle, spontaneous protest against established architecture.

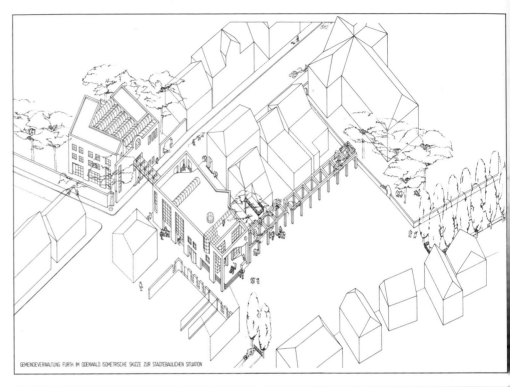

GEMEINDEVERWALTUNG FURTH IM ODENWALD ISOMETRISCHE SKIZZE ZUR STADTEBAULICHEN SITUATION

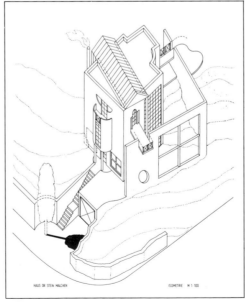

HAUS DR STEIN MALCHEN   ISOMETRIE M 1:100

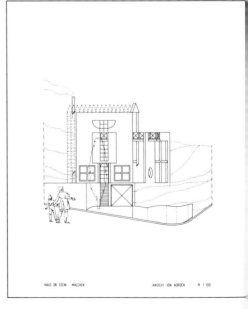

HAUS DR STEIN MALCHEN   ANSICHT VON NORDEN M 1:100

552-555. Malchen House (West Germany), 1976: internal and external views.

Peter Wilson

Melbourne (Australia) 1950.
Got his diploma at the Architectural Association in London in 1974.
Has been teaching at the AA since 1978.
Lives and works in London.

If describing the relationship of my projectural work to the history of architecture the.... words hover, like sand and rock, in the air. Their natural state. In rare instances, like the phosphorescent afterglow of the magicians slight of hand, they cease their random dance. Natural allegiances, structures and meanings appear seemingly implicit in their very nature. Such intimate certainties like buildings soon fall victim to time. Imperceptible earthquakes agitate both words and bricks. What we believe to be bonds become again voids. We must wait again in hope that when the writer stops writing and the juggler stops juggling, the words will fall in a sequence in truth and the bricks in the certainty of architecture.

The Water House 1976. Set against a neutral landscape this house is designed by reduction. Refusing referential or functional justification it relies instead on its archetypal forms and elemental material. The subconscious poetics of earth, fire, air and water exist as the common culture when the contemporary one is read as debased.
The Comfortable House 1977. A house as a mechanism that defines the relationship between its occupier and the world. An underground urban building, its real and virtual views correspond to the double reading of the architectural drawing.
Powerscourt 1979. An obviously historical context exploiting the theoretical and formal differences between the contemporary (the Villa Auto) and the classical villa (Powerscourt, a nineteenth century Irish stately home). Juxtaposed they share a common but empty center — there can be no center in the twentieth century. The old villa is now public, its owners having retreated to the two new and identical pavillions. The comic pavillion replacing a fountain in the formal garden is connected by an auto-path to the tragic pavillion in the ha-ha of the landscape garden.
Millbank Housing Competition 1977. The potentially infinite colonnade of housing forms a wall to the Thames. This and the various layers of the site behind are dense with popular and historical reference. These should not be specified, their layers of meaning exist as a provocation, enriching the spaces by implying potential rituals of occupation.

556-558. Project for the reconstruction of Powers Court (Ireland), 1979: general plan and elevations.

559. The water house, 1976.
560. A public convenience, 1977.

561. A comfortable house (for architectural speculation) in the metropolis, 1977: section.

Werner Christian Wontroba

Katowice (Poland) 1941.
Studied Architecture at the HBK of Berlin.
Teaches at the Berlin Academy of Fine Arts.

Ich lebe mein Leben in wachsenden Ringen / die
sich über die Dinge ziehen.
Ich werde den letzten vielleicht nicht vollbringen /
aber versuchen will ich ihn.
(Rainer Maria Rilke)

A thousand shadows joining /
make one more, /
like the shadow of a tree with its thousand leaves /
one thought covering the other, /
one culture burying the other, /
overlapping and stratified, /
forming a big hill: the culture of the present /
there is no chance of clearing away and
reconstructing those layers / without destruction.
Shadows of memory /
are source and root /
for a perpetual renewal.

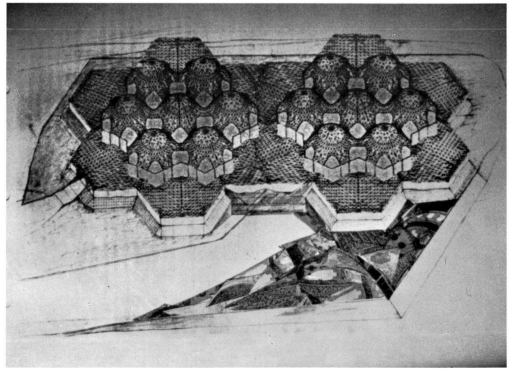

62. "Gothic-Classicism," 1971-1979.
63. "Markthalle-Bürgerforum," 1976.

564. "Gothic-Classicism", detail.
565. "Innenhofgestaltung," work on the house of A. Endell on Steinplatz, Berlin (West Germany).

The Corderia of the Arsenale

The Tana reopened: machines and workshops of the Arsenal of Venice
Manlio Brusatin

What is work before being conscience and ideology? It is wonder. Artificial privilege of the allure of manufacture, technique of a technique, marvellous and secret pretence: that's what Venice's Arsenal was. The primitive, infernal place in Dante's passage (1313) in Malebolge:
"e vidila mirabilmente oscura

....

bolle l'inverno la tenace pece"
original root and echo of the literature of images on the great workshop of the Arsenal, hovering over the incessant and frenzied drone of thousands of Arsenal workers; ever-praised work, narrated by fragments and impressions, actually never presented and described except through external figures as strategies of outward appearance (the main door) in cartographic drawings of enlargements planned and carried out like maps of former battles (overall plans).
After the archaic and motionless seven Wonders of the World, the Pyramid of Egypt, the Mausoleum of Halicarnassus, the Temple of Diana at Ephesus, the Colossus of Rhodes, the Statue of Zeus at Olympia, the Pharos of Alexandria, the Hanging Gardens of Babylon, the first Arsenal of Venice, a plain shelter for ships, becomes at the beginning of the 14th century (1303-1325) and throughout the one following, the site for every possible modern wonder: incessant work, where a ship can be built in one day or just for mere entertainment during a meal before the amazed eyes of a guest monarch, where some make oars, some make sails and others mill powders and cast guns, and everyone makes everything.
It is the myth of the eighth wonder and, at the same time, the historical depth of a *History of Industry* which is to be written sooner or later, not to run up, to a limited degree, against the classic terminology of the "history of capitalism:" accumulation of capital, production methods and ratios, conceptual analyses of technology with regard to the specific organization of work... An undertaking that – if we want to insist on the real limits of that "industry," not clearly commutable with the one of the last two centuries – would evince the objective limits of this same research. Certainly the industrial, modern and by now classic process, the "English way," reveals itself already in the 18th century through an effect of multiplicities and quantities: but how does it happen that a strong worker concentration of products and manufactured goods like the Arsenal of Venice, or concentrations of looms and spinning-mills in Florence or Bruges can produce, so to say, at the rate of a negative productivity, based solely on the concept of quality, which is non-comprehensive and non-limited? – to be quite clear, indivisible values of use and exchange. Ruggiero Romano has partly sketched the operating and counterpoising lines of the origins – by that time already explosive – of this pre-industrial industry, [1] showing, on the whole, a still mainly agrarian society: the same manufactured production had not taken on an autonomous technology or a "macchinalità" but was bound to end up absolutely dependent on mercantile activity. An unceasing flow of *Navires et Marchandises*

therefore, authentic *topos* of the historiography of the *Annales*, where the ship *is* merchandise, or, as it appears in the remarkable essay on Venice by Frederic Chapin Lane, flow of *Navires et Constructeurs*, [2] which I would appropriately re-entitle, from the original *topos*, *Navires et Marchands* since here we are, so far away from a productive technology and, finally, from that "technique of the technique" called *Armamento* (war in absence of war), in this case fundamentally of ships as today fundamentally of aeroplanes which is – going back to Clausewitz – the "rule" of political war "fought with other means."
This is the real explosive meaning beyond the historical one of the Arsenal over which economic history skims, attributing to this "monstrous" apparatus the good smell of wood and merchandise, comforting image of wonder as the traditional iconography of the Arsenal so often shows with its entrance, so architecturally definite and outlined, external *fabrica* to conceal the *internal* machina.
As a judgment-sentence of the strictly joined relationship between *fabrica* and *machina* in the 15th - 16th century cultural view, relationship by means of which the production of Italian machines seen as manufactured goods and inventive apparatuses is carried out – a process that I have already tried to explain but that, here, is worth summing up – [3] we could take that of Gottfried Wilhelm Leibniz, quoted in a letter (1671), addressed to the Duke of Hanover, later George II of England, where there is a programmatic extolling of German art which definitively tends to the building of moving and operating works in contrast to Italian art which is exclusively committed to the building of objects "without life, motionless, made to be beheld from the outside."
Opposing images that today end up by being platitudes when speaking of beautiful and ugly machines, of efficient and inefficient machines whose productive strain is still at the basis of a clash of cultures whose results now face each other in some memorable football matches, as in the breath and sweat of tourist masses who become Italian every summer. All the foreigners think it is impossible to work in Italy but they would like to live there, all the Italians think that abroad they can work and live only with difficulty. So flaunting these two last commonplaces, less common than a not merely German ritual between to be and/or to have, Italian culture is, by its nature, in a "Post-Modern" condition where we work to live, abrogating the dreadfully "modern" conception of living in order to work. Therefore those who make a cult of the avant-garde are invited to watch and sit down here, as long as they do not already fabricate, in their own analyses the conditions for the historical delays of Italian culture, which have been the subject of so many protests, first of all of which is the ignorance of our own arts and intelligence.
At the end of the 17th century Leibniz had decreed the exhaustion of the Italian *machina* and it was undoubtedly a functional and "modern" criticism; the result of Italian technical-artistic work brought about the "capo d'opera," the architectonic *fabrica*, where the employment of *labor* and effort – a distinction

outlined by Le Goff – required a result of the appearance in the *opus* (the monument, the finished work, the 16th-century town building itself): the final and immutable aspect, the unique result which rewarded even the role of the worker by means of a closed programme, coming to an achieved aim, defined by the design and by the different ambitions or manufacturing wills of those men who had produced it. The setting up of small and laborious dispersed and individual technologies (*pauper labor*) which had fixed their own image in the monument, (*magnum opus*) involved both the practical execution of drawing skills and the support of the political virtues of a prudent government the representation of the city-state as the visual making of its parts: palaces, roads, squares, forts perspectives, landscapes. So, at least, in the humanistic project of Italian art where the *machina* which dozes in Athens and seems to free itself of Platonic deadweights with Alexandrian mechanics gets to its own ethico-aesthetical working in the *fabrica*: external and meaningful token, final and erected construction, transposed into monument. All that after the intense activity of a great project which multiplies the human effort used and distributed within the "montatorie" and "tractorie" machines – as Alberti said – (or in Greek "acrobatiche" and "banausiche," that is hoisting and carriage machines) or of scaffoldings (the Brunelleschi "armadure"), such necessary temporary and subsidiary structures but destined to disappear with the disclosure of the building now to be beheld. A result not always achieved in an urban scene, very often not brought to a conclusion, as the holes and the "different" brick shapes of many façades of Italian buildings and churches show. In the holes left by the scaffolding we can read the interrupted moment of a drawing which "was to" have been accomplished with the definite stone facing, even after a great number of years ending up by never being completed, unless in the wide-open eyes of sharp observers.
In short in the Italian treatise on arts and constructions *fabrica* is a synonym for *architectura*, in particular in Leon Battista Alberti who, realizing such Vitruvian dubiousness (which will remain for the 16th century a programme of building production and quantity) wants to turn it into *res aedificatoria* in order to outline the possible field of the new mechanics of art in a diffuse and spoken construction. But *Fabrica* is *architectura* that should also be seen and beheld at the end of the 16th century characterized by the fever of erecting obelisks built by marvellous machines planned for their transport and setting up – gigantic towers which occupy the great printing plates of the "celebrated" architect who have invented them and, as any unique and unrepeatable work of wonder (effect of suddenness) they support the solitary obelisk which is as undamaged as it is vaguely superfluous by comparison with the apparatus of machines which have brought about its erection. After its construction (and *because of it*) the gigantic machines are bound to disappear. There is no longer a place for these machines.
The tenth book of *De Architectura* by Vitruvius is

1. Leonardo da Vinci, interior space in the Arsenale, ink drawing, ca. 1499, London, Queen's Gallery.

2. Light boats with multiple screws (above) and an unsinkable boat made of wood and oilcloth, watercolour in *De re militari* by Roberto Valturio, manuscript written in the middle of the XV century, Venice, Biblioteca Nazionale Marciana.

3. Machine for twisting ropes, engraving done at the end of the XVI century, in *Machinae Novae*, by Fausto Venanzio, Venice, undated, Venice, Biblioteca Nazionale Marciana.

completely devoted to *machine* and is, we think, the illustrative part of the text, unanimously believed to be the synthesis of Greek technical knowledge and of Roman mechanical learning. The historical reading in the end debases it. Francesco di Giorgio Martini gives an ideal summary — if compared to the better outcome of the first book and to the contemplation of the log cabin in the second book, offered as *idea* of architecture, birth of natural embellishments, virtual reunion of art to its natural origin. An archeological nature moralized before the dark, vibrating nature of the mechanical monster which is held separate and perhaps prevented from being completely "spoken," as it appears from the incomprehensible and unknown speech of the *machinae* described in the various Latin-Italian editions of Vitruvius from the 15th to the 16th century, as well as from the plates of Guido da Vigevano and Andrea Vesalio where out of the admirable anatomy of the *Humany corporis Fabrica* (15...), the mechanics of muscles could do nothing but be lost in a dead and decayed organism unless it does not recompose itself in its *fabrica*, worthy object of the exhibition and catalogue of autoptic science.

In fact the Italian translations of Vitruvius's tenth book differ greatly from the classical models of poetic-literary composition in order to achieve a style that is esoteric and defaulting at the same time as to the description of the working of the *machina*, an explicative formula which will approach the described subject only with the first illustrated editions.

Fra Giovanni Giocondo of Veneto (1511) is one of the first commentators of Vitruvius's *De Architectura*, which is provided with explanatory xylographies regarding above all the tenth book of *machinae*: however we are amazed at the archaic nature of these illustrative adaptations, taken, as it has been shown, from Byzantine models drawn from Alexandrian sources. The somewhat out-of-date aspect of this repertoire of *machinae* would not be justified if it had not been opportunely separated, as Fra Giocondo himself does, from the complete mechanical operations necessary, for example, for the reconstruction and enlargement of Veneto cities which had been rebuilt in a few months in 1510 under his jurisdiction and spurred on by the urge to withstand the return of Maximilian of Hapsburg. The Venetian dockyard organization and mechanized labour timetable of the Arsenal are for the first time exported out of Venice as requisites for a fast setting-up of the line of defence of the town which changed very rapidly in contrast to the sluggish display of urban inertia over several centuries.

The building timetables of the Arsenal and the rapid rhythms for the building of a ship are contrasted with the historic slowness of the building in post-medieval towns which employed entire generations of workers and architects: a condition that still affects the very slow manufacture times which can be found in Alberti, Francesco di Giorgio, Giuliano da Sangallo and also in Leonardo.

It would of course be useful if we could discuss the production times within the dockyard work for each building architecture achieved between the 15th

and the 16th century: the new employment of labour together with the mechanistic principles drawn from old ideas and technical minds, were all cases (which are not at all the times of the merchant) of production acceleration urged perhaps by the press of the war, elements of a system that would be completely inefficient if placed outside a great *casa-macchina* of industry like the Arsenal. This is the first point of discontinuity and laterality that the accelerating rhythm of the work of the Arsenal marks in the eternal clepsydra of production times of the artistic technique of the 16th century which is, as we have previously said, mainly *fabrica* in *architectura*. In all the cases concerning the complete divergence of application of production times — long for a church and a public building, short for a ship — the productive structure of the Italian workshop of the 15th-16th century is not indifferent to the production time. The foundry-workshop proposed by Vanoccio Biringuccio in *Pirotechnia* (Venice, 1540) already works by taking into account a specialization of the workers and an internal subdivision of the different work operations even if the construction site still remains tied to the necessity of working in the open, with rhythms slowed down according to the seasonal cycles, where time seems to be built with time. The *fabrica* actually lives on the construction calculation of its own working life, not on the minimum or reduced time which might be spent to build it: which is like creating our own virtues and fortunes out of our own immobility fixing in a state of rest the mobility of the *machina* "which moves for art's sake with many turns." So for Daniele Barbaro in *Dieci Libri dell'Architettura di M. Vitruvio tradutti e commontati* (Venice, 1561) the critical passage on the definition of the *machina* is translated in a very personal way if we look at the complicated description written for Raffaello by the "fixico" Fabio Calvo Ravennate (1514-15); here, in Barbaro's commentary, the "*machina* is a perpetual and continuous joining of material which has enormous strength, *i movimenti de i pesi*." At the foot of the definition we feel we should give a further concrete and contingent comment, this time wholly Barbaro's: "*Machina* is a *balancing*, or continuos joining of substance, *that is of wood*, which has immense strength, 'i movimenti de i pesi'."

The illustrative plates in Barbaro's Vitruvius still follow the outlines of the simple *machinae* dear to Alberti in *De re aedificatoria* (winches, windlasses, steelyards, wedges, pliers, pulleys) or implements listed in *Ludi matematici* of Leon Battista (fire and water watches, hydraulic gears and odometers). A general plate divided into six parts, restricts however a system of "modern" machines which establish their accelerated and multiplied engineering (water wheels, mills and grinders, Archimedean screws and norias, force and suction pumps) in contrast to the experimentation of the so-called "moti spirituali" and "automati" of Ero of Alexandria and to the toy-machines which can be found in other Alexandrian works of mechanics, reissued and annotated by Giambattista Aleotti, Federico Commandino and Bernardino Baldi in the middle of the 16th century. Only in this way — thought

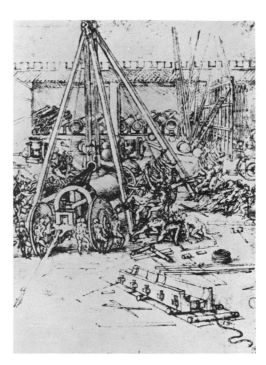

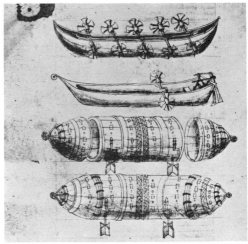

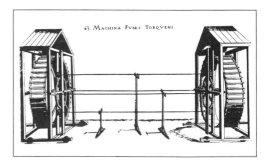

Daniele Barbaro — for the Arsenal: "Mars is chased off by Minerva" and this differently "to gain Reigns and Provinces." The presence of this new *ratio*, on the turning of a war industry into a state industry, acted upon or at least suggested by Daniele Barbaro, has been the object of useful and recent remarks by Ennio Concina.[4] Moreover the parallel reading of the *Quattro Libri* of Andrea Palladio and of the *Commento* on Vitruvius of his precious client would propose cores of condensation in Palladian criticism that would weigh down many utopian ideas, using the same key-words of this essay: *fabrica* and *machina*. At this point, we would also suggest some distinctions, within a list of intellectual technicians, which Filippo Pigafetta writes in a well-known introduction to the translation of *Mechaniche* (Venice, 1581) by Guidubaldo del Monte, whose editions of *machinae* and whose *canets* shared common interests with Giulio Savorgnan, a Veneto captain and officer of fortresses as well as of military machines. After the ancient mechanics of Ctesibio, the two Eros, Hero, Pappo, Carpo, Eliodorus, Oribasio and the modern Giordano Nemorario and Leon Battista Alberti, there is a set of three from Veneto: Niccolò Tartaglia, an algebrist rival of Gerolamo Cardano, known as the man who proposed Archimedean inventions for *Sulevare con ragione e misura ogni affondata nave* (1554); Vittorio Fausto of the Arsenal, the humanist who had proposed a naval colossus (the quinquereme) taking it from Archimedes and from Roman tradition, which was not a military success. Nevertheless it was the image of a project of restructuration of dockyard work which we would now call "integrated": horizontal (roofed-over and closed pavilions, standardization of pieces and tools, assembly lines) and vertical (forestry planning, territorial inventory of timber and pre-working, in loco, of naval pieces of equipment). Finally Daniele Barbaro, a frequent visitor to the Arsenal and an experimenter in this place of machines in the field of weight-lifting: unusual activities for a cardinal who had attended, with scrupolosity, the Council of Trent: his comment on Vitruvius's *Dieci Libri* or the *Pratica delle Prospettiva* (1589) was equally unusual as was the building of his villa at Maser (1557 onwards) which certainly involved setting up machines for the mere entertainment of the client and of his brother Marcantonio, even if nothing transpired in the final composition of the *fabrica* as was realized by Andrea Palladio.

This kind of intellectual mechanics had already begun to work in the Arsenal at the beginning of the 16th century, above all in the experimentation and ballistic patent of bombards and artillery, but the attempt of Vettor Fausto to impose an intellectual direction which was independent of tendencies if not of politics, is opposed by the *Proti* of shipyard workmen, of shipwrights and of art masters. Therefore in the running of the Arsenal there is the prevalence of a principle of defence of the workers' career and technical capacities exercised exclusively inside this state industry, inviting any free intellectual mechanic to become an "officer" of the Arsenal, in order to bind his technical knowledge to the regular internal operations. Now

is the time when — in the description of the functions which go beyond the Republic and the magistracies by Giorgio Contarini (1554) — the *fabrica* of the Arsenal becomes autonomous, a town within a town, with its own citizens, walls, government, simulacra of the official stability and of the production time. Only in this moment do the machine/ae, produced or to be produced, fix an image of organization prevailing over the organization which had dominated the production and the work of the society of the 15th and 16th century characterized instead, as we have explained, by the supremacy of the *fabrica* over the *machina*; here, on the contrary, the relationship changes, the internal "machinalità" of an Arsenal covered and organized for a continuous work, circumscribed by walls, becomes this time — and no longer archaically — the simulacrum of the modern "fabrica." This structure, however, does not invade the town but is run with the same specificity as the political organization of Venice (strictly kept far from any probable enemy or spy) in a structural tripolarity which distinguishes itself as founder of the genealogy of the statemanship of Venice: the Ghetto which organizes and does not exclude the ethnic diversity turning it into *tolerance*, the Lazzaretto which practises prevention and protection extending to *assistance*, the Arsenal which joins work and production in order to become *industry*. The map of the technical knowledge in Veneto, throughout the 16th century, is not uncertain in itself but is related to the Arsenal *machina* which appears as a distinct subject, object of convenient exemptions, compared to the history of internal institutions and to the effective "time" of the Arsenal, about which we know very little, which must be inferred from the parts of its own buildings with an expert scanning technique, to detect the slightest signs on the *body* of the monument, with even more cunning and application than the reading of archive papers which have undergone the filter of the word, order and law.

The capital towns of the technical knowledge between the 15th and the 16th century — in particular as to the pairing *fabrica machina*, pivot of our dissertation — are surely Florence and Nuremberg: the former for the specificity of the model, the specimen, the "supremacy of drawing," the latter with the secret and specialized mechanics of machine tools, suitable to construct the "uova" (pocket watches) and the "aquile" (automatons) made in Germany. Between these two poles, differing in their production and use of machines, Venice finds itself in a profitable position, playing upon intermediate technologies not precisely of the *machina* and of the finished article, but playing on the movement and transport of both and, paradoxically, of the shifting of one far from the other. What moves the effects of the *machina* from its product is some sort of side-technique which we will call "of fluidity;" internal movement of locations and still points with a flux of supplying and taking. In the great European commerce what Venice really "invents" is not the mechanism of finances, of credit and of accounts which belong to Florence (as it appears from the great number of petty

treatises on multiplication tables, or from the mathematical rules for the calculation of the volume of barrels to the spreading of the "rule of three" and of the "double entry" developed by Luca Pacioli), but the technique of transport and the regularity of trade. And this takes place despite a very particular and differentiated presence of goods on board distributed among merchants, shipowners and sailors (each of them is a producer of commerce) and an exacting and very meticulous drawing up of contracts of even the lowest importance, in contrast, for example, to the simplicity and brevity of Genoan bargaining formulas.

In addition this *fluidity* of traffic-transport does not occur only on the sea but also within the territory of the Republic which is crossed everywhere by waterways and canals, bridges, locks and quays: all that led the hydraulic-technical knowledge towards the territory trained to the idea of villa and to the policy of supporting the *low* technology compared with the *high* one of the Arsenal, from the 17th to the 18th century, as it appears, in particular, in the works of Alvise Cornaro, Daniele Barbaro, Vincenzo Coronelli, Bernardo Lodoli, Gianrinaldo Carli and Gianmaria Maffioletti.

The study of a well-known 15th-century manuscript, from the Marcian library, *De Machinis* (Lat. cod. VIII 40,2941), which assembles the inventions of the Sienese Jacopo Mariano, known as the Jackdaw, certainly not an autograph but a "duplicate" of a similar manuscript owned by Bartolomeo Colleoni and subsequently lost, evinces some interesting points by virtue not so much of its authenticity but of the additions of different styles which can be interpreted as a precise operation which concerns the 15th century Veneto mechanics. The curious inventions of Jacopo Mariano, recognizable in other manuscripts, are integrated with drawings taken from Francesco di Giorgio Martini and in particular from Roberto Valturio whose printed edition of *De re militari* came out in Verona in 1472. The drawing integrations are not at all complete if we compare them with a similar manuscript *Disegni di macchine diverse* (It cod. Z.86, 4817), from St. Mark's Library, the whole thing with the archaic and distant manuscripts of Vegezio and Sofiano which conjure up visions of sudden invasions, stratagems, surprise and wonder between the besieged and besiegers. These additions, with new drawings, declare a willingness and a technological programme deeply different from Florentine-Sienese *machinae*, at least in their insistence on metallic parts and on the exact assemblage of rolled and drawn iron in comparison with the traditional wood material. It is a matter of a deliberate metallurgical application already present in the fusion of bombards carried out by artists such as Donatello and by Paduan foundries. These are, however, only vague indications of the technical apparatus of the knowledge and work of the Arsenal, since the 17th century ends up in a visual, almost absolute void. Only two greatly meaningful images appear at the beginning and at the end of the dockyard production of this century which does not supply but rather erases images of itself. The first is one of

Leonardo's drawings, carried out probably during his Venetian stay (1499), fleeing from Milan, which was besieged by the French, that probably concerns the inside of the Arsenal of Venice. The drawing (now in the Queen's Gallery at Buckingham Palace) settles the theme of the lifting up and transport of a cannon ignoring none of the *machinae* and none of the energy expended on the work. The scene is enclosed by the typical walls of the Arsenal with canopies, where guns are lined up one on top of another. Proper sliding trolleys on round pallets serve to prepare the piece on the spot: in the middle the derrick crane, rich in technical details, where a pair of pliers held up by pulleys gathers the ropes that sling the nuts of the howitzer, to be laid on the gun-carriage or on the forecarriage of a cart with armoured wheels, much higher than the men who lock them. The enormous gun is lifted by the effort of four groups of workmen who alternately rotate an iron bar fixed in the rectangular heads of the two long winches: the rope wound round them is held back by two other groups of men for the slow manoeuvre of setting the piece on the gun-carriage.

The second image, engraved by the architect Giacomo Franco (1610) concludes very slowly the Leonardesque beginning which had been heavily under strain; it has an exhaustive and precise caption which brings out the window for the salary payment to the workers: "This is the door of the wonderful Arsenal where unceasingly galleys and other war vessels are built, and the people you see are the shipyard workmen who enter in the morning and go out in the evening, with perfect order." The worker satisfied with his hard-earned bag of coins stands again by the dignified and thoughtful group of craftsmen, everyone with his own tools or with the parcel of work clothes going out of the prestigious imposing door of the Arsenal: the place of secret and guarded work has, by now, become a modern factory with entry and exit working hours. According to the map of Venice by Jacopo de' Barbari (1500), the real construction of the Arsenal was carried out during the 16th century, in accordance with the maximum naval strength registered at the time of the Battle of Lepanto (1571). From 1516 the old Arsenal — behind its door towards the town — is inactive and the new Arsenal developed with powder and artillery units opens on Novissima Grande dock, the real 16th-century part, where the ordinary *squeri* (sheds) and the gigantic galleasses stretch away towards the lagoon, in front of the dock and the canal by the same name which easily doubles the basin of the old Arsenal. With the artillery workshop flanking the Corderia and the oar workshop jutting out townwards near the entrance but, above all, with the shelter and covered dock of the Bucintoro (1547) designed perhaps by Nicolò Sammicheli expressly for the golden galley of the Wedding of the Sea, the comprehensive structure of the Arsenal comes to a close. A further completion, half architectonic and half commemorative, is carried out only after the Battle of Lepanto with the Gaggiandre (1573), exceptional covers on the water that a long-standing tradition ascribes to Jacopo Sansovino, and with the rebuilding of the

House of Canevo or Corderia of the Tana carried out by Antonio Da Ponte (1583) — later architect of the Bridge of Sighs, — "the longest and broadest house I or anyone else has ever seen," as it is already defined by the traveller J. de Chambes in 1459, which is the wonder of wonders.
The name itself "the Tana," apart from its apparent and actual meaning, has always been linked to the town described by Marco Polo in *Livre des Merveilles* (chapter CLXI): "Tana is also a great kingdom... here there is a lot of 'bucherame' and cotton-waste (net and cotton rags)." But close to the real needs, the Tana building — one thousand Venetian feet long — as long as the longest hawsers which could be made, is the fittest place to house the *Machinae Novae* (about 1615) of the Dalmatian Fausto Veranzio who draws, in a curious collection of plates, a system of fountains for St. Mark's square, lenticular beamed bridges in iron and wood, "water-wheels," "movable-roofed towers" and "flying men" together with "machines which twist ropes" which, from his description, are doubtless destined for the Corderia of the Arsenal: "The machines which twist our great ropes these days, can only be worked by man with the greatest difficulty; operating with no particular art except the use of strength alone. Thus I have found this new Machina, which moves with my double wheel, with this wheel a man alone will do more than many using only their own physical strength." [5] This treatise of Fausto Veranzio along with another famous one, *Nuovo Theatro di Machine et Edificii* (Padua, 1607) by Vittorio Zonca, describes the Veneto mechanical knowledge still strongly mixed with architecture and useful arts, a note not present in *Diverse e artificiose machine* (1588) by Agostino Ramelli from Lugano, by now an expert in the continental military-technical knowledge, and not even in *Miracoli e meravigliosi effeci dalla natura prodotti* (Venice, 1560) by the Neapolitan Giambattista Della Porta, a catalogue of jokes and tricks where the Southern magical-scienfiic knowledge is going to become independent of that of the Northern towns of Tartaglia and Cardano. All this production of minds and machines is nearly the opposite (for the still radical opposition of the leading concepts *fabrica / machina*) of the first and most important illustrated treatise of the industrial era of the continent, not only of Germany; the treatise on the extraction of metals and on mining work, *De re Metallica* (1546) by Georg Bauer Agricola, physician and expert in fossils, who completed his studies in Padua and applied with unusual energy the principle of useful machines at all costs, over those typically Italian machines appreciated only for their outward appearance (or secret, which is the same). Also the Arsenal remains still, it does not develop, and multiplies like the small defective but active *machinae* of Agricola.
The 17th century is not so much an inactive century for the Arsenal as the silent transformation into a secret state prison and the often denigrating images of the "false government" of the Republic of Venice spread before the European principles in the 17th-century anonymous *Squitinio della libertà originaria di Venezia* (Cologne ed., 1681), are stressed, even

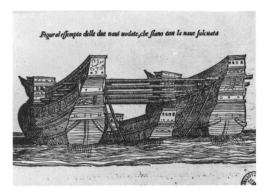

Figural essempio delle due naui uodate, che stano con la nsue sulcuata

Figural essempio delle due naui piene di acqua, per sulcuarre la naue affondata

too peremptorily, by Luigi Helian with very hard words; "... They compel their subjects to carry materials for their public works, as if they were so many horses or donkeys, they force them to go to war, or serve in their galleys where they are beaten. They are charged with duties and gabelles; Governors and Officers are sent to the towns of their Dominion: men who have spent their youth, not in Padua or in Paris, but on the Sea and on Tanai, who, instead of studying Philosophy or the Law, or our Religion, have learnt to squeeze the peoples dry and to heap money using any means, assuming Barbarous manners and Mohammedan superstitions and customs." [6] The comment of the Pole Billewicz in a nearly contemporary diary (January 1678) does not differ very much: "I went to the galleys where I saw masses of people in slavery, some sold, some captured, coming from different countries... And here they are in deep indigence, always working enormously and surviving miserably with abominable clothes, always fettered, never free, except during the battles, when a galley clashes with another one, then they are freed of their chains." Womb of a great galley of ignominy and slavery, a subject still to be probed, the Arsenal hardly recognizes itself in the recomposed image of the fresco that Angelo Diedo ordered for his villa of Breganze: result of an enlightened rearrangement (1675), which is revealed through the ordered matter of a reformistic enterprise that remained perhaps unrealized or emblematically realized in the entrance yard (1687) with new Constantinople insignia.

Carlo Contarini, in a precious *Relazione sulle condizioni dell'Arsenale di Venezia* (1662) had already enquired into the causes of the decadence of the House of the Arsenal "reduced to such a miserable state that where the superflous abounded, now the necessary is missing," [7] and finds a way out speaking with sadness as if he were in front of a mirror, in his own words — by now corroded, where one do can nothing but contemplate the nation's calamities. After the survey and estimate of the potential of the fleet (of eight galleys called *galleazze* not even one is operating) the inquiry goes into the question of the analysis of timber requirements: English oak used for planking is abundant, fir-trees for the masts grow in a protected place in Carnia, while walnut for rudders, beech for oars (this is strictly linked also to a good craftmanship), elm for forecastles, the supports and ship findings, ash for pontoons and for the moving parts must be seriously subject to quota restrictions together with the tow for the necessary rigging and *canevo* and pitch (*pegola*) for the tarring and caulking of keels, everything imported from the Near East. The plan, however, turns out inexplicably defective as to the whole metallurgical system and the co-ordination of iron manufactures coming from the Brescia and Agordo mines — seafarers seem to hate metals. But a territorial policy and a policy for the promotion of cultivation (hemp) and woods (oaks and beeches) shows itself ahead of time, a policy which was to be systematically described by Bernardo Lodoli in his *Cuore veneto legale* (1703) and his mnemonic tables relative to this government: "Oaks and

10. La Tana or Corderia in the Arsenale, lithograph, in *Vedute e prospettive degli interni de' migliori tempi e delle situazioni più pittoriche della città di Venezia disegnate da Andrea Tosini e incise all'acqua tinta da Antonio Lazzari*, Venice, 1829, Venice, Museo Correr.

11. Interior space in the Corderia (photograph by Antonio Marticelli).

12. Ignazio Colombo. Explosion in the Arsenale, engraving, 1793, Venice, Museo Correr.

canepi are the favourite ones," towards the programmed rationalism and physiocraticism of the culture of Veneto at the height of the 18th century. And throughout the entire 18th century it is hard to find deep signs of decadence in the Arsenal except in the warnings of disturbances and hierarchical overthrows on which the Arsenal broods without displaying, and which appear only in the *Carceri* of the Venetian architect Piranesi. [8] How is it possible not to see fearfully in the mankind segregated in that space which Giambattista frequented as a boy with Giovanni Scalfurotto, *proto* of the Arsenal masons (from 1711), that monstrous truth of the former times and places of a structure which slows and reveals itself, as in prophecies, only to children and crack-brains? We think that the discovery which most injures im childhood is the diversity of sexes, hence — inferring from Freud — the discovery of class diversity and oppression, and that the object of affection which we carry with us is without exception, the last one of this terrible ascertainment: for Piranesi the *irreverential* object of his ancient-obsessive history in the Arsenal. And the exalting in front of those differently productive ruins, costs precisely the very high price of the absolute truth which generally loathes itself, and in itself, is not true for any rationalist who sees in the present only the image of a prospective way out. Also Piranesi's *Carceri*, like the Venetian Arsenal, are the concealed part, burdened with dead-weight, far from the "civil" history view. Even figuratively, not to fall in ideological suggestions, the state of hard labour, normally in force at the beginning of the century of revolutions, finds itself in an almost unjustified expansion, in that unlimited and cell-shaped space which is used for building galleys and where generally everyone falls back but which must yield to the statute of modern factory. This helps us to say that this workplace — the operating factory — will become the best government machine precisely when the lightness of sentences will be asked for since the former

harshness could no longer be applied, but it works through the duration and the "form" of the same production time.

And the ruin, the dead and useless part of the Arsenal is the original image and genealogy of a scene of figures of the prison work that the young Piranesi, fleeing from Venice (1740), carries with him. His *Carceri* are not only the works of a nature stronger than time, stronger than art but are the reject usefully abandoned which rests on itself and ferments. There is the suspension typical of Piranesi that this surface breaks against something repudiated and impeded, something set punitively to nourish the great energy, on the level of moral and civil ground of the reason which arranges and fosters speeches out of those ruins, picking up all the pieces which serve for a new state, no longer as small as a town, marking unfailingly the borders (which cannot be limited) of its empire.

After the angry escape of Piranesi, there are those who remain — will they be the culprits? Those who go on working for the Arsenal after Piranesi, Giuseppe or Tommaso Scalfurotto (a relative of the same *proto* Giovanni Antonio and Matteo Lucchesi) who will accomplish the true construction, typical of the Enlightenment, inside the Arsenal, in coincidence with the reformism wave of Veneto rationalists in the 1780's. It is the Squadratori Building (1788) near the Galeazze basin; school and workshop at the same time, like what architects and drawing masters tried to set up for "masons, stone-dressers and carpenters" elsewhere in the Veneto. Also the Tana had been ennobled in 1779, perhaps by Filippo Rossi, the *proto* in the factories, with a massive entrance door, in order to disclose the exactness of old and moralizing principles. The Englishman, J. Patisson, assisted by the Venetian Domenico Gasperoni, builds inside the Arsenal a museum like a garden of scrap-iron, setting the cannon-balls with the taste of a French sweet-shop, taken from *Le pâtissier pittoresque* of A. M. Câreme, by gathering, lining up and raising the

cannons scattered through the Arsenal, nearly a new set of columns, careened with gun parts and springals like skewers and spits, together with mural formations of Saracen armours like motionless shoals of lobsters and shrimp shells; the prototype of the most crackling barracks art of the ancien régime, *Wunderkammer*, properly cooked and served with an apple in the mouth. It is impossible not to appreciate it.

Professor Giammaria Maffioletti, elsewhere, will impartially document in the unpublished work *Brevi e succinti principi agrari Boschivi a lume degli Scolari di Naval Architettura nell'Arsenal di Venezia* [9] the old programme of the conservation of territory promoted by a constant branch of politics in the management of the Arsenal, together with a rare essay on wood technology which stands as a hibernated exemplar like technical knowledge soon swept away, with the destruction of the Arsenal, by the "French fury" in 1798. An essay which the abbot Maffioletti will rearrange "before" and "after" in two decorative plates dedicated to Francesco II of Austria.

Explosion and frightful destruction; reassembled during the second French domination of Venice, in 1810-1811, with a great intervention of maritime settling and with the building of a tower, whose exclusive function was the hoisting of ships: paradoxical and unique building, open onto the Porta Nuova, like an absurd architecture by J. J. Lequeu on the water — a real architectonic museum near the Gaggiandre of Sansovino.

How could they not think of bringing this authentic stronghold of guilds to life again, replacing the bell for shipyard workmen, rebuilding the pointed vaults in the *squeri*, reforging the wrought irons in that theatrical Gothic style which conjured up Fascist Italy in the Arsenal life and in the Arsenal workers — one is reminded of D'Annunzio — when in the morning they set off with very long strides for their "war work"?

The great silence after waves of dispersed steps, is now engraved, in front of the store of aquatic reassembled material: "The country is to be served above all in silence, in humility and discipline, without rhetoric phrases but with continuous daily work."

To behold this silence is the last itinerary whispered by the dark Arsenal of Venice in its greatest building ever seen: the Tana re-opened.

1. Ruggiero Romano, *Industria: storia e problemi*, Turin, 1978.
2. Frederic Chapin Lane *Navires et constructeurs....*
3. Manlio Brusatin La macchina come soggetto d'arte in *Annali della Storia d'Italia*, Turin, 1980, vol. III.
4. Ennio Concina "Dal 'tempo del mercante' al 'Piazzale dell'Impero': l'Arsenale di Venezia", in *Progetto Venezia*, Venice, 1980.
5. Fausto Veranzio *Machinae Novae....*
6. Anonymous, *Squitinio della libertà originaria di Venezia*, Cologne, 1681, pp. 214-15.
7. Carlo Contarini "Relazione sulle condizioni dell'Arsenale di Venezia" (1622), in *Nozze Canali-Benotto*, Venice, 1882.
8. Manlio Brusatin, *Venezia nel Settecento: stato, architettura, territorio*, Turin, 1980, pp. 339-41.
9. Giammaria Maffioletti, *Brevi e succinti Principi Agrari Boschivi a lume degli Scolari di Naval Architettura nell'Arsenale di Venezia dettati loro dall'Ab. Maffioletti... in ubbidienza e nova commisione ingiuntasi dall'ordinanza Inquisitorial approvata dall'Ecc.mo Senato* (about 1790), Author's property.

Index

The names in italics indicate the exhibiting artists. The names in Roman letters are the artists to whom reference is made in this catalogue.

Aalto Alvar, pp. 28, 31.
Alberti Leon Battista, pp. 33, 246, 275, 342, 343, 344.
Anselmi Alessandro, p. 164.
Aprile Marcella, p. 251.
Architektengroep VDL. p. 79.
Asplund Gunnar, p. 81.
Aymonino Carlo, pp. 12, 306.

Barabino Carlo, p. 50.
Barbaro Daniele, pp. 343, 344.
Basile Ernesto, p. 12.
Batey Andrew, p. 81.
Beeby Thomas Hall, p. 84.
Behrens Peter, pp. 12, 28, 304.
Benamo Georgia, pp. 35, 89.
Bernini Gian Lorenzo, pp. 134, 189.
Bétrix Marie-Claude, p. 271.
Bigelman David, p. 297.
Bisconti Adriana, p. 251.
Biurrun Salanueva Francisco, p. 93.
Blatteau John, p. 95.
Bofill Anna, p. 98.
Bofill Emilio, p. 98.
Bofill Ricardo, pp. 18, 28, 29, 34, 38, 98.
Bonet Pep, pp. 103, 115.
Borromini Francesco, p. 285.
Botta Mario, p. 334.
Boullée Etienne-Louis, p. 212.
Brancusi Costantin, p. 24.
Breuer Marcel, p. 15.
Brown Frank E., p. 16.
Brunelleschi Filippo, p. 31, 342.
Brusatin Manlio, p. 106.
Buffi Jean-Pierre, p. 110.
Burnham Daniel Hudson, p. 84.

Campi Mario, p. 271.
Candilis George, p. 234.
Carniaux J.P., p. 98.
Castagnetti Franco, p. 251.
Cellini Francesco, pp. 38, 112, 134.
Chiatante Paola, p. 164.
Cirici Christian, pp. 103, 115.
Ciucci Giorgio, p. 306.
Clotas Salvator, p. 98.
Clotet Lluis, pp. 103, 115.
Coenen Jo, p. 118.
Cohen Stuart, p. 120.
Collado Ramon, p. 98.
Collovà Roberto, p. 251.
Colombari G., p. 270.
Colucci Gabriella, p. 164.
Consolascio Eraido, p. 271.
Consuegra Guillermo Vazquez, p. 123.
Coronelli Vincenzo, p. 344.

Cosentino Nicoletta, p. 125.
Culot Maurice, pp. 17, 128, 217.
Czech Hermann, p. 132.

Dal Co Francesco, p. 306.
D'Amato Claudio, pp. 38, 134.
Da Ponte Antonio, p. 345.
D'Ardia Giangiacomo, p. 143.
Dardi Costantino, pp. 9, 38, 137.
Da Sangallo Giuliano, p. 343.
Da Vinci Leonardo, pp. 343, 345.
De' Barbari Jacopo, p. 345.
De Boni G., p. 270.
De Bretteville Peter, p. 222.
De Chirico Giorgio, pp. 18, 33.
Delacroix Eugène, p. 224.
De Portzamparc Christian, pp. 35, 38, 89.
Digerud Jan G., p. 200.
Di Giorgio Martini Francesco, pp. 343, 344.
Dillon Patrick, p. 98.
Di Noto Anna, p. 164.
Dixon Jeremy, pp. 36, 146, 203.
Drew Egbert Donald, p. 328.

Eisenman Peter, pp. 17, 30.
Erith Raymond, p. 300.
Eroli Pierluigi, p. 164.
Erskine Ralph, p. 36.

Farina Paolo, p. 148.
Farrel Terry, p. 150.
Feugas Jean Pierre, p. 297.
Filarete (Antonio Averulino), p. 275.
Franco Giacomo, p. 345.
Friday, p. 152.
Fuller Richard Buckminster, p. 59.

Gardella Ignazio, pp. 12, 50, 52, 57, 61.
Garnier Tony, p. 246.
Gasbarian John Joseph, p. 295.
Gasperoni Domenico, p. 348.
Gaudì Antoni, pp. 18, 28.
Gehry Frank O., pp. 18, 31, 38, 61, 154, 306.
Genovese Federico, p. 164.
Gerard Patrick, p. 98.
Giocondo fra' Giovanni, p. 343.
Giovannoni Gustavo, p. 50.
Godard Keith, p. 222.
Gold Michael, pp. 158, 203.
Grashorn Burkhard, p. 161.
Grassi Giorgio, p. 33.
G.R.A.U. Studio, pp. 38, 164, 165.
Grau Xavier, p. 98.
Graves Michael, pp. 19, 29, 31, 38, 61, 170, 306.
Greenberg Allan, pp. 16, 18, 38, 176.
Gropius Walter, pp. 15, 23, 28, 320.
Grossi Giuseppe, p. 181.
Grumbach Antoine, p. 184.

Guimard Hector, p. 28.

Hejduk John, p. 30.
Hilberseimer Ludwig, p. 306.
Hilmer Heinz, p. 187.
Hodgetts Craig, p. 222.
Hodgkinson Peter, p. 98.
Hoffmann Joseph, p. 12.
Hollein Hans, pp. 35, 36, 38, 189.
Hood Raymond, pp. 31, 214.
Horta Victor, p. 28.
Huet Bernard, p. 297.

Inigo Jones, p. 300.
Isozaki Arata, pp. 38, 194.
Izenour Steven, pp. 17, 328.

Jahn Helmut, p. 198.
Jan & Jon (Jan G. Digerud, Jon Lundberg), p. 200.
Jansana J., p. 98.
Jefferson Thomas, p. 306.
Johnson Philip Cortelyou, pp. 12, 19, 30, 31, 59, 61, 62.
Jones Edward, p. 203.

Kahn Louis I., pp. 16, 17, 18, 24, 26, 27, 29, 30, 165, 289, 297, 306, 314, 334.
Kallmann Gerhard, p. 30.
Kawahara Ichiro, p. 205.
Kijima Yasufumi, p. 205.
Kleihues Joseph-Paul, pp. 12, 18, 38, 161, 208, 217.
Klotz Heinrich, p. 334.
Koolhaas Rem, pp. 9, 19, 33, 34, 35, 38, 214.
Krier Léon, pp. 15, 17, 19, 33, 34, 35, 38, 106, 131, 217, 306, 334.
Krier Robert, pp. 15, 17, 19, 35, 306, 334.
Kroll Lucien, p. 36.
Kupper Eugene, pp. 31, 222.
Kupper Gérard, p. 224.

Labatut John, p. 328.
Labrouste Henri, pp. 16, 17, 212.
Lamunière Jean-Marc, pp. 224, 227.
La Rocca Teresa, p. 251.
Laugier Marc-Antoine, pp. 33, 35.
Le Corbusier, pp. 15, 17, 18, 24, 28, 30, 31, 33, 35, 246, 334.
Ledoux Claude-Nicolas, pp. 31, 34, 212.
Legache Catherine, p. 228.
Leoncillo (Leoncillo Leonardi), p. 165.
Leonidov Ivan, p. 214.
Lepère Yves, p. 228.
Lequeu Jean-Jacques, p. 348.
Leroy Bernard, p. 297.
Lissitzky El, p. 319.
Llistaseila Xavier, p. 98.

Lodoli Bernardo, pp. 344, 346.
Loerakker Ben, p. 79.
Lombardo Fabio, p. 251.
Loos Adolf, pp. 33, 81, 189, 334.
Lucchesi Matteo, p. 348.
Luckhardt Wassilly and Hans, p. 69.
Lundberg Jon, p. 200.
Lutyens Edwin, pp. 16, 18, 20.
Lyndon Don, pp. 240, 314.

Machado Rodolfo, p. 230.
Mackintosh Charles Rennie, p. 28.
Mack Mark, p. 81.
Magnaghi Alberto, p. 110.
Mainini Giancarlo, p. 143.
Mallas Frank, p. 152.
Mallet-Stevens Robert, p. 234.
Manieri-Elia Mario, p. 306.
Marchioni F., p. 112.
Mariotti Roberto, p. 164.
Martini Massimo, p. 164.
Masheder M., p. 159.
Matzkin Donald R., p. 152.
Maybeck Bernard Ralph, p. 18.
Meier Richard, pp. 17, 30.
Melnikov K., p. 214.
Meyer Hannes, p. 23.
Migliore Omar, p. 98.
Milani Pino, p. 164.
Minardi Bruno, p. 181.
Moholy-Nagy Laszlo, p. 24.
Mondrian Piet, p. 165.
Moneo Rafael, p. 306.
Montes Fernando, p. 234.
Montuori Francesco, p. 164.
Mooney Kemp, p. 237.
Moore Charles W., pp. 16, 17, 18, 32, 34, 35, 38, 240, 306, 314.
Morris William, p. 212.
Mozuna Monta (Kikoh), p. 246.
Mulas Franco, pp. 164, 165.

Neumann Gerd, p. 249.
Newman Arnold, p. 59.
Nicolin Pierluigi, p. 251.
Nicolosi Patrizia, p. 164.
Niemeyer Oscar Soares, p. 35.

Olbrich Joseph Maria, p. 28.
Oliver Richard B., p. 254.

Palladio Andrea, pp. 31, 34, 125, 134, 228, 300, 343, 344.
Pareja Hilario, p. 98.
Passi Dario, pp. 143, 144.
Patetta Luciano, p. 256.
Patisson J., p. 348.
Patrizi Giampietro, p. 164.

Paxton Joseph, p. 212.
Pei Icoh Ming, p. 30.
Peili Cesar, p. 30.
Pfeiffer Herbert, p. 259.
Pierluisi Franco, p. 164.
Pietilä Reima, pp. 27, 28.
Piranesi Giambattista, pp. 35, 348.
Placidi Corrado, p. 164.
Podrecca Boris, p. 262.
Polet Joseph, p. 228.
Poncet Alain, p. 224.
Porro Ricardo, p. 297.
Portman John, pp. 30, 31.
Portoghesi Paolo, pp. 12, 18, 27, 28, 38, 52, 68, 224.
Pugin Augustus Welby, pp. 37, 212.
Purini Franco, pp. 38, 265.

Rauch John, pp. 237, 328.
Recevsky Thierry, p. 98.
Reichlin Bruno, p. 271.
Reinhart Fabio, p. 271.
Repton Humphrey, p. 35.
Ricchino Francesco Maria, p. 52.
Ridolfi Mario, pp. 12, 13, 61, 68, 69, 71.
Rijnboutt Kees, p. 79.
Robertson Jaquelin, p. 17, 18.
Rocamorra M.D., p. 98.
Rocias J.M., p. 98.
Rodin Auguste, p. 304.
Rogers Ernesto Nathan, pp. 59, 275.
Rosato Enzo, pp. 164, 165.
Rossi Aldo, pp. 10, 12, 13, 18, 19, 21, 22, 24, 33, 34, 35, 38, 271, 275, 306, 334.
Rossi Filippo, p. 348.
Rota Italo, p. 251.
Rowe Colin, pp. 33, 34, 35, 36.
Ruijssenaars Hans, p. 79.
Ruskin John, p. 212.

Saarinen Eliel, p. 28.
Samuel Danny Marc, p. 295.
Sanmicheli Nicolò, p. 345.
Sansovino Jacopo, pp. 345, 348.
Santelli Serge, p. 297.
Sattler Christoph, p. 187.
Scalfurotto Giovanni Antonio, p. 348.
Scalfurotto Giuseppe, p. 348.
Scalfurotto Tommaso, p. 348.
Scarpa Carlo, p. 12.
Schindler R.M., p. 189.
Schinkel Karl Friedrich, pp. 12, 33, 34, 36, 81, 212.
Schlaun Johann Conrad, p. 259.
Schnebli Dolf, p. 271.
Schwartz Patrick, p. 224.
Scolari Massimo, pp. 106, 281.
Scott-Brown Denise, p. 17, 18, 328.
Sellers David, p. 20.
Semper Gottfried, pp. 246, 320, 321.
Serlio Sebastiano, pp. 19, 33.
Sert José Llouis, p. 30.
Silvetti Jorge, p. 230.

Slovic David S., p. 152.
Smith Thomas Gordon, pp. 16, 18, 31, 38, 285.
Soane John, p. 300.
Staderini D., p. 270.
Stephen Douglas, p. 214.
Stern Robert A.M., pp. 9, 15, 16, 18, 29, 31, 34, 38, 61, 289, 306.
Stirling James, pp. 18, 28, 35, 36, 37, 217.
Sullivan Louis Henry, pp. 84, 306.

Taft Architects, p. 295.
Tafuri Manfredo, p. 306.
Tange Kenzo, pp. 194, 205.
T.A.U. (Théorie-Architecture-Urbanisme), p. 297.
Taut Bruno, pp. 12, 69.
Terragni Giuseppe, p. 334.
Terry Quinlan, pp. 33, 300.
Tesar Heinz, p. 304.
Thermes Laura, p. 265.
Tigermann Stanley, pp. 19, 29, 30, 38, 306.
Timme Robert Howard, p. 295.
Torchinsky Bernard, p. 98.
Torre Susana, p. 312.
Turnbull William, pp. 240, 314.
Tusquets Oscar, pp. 93, 115.

Ungers Oswald Mathias, pp. 17, 28, 33, 35, 38, 306, 319, 334.
Utzon Jørn, pp. 28, 29.

Van Bogaert George, p. 224.
Van der Rohe Mies, pp. 16, 23, 24, 28, 30, 31, 59, 84, 214, 306, 334.
Van de Velde Henri, p. 23.
Van Eyck Aldo, p. 28.
Vasari Giorgio, p. 320.
Venezia Francesco, p. 325.
Venturi Robert, pp. 9, 15, 16, 17, 18, 19, 21, 22, 24, 28, 31, 38, 208, 237, 306, 328.
Vergano Serena, p. 98.
Viollet-le-Duc Eugène Emmanuel, pp. 33, 214.
Vitruvius, pp. 33, 320, 342, 343.
Von Kostelac Ante Josip, p. 334.

Wagner Otto, p. 36.
Weinbrenner Friedrich, p. 33.
Whitaker D., p. 240.
Wilson Peter, p. 336.
Wines James, p. 306.
Wontroba Werner Christian, p. 339.
Woods Sh., p. 234.
Wright Frank Lloyd, pp. 17, 18, 20, 28, 59, 214, 306.

Zenghelis Elia, pp. 34, 214.

contents

The end of prohibitionism
Paolo Portoghesi 9

How things got be the way they are now
Vincent Scully 15

Towards an authentic architecture
Christian Norberg-Schulz 21

Towards radical eclecticism
Charles Jencks 30

The "Strada Novissima" 38

**Homage to
Gardella, Johnson, Ridolfi** 49

The fascination of the present
Paolo Farina 50

Philip Johnson: images
Emilio Battisti 59

The craft of Mario Ridolfi
Francesco Cellini, Claudio D'Amato 68

Participants 77

Architektengroep VDL 79

Andrew Batey/Mark Mack 81

Thomas Hall Beeby 84

Georgia Benamo /
Christian de Portzamparc 89

Francisco Biurrun Salanueva 93

John Blatteau 95

Ricardo Bofill 98

Pep Bonet / Christian Cirici 103

Manlio Brusatin 106

Jean-Pierre Buffi 110

Francesco Cellini 112

Luis Clotet / Oscar Tusquets 115

Jo Coenen 118

Stuart Cohen 120

Guillermo Vazquez Consuegra 123

Nicoletta Cosentino 125

Maurice Culot 128

Hermann Czech 132

Claudio D'Amato 134

Costantino Dardi 137

Giangiacomo D'Adria 143

Jeremy Dixon 146

Paolo Farina 148

Terry Farrel 150

Friday 152

Frank O. Gehry 154

Michael Gold 158

Burckhardt Grashorn 161

Studio G.R.A.U. 164

Michael Graves 170

Allan Greenberg 176

Giuseppe Grossi / Bruno Minardi 181

Antoine Grumbach 184

Heinz Hilmer / Christoph Sattler 187

Hans Hollein 189

Arata Isozaki 194

Helmut Jahn 198

Jan & Jon 200

Edward Jones 203

Yasufumi Kijima 205

Joseph - Paul Kleihues 208

Rem Koolhaas Elia Zenghelis 214

Léon Krier 217

Eugene Kupper 222

Jean - Marc Lamunière 224

Yves Lepère 228

Rodolfo Machado / Jorge Silvetti 230

Fernando Montes 234

Kemp Mooney 237

Charles W. Moore 240

Monta Mozuna 246

Gerd Neumann 249

Pierluigi Nicolin 251

Richard B. Oliver 254

Luciano Patetta 256

Herbert Pfeiffer 259

Boris Podrecca 262

Franco Purini / Laura Thermes 265

Bruno Reichlin / Fabio Reinhart 271

Aldo Rossi 275

Massimo Scolari 281

Thomas Gordon Smith 285

Robert A. M. Stern 289

Taft Architects 295

T.A.U. 297

Quinlan Terry 300

Heinz Tesar 304

Stanley Tigerman 306

Susana Torre 312

William Turnbull 314

Oswald Mathias Ungers 319

Francesco Venezia 325

Robert Venturi / John Rauch /
Denise Scott-Brown 328

Ante Josip von Kostelac 334

Peter Wilson 336

Werner Christian Wontroba 339

The Corderia of the Arsenale 341

The Tana reopened: machines
and workshops of the Arsenale
of Venice
Manlio Brusatin 342

Index of names 349

We wish to thank all of those who so kindly put at our disposition the material used the illustrations in this catalogue, and to especially thank:
ASAC - Laboratorio Fotografico della Biennale di Venezia, Archivio Fotografico del Museo Correr, Archivio Fotografico del Museo Storico Navale, Nasa Arai, Morley Baer, Thomas Bernard, Orlando Cabanban, Giorgio Casali, Francesco Cellini, Claudio D'Amato, Faust-Piqueras, Roberto Freno, Fujitsura, Heinrich Helfurstein, Franz Hubmann, Steven Izenour, Howard Kaplan Rollin R. La France, Antonio Martinelli, Martinotti, Alan Mac Gee, Norman Mc Grath, Thilo Mechau, Jean Mohr, Arnold Newman, Patrizia Nicolosi, Overas Photo As, George Pohl, Paolo Portoghesi, Ryoohata, Sergio Rossi, Sadin-Karant, Julius Shulman, Bob Super, Jerzy Surwillo, James Steinkamp, Gerald Zugman.

Printed in Italy by Fantonigrafica, Venice.